GOD'S HAND
ON
AMERICA

GOD'S HAND

～ ON ～

AMERICA

Divine Providence in the Modern Era

Michael Medved

CROWN
FORUM
NEW YORK

Copyright © 2019 by Medved Communications, Inc.

Published in the United States by Crown Forum, an imprint of Random House,
a division of Penguin Random House LLC, New York.

crownpublishing.com

CROWN FORUM with colophon is a registered trademark
of Penguin Random House LLC.

ISBN 978-0-451-49741-3
Ebook ISBN 978-0-451-49742-0

Printed in the United States of America

1 3 5 7 9 8 6 4 2

First Edition

For my immigrant grandparents

Harry and Sarah Medved

Saly and Bella Hirsch

They came to this favored land

And saw God's Hand on America

Contents

I always consider the settlement of America with Reverence and Wonder—as the Opening of a grand scene and Design in Providence, for the Illumination of the Ignorant and the Emancipation of the slavish Part of Mankind all over the Earth.

—JOHN ADAMS, 1765

As to great and commanding talents, they are the gift of Providence in some way unknown to us. They rise where they are least expected.

—EDMUND BURKE, 1791

If ever I feel the soul within me elevate and expand to those dimensions not wholly unworthy of its Almighty Architect, it is when I contemplate the cause of my country. . . .

—ABRAHAM LINCOLN, 1840

I, for one, believe more profoundly than in anything else human, in the destiny of the United States. I believe that she has a spiritual energy in her which no other nation can contribute to the liberation of mankind.

—WOODROW WILSON, 1919

GOD'S HAND
ON
AMERICA

WILLIAM HENRY JACKSON exploring Wyoming's Teton mountains in 1872, the
year before his famous photograph of the Mount of the Holy Cross. A Gettysburg veteran,
gifted painter, and geological surveyor, he served as a "technical advisor" for the filming of
Gone with the Wind and is buried in Arlington National Cemetery.

1

The Message in the Mountainside

"His Sign, His Seal, His Promise"

Wonders, legends, and mysteries spurred American adventurers of every era to explore dark, remote corners of their continent. On rare occasions, miraculous rumors turned out to be true, shaping the young nation's mystical sense of itself.

Such discoveries became especially important after the devastation of the Civil War, reassuring the weary populace that America maintained its special place in God's master plan. Then, as now, a bitterly divided nation, plagued by recent bloodshed and polarizing politics, longed for some unequivocal sign that providential protection still applied to this once favored land.

"NATURE ITSELF HAD SPOKEN"

As early as the 1840s, explorers in the Rocky Mountains heard persistent reports of one such sign—a colossal cross of snow that appeared for a few months each year on the flank of an uncharted Colorado peak. Indians, prospectors, and mountain men spoke in awe of this gleaming vision produced by the late spring thaw on a sheer rock cliff, largely obscured by surrounding pinnacles that equaled or exceeded its commanding height. According to breathless accounts, the magical sight disappeared whenever wanderers approached too close to its sparkling magnificence.

The first credible sighting of this elusive marvel came from a Massachusetts newspaperman who ventured west in an effort to restore his failing health. In August 1868, Samuel Bowles, the respected abolitionist editor of the Springfield *Republican* and a close friend of the poet Emily Dickinson, set out to tour the sparsely settled Colorado Territory. Like other true believers in the sacred Union cause, he couldn't shake his postwar funk following the wrenching tragedy of Lincoln's assassination and the chaotic, disappointing steps toward racial justice and Reconstruction.

In the Rockies, Bowles hoped to rediscover his sense of wonder by climbing to the forbidding, fourteen-thousand-foot summit of Grays Peak. With two companions and a single pack mule, he ascended fifteen miles and camped overnight in the brisk, starry mountain air before the next morning's final push through snowdrifts fifteen feet high. After struggling over loose, treacherous rocks for the last mile, they came to a viewpoint that stirred their deepest emotions.

"It was not beauty, it was sublimity," Bowles wrote. "It was not power, nor order, nor color, it was majesty; it was not a part, it was the whole; it was not man but God, that was about, before, in us. Mountains and mountains everywhere . . . Over one of the largest and finest, the snow-fields lay in the form of an immense cross, and by this it is known in all the mountain views of the territory. It is as if God has set His sign, His seal, His promise there,—a beacon upon the very center and height of the Continent to all its people and all its generations."

Despite this rapturous description, later published in his popular book *The Switzerland of America*, Bowles left no indication of the mystical mount's precise location. Without a map or firm coordinates to recall the perilous path to the breathtaking view, travelers who attempted to retrace his steps found only frustration in their attempts to locate the sacred, solemn site the New England journalist had so memorably acclaimed.

Finally, five years later, under the auspices of the United States Geographical and Geological Survey, an expedition secured lavish federal funding to the tune of $75,000 to expose the truth behind the phenomenon already labeled "the Mount of the Holy Cross." Its intrepid leader, Ferdinand Vandeveer Hayden, boasted a national reputation as a decorated Civil War doctor, university professor, and "notorious unbeliever" celebrated for his previous exploration of the stunning landscape of Yellowstone. His new probe of the Rockies and its mythic religious symbol involved botanists, fossil collectors, mineralogists, topographical artists, scouts, philologists, cartographers, and geologists like Hayden himself.

It also attracted a pioneer photographer named William Henry Jackson, who had trained as a landscape painter before fighting at the Battle of Gettysburg at age twenty. After the war, he risked his life again to shoot the completion of the transcontinental railroad from the cowcatcher of a moving locomotive, and then accompanied Hayden on his celebrated journey to Yellowstone that inspired Congress to create the first national park. For Jackson, the desire to capture the first images of the Cross in the Mountainside became a professional obsession as well as a spiritual quest.

In this pursuit, he trekked into the Rockies with nearly a hundred pounds of equipment on an aging, overburdened mule. The baggage included three cameras and heavy glass photographic plates of various sizes, some as large as eighteen by twenty-two inches. These fragile panes had to be coated, exposed, and developed on-site, with no light-metering equipment or predetermined emulsion speeds, requiring "inspired guess work" from the explorer and artist.

Breaking apart from the main body of the expedition, Jackson struggled with his bulky equipment and his balky mule for two days of rugged climbing across Tennessee Pass and the Eagle River. Exhausted, he staggered across the shoulder of forbidding Notch Mountain, to approach the fabled but still-undocumented cross that Samuel Bowles had described. For most of the way, mist rising from the valley below blocked his sight lines, but the air began to clear as he continued his climb.

"I emerged above the timber line and the clouds," Jackson later recalled, "and suddenly, as I clambered over a vast mass of jagged rocks, I discovered the great shining cross dead before me, tilted against the mountainside." The snow, buried deep in the fissures of the dark gray rock, glistened like polished silver in the midmorning sun, refracting the light toward the slack-jawed photographer. Jackson stood and caught his breath, silently contemplating "the Holy Cross in all its sublime impressiveness . . . the marvelous mountain on which nature had drawn with mighty lines of snow the symbol of the Christian world."

Jackson's weary colleagues straggled up behind him and witnessed a sudden signal that served to confirm the cosmic significance of their discovery. As they caught their first view of the spectacle, a gleaming rainbow shot into the cloudy sky, vaulting out of the thick, low-lying fog, framing the great cross and reminding them of God's covenant with Noah. As Yale professor William H. Goetzmann described the scene in his 1966 book *Exploration and Empire*, that rainbow's brief, eerily timed appearance represented "one of those sublime moments so sacred to the nineteenth-century romantic imagination. . . . Trivial though it seems as a discovery per se, the Mount of the Holy Cross had meaning for all the many thousands who saw its various representations. To the religious mind of the day it was worth as much as all the moving sermons delivered by Henry Ward Beecher. . . . Nature itself had spoken."

But for William Henry Jackson to capture that solemn pronouncement for posterity, he first had to unpack his skittish mule, Hypo, and set up the complicated camera equipment. By that time, the rainbow had dissolved as quickly as it had appeared, and dank mist once more shrouded the face of the mountain. The determined photographer resolved to wait out the forbidding weather, spending a wet, shivering night near his cliffside perch high on the slopes of Notch Mountain, struggling to keep both his soggy campfire and fading hopes alive.

The next morning dawned clear and crisp: a suitable blessing for Sunday, August 24, 1873—the Lord's Day, of course. Jackson rose with the sun to seize his opportunity. He once more arranged his camera equipment and prepared the mountainside darkroom he would need to develop the images properly. Somehow, he managed to expose all eight plates he had wrapped protectively for his climb, and with the largest pane of glass generated what his 1988 biographer P. B. Hales anointed "the most famous image ever made of an American mountain."

The photo of the Mountain of the Holy Cross, formally presented to Congress and to President Ulysses S. Grant, received wide distribution and caused a national sensation. It became the subject of thousands of reproductions, postcards, souvenirs, and even a U.S. postage stamp in 1951. A framed print of the world-famous photo made its way to Rome, placed prominently in the pope's private apartment in the Vatican.

"THE GREAT SHINING CROSS THERE BEFORE ME, TILTED AGAINST THE MOUNTAINSIDE": The first photograph of the legendary Mount of the Holy Cross in Colorado, dubbed "the most famous image ever made of an American mountain." Captured under near-impossible circumstances by William Henry Jackson on Sunday, August 24, 1873.

"THE CHASM BETWEEN REPUTATION AND IMMORTALITY"

This vision also inspired a friend of Jackson's to make his own trek into the wilderness to try to capture the grandeur of the now-famous scene in an epic work of art. The British-born painter Thomas Moran had previously accompanied Hayden and Jackson on their expedition to Yellowstone, where he fashioned a series of celebrated canvases that colorfully conveyed the glories of the future national park. Moran hoped to achieve similar success in capturing the Mount of the Holy Cross, but the constant drizzly and cloudy conditions made it impossible for him to paint on-site. Nonetheless, he managed a series of fanciful sketches: in one draft, for example, he added a stairway of roaring cataracts at the base of the cross where none, in fact, existed. Moran remained single-mindedly committed in all his work to expressing the "truth" and "meaning" of each dramatic scene rather than recording realistic details. He went on to fashion his dramatic sketches into a gigantic masterpiece, seven feet tall and five feet wide.

This grand production became a wildly popular attraction that occupied pride of place at Memorial Hall, the central exhibit gallery of the Philadelphia Centennial International Exposition of 1876. To celebrate the first full century of American achievement, this dazzling world's fair occupied 450 crowded acres in Fairmount Park and drew ten million awestruck visitors from around the globe. An estimated one in five Americans made the pilgrimage to Philadelphia to honor the city where independence began, and to gasp at scientific breakthroughs like Alexander Graham Bell's world-changing telephone or the Remington #1 Typographic Machine (the first commercially successful typewriter).

Fairgoers also turned a disproportionate amount of their hungry attention to Thomas Moran's indelible image of the miraculous and magnificent mountain in the wilderness. That image touched the happy hordes as freshly revealed evidence that God looked with special, clearly expressed favor on the works and ways of the new nation that celebrated its first glorious century of existence.

Moran himself grandiloquently promoted the significance of the "holy site" he had skillfully enhanced, declaring in the Centennial catalog that "the Mountain of the Holy Cross is in some respects the most remarkable peak on the American continent." A New York reviewer, overwhelmed by the spiritual power of the prized canvas, solemnly concluded: "Beyond question, in the painting of this picture, Mr. Thomas Moran has made one of those exceptional leaps which bridge the chasm between reputation and immortality."

"THIS MARVELOUS TESTIMONY TO
HIS SOVEREIGNTY"

Ernest Ingersoll, a tireless, Harvard-educated naturalist and explorer, later summarized the profound impact that the Mount of the Holy Cross made upon the public consciousness. "What matters it whether we write 'God' in the Constitution of the United States," he asked, "when here in the sight of all men is inscribed this marvelous testimony to his sovereignty?" In his popular books and lectures, Ingersoll stressed the significance of the sign on the mountainside as an undeniable message from the Almighty.

The cross of the Rockies served as the country's ongoing reminder of an unbroken covenant, and with Ingersoll's enthusiastic support, the Thomas Moran painting toured the nation and the world, on exhibit in major cities throughout Europe and North America. Eventually purchased by a wealthy Irish Canadian physician, it became the proudest feature of his Manitou Springs mansion in Colorado. The estate went up in flames in 1886, but firefighters, in a rescue deemed "miraculous," salvaged the famous canvas by cutting it from its frame, rolling it up, and passing it through an open window. Ultimately, the legendary work of art became the property of a western legend of another sort: singing cowboy and Hollywood mogul Gene Autry, who added it to the permanent collection of his Western Heritage Museum.

By that time, this mountain with the monumental symbol seared upon its side had become such an established feature of popular culture that the beloved poet Henry Wadsworth Longfellow invoked it as a title of a moving, celebrated sonnet, "The Cross of Snow." Captivated by a reproduction of Moran's painting in an expensive art book he had acquired, Longfellow compared the shimmering image with his "changeless" mourning for the young wife who had died before his eyes in a household fire many years before:

> *There is a mountain in the distant West*
> *That, sun-defying, in its deep ravines*
> *Displays a cross of snow upon its side.*
> *Such is the cross I wear upon my breast*
> *These eighteen years, through all the changing scenes*
> *And seasons, changeless since the day she died.*

THE MOUNTAIN'S MYSTERIES

While Longfellow focused on the peak's poetic power, other Americans cherished its potential as a source of mystical healing. The first organized pilgrimage occurred in July 1912, when the Episcopal Bishop of Western Colorado performed a Holy Eucharist from the peak of Notch Mountain, where participants turned their gaze toward the giant cross, some 1,500 feet in height, less than two miles away. The snowfield to the right of the cross became "the Supplicating Virgin" for its suggestion of the Madonna reaching out in compassion toward the crucifixion. The deep pond that absorbed melting snow from the face of the sheer cliff won designation as "the Bowl of Tears" to recall the chalice catching the blood of Christ. The meandering stream that descends from this small, still body of water became known, inevitably, as Cross Creek.

Tourists visited the mountain in increasingly popular pilgrimages. Frederick Gilmer Bonfils, editor of the *Denver Post*, promoted and sponsored these faith-infused journeys, with two hundred devotees from twenty-five different states hiking to the summit of Notch Mountain in 1928. Two years later, the *Denver Post* reported: "There is an unusual number of persons this year who are afflicted with serious maladies that have defied the best efforts of medical science: they hope that sight of the Holy Cross, coupled with firm faith in divine power, will accomplish cures. Certainly such cures have resulted from pilgrimages of the last two years." One frail sixty-six-year-old woman who had been unable to leave her bed for eight full years insisted that a horse and wagon haul her high enough up the mountain to catch at least one hopeful glimpse of the mystical symbol. After gazing at the marvel before her, and praying for renewed health, she astonished her companions by walking back down the trail without aid or support.

Such reports encouraged a charismatic Denver pastor to promise his ailing congregants that they would be healed if they faced the peak and knelt in prayer at the appointed hour, while he climbed the holy mountain on their behalf. Swamped with grateful assertions of cures following his return, he resolved to carry "healing handkerchiefs" with him on the next pilgrimage to benefit those too weak to make the trek themselves. By 1932, he had received more than two thousand handkerchiefs from across the country, and asked for assistance from the U.S. Forest Service in lugging the load to the top of Notch Mountain. There, they would receive the potent, site-specific blessing, with each of the assembled hankies dipped in the "holy water" pooled in the greenish, glacial runoff collected in the Bowl of Tears.

Those who sought a more intimate encounter with the mountain's mysteries than a sanctified square of cloth continued to struggle with primitive roads and poorly maintained trails. Nevertheless, they trekked to the site each summer, visiting the only facility to accommodate such dedicated travelers on the southern ridge of Notch Mountain: a rude, tiny cabin assembled entirely of stone, known since the mid-1920s as "the Pilgrim's Hut." It provided shelter from the high-altitude chill and a facility for small groups to convene religious services, particularly on Sundays. The only window—a small opening in the rough rock wall—offered a view of the Holy Cross when mist and storms permitted.

Despite the small numbers who took the trouble to approach the mountain personally, the government in faraway Washington still took notice of the peak's enduring hold on the national imagination. In his first two months of office, President Herbert Hoover used his executive power under the Antiquities Act to declare the "Holy Cross National Monument." Five months later, the stock market crashed and the nation began sliding toward the Great Depression, depriving the federal bureaucrats of the funds they needed to develop the attraction as planned. Hoover's successor, Franklin D. Roosevelt, did manage to dispatch two hundred youthful workers from the Civilian Conservation Corps to build a log lodge at the cost of $120,000, but it wasn't enough to sustain the pilgrimages during economic hard times and the gathering war clouds in Europe and Asia. In 1934, the tally of midsummer pilgrims reached its all-time high of three thousand; that number declined precipitously in the face of bureaucratic neglect and dwindling enthusiasm by the local press—especially after the death of *Denver Post* editor Bonfils, the site's most fervent promoter, in 1933.

THE FABLED (AND FALLEN) CROSS

As the number of visitors fell off, so did a crucial element of the cross itself: its right arm collapsed in rock slides or avalanches at some point after 1941. Because snow covers all of the mountain for much of the year, and few climbers ever attempted close-up inspections of the huge fissures that shaped the cross, the exact moment of its demise, like so much else about it, remains a mystery.

One theory blames the U.S. Army, which established Camp Hale nearby for winter warfare and mountain combat training in World War II. This facility directly abutted the boundary of the national monument and, according to persistent rumors, authorized firing of artillery on a few occasions that inadvertently ruined the right arm of the famous cross. A 1968 investigation of army records produced no evidence to support such speculation, but the photographic record shows an unmistakable deterioration of the symbol during the war years. In any event, no subsequent image by any photographer ever showed the cross with the vivid and startling clarity of William Henry Jackson's first rainbow-heralded image of 1873.

Ironically, Jackson himself may have outlived the natural wonder he did so much to popularize: he worked well into his nineties and finally succumbed at age ninety-nine in June 1942. For those who continue to ascribe supernatural power to the Mountain of the Holy Cross, it's worth noting that the three deeply devoted true believers who did the most to emphasize its significance all led unusually long and richly rewarding lives: eighty-nine years for Thomas Moran, ninety-four for Ernest Ingersoll, and nearly a century for Jackson.

None of them lived long enough, however, to protest the decision by Congress to strip the Mountain of the Holy Cross of its national monument status in August 1950.

In a quietly enacted "cost-cutting measure," the people's representatives reassigned the mountain from the purview of the National Park Service (and the Department of the Interior) to the less restrictive supervision of the Forest Service (and the Department of Agriculture). Even the superintendent of Rocky Mountain National Park supported the downgrade, because he claimed that fewer than fifty people visited the monument in the course of any year and it would cost pilgrims "a climb worth half your life" to ascend Notch Mountain to catch the disappointing view of the fabled (and now fallen) cross.

In the intervening decades, few voices have demanded new attention for the symbol in snow that once caused such an intense national sensation; after all, today's secularized society expends far more energy in protesting crosses on public land than on protecting them.

Even in an era of rampant conspiracy theories, no one suspects human agency in any of this: how could some secret society or devious hoaxer claim credit for either making or marring the religious imagery dramatically identified, then desultorily disregarded, on a craggy peak some fourteen thousand feet above sea level?

But it seems odd, if not utterly amazing, that a mere seventy-five years after Samuel Bowles first described the cross and hailed its immortal importance, that "sign," "seal," and "promise" had been swallowed up by the same grinding ice and rock that had created it in the first place. Bowles once reverently proclaimed the site as "a beacon upon the very center and height of the Continent to all its people and all its generations," but a mere two generations later that beacon no longer illuminated the landscape.

This strange tale of the disappearing symbol parallels the deeper, more disturbing story of the nation's dissolving faith in its own divinely ordained destiny. To those inclined to find significance in omens and portents, the message from the mountainside seemed unmistakable: just as some vast power had once carved a benediction, that identical force now engraved a warning of collapse and confusion.

"AN OVERRULING PROVIDENCE"

In the decades following World War II, Americans at large never outright rejected the old idea that an Almighty God provided unique blessings and reliable protection for our country, but they certainly seemed to discuss it less frequently.

In my previous book *The American Miracle*, I emphasized the confidence of America's earlier leaders in the divine direction of their endeavors and recounted twelve stories of crucial turning points in the rise of the Republic. Each of these events involved elements so unlikely, so bizarrely beneficial to the new nation, that participants in these decisive developments felt little doubt they had profited from supernatural assistance.

Thomas Jefferson, though widely criticized in his time for skeptical, unconventional religious views, never questioned that a higher power had selected the United States as a chosen instrument of human betterment. Denounced by his archrival Alexander Hamilton as "an atheist in religion and a fanatic in politics," the third president nonetheless praised the nation in his First Inaugural Address for "acknowledging and adoring an overruling Providence, which by all its dispensations proves that it delights in the happiness of man here and his greater happiness hereafter."

To Jefferson, no place on Earth stood a better chance of achieving such satisfactions than the United States, "kindly separated by nature and a wide ocean from the exterminating havoc of one quarter of the globe . . . possessing a chosen country, with room enough for our descendants to the thousandth and thousandth generation."

Neither the nightmarish carnage of the Civil War nor the unspeakable tragedy of Lincoln's assassination could shake that belief in God's guiding hand and its felicitous arrangement of American affairs. Concerning the horrors of the sectional struggle, Lincoln himself used his Second Inaugural Address to suggest weighing the war as possible blood atonement for the long-standing sin of slavery. And when an assassin's bullet fatally wounded the president (hauntingly, on Good Friday) at the very moment of ultimate Union victory, the newly rejoined Republic came to see his death as a singular, sacred instance of redemptive and unifying martyrdom.

God's Hand on America takes up the story in the years immediately following that sublime sacrifice, beginning with an astounding addition to the nation's territory, orchestrated by Lincoln's closest associate, shortly after he barely survived two near-fatal experiences.

Just two years later, a marvel of vision and leadership from a forgotten (and doomed) American hero, written off as "crazy" by most of his contemporaries, succeeded in binding the Republic from coast to coast and creating, for the first time, a true continental Republic.

Afterward, tidal waves of immigration broke on American shores and helped to fill the empty land, including millions of east European Jews, whose sudden, unexpected arrival served to fulfill biblical prophecies and to confer an otherworldly advantage.

In the twentieth century, three titanic figures—two great presidents along with the greatest Englishman of the age—each escaped death on American soil due to extraordinary good luck that struck observers even at the time as illogical and unnatural.

During World War II, the bloodiest conflict in human history, five minutes of midair miracles near three desolate islands in the Pacific changed the tide of battle irrevocably, and a bizarre turn of events at a Chicago convention combined with an oddly indecisive president to keep a manifestly unsuitable, possibly dangerous figure from the White House.

Finally, a revered clergyman whose mere survival repeatedly beat the odds lived to fulfill what he himself recognized as a prophetic and providential role, to begin the correction of the nation's "original sin" of slavery and racism.

As strange and haunting as such tales may seem in retrospect, they failed to provoke the awe and wonder generated by similar stories in the first century of the Republic's history. The different reactions reflected changes in the nation's status: by the time the United States emerged from civil war and approached the grand celebrations of its 1876 Centennial, Americans began to take their success and good fortune more and more for granted. Moments of favoring fate and dramatic deliverance looked far more noteworthy and necessary to a fragile, struggling, infant enterprise, like the United States in its early years, than to a rising economic and military powerhouse reaching for dominance on the world stage.

In other words, after the Civil War, the happy accidents and coincidences that characterized the beginnings of the American experiment began to look normal, even reliable, and felt far less startling and illogical. Acclimatized to a long, unprecedented, seemingly preordained winning streak, Americans began to imbibe the advice later championed by educator Laurence J. Peter: "Don't believe in miracles. Depend on them."

"SURE ABOUT THE COUNTRY"

To search for such moments of inflection, to look for indications of divine direction, isn't indulgent or superstitious. It remains a useful, even noble endeavor for citizen, statesman, or scholar to try to make sense of significant patterns in seemingly unconnected events, considering hints or signs wherever they appear.

With a healthy hunger for such symbols, it's hardly surprising that the nation in the 1870s took eager notice when Samuel Bowles and William Henry Jackson sighted the shining, perpendicular lines of an icy cross carved into a Colorado mountainside shortly after the costly victory in the war to save the Union.

But that discovery offered no sure, sacred proof of heavenly approbation, any more than it signaled the country's diminished goodness some eighty years later when federal bureaucrats, annoyed or embarrassed by the symbol's deteriorating condition, callously stripped its national monument status.

After the end of that designation in 1951, the sign never disappeared entirely, but it became murkier, more difficult to read and identify. So, too, spotting the entanglement of providence in America's affairs, recognizing the nation's role in constructive cosmic plans, counts as more complicated in recent years.

At the same time, it makes sense to hope that providence would continue to use the United States to achieve its higher purposes. It's a matter of utility more than reward. After all, as an instrument for changing the world, the Republic's continued power and prosperity still make it the most convenient tool around.

Lincoln himself incorporated a similar concept of instrumentality in describing his own part in God's plan for his country. In the month before he took the oath of office for his first term, he traveled by rail from his home in Springfield, Illinois, speaking frequently along the way. Twice in Indianapolis, Lincoln referred to himself as an "accidental instrument." In Trenton, he spoke to the New Jersey legislature and declared himself "happy indeed if I shall be an humble instrument in the hands of the Almighty, and of this, his almost chosen people, for perpetuating the object of that great struggle." Three years later, near the conclusion of the Civil War, he confessed in a famous letter to a Kentucky newspaper editor: "I claim not to have controlled events, but confess plainly that events have controlled me."

That such events should so regularly bless and benefit the United States defies the ordinary odds but conforms to our lived experience, as the pages that follow will show. Otto von Bismarck, Germany's "Iron Chancellor," alluded to this unearned aspect of America's shielded status with a famous formulation at the end of the nineteenth century. "God provides special protection," he said, "for drunkards, imbeciles, small children, lost dogs and the United States of America."

Joe Biden, during more than forty years in elective office, liked to put his own spin on that reassuring maxim. "My grandfather used to say that God looks out for drunken Irishmen and the United States of America," the senator, vice president, and perennial pursuer of the presidency often observed.

Biden's optimism persisted in the face of personal tragedies and professional disappointments. When he concluded his two terms as vice president in 2017 and welcomed a new administration he intensely distrusted, the *New York Times* asked Biden if he still believed the old line he had always favored.

"I'm not sure about the Irishmen," he answered. "But I'm sure about the country."

"MANAGED IN THE GO-AHEAD WAY OF THE AMERICANS": *Signing of the Alaska Treaty* (after midnight, March 30, 1867). This idealized depiction of the great occasion by Emanuel Leutze (the German American painter best known for *Washington Crossing the Delaware*) shows Secretary of State William Henry Seward seated to the left of the globe and the fraudulent aristocrat Baron Eduard de Stoeckl, Russian ambassador, standing to the right. At the far right sits Fred Seward, assistant secretary of state, recovered from the coma he endured when trying to defend his father from a would-be assassin.

2

"North to the Future"

The Irrational—and Essential—Acquisition of Alaska

Two frightening carriage accidents shaped one uniquely consequential American life and inarguably altered the destiny of the Republic.

Those twin catastrophes, separated by forty-one years of turbulent history, illustrate the peculiar pattern by which favoring fate has led the nation, again and again, through episodes of horror and pain toward prosperity and power. They show the way that seemingly random occurrences and unlikely, operatic plot twists have repeatedly transformed disaster into deliverance.

The two roadway mishaps both threatened the life of William Henry Seward, best known as Lincoln's secretary of state. Had either of the accidents never occurred, or had they produced even slightly different outcomes, a map of the United States would look vastly different today. Arguably, the Cold War with Russia could have concluded with Soviet victory and American subservience. In fact, had Seward somehow avoided either one of these dangerous episodes, it's hard to imagine how America could have fought, let alone won, the most important naval engagement of World War II.

"WALKING ABOUT TOWN, AFTER HE IS DEAD"

The first accident occurred in 1824, when Seward was twenty-three years old. A recent bridegroom and newly minted lawyer in upstate New York, he invited his proud parents to join him on an excursion to Niagara Falls. On the way to behold this celebrated wonder of nature, the "spacious stage coach" transporting them through the streets of Rochester suddenly lost a wheel when a linchpin gave way. The carriage banged and skidded on the muddy road near the rushing Genesee River before tumbling down a steep, slick ravine, leaving its occupants terrified but uninjured. The passengers nonetheless needed help in extricating themselves from the wreck and clambering back up the treacherous embankment, feeling grateful when local bystanders rushed to their aid. Nearly fifty years later, Seward recalled: "Among a crowd, which quickly assembled, one taller and more effective, while more deferential and sympathizing, than the rest, lent the party his assistance. This was the beginning of my acquaintance with Thurlow Weed."

The lifelong friendship that followed became one of the most significant political partnerships of the nineteenth century. Weed, a shambling, ink-stained newspaperman four years older than Seward, became an influential editor and behind-the-scenes party organizer for the Whigs and, eventually, the Republicans. He entered the New York State Assembly just months after meeting Seward and almost immediately began promoting his brilliant, ambitious new friend for a series of public offices. Weed declared himself profoundly impressed by the fidgety little man (only five feet six inches tall) that he met on that slippery slope.

Seward's infectious energy and unshakable amiability struck all of his contemporaries as noteworthy; Henry Adams later described him as "a most glorious original." With his distinctive, avian lightness in gait and gestures, combined with his sharply beaked countenance and shock of unruly red hair, he reminded observers of an arrogant parrot or a curious jay. In correspondence, Weed enthused over his young colleague's "stern integrity, earnest patriotism, and unswerving fidelity.

I saw also in him a rare capacity for intellectual labor, with an industry which never tired and required no relaxation."

Under Weed's tutelage and sponsorship, Seward won election to the legislature and served two terms as governor of New York and two as U.S. senator. After Seward and Weed left the collapsing Whig Party in 1855, they identified with the newly organized Republicans. Senator Seward's elegant oratory combined with Weed's expert machinations to make him the prohibitive favorite for the presidential nomination in the crucial election of 1860.

The national convention in Chicago dashed these hopes, when wary delegates shifted on the third ballot to the upstart "rail-splitter" candidate, Abraham Lincoln, a little-known prairie lawyer and one-term congressman who provided a less polarizing, more electable alternative to the fiercely anti-slavery Seward. Deeply disappointed, the senator felt like something of a ghost when he ventured back onto his hometown streets of Auburn, New York, where he enjoyed overwhelming popularity. "I had the rare experience of a man walking about town, after he is dead, and hearing what people would say of him," he wrote. "I confess I was unprepared for so much real grief, as I heard expressed at every corner."

Nevertheless, the defeated candidate overcame that grief and followed Weed's advice to mask his sense of betrayal while campaigning for "Honest Abe" in northern states, drawing huge, enthusiastic crowds. The united Republicans offered a striking contrast to the hopelessly divided Democrats, and the victorious Lincoln followed a well-established tradition by giving the top slot in his cabinet to the leading figure in the national party, installing William Henry Seward as secretary of state.

The New Yorker initially expected to dominate the administration, employing his vastly superior education, experience, and Capitol Hill connections in an attempt to guide the rough-hewn newcomer from the Illinois frontier. But within weeks of Lincoln's installation in the White House, with the secession crisis presenting the gravest possible test of presidential leadership, Seward generously acknowledged the intellect of his onetime rival as easily equal to his own. In a private letter to his wife in June 1861, the secretary of state declared: "Executive skill and vigor are rare qualities. The President is the best of us; but he needs constant and assiduous cooperation."

Seward determined to provide that cooperation, soon becoming Lincoln's most indispensable supporter within the government. Noah Brooks, the California reporter who became Lincoln's friend and an astute observer among the Washington press corps, noted that Seward developed a closer relationship with the president and spent more time in private conversation with him than did any other member of the cabinet. His son Frederick Seward, who served as assistant secretary of state, recalled that whenever Lincoln and his father "sat together by the fireside, or in the carriage, the conversation between them, however it began, always drifted back into the same channel— the progress of the great national struggle. Both loved humor, and however trite the theme, Lincoln always found some quaint illustration from his western life, and Seward some case in point, in his long public career, to give it new light."

Lincoln reacted with bemused affection to his associate's irresistible impulse to recall past triumphs. "Mr. Seward is limited to a couple of stories which from repeating he believes are true," he drawled to a visitor. Seward knew the president well enough to make good-natured sport of the chief executive's own peculiarities. He addressed an English journalist in Lincoln's presence and confessed that he "always wondered how any man could ever get to be President of the United States with so few vices. The President, you know, I regret to say, neither drinks nor smokes."

Seward, on the other hand, more than made up for him with his indulgence in both habits—building up an official State Department cellar of fine wines and puffing through nearly a dozen of the best Cuban cigars every day. In 1863, Brooks described him as "affable and pleasant, accessible—from a newspaperman's point of view—smoking cigars always, ruffled or excited never, astute, keen to perceive a joke, appreciative of a good thing, and fond of 'good victuals.'"

None of this endeared him to Mrs. Lincoln, who was jealous of the secretary of state's easy access and intimate conversations with her husband. She dismissed Seward's wife, who had established their homestead in Auburn, New York, as a way station for escaped slaves on the Underground Railroad, as a "dirty abolition sneak." She instinctively resented the lavish diplomatic dinners the Sewards occasionally hosted at the three-story redbrick home, known as "the Old Club House," that he had rented at the edge of Lafayette Square, just steps away from the White House. She instructed coachmen never to drive her past the front of the Seward home, and on several occasions she demanded that Lincoln reshuffle his official family to drop the secretary of state from his privileged position. She opined to one startled reporter that if the president kept Seward at the head of his cabinet "the country would be ruined within three months."

Contrary to this dire prediction, the secretary's able diplomacy and sagacious counsel helped the nation survive four agonizing years of turmoil, tragedy, and slaughter. The torment seemed unending until the arrival of April 1865, which suddenly brought brightening days to the federal capital. On Monday the third, word reached Washington in the morning that General Grant's blue-coated troops had finally entered Richmond, the seat of the Confederate government, some one hundred miles away. "The great news spread like wildfire through the city. . . . Almost by magic the streets were crowded with hosts of people, talking, laughing, hurrahing, and shouting in the fullness of their joy," Noah Brooks reported. Seward received the news at the War Department, where he had been monitoring the latest telegraphic dispatches. He later joined Secretary of War Edwin Stanton on the balcony for impromptu remarks to a raucous, jubilant crowd that spontaneously gathered below. They concluded by leading the emotional throng in a reverent rendition of "The Star-Spangled Banner."

"IN THE GREATEST ANXIETY ABOUT FATHER"

Two days later, the secretary of state suffered the second carriage accident that changed the course of his life and affected the fate of the Republic.

With the president still in Virginia, conferring with his generals and touring the conquered rebel capital, the secretary of state impatiently awaited Lincoln's return. He needed the chief's quick approval for crucial diplomatic dispatches. At four in the afternoon of Wednesday, April 5, Seward gave in to his restlessness and set off for a brief spring outing in the company of three young people he thoroughly enjoyed: his son Fred, his adoring and much-adored twenty-year-old daughter, Fanny, and Fanny's young friend Miss Mary Titus. The little group rode in a two-horse coach up Vermont Avenue from the Seward home near the White House. Troubled by a rattling, improperly closed carriage door that kept flying open, Seward ordered the coachman to stop to repair the problem before they went farther. As the driver, Henry Key, got down from his perch and attempted the repair, something startled the horses and they galloped away, pulling the reins out of the driver's hands and leaving him sprawled helplessly on the street.

Noting the obvious danger, Fred Seward promptly jumped out of the cab to try to slow the panicked beasts. He fell to the ground, while the carriage careened along the avenue, with the loose reins snapping wildly behind the frightened and desperate animals. As Fanny Seward described the chain of events: "The horses turned round with a rapid sweep & went on increasing their speed. Father had some idea of being able to stop them, & sprang from the carriage in spite of my entreaties that he would not jump." She couldn't see the outcome of his leap, but the heel of his shoe caught on the carriage step, spinning him facedown onto the street. A newspaper account later reported that he "fell violently to the ground upon his right side, breaking his arm close to the shoulder joint, bruising his nose, cheek and jaw in a terribly painful manner."

When a passing soldier risked trampling and finally managed to halt the carriage, Fanny got out and "hastened back to look for Father," where she "met a crowd of men carrying him, & I thought he was dead, but they told me no." She led the men back to the Sewards' rented residence.

The family physician, Tullio Verdi, arrived within minutes and found Seward with "his lower jaw completely fractured on both sides, his right arm also fractured, near the shoulder." According to later medical reports, the blood that gushed from his nose had almost drowned him, cutting off his breathing. The injuries struck physicians as life-threatening for the sixty-three-year-old secretary of state, and Dr. Verdi deemed his condition "perilous in the extreme."

"About six o'clock," Fanny reported, "I went into the room—he was so disfigured by bruises, his face so swollen, that he had scarcely a trace of resemblance to himself. His eyes were closed by immense swellings. . . . I sat up till three o'clock in the morning—Father was restless, & talking constantly, in his sleep—holding my hand."

The biggest challenge for the doctors involved the need to hold together the shattered pieces of his badly broken jaw in order to promote healing. At first, they tried to do the job with heavy bandages, but then replaced them with a complicated, specially designed brace of metal, canvas, and wires anchored to back teeth on both sides of Seward's face. With this contraption covering the lower half of his face, and taking potent medication to try to reduce his pain, the secretary of state could barely speak and became delirious and incoherent each night after dark.

In upstate New York, Seward's wife, Frances, received telegraphic notice of her husband's dire condition and boarded the first available train to Washington. She greatly preferred the comforts of their elegant, spacious country residence outside the town of Auburn and never made a serious attempt to adjust to the frantic social whirl of the capital city. During forty years of marriage, the Sewards had spent more than a decade living apart.

When Frances arrived the second night after the accident, she made her way to her husband's rented house on Lafayette Square near the White House. Fanny tried to prepare her for the worst. "I told Mother before she saw father something of his appearance," she recalled, "still she was much shocked by it. . . . Later . . . she took a cup of tea in the dining room. . . . She had been sick on the way, but was looking well then—& was in the greatest anxiety about father."

In the days that followed, Secretary of War Edwin Stanton became a particularly frequent visitor at the sickbed of his stricken colleague, reporting the latest news on the final stages of the war, trying to convey comfort and cheer. He also cabled updates on the secretary of state's condition to the worried Lincoln, who remained in Virginia with his generals. One afternoon, struggling to speak through his brace and his bandages, Seward managed to croak the words "God bless you, Stanton," but his friend immediately stopped the painful effort. As Fanny remembered the interchange, Seward nonetheless stammered: "You have made me cry for the first time in my life I believe."

At dusk on Palm Sunday, April 9, the president finally returned from Virginia and went directly to the Sewards' house. Frederick, the secretary's son and devoted assistant, remembered that "it was in the evening and the gas-lights were turned down low, and the house was still, every one moving softly, and speaking in whispers." Lincoln climbed the stairs to his friend's room and sat down at the edge of the bed to announce to his secretary of state that their wartime ordeal approached its conclusion. "I think we are near the end, at last," the president declared.

As Seward later recalled the interchange to a friend: "After a few words of sympathy and condolence, with a countenance beaming with joy and satisfaction, he entered upon an account of his visit to Richmond, and the glorious success of Grant,—throwing himself, in his almost boyish exultation, at full length across the bed, supporting his head upon one hand, and in this manner reciting the story of the collapse of the Rebellion." For the better part of an hour, the president stretched alongside the suffering secretary, keeping his head near Seward's so he could hear the brief, breathy, tortured responses from his bandaged lieutenant. Sensing the obvious exhaustion of the convalescent, the president finally bade good night, made his way down the stairs, and walked across Lafayette Square to the White House. The two friends, and onetime rivals, never saw each other again.

Some two hours after the president's Sunday night visit, with most of the capital city already settled into sleep, Secretary of War Stanton roused the Seward household with the glorious news that Lee had surrendered to Grant earlier in the day. "God be praised!" the secretary of state croaked through his broken jaw. The following morning, he "felt better" according to Fanny's report and "sat up twice during the day."

"LIKE THE SCENES OF SOME HIDEOUS DREAM"

On Good Friday of that monumental Holy Week, Seward managed to consume a healthy breakfast for the first time since his accident nine days before. Despite his fragmented jaw, he swallowed most of a soft egg, toast soaked in milk, some thin slices of fish, and a cup of coffee. By midday, Frederick returned from the cabinet meeting he had attended in his father's place, where Lincoln had spoken to his official family about the haunting dream that struck him as he awoke that spring morning. "I had a dream last night," he told the assembled cabinet officers and the visiting General Grant. In this vision, which the president said he experienced on many previous occasions before momentous events, "he seemed to be in some singular, indescribable vessel . . . moving with great rapidity towards an indefinite shore."

Fred also reported on the president's "kindly feeling toward the vanquished, and hearty desire to restore peace and safety at the South, with as little harm as possible to the feelings or the property of the inhabitants." With the secretary of state making daily progress from his painful and devastating injuries, he yearned to return to his post and to resume his prominent role in that process.

As Seward recovered, Fanny helped her father pass the rest of the day by reading to him from Tennyson, a poet he greatly admired. A tall, slender, artistic, and strongly opinionated young woman, Fanny had kept a private diary for the six years since she turned fourteen, in part to ensure an intimate record of her father's role in the great events unfolding around her. At the nearby White House, President Lincoln took advantage of the light official schedule that Good Friday after-noon to take a carriage ride with his wife, Mary, before dinner and their scheduled visit to Ford's Theatre in the evening.

By ten that night, the weather had turned drizzly, and Fanny Seward turned down the gaslights to darken her father's bedroom. In the deep shadows, she sat at his bedside to watch over his still-labored breathing. To assist her, and to take over the guardian role when she tired, the army had assigned Sergeant George Robinson, a wounded combat veteran now serving as a military nurse.

From the third-story bedroom, she didn't hear the bell that rang at the front door or catch the content of the late-night argument that erupted in the entry hall. The nineteen-year-old black servant who answered the urgent knocking and ringing confronted a tall, powerfully built visitor in a long coat, well-shined boots, and a black, broad-brimmed hat. The stranger announced that he carried an important bottle of pain-relieving medicine and that Dr. Verdi himself had instructed him to deliver it personally to the secretary of state, along with directions for its proper use. Considering the late hour, the young servant, William Bell, sensibly insisted that the master of the house couldn't be disturbed, but the bold, imposing messenger refused to leave until he had completed the mission he said he had been assigned.

Hearing the commotion, Frederick Seward strode out to the stairway to take charge. He offered to receive the carefully wrapped package on his father's behalf, but the intruder, who gave "the impression that he was rather dull or stupid," stubbornly and endlessly repeated his strange demand to see the older Mr. Seward immediately, and in person.

When Fred continued to deny entry to the sickroom at the top of the stairs, the messenger seemed to hesitate.

"Very well, sir, I will go," he finally announced after a tense, awkward moment of silence. The tall, broad-shouldered stranger slowly retreated a few steps, descending from the landing toward the front door and the dark street, but then whirled suddenly and leapt upward, lunging directly at Frederick Seward. Pulling a .36-caliber Whitney revolver from his belt, where it had been hidden by the overcoat, the intruder took direct aim at young Seward's face.

"And now, in swift succession, like the scenes of some hideous dream, came the bloody incidents of the night," Fred recalled much later. With the barrel leveled at his forehead from a distance of perhaps two feet, the gun misfired when the would-be assassin pulled the trigger. Five bullets still remained in the cylinder, but instead of firing a second time and killing his target, the intruder gave vent to his rage and frustration, clubbing Fred Seward with the barrel of his pistol. He struck him so savagely, so insistently, that the force of the blows shattered both the victim's skull and the assailant's weapon. The repeated blows left young Seward's face covered in a sheet of blood as he staggered, falling to the floor with grievous head injuries resulting in a coma that kept him incapacitated for two months.

Leaving his first victim unconscious on the stairs, the assailant, Lewis Powell, rushed forward through the shadowy hallway toward the sickroom of the secretary of state.

Powell had invaded the Seward residence as part of the synchronized assassination conspiracy devised by the famous actor John Wilkes Booth. Hailed by theater critics and his many admirers as "the handsomest man in America," Booth had become an impassioned supporter of slavery who harbored a fanatical determination to kill Lincoln and wreck the "tyrannical" federal government. The acclaimed twenty-six-year-old thespian naturally assigned himself the starring role in the evening's gory drama. He would kill the president, while two of his loyal associates would simultaneously murder the two other most significant figures in national office: Vice President Andrew Johnson and Secretary of State Seward. George Atzerodt, the morose German immigrant designated to slaughter the newly installed vice president in his unguarded hotel room, lost his nerve and spent most of the night drinking instead of killing.

Powell received only third billing in the highly theatrical production, despite far more direct experience in murder and cruelty than any of his associates. The youngest son among eight children of an itinerant Baptist preacher from Alabama, Lewis lied about his age when he first volunteered for the fight shortly after his seventeenth birthday. With two brothers dying on the field of glory, and a third suffering horrible wounds while losing a limb during the siege of Petersburg that preceded Lee's surrender, the family's sacrifices consecrated the Confederate cause in Powell's eyes. By all accounts a ferocious, implacable warrior, Lewis developed searing hatred for the enemy. According to one disturbing (and often discounted) story, he carried with him the skull of a fallen Yankee and used it to collect ashes from his cigars.

At Gettysburg, Powell himself suffered serious wounds and became a prisoner-of-war, but later escaped to carry on the struggle with a fiercely effective band of irregulars, the notorious Mosby's Rangers.

In the last years of the war, he also may have involved himself with the Confederate secret service before falling in with Booth. By the time he rang the bell of the Old Club House with the fake bottle of medicine from Dr. Verdi (Booth had gleaned the physician's name from newspaper accounts), Powell still stood a week shy of his twenty-first birthday. Despite the gruesome, grisly experiences that scarred his war years, he counted as only eight months older than the other twenty-year-old in the fateful Good Friday confrontations: the ethereal and fragile Fanny Seward.

The sounds of struggle at first made Fanny think that servants "were chasing a rat in the hall," as the noise gradually aroused the rest of the household. Alarmed, the secretary's daughter opened the door of her father's darkened room and recognized in horror her brother's badly bloodied figure, with his skull an open wound.

Lewis Powell recognized the opened door as his opportunity. He pushed past the slender girl, punching her in the face as he ran toward the helpless secretary of state immobilized at the far corner of his bed. The intruder now brandished a Bowie knife in his right hand and held the remnants of the revolver in his left, with the butt still useful as a club. When Sergeant Robinson, the army nurse, tried to stop him, the blade crashed down into the sergeant's forehead and he fell to the floor.

With Fanny shouting "Don't kill him!" Seward began to grasp the situation through the haze that clouded his mind during the nights of his recovery. He later said "he knew the man sought his life, still he feared for Fanny and, with great effort, rose up in his bed to interpose his shattered frame as a protection." This movement only served to help the attacker locate his prey in the darkened room, pinning him to the bed with his powerful left arm, then raising the knife high above his head and bringing the blade down three or four times with full force. Both of the first two strikes missed the small and feeble Seward entirely, ripping sheets and mattress instead of human flesh. Another blow plunged deep into the right cheek of the secretary of state, nearly severing it from his face, leaving a flap of partially detached flesh and unleashing a great gush of blood.

That thrust and, very possibly, others, may have been blocked or turned aside by the metal-and-canvas contraption that the doctors had designed to allow Seward's broken jaw to heal. As biographer Walter Stahr wrote in his vivid 2012 account, *Seward: Lincoln's Indispensable Man*, the secretary was "fortunate to be wearing the brace on his jaw: although accounts differ on this point, it seems likely that the brace deflected one or more of Powell's blows." In Fanny's opinion, that splint was the only thing that prevented the blade from penetrating his jugular vein and ending his life. Stahr added: "Finally, Seward was fortunate that his doctors (in order to allow his broken arm to

"I'M MAD, I'M MAD": The words of Lewis Powell, age twenty, moments after he repeatedly stabbed Secretary of State Seward and bludgeoned the secretary's son Fred. Captured three days later and held in federal custody for less than three months, the former Confederate raider died by hanging for his role in the Lincoln assassination conspiracy.

hang freely) had placed him on the edge of his bed farthest from the door. This may well have caused Powell's first blow to miss; it also allowed Seward to fall or to roll himself off the bed, out of Powell's reach, at least for a moment."

In that instant, Sergeant Robinson found his feet, shaking off the wound to his forehead and throwing himself at the knife-wielding would-be killer. While they struggled, Fanny wailed in horror and despair, pleading for help. Her brother Augustus, asleep in a nearby bedroom, awoke to the chaos and ran to the room in his nightshirt. A thirty-eight-year-old West Point graduate and a major in the army, Gus joined Robinson in grappling with the intruder. As the two Union veterans wrestled the former Confederate raider out of the room and into the hall with its hissing gaslight, Powell pronounced his first words since commencing the attack. "I'm mad, I'm mad," he declared, with an air of unnatural calm and control, before rushing down the stairs. He slashed and stabbed at others who tried to stop or pursue him, including the teenaged servant, William Bell, finally escaping from the three-story residence he had transformed into a "house of horrors." After pushing through the open front door, he dropped his bloody blade on the street, strode into the shadows of Lafayette Square, found the tethered horse intended for his getaway, and rode off into the darkness.

The military investigators from the Department of War didn't find him till three nights later but managed to take him into custody without a struggle. Powell's trial took only a month, followed by his execution, with three other coconspirators, just a week after the verdict. Eyewitnesses watched him struggling for nearly five minutes on the gallows, kicking and swinging wildly, before the noose finally strangled him.

"IF HE HAD BEEN ALIVE HE WOULD HAVE BEEN THE FIRST TO CALL"

On the night of the attack, Fanny Seward knew nothing of the assailant, or of the simultaneous shooting of the president at Ford's Theatre ten blocks away. Near eleven o'clock, after Powell had bolted from the secretary of state's home, Fanny ran back into the sickroom of her wounded father and saw her brother Gus with "his forehead covered with blood. It seemed to me that every man I met had blood on his face." She felt desperate as she searched for her father's body in the midst of the chaos. "I remember running back, crying out 'Where's Father?' seeing the empty bed. At the side I found what I thought was a pile of bed clothes—then I knew that it was Father. As I stood my feet slipped in a great pool of blood. Father looked so ghastly I was sure he was dead, he was white & very thin with the blood that had drained from the gashes about his face & throat."

Sergeant Robinson, ignoring his own wounds, gently lifted the soiled, torn, seemingly discarded "pile of bed clothes" back onto the bed. Coughing blood, the secretary of state managed to speak and, remarkably, took command.

"I am not dead," he announced, deliberately and authoritatively. "Send for a doctor, send for the police. Close the house."

When Dr. Verdi arrived, he described Seward as the only one in the room whose face "did not express fear." Fanny watched her father "reach out his hand towards me in a soothing way, as if to bid me to be calm and reassure me." Later, another physician "sewed up the great gash in father's cheek—which had lain open."

The doctors worried most about Frederick Seward, who remained unconscious. They expected that even if he survived, his brain injuries would lead to gravely reduced mental faculties. As it happened, he recovered completely and continued as his father's irreplaceable aide for another four fateful years, returning to serve President Rutherford B. Hayes as assistant secretary of state eight years after that. He lived until 1915, dying with abundant honors at age eighty-four.

On the drizzly, grim Saturday morning after Powell's rampage, it was Secretary of War Stanton who brought news to the Seward household of the night's other terrors. When Seward's wife, Frances, finished reporting to the ashen visitor on the state of her immediate family, she asked "as to whether anything later had been heard from the President."

"Yes," the bearded secretary quietly replied. "He is dead."

Initially, family and physicians kept the ghastly news from Seward to prevent a blow to his recovery. According to an account by Noah Brooks five days after the assassination, the secretary of state had asked that his bed be moved to give him a view of the intermittent spring sunshine through the window. Eventually "his eye caught the stars and stripes at half-mast on the War Department." Seward then reportedly told an attendant who came in to check on him that he inferred that "the President is dead." In response, the assistant "stammered and changed color as he tried to say nay" but Seward insisted: "If he had been alive he would have been the first to call on me; but he has not been here, nor has he sent to know how I am, and there's the flag at half-mast." The secretary "lay in silence, the great tears coursing down his gashed cheeks, and the dreadful truth sinking into his mind."

Other dreadful truths soon afflicted the Seward family. In mid-May, the *New York Herald* announced that the secretary's wife of forty years had "been made quite ill by mental anxiety and unremitting attention to her husband and son." Fanny sat at Frances's bedside on June 21, just nine weeks after Lincoln's assassination and her husband's attack, when "she lay still and beautiful, only breathing more and more lightly till she ceased to breathe at all."

A year later, Fanny herself suffered from an increasingly painful cough, but nonetheless traveled to be at her frail father's side in Pennsylvania as he campaigned for congressional candidates allied with the new president, Andrew Johnson. The electoral outcome amounted to a massive rejection of Johnson, and of Seward, and the exhausting trip seemed to drain Fanny's strength. She managed to return to Washington but never recovered from her illness, almost certainly tuberculosis. She died on October 29, at age twenty-one.

After the troop of terrors that nearly trampled William Henry Seward in 1865—the near-fatal carriage accident, the assault on his person by a would-be assassin, the murder of his closest associate in government, the dreadful injuries to his son Frederick, the sudden death of his wife—it was this loss of his brilliant, deeply devoted daughter that struck him with the most punishing force. He wrote to a friend, the diplomat Henry Sanford: "No one can ever know or conceive how precious in my sight was the treasure that you so truly say was removed." To an actress that Fanny had greatly admired, he explained that he knew he should "rejoice that she was withdrawn from me to be reunited with the pure and blessed spirit that formed her own. But, unfortunately I am not spiritual enough to find support in these reflections."

"IN A VERY FEW YEARS THE CONTROLLING INFLUENCE OF THE WORLD"

He was, however, "spiritual enough" in his soul-deep faith in America's destiny to continue his work at the State Department, despite the personal disasters that might otherwise have overwhelmed him. Like his fallen friend, Lincoln, and other luminaries in the young nation's past, Seward hardly counted as conventionally devout or an avid churchgoer. But as with Washington, Franklin, Jefferson, Hamilton, John Quincy Adams, Jackson, and so many more, he combined his highly personal, unorthodox theology with fervent faith in his nation's supernatural significance. Seward never doubted that the rise of the Republic reflected the divine will, or questioned the idea that even greater grandeur would characterize the American future.

In 1846, three years before his elevation to the Senate, and before his country had secured its claims to California and Oregon, young Seward sketched dazzling visions of national splendor. "Our population is destined to roll its resistless waves to the icy waters of the North and to encounter oriental civilization on the shores of the Pacific," he declared.

Later that same year, he told enraptured listeners in Minnesota that America would one day swallow the struggling, straggling Arctic settlements then known as "Russian America."

"I see the Russian," the rising politician declared, "as he busily occupies himself in establishing seaports and towns and fortifications on the verge of this continent, as the outposts of St. Petersburg; and I can say, 'Go on and build up your outposts all along the coast, up even to the Arctic Ocean; they will yet become the outposts of my own country—monuments of the civilization of the United States in the Northwest.'"

As a U.S. senator, he hoped to advance this prophecy by proposing in 1852 a naval survey of the Bering Strait and the yet uncharted waters of the frigid North Pacific. The next year, he declared that "the borders of the federal republic . . . shall be extended so that it shall greet the sun when he touches the tropics, and when he sends his gleaming rays toward the polar circle, and shall include even distant islands in either ocean." He visualized the American people "entering on a career of wealth, power and expansion" that would make them "in a very few years the controlling influence of the world."

After Lincoln's murder and Union victory in the Civil War, fate seemed to provide the secretary of state with a unique opportunity to pursue bold schemes that had inspired his lyrical rhetoric for two decades. He had returned to work and recovered from his injuries— though he wouldn't allow himself to be photographed from the right side, where Powell's deep slice into his cheek left him permanently disfigured. Nonetheless, Seward struck his contemporaries as more impressive than before his near-death experience. John Hay, one of Lincoln's two personal secretaries and himself a future secretary of state, described him as "splendid in his present temper—arrogant, in-solent, implacable—thoroughly in earnest—honest as the day." He stood out as the most prominent survivor of the most formidable as-sassination conspiracy in the nation's history, somehow protected from the death all around him and preserved, so it seemed, for a higher purpose.

Seward pursued that purpose in controversial efforts to acquire vast tracts of undervalued real estate that could establish America's dominance across the Pacific and throughout the Western Hemi-sphere.

He developed a particularly fierce focus on nearly six hundred thousand square miles of desolate, seemingly worthless wilderness in the far northwestern corner of the continent. Horace Greeley's *New York Tribune* later derided this territory as "Walrussia . . . a hideously expensive and tax-burdensome folly," suitable only for the walruses who thronged there in abundance and the few dozen hairy, hardy Russian fur traders who shivered in struggling settlements they had tried to plant in its frozen wastes.

Despite such ridicule, Seward saw three elements of fortuitous timing that impelled him to make Russian America—the province later known as Alaska—the primary target of his imperialist appetite.

Most poignantly, he longed for the quick fulfillment of Lincoln's call (in his Second Inaugural Address) to "bind up the nation's wounds," reuniting North and South in a new sense of common identity and shared goals. Russian America offered a grand arena for such nationalistic dreams, far removed from the recent scenes of sectional conflict, and with a land area more than double the size of the Lone Star colossus of Texas. Seward expected that securing Alaska's more than five thousand miles of Pacific coastline would ensure American dominance of the entire ocean and its profitable commerce with all of Asia, while inspiring a new burst of unifying patriotism.

Second, a shift in the status of British North America suggested that the reorganized Dominion of Canada might make its own move on the czar's American holdings if Seward failed to act quickly. The Canadian Confederation of July 1, 1867, for all practical purposes, established an independent nation on the northern border of the United States, and that rising entity might logically seize or purchase the lightly settled, neighboring domain of Russian America. Britain and Russia had fought on opposite sides of a multinational war in Crimea as recently as 1856 with at least half a million casualties, and distrust and resentment continued to poison relations between the rival powers. The czar and his ministers in St. Petersburg appropriately worried that even a small flotilla of British (or British Canadian) ships could seize all of the shaky Russian outposts in North America in a matter of weeks, leaving the Romanov regime helpless and humiliated.

This led to the most important force pushing Seward toward the quick, if controversial, purchase of Alaska: the Russian government's ardent desire to unload the remote and forbidding territory as expeditiously as possible. Even before the Civil War, the authorities noted that sea otters, the chief quarry for Russian America's fur traders, had been hunted to the point of extinction. Moreover, the most influential military and diplomatic leaders feared America's undisguised appetite for new land. Admiral Andrei Popov, commander of the Russian fleet in the Pacific, commented on the Yankee "doctrine of manifest destiny" that "is entering more and more into the veins of the people, and new generations are sucking it in with their mother's milk, and inhaling it with every breath of air they inhale. There are twenty millions of Americans [the Census Bureau actually reported more than thirty million], every one of them a free man and filled with the idea that America is for Americans. They have taken California[,] Oregon, and sooner or later will get [Russian America]. It is inevitable."

The brother of the czar, Grand Duke Constantine, echoed those sentiments. After Union success in putting down "the Great Rebellion," he told the foreign minister, Prince Alexander Gorchakov: "It cannot be said that cession to the United States of these remote colonies, which have no essential ties with Russia and which we cannot defend in case of need, would not satisfy the need of foresight and common sense."

To address that need for foresight and common sense and to close a deal with the victorious Americans, the grand duke and the prince could rely on the suave, cosmopolitan wiles of His Excellency Baron Eduard de Stoeckl, one of the most preposterous phonies in the history of Russian diplomacy. This shameless impostor represented the czarist empire for nearly twenty years in Washington, though his claim to Russian nationality was dubious at best and his right to an aristocratic title was nonexistent. The son of an Austrian diplomat who wed a Russian translator's daughter in Constantinople, Stoeckl added "de" to his name to sound more French and fabricated the title "Baron" to impress the gullible Americans.

During his long service in the Russian legation in Washington and then as the czar's ambassador to the United States, he developed flawless English and fast friendships with leading members of Congress, including then-senator William Henry Seward. These politicos admired Stoeckl's fashionable Parisian clothes and silky side-whiskers, while sharing his near-boundless enthusiasm for fine wines and good cigars. Stoeckl's statuesque new American wife (from Springfield, Massachusetts) only added to the ambassador's popularity with the capital's social set.

These aristocratic airs corresponded to Stoeckl's unabashed eagerness to enrich himself with the sums he would receive if he negotiated an advantageous deal to sell Alaska, including a secret 25,000-ruble reward from the imperial court. At the beginning of 1867, the timing seemed perfect to conclude the sort of transaction the Russians had contemplated for years. With a weakened President Johnson embroiled in consuming conflict with Congress over Reconstruction policy for the South—a conflict that led within a year to an impeachment crisis—Seward enjoyed a free hand with foreign policy to explore his expansionist aspirations. As the president's most conspicuously loyal (and increasingly lonely) ally, the secretary of state also hoped that a major achievement on the diplomatic front could distract attention from the administration's deteriorating situation on Capitol Hill.

Seward therefore pursued his largely unauthorized negotiations in total secrecy, delighted to see that his old friend "Baron" de Stoeckl seemed to crave success as much as he did. When they agreed to a draft of a potential treaty, they transmitted it by telegraph to St. Petersburg, using the newly installed transatlantic cable at a cost of almost $9,000, paid, at Seward's insistence, by the U.S. government. As Stoeckl explained to his associates at the imperial court, "This whole affair has been managed in the go-ahead way of the Americans."

Five days later, on March 29, a Friday night, Stoeckl got the approval he needed from the Foreign Ministry and walked immediately from his temporary lodgings across Lafayette Square to Seward's residence in the Old Club House. Seward interrupted a game of whist with his family and friends to welcome the news and the ambassador's suggestion that he would appear at the secretary's office the following morning to agree on final language and execute the treaty. But the energized and excited secretary of state saw no reason to delay.

"Why wait till tomorrow, Mr. Stoeckl?" he famously declared. "Let us make the treaty tonight."

"But your department is closed," the baron protested. "You have no clerks, and my secretaries are scattered about the town."

"Never mind," the secretary of state assured him. "If you can muster your legation together before midnight, you will find me awaiting at the department, which shall be open and ready for business."

With that, he dispatched his son Fred, who had returned to his duties as assistant secretary after recovering from his coma, to undertake the unenviable task of a late-night mission to the imperious Charles Sumner, senator from Massachusetts and chairman of the Foreign Relations Committee, to inform him of the proceedings.

Though the distinguished New Englander proved unavailable for the occasion, the convivial comrades who actually showed up at the State Department worked indefatigably between midnight and 4:00 a.m. and successfully concluded the largest real estate transaction since the Louisiana Purchase. At a price of $7,200,000—approximately $125 million in today's dollars—the Russian Empire ceded all its property in North America to the United States for 1.973 cents per acre, to be exact. Shortly after sunrise on that fateful Saturday morning, Seward walked the signed documents over to the White House, where the president expressed his enthusiastic approval. Andrew Johnson composed a brief message to attach to the documents urging rapid ratification before the Senate's imminent adjournment for its spring recess.

"THE CITIZEN THROBS ANEW"

Despite his differences with President Johnson over the issues of Reconstruction, Senator Sumner took up the cause of winning support for the purchase of Russian America. Before the Foreign Relations Committee, which he chaired and dominated, the senator encountered considerable grumbling about the dominant role of Seward in arranging the whole transaction; most Republicans had come to resent his unwavering support for the embattled president. William Fessenden of Maine told his fellow senators he would support the treaty only "with an extra condition that the Secretary of State be compelled to live there, and the Russian government required to keep him there." Though his colleagues failed to attach that particular provision, and Senator Fessenden remained grumpily opposed, the treaty cleared the Foreign Relations Committee within a week, drawing a vote of four to two with one abstention.

Voices in the press divided sharply on the issue, with the *New York Tribune* continuing to attack the addition of "Walrussia" to the federal Republic. "There is not, in the history of diplomacy, such insensate folly as this treaty," editor Greeley thundered. The *New York Herald* took a more balanced approach but still characterized the vast territory as "an ice house, a worthless desert, with which to enable the Secretary of State to cover up the mortification and defeats he has suffered with the shipwrecked South Policy of Andrew Johnson." Opponents also ridiculed the proposed acquisition as "Seward's Ice Box" or "Johnson's Polar Bear Garden," but, as biographer Walter Stahr points out, the term "Seward's Folly," often cited in modern history texts, never became popular until years later.

Moreover, much of the press did offer enthusiastic approval of the proposed deal, with the *Boston Herald* summarizing the most important argument in its behalf: "There can be but one opinion: it is dog cheap." Nevertheless, the efforts to assure ratification proved notably expensive: Seward hosted a series of five dinner parties for wavering senators where, the *New York Herald* observed, "terrapin and Château Margaux will doubtless assist in the elucidation of this already knotty subject."

By the time Senator Sumner delivered one of his typically florid and grandiose orations on the Senate floor, commanding the attention of his colleagues for more than three hours as his stentorian voice boomed out nearly fifty pages of text, approval seemed all but assured. He began his remarks by acknowledging the arguments against the purchase. "The immense country is without form and without light, without activity and without progress," he allowed. "Its life is solitary and feeble. Its settlements are only encampments or lodges."

Nonetheless, he insisted that the acquisition would help the nation recover from the dispiriting devastation of the recently concluded sectional conflict. "With an increased size on the map there is an increased consciousness of strength, and the citizen throbs anew as he traces the extending line."

At the end of his epochal address, Senator Sumner declared that after the treaty's confirmation, the familiar designation of "Russian America" must no longer apply to newly purchased property of the United States. Instead, the erudite and Harvard-educated legislator suggested the word that Aleutian Islanders used to refer to the continental vastness of the mainland, a term he translated more elegantly as "the great land." That word was "alaska."

With the Senate voting twenty-seven to twelve to ratify the treaty—one vote above the constitutional requirement of two-thirds—members of that august body joined with leading representatives of the press to embrace Sumner's ingenious suggestion. But even with its lyrical new name—so clearly preferable to "Seward's Ice Box"—Alaska faced a tough sell in the House of Representatives, which needed to appropriate the money to pay off the Russians before the United States could complete the transaction. A minority report in the Foreign Relations Committee complained of the new territory that "its timber [is] generally of poor quality and growing on inaccessible mountains" and described the region as "a nation of savages in a climate unfit for the habitation of civilized men."

Fortunately, Secretary of State Seward had displayed the foresight—or cynicism—to prepare the pro-treaty forces to overcome such objections. In his post-midnight negotiations with Stoeckl, the two men had agreed on the peculiar price of $7,200,000, with the extra $200,000 explicitly assigned to cover the baron's unspecified "expenses" associated with the sale. The Russian ambassador quietly approached his personal friends at the Riggs Bank in Washington and persuaded them to advance him the money, personally, against the credit of the U.S. government.

Undoubtedly, some of these funds ultimately found their way into the personal treasury of the Stoeckl family, but the baron also used the windfall to recruit a discreet cadre of well-paid lobbyists, who showed no more scruples in the nineteenth century than similar agents of influence display in the twenty-first. A congressional investigation two years after the contested vote confirmed that the purchase promoters paid money legally to reward journalists for favorable reports about "the great land" Seward sought for his country, but the investigators dismissed accounts of outright bribery as "nebulous gossip."

Subsequent historians have found much stronger evidence of House members enriching themselves through generous gifts taken from the fund for special expenses allotted to the wily Baron de

Stoeckl. President Johnson himself, for instance, scribbled down notes of a carriage ride he took with Seward as a friendly Sunday outing. The two men stopped for "refreshments" (and both were known to enjoy midafternoon libations, after which the secretary of state assured him of a favorable outcome in the House of Representatives because of direct payments to key members. John Bigelow, a distinguished diplomat and a close friend of Seward's, reported a similar conversation in his diary. After a typically elegant dinner at the Old Club House, the secretary mentioned encouraging ten different representatives to back the treaty, some of whom received as much as $10,000—the equivalent of nearly $200,000 in today's money.

In any event, the bill to fund the purchase of Alaska went through easily, by a vote of 113 to 43. His great work accomplished, His Excellency Baron de Stoeckl promptly left town before anyone could pummel him with uncomfortable questions and resigned from the Russian diplomatic service. He spent the final years of his life in Paris, where his "expenses" from the treaty and his 25,000-ruble bonus from the czar allowed him to indulge his elegant and artistic tastes.

"PEACEFULLY BENEATH THE SHADOW OF ITS WINGS"

None of these grubby background details prevented prominent voices in the press and public from exulting at the sheer scope of Seward's addition to the national landscape. Much as he had hoped, the deal with the Russians stirred nationalistic impulses, even in southern states that had recently fought with desperate valor against the same federal government that now claimed the vast new prize. In an editorial applauding the treaty, the Charleston Daily News in South Carolina cited the good fortune of "Brother Jonathan" (an early version of Uncle Sam) in comparison to his European counterparts:"Now while French and English, Austrians and Prussians, Russians and Italians, are quarreling over Eastern questions and German questions, Brother Jonathan can sit with sublime indifference on the top of the Alleghenies and spit his tobacco into either the Atlantic or Pacific, whitling huge California timber with a clasp knife made of iron out of his

mountains, and mix his cobbler with lemons grown in his own tropics, and cooled with ice brought from his own Arctic Circle." The same
writer also reported, with some exaggeration, that Alaska "is said to
contain the highest mountain in the world ... a fit pinnacle from
which the American Eagle can, when the days of good feeling come
back, 'spread itself' over the immense country that will then lie peacefully beneath the shadow of its wings."

William Henry Seward got a bald eagle of his very own as a me-
mento of the epic journey to Alaska that he undertook shortly after
he left office as secretary of state. Despite his weakening health and
the approach of his seventieth birthday, he noted that "at my age, and
in my condition of health, 'rest was rust,' and nothing remained, to
prevent rust, but to keep in motion." In June 1869, he crossed the
country on the transcontinental railroad that had been completed
only weeks before. Steamships carried him from San Francisco to the
remote settlements of the Pacific Northwest and then up to the "Arctic Province" that constituted his great gift to the Union. He delivered
a lengthy address to the citizens of Sitka, described by Frederick as
"Russians in their national dress, United States soldiers in their blue
uniforms, Indians in blankets and feathers, and traders and travelers
clad in the latest style."

He came home to Auburn bearing the captive bird from Sitka in
a huge cage, more than ten feet square. Another trip took him around
the world, allowing him to walk on the Great Wall of China and to
visit all the European capitals. When he returned, he claimed to have
traveled more than seventy-two thousand miles. As soon as he made
it back to his comfortable country home, greeted by his dogs, his servants, his family and friends, he began demanding, "Show me the
bird." He immediately went to the national symbol, and a visitor reported that the eagle "winked at Mr. Seward with his weather eye and
seemed to say 'Mr. Secretary, you and I understand each other.'"

He spent the next year beginning his memoirs with Fred, while
simultaneously writing accounts of his travels. On October 10, 1872,
he spent the morning, as usual, working at his desk, when he began to
feel weak and took to his bed. He died that afternoon with the reputed last words: "Love one another."

"THE ALASKA WE'VE LOST"

Had he died seven and a half years earlier, during the attack by Lewis Powell on the night of Lincoln's murder, there is scant chance that the United States would have acquired the largest state in the union. It's not hard to imagine that Alaska today would be a prized part of Russia or, very possibly, another province of Canada. As historian Richard Kluger summarized the situation: "The truth was that no one else in the federal government had any interest in the project." Seward's personal obsession with territorial expansion led him to ignore a weakened and distracted president, and then to employ every available means to sell his deal to a balky Congress.

Harvard historian Oscar Handlin identified Seward's lonely, relentless determination to complete his grand bargain as one of the key "turning points in American history" described in his 1954 book *Chance or Destiny*. "Had this opportunity been passed by, the Russians might never have been dislodged," he writes. "By the end of the century the whole situation had changed. The discovery of gold and other mineral resources suddenly gave the territory a new and unexpected value. . . . Furthermore, the Czar was now acquiring the means to defend it. For the construction of the trans-Siberian railroad, which was completed at the turn of the century, narrowed the distance between St. Petersburg and the Pacific, and allowed the Russians to establish naval bases at Port Arthur and Vladivostok, which soon became important centers of power in the area. Not many years after 1867, the Russians might have been far from willing to give up Alaska."

In a 1967 piece in the British journal *History Today*, Louis C. Kleber ponders the world-shattering importance of Seward's survival and vision: "What if Seward had been an inward-looking Secretary of State? It is entirely conceivable that the Soviet Union, as successor to Imperial Russia, might possess Alaska today. . . . For Americans it would be far worse than a Cuba in the north, for though Cuba may be hostile, it is still a country that on its own represents an insignificant threat compared to a Soviet Union holding Alaska as her own sacred territory. From the southern reaches, Russia would be able to launch missile and bomber attacks in a wide arc at vital industrial centres."

Russian nationalists in the post-Soviet era share the assumption by Kleber and Handlin that Baron de Stoeckl's dealings with Seward may have advanced his own interests but badly damaged those of the motherland. In 2017, 150 years after the czar sold off his American real estate at a fire-sale price, Sergei Aksyonov, the prime minister of Crimea, told a television interviewer: "If Russia was in possession of Alaska today, the geopolitical situation in the world would have been different." The magazine *Military-Industrial Courier* echoed his sentiments with a two-part series, "The Alaska We've Lost." In a 2016 poem addressed to Czar Alexander II, Putin's deputy finance minister, Vladimir Kolychev, angrily declaimed: "Along with Alaska, you sold out your Russian people."

While Russians have only recently recognized the magnitude of the northern edge they handed to the United States, it also took at least three generations before Americans caught up with Seward in seeing Alaska's importance and potential. Though the 1896 discovery of gold in the nearby Canadian Yukon brought one hundred thousand prospectors into the region, few of them made the great land their permanent home. When Congress finally granted Alaska territorial status in 1912, barely fifty thousand people lived there—the sort of crowd you'd see at a contemporary football stadium—spread out over an area twice the size of Texas. Only after the Japanese seized the remote Aleutian Islands of Kiska and Attu in 1942 did the authorities and the public begin viewing Alaska as American soil and commit major military resources to the recapture of the occupied territory.

Subsequent statehood (in 1959), the development of a prodigiously productive oil industry, a growing population, and booming tourism now belie Greeley's description of the purchase of "Walrussia" as a "hideously expensive and tax-burdensome-folly." In 1967, the centennial celebration of that no longer controversial transaction, the state of Alaska affirmed its status as a preordained piece of the nation's destiny by adoption of a new, official state motto: "North to the Future." Newspaperman Richard Peter, who originated the slogan and pushed it through the legislature, saw the words as "a reminder that beyond the horizon of urban clutter there is a Great Land beneath our flag that can provide a new tomorrow for this century's 'huddled masses yearning to breathe free.'"

CLAIMING SPECKS IN THE OCEAN

The reference to the Statue of Liberty and the poetic inscription on its base makes clear that it's as natural today to view Alaska, in all its immensity, as inevitably American—as much a part of our present identity as New York or Colorado. But no other territory joined the federal union based so exclusively on the efforts of one man. Without Seward, there would have been no state of Alaska, and without the two crucial carriage accidents that afflicted him as a young man and then as an aging public servant, there would have been no Seward—at least not in a position to wield such a powerful influence on the shape of the United States. Without the first mishap, he might never have struck up the political partnership with Thurlow Weed, which made possible his emergence as governor, senator, presidential candidate, and secretary of state.

And without the second incident—the horrible injury that nearly killed him on April 5, 1865—he never would have worn the metal-and-canvas splint that protected his jugular vein from the stabbing thrusts of a crazed would-be assassin some nine days later. That seemingly catastrophic injury not only spared his life but actually served to save it. Seward, of course, took great pride in his irreplaceable role in adding so much resource-rich real estate to the nation he revered. But he also felt frustration at the failure of his other attempts to build the American empire. At various times during his service as secretary of state, he pushed for adding Panama, Hawaii, the Danish Virgin Islands, part of Santo Domingo, and even Iceland and Greenland to United States territory. Aside from Alaska, the addition of only one other tiny tract of land can be credited entirely to Secretary Seward, attracting scant notice from the public or, for that matter, from historians.

The day after the Fourth of July in 1859, an American captain of a small, hardy seal-hunting ship sighted a desolate Pacific atoll. He claimed the 2.4 square miles of territory under the obscure Guano Islands Act of 1856, which authorized Americans to take possession of uninhabited islands to collect valuable guano, or bird droppings. Though no one ever bothered to try to harvest the guano in question, Seward noted this forgotten claim from eight years earlier in State Department files and identified an important opportunity: here were a few specks of land at almost dead-center of the Pacific, 1,200 miles northwest of Hawaii (which he coveted), with no cost to the public treasury and no rival power to contest its seizure. At the secretary's urging, and through reliance on the Guano Islands Act, Congress approved annexation in August 1867, and a navy ship took possession shortly thereafter. This little-noted maneuver occurred at the very height of Seward's consuming battle to win approval for the acquisition of the 600,000 square miles of Russian America.

Only later did the lonely guano atoll win the designation "Midway Islands."

Just seventy-five years after the visionary secretary of state thought to add them to the American map, his countrymen fought the most important naval battle in their history over these insignificant dots in the ocean in one of the long series of blessings and amazements that have continued to shield and sustain the United States of America.

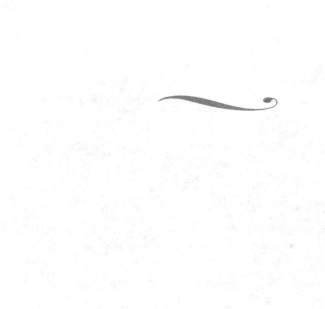

"WE HERE CONSECRATE THIS GREAT HIGHWAY FOR THE GOOD OF
THY PEOPLE": Celebrating the "Golden Spike" at Promontory Summit, Utah Territory,
May 10, 1869, marking completion of the world's first transcontinental railroad.
One enraptured clergyman proclaimed that "this Pacific Railway is a means,
under Divine Providence, for propagating the Church and the Gospel."

3

"The Lightening Stands Ready"

Transcontinental Tracks and a Reborn Benediction

Americans of 1869 hailed the completion of the transcontinental railroad as a spiritual milestone, not just a mechanical accomplishment.

For the hundreds who gathered in the high desert of Utah Territory, and for the millions who celebrated the magical moment through telegraphic connection in cities and villages across the country, the pounding of the Golden Spike amounted to an open miracle.

Dr. Hartwell Carver of Rochester, New York, had been promoting the great project with messianic enthusiasm for more than thirty years. To him, the rail connection to the Pacific represented nothing less than "the means of uniting the whole world in one great church, a part of whose worship will be to praise God and bless the Oregon railroad."

At age eighty, Dr. Carver managed to make the arduous journey to Promontory Summit to personally bless the completed task. A telegraph wire had been attached to the fateful golden nail, with another fastened on the designated sledgehammer. At the precise moment that the breathlessly awaited blow finally fell, a signal would spark instantaneously through a web of cables, informing every corner of the continent that the great work had reached its official completion, linking Atlantic to Pacific with a superhighway of iron bars. That message would provoke roaring cannon, blaring brass bands, and church choirs erupting into exultant hymns of praise at the midafternoon moment that the assembled multitudes received it.

"HATS OFF; PRAYER IS BEING OFFERED"

But first they prayed. At Promontory Summit, nearly a mile above sea level, Reverend Doctor John Todd of Massachusetts stepped before the crowd. A telegraph operator who had traveled to the site from Ogden, Utah, tapped out a series of dispatches to calm impatient participants from coast to coast, who waited for assurance that their jubilation could commence. "Almost ready," one telegram declared. "Hats off; prayer is being offered."

Reverend Todd then praised God's "wonderful name" and asked "that this great work, so auspiciously begun and so magnificently completed, may remain a monument to our faith and good works. We here consecrate this great highway for the good of thy people."

The next telegraphic message combined a sense of excitement with obvious relief. "Done praying," it tersely declared. "The spike is about to be presented." And then, more fretting before the grand climax: "All ready now. The spike will soon be driven. The signal will be three dots for the commencement of the blows."

Leland Stanford, a Sacramento store owner who'd served a term as governor of California and would go on to found a great university, got the privilege of initiating those blows. As one of the principal investors in the Central Pacific Railroad, he dressed in top hat and formal suit, an incongruous outfit for the remote, desolate, and windy location. He paused for a moment to contemplate the grandeur of the occasion, lifted the hammer above his portly frame, then swung toward the ceremonial spike. But somehow, he managed to miss it entirely. Still, the blow clanged against rail, producing applause and hurrahs, and causing the telegraph operator to click out his awaited notification—"Done!"—as cannon and choruses exploded from coast to coast.

In Washington, D.C., more than one hundred artillery pieces discharged simultaneously, producing a thunderous roar that residents never forgot. Several reporters estimated that the celebratory volleys across the country delivered more firepower in a single hour than all the booming cannon of Union and Confederacy combined, in all three days of the recent Battle of Gettysburg.

Inside New York City's venerable and elegant Trinity Church, near the corner of Broadway and Wall Street, Reverend Doctor Morgan Dix ascended the pulpit to announce that "the extreme borders of our land have been joined and brought nigh together, and a pathway opened between remote parts of the earth, both for the commerce of the nation and for a highway and a way whereby Thy Gospel may have free course, and Thy holy name may be glorified."

His colleague, Reverend Doctor Francis Vinton, agreed in viewing the completion of the amazing new railroad as an occurrence of cosmic significance. "When we contemplate this achievement, we can hardly realize its magnitude" as "a means, under Divine Providence, for propagating the Church and the Gospel from this, the youngest Christian nation, to the oldest lands in the Orient, now sunk in Paganism and idolatry."

Across the country, citizens praised the new transcontinental connection as an indication of America's divinely designated destiny.

Philadelphians heard the bells pealing in Independence Hall, echoing immediately at nearby fire stations and "drawing a crowd into the streets." An eyewitness reported that "flags were immediately hoisted everywhere. A large number of steam fire-engines were ranged in front of Independence Hall, with screeching whistles, horse carriages, bells ringing, &c. Joy was expressed in every face at the completion of the great work of the century."

In Chicago, workers left their jobs early to pour into the streets upon word that the Golden Spike had completed the great task. A parade commenced, described by reporters as "entirely impromptu," involving "almost every man and woman and child in the city" in an unprecedented procession that stretched for seven miles, according to the lowest estimate.

Special pride marked the emotional response in Salt Lake City, the permanent settlement closest to the ceremony at Promontory

Summit. Brigham Young's Mormon capital felt a proprietary stake in the achievement because of the prominent part played by some five thousand tireless Latter-day Saints who had labored in laying track. An astonishing seven thousand worshippers jammed into the Mormon Tabernacle, representing an apparent majority of the young town's population of twelve thousand, to hear an elderly church leader from England, John Taylor, exulting in the supernatural nature of an accomplishment "so stupendous that we can scarcely find words to express our sentiments or give vent to our admiration."

Taylor went on to recall his boyhood in another country and another epoch. "I can very well remember the time when there was no such thing as a railroad in existence," he told the astonished throng. "I rode on the first train that was ever made, soon after its completion; that was between Manchester and Liverpool, England."

At the time, that primitive but functional steam engine railway ran just over thirty miles and began carrying passengers in 1830, astonishing the world and inspiring a frenzy of copycat construction. Less than two years later, the first train service came to the United States with ambitious little lines in South Carolina and upstate New York. Even before this wondrous new technology made its way into isolated villages and farms, glowing newspaper accounts excited dreamers and schemers across the country.

"A PERFECT PASSION FOR RAILROADS"

One young Illinois shopkeeper, for instance, grew up in remote frontier settlements in Kentucky and Indiana and never glimpsed a train of any kind but nonetheless spoke earnestly to his neighbors about the need for governmental support to bring a railroad to their region. Twenty-three-year-old Abraham Lincoln made his first run for public office in 1832 with a platform that emphasized enthusiastic support for a rail connection between the new town of Springfield and the Illinois River.

He lost that election, finishing eighth of thirteen candidates, but he never lost his passionate interest in rail transportation. In the legal practice that later punctuated and propelled his political progress,

Lincoln earned his best fees as a railroad lawyer, especially during seven years as counsel to the powerful Illinois Central. His work not only helped to settle complex shareholder disputes but also allowed the company to escape onerous tax burdens and to build the crucial infrastructure that made it the dominant corporation in the state. Throughout his political and legal battles, Lincoln exemplified the enraptured attitudes that led French economist Michel Chevalier to observe in 1850: "The Americans have a perfect passion for railroads."

In February 1859, as a recently defeated senatorial candidate, Lincoln poetically expressed that passion in a memorable lecture on "Discoveries and Inventions" delivered in Jacksonville, Illinois. The local Literary Society received the lanky visitor with "repeated and hearty bursts of applause" from an eager audience conscious of his celebrity status. Although he lost his bid for the Senate seat, Lincoln had conducted an unexpectedly strong challenge to the powerful incumbent senator (and outspoken railroad advocate in his own right) Stephen Douglas, generating rumors of a potential run for the presidency. That long-shot campaign installed Lincoln in the White House barely two years after the talk in Jacksonville, where the future president sought to invoke the spirit of restless youth.

"We have all heard of Young America," Lincoln told the curious crowd. "Is he not the inventor, and owner of the *present*, and sole hope of the *future?*"

Honest Abe harbored no doubt what form of transportation would deliver "Young America" to that future. "The iron horse is panting, and impatient, to carry him everywhere, in no time; and the lightening stands ready harnessed to take and bring his tidings in a trifle less than no time. He owns a large part of the world, by right of possessing it; and all the rest by right of *wanting* it, and *intending* to have it. . . . He is a great friend of humanity; and his desire for land is not selfish, but merely an impulse to extend the area of freedom."

Warming to his theme on that freezing winter night, Lincoln continued to celebrate his countrymen's unparalleled ability to innovate and improvise. "We, here in America, think we discover, and invent, and improve, faster than any of them," the future emancipator declared. "It is in this view that I have mentioned the discovery of America as an event greatly favoring and facilitating useful discoveries and inventions."

From the perspective of the antebellum era, no invention looked more useful or revolutionary than a steam locomotive on railroad tracks. Before that marvelous technology appeared in the British Midlands, no human being could travel on land at greater speed than the charioteers who followed the biblical Pharaoh in pursuit of the escaping Israelites more than three thousand years earlier.

"THE PROPHET OF PEACE, THE MESSENGER OF CIVILIZATION"

For Americans, rail transport promised a deliverance even more miraculous than the rescue at the Red Sea. Suddenly, fire-breathing, belching metallic behemoths could transport whole crowds of human cargo, along with nearly unlimited freight, at sustained speeds of more than twenty miles per hour—covering long distances four times faster than even the strongest horse. By the time of Lincoln's Jacksonville speech, locomotives could hit speeds of sixty miles per hour on sections of straightaway track, topping the furious gallop of racing thoroughbreds at their moments of greatest exertion.

Trains revolutionized the nation's continental vision. During the California gold rush of 1849, thousands of adventurers made the arduous and uncertain overland trek from the eastern seaboard to the gold fields. Some traveled in wagons pulled by oxen or mules, risking life and health in a perilous journey requiring a minimum of four months, and often lasting more than half a year.

Traveling by ship cost far more, following a route of fifteen thousand miles around Cape Horn at the tip of South America, with weary travelers hoping to be successfully deposited in San Francisco three to five months later, depending on winds and tides.

The "Panama Shortcut" trimmed eight thousand miles of ocean travel but required a dangerous jungle passage on routes near the site of the modern canal, with serious risks of malaria, yellow fever, and cholera, as well as significant difficulties in boarding a second ship on the Pacific side of the isthmus. If all went well, the survivors could arrive in the Golden State within two months.

Advocates for a Pacific railway promised passage in as little as a week, with an unprecedented ability to barrel through unilluminated darkness and inclement weather toward even the most distant destination. That power could change everything, transforming the United States for the first time into a truly continental confederation.

In 1849, President Zachary Taylor had offered Abraham Lincoln a promising appointment as governor of the Oregon Territory, but the former congressman turned it down because of the settlement's remote status in a dank, untamed corner of the map, far removed from civilization. With regular train service, the settlements in California, Oregon, and the new Washington Territory would no longer qualify as the equivalent of isolated, vulnerable overseas possessions; a trip to the West Coast need not resemble some risky intergalactic voyage through endless nothingness to a space colony in another solar system.

No wonder that nineteenth-century Americans looked upon trains with the same awe and wonder with which later generations viewed fanciful spacecraft in science fiction movies. John McDowell Leavitt, the Episcopal clergyman, popular novelist, and president of Lehigh University, memorably celebrated the locomotive as a godly and redemptive instrument, "the prophet of peace, the messenger of civilization, the herald of the millennium, the conqueror of humanity ... raising the valleys, leveling the mountains, and making the crooked straight and the rough plain, for the monarch of the universe."

The shining new path between the seas could, in other words, alter the nature of the landscape itself, by changing the great empty core of the continent from an affliction to an opportunity. True believers expected that a transcontinental railroad would not only bind the Pacific states to the rest of the country but also fill the empty land in between with farms and free men.

Before the Civil War, however, this middle core looked remote, even forbidding. When New York newspaper titan Horace Greeley followed his own advice to "Go west, young man," and traveled by wagon and stagecoach across the continent, he judged much of the terrain unfit for human habitation. "I thought I had seen barrenness before," he wrote of the parched, rocky territory of Nevada, noting that there "famine sits enthroned and waves his scepter over a domin-ion expressly made for him."

Twenty years later, even after the railroad had crossed the prairie, Scottish writer Robert Louis Stevenson made similar observations about his passage through the otherworldly landscape of the upper Midwest. "We were at sea—there is no other adequate expression—on the plains of Nebraska," he wrote. He marveled at the idea that settlers could somehow survive "in this spacious vacancy . . . this straight, unbroken, prison-line of the horizon."

"HE SHELLED MY WOODS COMPLETELY"

Lincoln journeyed to the edge of this same "spacious vacancy" in Au-gust 1859, to make a political speech and to scout potential origina-tion points for a grand Pacific railroad. He rode the existing lines all the way to their western terminus in Council Bluffs, Iowa, just across the Missouri River and a ferry ride away from the bustling frontier town of Omaha, Nebraska. He had become involved in a complicated land deal with one of his political and business partners in Illinois, who had acquired some lots on the Iowa side of the river. Naturally, this property would greatly increase in value if construction of a rail-road to California ever actually commenced.

The day after his well-attended address at the local concert hall, Lincoln met with a group of business leaders on the broad, sagging porch of a grand but rickety hotel known as Pacific House. He took a particular interest in twenty-eight-year-old Grenville Dodge, who had earned a reputation as the leading railroad engineer of the region. Taking him aside, the railroad lawyer already known as Honest Abe posed a pertinent question: "Dodge, what's the best route for a Pacific railroad to the West?"

They spoke for more than two hours on that hotel porch, locked in earnest conversation about the plans and prospects that Dodge had developed over the course of several years. "Mr. Lincoln sat down beside me and, by his kindly ways, soon drew from me all I knew," Dodge recalled years later. "He shelled my woods completely and got all the information I'd collected.... This interview was of the greatest importance to me. It was a milestone in my life and Mr. Lincoln never forgot it."

Dodge knew that Lincoln remembered their talk because he referred to it at the height of the Civil War when he twice summoned the young engineer to the White House. By that time, Dodge had established himself as one of the most capable and versatile generals in the Union Army, becoming a key lieutenant to the rising commander Ulysses S. Grant. He repaired bridges and track that retreating Confederates attempted to destroy, constructing new railroads for the rapid transportation of federal troops.

Grenville Dodge also demonstrated conspicuous valor on numerous battlefields along with an uncanny ability to survive enemy bullets that ripped through his body on three different occasions. During each of the general's hospitalizations, politicians and businessmen tried to persuade the wounded officer to resign from the army to concentrate on constructing rail lines that would make their own contribution to the federal cause. Each time, Dodge refused. "Nothing but the utter defeat of the rebel armies will ever bring peace," he declared. "I have buried some of my best friends in the south, and I intend to remain there until we can visit their graves under the peaceful protection of that flag that every loyal citizen loves to honor and every soldier fights to save."

While the war delayed Dodge's personal participation in laying track to the West Coast, it played a larger role in hastening that epic project. For more than twenty years before the conflict, Washington politicians had debated the prospects for such a line but sectional rivalry had blocked consensus. In 1853, Congress authorized an analysis of various potential routes and Secretary of War Jefferson Davis dispatched four teams of surveyors to report on four of them.

As a loyal Mississippian (and future president of the Confederacy), the secretary strongly favored a southern route, hugging the Mexican border and culminating in San Diego. Southerners like Davis felt confident that such a path would not only provide economic advantages for their region but help assure the extension of slavery—from Texas through the New Mexico and Arizona territories and, perhaps, into Southern California. Free-state members of the Senate and House hated the idea of a southern railroad precisely for that reason, insisting on a route through the Great Plains that would take freight and passengers all the way to Sacramento.

The disagreement proved no easier to resolve than any other aspect of the sectional dispute until the southern states made their fateful decision to leave the Union. Secession may have been a disaster for the nation, but it proved an immediate boon to the prospects of a transcontinental rail line. When representatives from eleven slave states abandoned the federal Congress, all opposition to the northern line literally left the building.

But even as the political obstacles disappeared, the practical problems remained—especially the near-universal skepticism about building a railroad that could transit the steep, jagged heights of the Sierra Nevada. That range presented a formidable and sometimes deadly challenge to all would-be pioneers who tried to take their ox-drawn carts and wagons through the passes; the difficulty of building tunnels and bridges that could accommodate huge, unwieldy locomotives looked even worse. The irresistible enthusiasm about rail transportation in general now confronted a seemingly impassable obstacle in the form of the menacing mountains that blocked access to California. Hubert Howe Bancroft, then a recent arrival in San Francisco and later a distinguished historian, commented that the challenge struck savvy observers as so "stupendous and hazardous an enterprise it appears an act of madness or of inspiration."

"THERE COMES CRAZY JUDAH!"

Public opinion tilted so heavily toward lunacy as the explanation for the improbable project that Californians spent years deriding its chief advocate and architect with an unshakable nickname that presumed his insanity.

Theodore Dehone Judah became known as "Crazy Judah" for his focused, feverish obsession with the transcontinental project. A visi-

"THERE COMES CRAZY JUDAH!": Theodore Dehone Judah (1826–1863), the indispensable, obsessed, but underappreciated driving force in championing and engineering the world's first transcontinental railroad. He described the venture as "the most magnificent project ever conceived."

tor to Sacramento named John McIntire recalled standing on Seventh Street with grocer Newton Booth, who suddenly exclaimed, "There comes crazy Judah!" McIntire watched with bemused interest, recalling that he had never before met "an insane man." As the stranger approached, McIntire felt mildly disappointed to meet a well-dressed gentleman with a neatly trimmed beard, glittering eyes, and an earnest manner. After concluding the brief encounter, Booth explained that Ted Judah exemplified a special sort of madness—he had become notorious as "Pacific Railroad crazy," utterly insufferable and monomaniacal about his visions for a grand and preposterous project. Booth and other locals had endured his rants so often that they banned the determined engineer from ever raising the subject in any respectable social context.

These restrictions may have limited Judah's conversation but they did nothing to cool the animating passion of his life. The son of an Episcopal clergyman from Connecticut, young Theodore nursed dreams of military glory. When the boy was only thirteen, after his father's death, his brother got the chance to enroll at West Point while Ted began working with local railroads. He later studied engineering at New York's Troy School of Technology (later Rensselaer Polytechnic Institute) but more important gained hands-on experience in every aspect of railroad construction and design.

At age twenty-one, Ted married the elegant, accomplished Anna Ferona Pierce, a cousin of future president of the United States Franklin Pierce. The young lady, considered a prized catch, showed talent as a skilled painter and a confident writer while sharing her husband's boundless energy and adventurous spirit. In her memoirs, she recalls some of their blissful joint excursions into unexplored corners of the continent, where he measured and tracked potential rail lines while she painted detailed landscapes to celebrate the rustic scenes.

Ted enjoyed his first great success while still in his twenties when he built the Niagara Gorge railroad that helped make the famous falls accessible to hordes of new tourists and constituted one of the purportedly impossible engineering feats of the 1840s. To skeptical investors who doubted his ability to overcome the obvious obstacles, Ted Judah boldly declared: "Gentlemen, raise the money and I will build your road."

This triumph prepared him for an even more imposing opportunity. During a business trip to New York City in 1854, Ted sent a telegram home to his wife ordering her to pack her bags. When he returned late that night, he shouted out his great news before he could even walk through the door. "Anna, I am going to California to be the pioneer railroad engineer of the Pacific coast," he announced in his booming voice.

Meanwhile, in the gold rush town of Sacramento, already established as the new state's capital city, a group of enterprising merchants considered how they could possibly bring the modern marvel of train transport to the isolated Pacific Coast. At that point, no tracks traversed any portion of the Golden State and no locomotive had ever sounded its haunting whistle to pierce the wilderness silence west of the Missouri River; across nearly three million square miles of the American West, the railroads simply did not exist. The group of merchants resolved to correct that situation.

They summoned Ted Judah to build track to cover the short distance to the gold fields in the nearby Sierra foothills. The purpose would be to transport picks, shovels, tents, blankets, food, tobacco, booze, and other necessities to the hordes of hungry miners who still searched for sudden wealth as they struggled to stay alive. To build even so modest a railroad, Judah first needed to haul all locomotives, train cars, rails, and other equipment from the East Coast to the West by piling it onto ships for the months-long journey around the far tip of South America. Once arrived in San Francisco Bay, the cargo could be reloaded onto riverboats to steam the final ninety miles to the frontier capital, best known for its saloons, gambling dens, bawdy houses, criminal gangs, and, of course, ambitious politicians.

Immune to such distractions, Ted Judah focused with single-minded ferocity on his mission to build railroads that would conquer and civilize the untamed, awe-inspiring landscape that surrounded him. He felt especially challenged and inspired by the Sierra Nevada, later described by naturalist John Muir as "The Range of Light . . . miles in height, and so gloriously colored and so radiant, it seemed not clothed with *light,* but wholly composed of it, like the wall of some celestial city."

Judah understood that however heavenly its appearance, the mighty Sierra constituted formidable walls that blocked his ambitions. The looming snow-packed peaks represented the most significant barrier separating the Golden State's boomtowns and mineral wealth from the crowded cities and productive farmland that beckoned so seductively to the east. He began badgering anyone who would listen about his unique ability to breach that barrier if only he received the financing he required. With long, florid dispatches that he published regularly in the *Sacramento Union,* he enhanced his reputation as a mad obsessive by insistently arguing for the immediate implementation of his soaring schemes.

"WE MUST KEEP THE BALL ROLLING"

These newspaper appeals soon provided the basis for Judah's self-published, book-length pamphlet with which he hoped to persuade a skeptical world of the feasibility and grandeur of his plans. By the time of its publication, Ted had already completed work on the small-scale but instantly successful Sacramento Valley Railroad, which provided the first-ever train service in the western United States.

At his own expense, he printed enough copies of his magnum opus, *A Practical Plan for Building the Pacific Railroad*, so that he could distribute one to each member of Congress, relentlessly campaigning to secure federal sponsorship for the daunting task of further rail construction. He insisted that any project on this scale required comprehensive governmental support and he pushed for a painless means of providing it. The federal authorities owned limitless tracts of empty land between Omaha and California, and it would cost them nothing to reward private entrepreneurs by giving them title to generous acreage on either side of any track they built. After all, that previously worthless real estate would instantly gain value by its proximity to the new coast-to-coast rail line, so it made some rough sense to transfer the land to the companies whose imagination and hard work had incontestably enhanced its worth. Judah also acknowledged that the builders of any new line would need federal help in underwriting the mammoth loans required to pay for matériel and the thousands of workers who would toil across the prairie.

During 1856 alone, "Crazy Judah" and Anna, his long-suffering but always adoring wife, made the arduous trip between California and the nation's capital three times. To save extra months in transit, they sailed to Panama and cut through the steaming, mosquito-infested jungles of the isthmus, just as they had when they first traveled to the Golden State. In Washington, Ted became a tireless lobbyist, haranguing congressmen and department officials and pleading for the legislation to fund his schemes. Eventually, he secured a White House meeting with an elderly, eternally dithering President James Buchanan, who proved no more decisive or effective in advancing the Pacific railroad than he did in averting civil war.

At the same time, the transcontinental project managed to attract some energetic support in Congress, especially from representatives of the western states, who assigned Judah an unused room in the Capitol to help him plead his case. There, he followed his wife's recommendation to establish "the Pacific Railroad Museum," announced to the waiting world with considerable fanfare and typically over-blown grandiosity. The jammed chamber displayed maps, plans, geological surveys, mineral samples, and a handsome collection of Anna's paintings, portraying some of the spectacular landscape Ted's railroad would traverse.

Politicos visited out of curiosity or bemusement and generally stayed to listen to Judah's persuasive presentations. Congressman John C. Burch, a California Democrat, remembered that Ted's "knowledge of his subject was so thorough, his manners so gentle and insinuating, his conversation on the subject so entertaining, that few resisted his appeals."

Judah also succeeded in changing minds back home in California. He pushed the state legislature to summon an official "Railroad Convention," where representatives of the western states, along with delegates from the Arizona and Washington territories, would officially petition the feds to get on with the Pacific railroad. Unsurprisingly, the convention officially selected then-thirty-three-year-old Ted Judah to represent their cause in the federal capital.

Between his cross-country trips, he continued his surveys in the mountains as he refined his detailed plans to conquer the Sierra. Anna recalled these joint expeditions with special fondness, as they camped together in the high country and worked tirelessly toward their common goal. They would awake to crisp mountain air, heavily scented with pine needles, a burning campfire, and strong coffee, and then spend the days with Ted scouting routes while she dabbed joyously at one of the paintings she produced to commemorate the process.

In October 1860, as the rest of the country hurtled toward the presidential election that installed Lincoln in the White House and pushed the southern states to secede, Judah had his own fateful encounter with a grizzled, gaunt, black-bearded mountain man with burning, dark, prophetic eyes. Daniel Webster Strong, universally known as "Doc," dispensed drugs and folk remedies in a rough, newly established miners' town known as Dutch Flat. Before the two met, Doc Strong wrote to Judah that he had found the solution to build a viable rail line to the east and invited the engineer to see the path for himself. Judah rode out to Dutch Flat, and together they ventured toward a pass through the crags more than seven thousand feet above sea level.

They slept for the night in an abandoned shepherd's hut. The next morning, Ted gazed out, and through a chill rain he saw his destiny. Doc Strong showed him the old "emigrant road" where, fourteen years before, one of the most notorious incidents in western history placed a purported curse on the ill-fated route.

In May 1846, the Donner Party headed for California by wagon train with eighty-seven men, women, and children, hoping for a new life on the Pacific Coast. By November, they became trapped for four months in heavy snowfall around the body of water now known as Donner Lake. At least thirty-five members of the party died of starvation, illness, or the freezing cold. The survivors, according to most accounts, kept themselves alive by cannibalizing the bodies.

This grisly tale was frequently recounted and had already become well known by the time Theodore Judah first beheld the haunted ground of Donner Pass. But not even the most horrid associations could stop him from recognizing the site's potential. Along the same ridge that had trapped the Donner Party, Judah could build a path over the Sierra with bridges, tunnels, and overpasses that would keep the track at a gentle enough grade to accommodate the locomotives of that time.

While others might have shunned the route for its taint of bad luck, the Donner Pass might have spoken with special force to Ted Judah, with his abiding belief in the power of rail transport to transform every aspect of reality. This grim, forbidding place where wagon-bound travelers had suffered deadly immobility for months could now give way to a highway of iron that rail passengers might travel safely, securely, and regularly, chugging their reliable, civilized course through the mountains and their mysteries.

Back at Doc Strong's cabin, the two men drew up a contractual agreement creating a partnership that later became the Central Pacific Railroad. Ted Judah also began to sketch out a huge map that extended to ninety feet, showing every detail of a plausible route through the mountains and beyond. He eventually carried this sacred scroll back to the Pacific Railroad Museum as a tool of final persuasion for doubtful politicians and queasy investors.

In San Francisco, the leading business figures had already turned Judah down. But he finally won the support of four Sacramento shop-keepers whose nervous backing for Crazy Judah ultimately made them rich and famous. Leland Stanford, Collis P. Huntington, Mark Hopkins, and Charles Crocker, later known as "the Big Four," became the dominant figures in Ted's newly chartered Central Pacific Rail-road and eventually won places of honor among the nation's wealthi-est families.

In the beginning, however, they nursed more modest ambitions: they knew that any development of transportation to the east would greatly boost their Sacramento businesses. Even a failed railroad could still provide a good return on their investment: before laying track for his transcontinental line, Judah first proposed to grade a wagon road for moving the needed workmen and equipment into place. That route would naturally connect to some of the rich, busy silver mines in Nevada, which would buy supplies from the California merchants, while producing considerable revenue from tolls even be-fore any laying of rails or importing of locomotives. As Charlie Crocker later confessed about the celebrated Big Four: "We none of us knew anything about railroad building, but at the same time were enterprising men, and anxious to have a road built, and have it come to Sacramento."

For Judah, a muddy, rutted, frontier wagon path could hardly ful-fill his aspirations: he looked upon horse-drawn transportation as an ancient, outmoded technology that represented only a temporary ex-pedient on the way to the futuristic glory of trains. His wife, Anna, recalled years later: "Everything he did from the time he went to Cali-fornia to the day of his death was for the great continental Pacific railway. It was the burden of his thought day and night, largely of his conversation, till it used to be said, 'Judah's Pacific Railroad crazy,' and I would say, 'Theodore, those people don't care,' or 'you give your thun-der away.' . . . He'd laugh and say, 'But we must keep the ball rolling.'"

"A WORK OF GIANTS"

With Theodore Judah pushing, that ball kept rolling right over a suddenly pliant Congress: when the railroad true believer Abraham Lincoln assumed power in the White House, and balky Southern representatives left the legislature along with their seceding states, the once far-fetched fantasy of a cross-continent rail line suddenly enjoyed lopsided support.

The commander in chief's unwavering determination finally forced the issue to its climax. Amid the bloody battles that transfixed the country, the president made the vision of a gleaming, metallic highway to the distant West into a pressing, practical priority. In one of his White House meetings with General Grenville Dodge, Lincoln insisted that the construction of a coast-to-coast rail line had become an urgent imperative "not only as military necessity, but as a means of holding the Pacific Coast to the Union."

In May 1862, the House passed the Pacific Railroad Act by a vote of seventy-nine to forty-nine, with the Senate following suit six weeks later by an even more comfortable margin of thirty-five to five. The terms closely followed the idea of a public-private partnership outlined in Judah's *Practical Plan* introduced five years earlier. The engineer's newly organized firm, the Central Pacific Railroad, would follow the route sketched in his ninety-foot-long "sacred scroll" to blast tunnels, raise trestles, and traverse mountaintops in crossing the Sierra from west to east, starting from Sacramento. Meanwhile, an even more recently organized firm, the patriotically named Union Pacific, would begin in Omaha and head west across the Rockies. The two companies would race to meet at some undetermined point in Utah Territory, encouraged by the new legislation to put down track as promptly as possible.

The rewards for their speedy progress amounted to the largest corporate land grant in history. With the two roads moving exclusively through unclaimed, unsettled federal land, the railroads received a right-of-way amounting to two hundred feet of property on both sides of any track they built. As a bonus, they also claimed an additional ten square miles of nearby land as reward for each mile of completed grade. The concept gave the companies control of a real estate empire of nearly two hundred thousand square miles— considerably larger than the state of California. The best way to profit from this property would require the railroads to encourage rapid settlement all along the long, lonely route to the Pacific. In addition, the two corporations could finance their gigantic endeavor with government-backed, interest-bearing bonds, delivering instant capital in amounts ranging from $16,000 per mile for relatively level territory to $48,000 per mile to traverse the treacherous passes over the Rockies and Sierra peaks.

For those who questioned this wartime federal largesse to profit-hungry railroad entrepreneurs, William Tecumseh Sherman had a ready answer. A onetime banker and railroad backer in California, who later became a legendary commander in the Civil War, he wrote to his brother John Sherman, at the time a congressman from Ohio, that the proposed rail line must be "a work of giants. And Uncle Sam is the only giant I know who can grapple the subject."

On January 8, 1863, that grappling began in earnest when a jubilant crowd gathered at the K Street waterfront of the Sacramento River to cheer the groundbreaking ceremony for Crazy Judah's Central Pacific Railroad. Judah himself missed the celebration, trekking yet again into the dangerous snowbound Sierra to perfect his measurements and finalize the plans for the construction to come. Leland Stanford, in his second year as governor of California, presided over the festivities and delivered a windy and grandiose address, promising "no delay, no backing, no uncertainty in the continued progress." The crowd offered lusty cheers, despite the tedious oratory, drenching rain, and bitterly cold conditions. A brass band blared "Wait for the Wagon" and the participants applauded a bold banner that showed a map of the continent, with two arms reaching toward a handshake at its center. "THE PRAYER OF EVERY LOYAL HEART," the inscription read. "MAY THE BOND BE ETERNAL."

"TO COMBINE ALL THE GOOD OF THE PAST"

Eleven months later, similar sentiments pervaded the parallel ground-breaking celebration as the newly organized Union Pacific Railroad began its westward march from the Nebraska Territory town of Omaha. Local dignitaries read congratulatory messages from President Lincoln and Secretary of State William Henry Seward, both enthusiastic backers of the coast-to-coast railway. "When this shall have been done disunion will be rendered forever afterward impossible," Seward promised. "There will be no fulcrum for the lever of treason to rest upon."

The featured speaker, George Francis Train, provided even loftier exhortations in a stem-winding, rambling, impromptu address that seemed to shuttle between memorable rhetoric and meandering mania. Train had already established an international reputation as a mad and irrepressible eccentric, having earned and lost several fortunes with controversial ventures in shipping, horse-drawn tramways, and railroads in the United States, Australia, and Great Britain. He had recently applied his organizational genius to the Union Pacific, which would earn him millions in profits from selling off the generous land grants that the federal government provided in return for completed track. Later in life, Train spent time in French jails for his revolutionary activities in backing the Paris Commune, ran an independent campaign for the American presidency on a radical platform of women's rights and alcohol restrictions, reputedly turned down offers to rule a new "Republic of Australia" as its dictator, and faced arrest on charges of "dangerous insanity" at the very height of his fame.

At Omaha, the remarks recorded by reporters rose to an unmistakably hysterical pitch as Train thrilled to "the inauguration of the greatest enterprise under God the world has ever witnessed." He repeatedly referenced the Egyptian construction of the pyramids and suggested that the new rail line amounted to a greater, more long-lasting achievement. To Train, and to his reportedly enraptured listeners, the providential plan seemed unmistakable: "America was reserved to combine all the good of the past—Industry, Law, Art, Commerce—with the grander mission of representing the grand Pacific Railway idea of progress." Though the effervescent orator far exceeded his allotted time, restive spectators saw no way to stop the runaway Train. He approached his grand finale by describing the hand of the Almighty in preparing a path for the all-conquering locomotives to come, "making a plateau of boundless prairie, expressly for the track of the great Union Pacific Railway of America. . . . As sure as the rainbow is the autograph of God, the Union must and shall be preserved."

Train confidently predicted that the cross-country railroad would be complete by the year 1870, an outrageously optimistic prophecy that drew derisive laughter from the edges of the crowd. The timetable discussed in congressional debate had allotted at least six years more, foreseeing completion of the mammoth undertaking in time to celebrate the Centennial of the nation's founding in 1876. But the lure of earning extra money and claiming additional land for every mile of track produced a fanatical focus on speed and competition as the eastbound crews raced the westbound workers to see which company could gobble up more of the promised rewards.

"SHOVELING, WHEELING, CARTING, DRILLING AND BLASTING"

The first challenge for both corporations involved transportation of vast quantities of equipment and matériel to the current construction sites as the work crews advanced farther into wild and unsettled territory. Laying track across the empty stretches of the continent required moving 110,000 tons of iron rails, 2 million bolts, 15 million spikes, and 3.5 million cross ties to the ever-shifting leading edge of construction. For the Central Pacific, Ted Judah had also ordered eight locomotives, eight passenger cars, and sixty freight wagons that had to be carried on ships from New York and sailed around South America into San Francisco Bay.

Another major obstacle concerned the effort to recruit the huge armies of workmen required to take on the gargantuan task. With work beginning in 1863, at the very height of the Civil War, most able-bodied males were already serving in armies devoted to the business of killing rather than the job of construction. The labor shortage meant that even the promise of good pay (which amounted to as much as three dollars a day) couldn't lure workers who had so far avoided military service to leave home for months at a time, facing prodigiously difficult tasks that sounded nearly as perilous as war itself.

For the California-based Central Pacific, the answer came unexpectedly from the other side of the ocean. During the six years of railroad building, more than ten thousand Chinese laborers poured into California to join the already substantial Asian population drawn by the gold rush nearly twenty years before. Though initially derided for their smaller stature and limited grasp of English, these hardy and uncomplaining newcomers took on the dangerous assignments shunned by most of the local workforce. Historians agree that some 75 percent of those who toiled on the Central Pacific were Chinese nationals, accomplishing the seemingly impossible feat of laying more than five hundred miles of track at elevations above five thousand feet. This meant snowdrifts of fifteen feet or more and avalanches that regularly buried their flimsy campsites, destroying huts and tents and, on several occasions, taking the lives of the workers.

When necessary, the Chinese workmen volunteered to climb into baskets that were then lowered by rope down sheer cliffs, suspended as much as a thousand feet above the jagged rocks that loomed below. Dangling from such precarious perches, they picked and chipped at the solid granite to make holes deep enough to accommodate the insertion of explosives. After they lit the fuses, their survival depended on whether their comrades hauled them up swiftly enough to escape the full force of the blasts that followed.

Such prodigious feats suitably impressed their supervisors but did little to quell the distrust of suspicious locals, who railed against the Asians and their "heathen" cultures, while resenting the work ethic and modest demands that allegedly depressed local wages. A visiting reporter from the New York Tribune reflected the combination of race-based contempt and grudging respect that characterized the prevailing attitude toward the "coolie gangs" that successfully performed the most difficult and dangerous undertakings. He described the Chinese workers as "shoveling, wheeling, carting, drilling and blasting rocks and earth, while their dull moony eyes stared out from under immense bucket hats, like umbrellas." Shortly after the railroad's completion, agitation for "Oriental Exclusion" began in earnest and led the Golden State to the most restrictive and discriminatory immigration policies in U.S. history.

On the other side of the Continental Divide, General Grenville Dodge took the post of chief engineer for the Union Pacific as soon as the war ended and he had finally recovered from his multiple wounds. Together with the other principals of that newly chartered line, he relied on a different sort of marginalized immigrant labor: Irish Americans from big cities in the East and Midwest provided the bulk of the brawn for the construction crews that headed west from Omaha. As soon as the war ended, the prospect of steady work, decent pay, and frontier adventure drew "Paddies" who had fought on both sides of the conflict. With surprisingly little rancor, former Confederates joined with Union veterans for the common cause: to conquer both space and time by rapidly rolling out the new railroad.

The military experience of most of the men helped protect their work from roving bands of Sioux, Cheyenne, and Arapaho who attacked surveyors or scouts, stole equipment and livestock, and even managed to tear up some of the track to derail approaching locomotives. The Indians realized that the huge, fire-belching machines and the hordes of strangers who prepared the way for them would alter their lives beyond recognition. To the natives, the brawny railway builders with their soldierly organization looked like invaders because, in fact, they were. Within a generation of the completion of their work, the buffalo so central to Plains Indian culture had been hunted close to extinction. The U.S. cavalry, along with government-aligned Pawnee warriors, occasionally protected workers from hit-and-run marauders from the threatened tribes, but for the most part the work crews had to defend themselves. More than a hundred of them reputedly died in the process.

As they pushed across the plains, the largely Irish army also attracted less heroic participants in its progress. The workers' long trains bearing necessary equipment and nourishment included some "special cars" that unofficially transported liquor, makeshift bars, prostitutes, musicians, dance hall girls, and gambling facilities to provide after-work diversions for the weary young men in their lonely prairie camp-sites. These rolling, rollicking trouble trains became widely known as "hell on wheels" for their ability to transport temptation. They accompanied the work crews all the way to their date with destiny at Promontory Summit and gave a colorful, durable new phrase to the American idiom.

"JUST LIKE AN ARMY"

In the last stages of construction, some of the most significant contributions came from workers who scrupulously avoided the distractions of alcohol, bawdy houses, gambling, and other taints of corruption. Salt Lake City, the capital of a Mormon commonwealth and the only significant settlement anywhere near the railway's route to the coast, played an outsized role in both promoting the project and providing essential labor for its completion. Brigham Young, the all-powerful president of the Church of Jesus Christ of Latter-day Saints, invested in the Union Pacific at the very beginning and had long advocated a cross-country railroad. In one sermon Young delivered at the Mormon Tabernacle, the president, prophet, seer, and revelator thundered: "Speaking of the completion of this railroad, I am anxious to see it, and I say to the Congress of the United States, through our delegate, to the company, and to others, hurry up, hasten the work! We want to hear the iron horse puffing through this valley. What for? To bring our brethren and sisters here."

To those who worried that the railroad might threaten the church by ending its isolation, bringing new settlers with anti-Mormon sentiments and corrupt personal habits, President Young boldly declared that Mormonism "must indeed be a damned poor religion if it cannot stand one railroad!"

At his direction, more than five thousand of the faithful went to work for both the Central Pacific, after that line crossed the Sierra, and the Union Pacific, when that road passed over the Rockies.

On both projects, the devout Mormon laborers pointedly distanced themselves from their often rowdy counterparts, setting up separate camps. A reporter from the *Deseret News*, Edward Lennox Sloan, visited work sites at Echo and Weber canyons and noted the Latter-day Saints' conspicuous good manners and strict avoidance of profanity even by those who had toiled for long hours laying track. "After the day's work was done, the animals turned out to herd and the supper over, a nice blending of voices in sweet singing proved that the materials exist among the men for a capital choir, and there is some talk of organizing one," he proudly reported.

No wonder these well-disciplined believers made such a positive impression on their employers. In a fascinating 1969 monograph about Utah's role in constructing "The Iron Trail to the Golden Spike," Mormon historian John J. Stewart noted: "In the 1860s the officials of Union Pacific and Central Pacific were almost the only non-Mormon citizens of the United States who had warm, friendly feelings toward the Mormons. So successful had anti-Mormons been in their hate-crazed propaganda campaign that almost no one understood or appreciated the Utah pioneers."

In completing their work on the world's first cross-continent rail link, these three despised and frequently persecuted groups—Chinese peasants, Irish laborers, and fervent Mormon settlers—managed to collaborate with unexpected ease and efficiency. Near the end of April 1869, a reporter for the *San Francisco Evening Bulletin* accompanied Charlie Crocker, one of the Central Pacific's Big Four, to witness the feverishly intensifying work shortly before the crews from the two railroads approached their long-anticipated rendezvous. Big shots from both sides went so far as placing a thousand-dollar bet—some sources say much more—over which work crews could lay the most miles of tracks in a single day between sunrise and sunset, with only an hour break for lunch.

"The scene is a most animated one," the *Bulletin* reported. "From the first pioneer to the last tamper, perhaps two miles, there is a thin line of 1,000 men advancing a mile an hour; the iron cars ... running up and down; mounted men galloping backward and forward. Alongside of the moving force are teams hauling tools, and water wagons, and Chinamen, with pails strung over their shoulders, moving among the men with water and tea."

One army officer who had ridden out to see the epic contest, grabbed Charlie Crocker's arm and noted, "I never saw such organization as this; it is just like an army marching across over the ground and leaving a track built behind them."

The eyewitness testified to their superhuman effort and breathless pace. "When the whistle blew for the noon meal, at 1.30 PM, the CP workers had laid 6 miles of track.... By 7 PM, the CP was 10 miles and 56 feet farther east than it had been at dawn. Never before done, never matched."

According to subsequent calculations, this feat meant that the determined, sweating, perfectly collaborating Chinese and Mormon teams from the Central Pacific not only won the wager for their bosses but laid out and spiked a full length of track (two parallel rails of fifteen feet each) *every twelve seconds* during that particular workday.

Less than two weeks later, the twin hordes, implacably advancing from both east and west, finally collided not in conflict but in celebration.

In the last days before the completion of the much-anticipated line—more than six months ahead of George Francis Train's insanely optimistic prediction—most of the country, and indeed the world, focused on the fateful finish. Initially scheduled for May 8, the ceremonies experienced a two-day postponement with an official explanation of heavy rains damaging key bridges. Actually, a brief, bitter rebellion regarding overdue pay by some of Union Pacific's angry Irish workers probably played a more significant role.

When the lines extending 690 miles west to Sacramento and 1,085 miles east to Omaha had already been completed, both companies delivered a handsome and well-polished locomotive for the occasion, waiting for the installation of the last two track lengths as part of the ceremonial consummation, appropriately billed as "the wedding of the rails."

As part of this long-awaited union, a special railroad tie had been prepared of polished California laurel wood with a silver plaque. Four holes had been drilled in advance to accommodate the four ceremonial spikes: two of gold, one of silver, and one of iron plated with gold on the head and silver on the shaft. The principal spike of solid 17.6-carat gold had been inscribed with a prayer: "May God continue the unity of our Country as this Railroad unites the two great Oceans of the world."

"TREMBLING WITH POWER"

The lofty sentiments that prevailed during the countdown to consummation echoed the prior poetic flights that inspired even pedestrian politicians who became enchanted by the possibilities of rail travel to transform the continent. A farmer and surveyor named Charles Cathcart, who represented Indiana for two terms in the House of Representatives, rose on the floor to address the glories of the new technology on February 6, 1846. "The Iron Horse with wings of the wind, his nostrils distended with flame, salamander-like vomiting fire and smoke, trembling with power, but submissive to the steel curb imposed upon him by the hand of man, flies from one end of the continent to the other," the congressman triumphantly prophesied. "In storm and darkness, in the heat of a torrid sun or the chilling blasts of a Siberian winter, this mystical symbol of man's intelligence speeds its onward way." The Golden Spike, at last, fulfilled such radiant dreams for "this mystical symbol of man's intelligence," and the nation's most celebrated poet erupted in exultation at an event of cosmic, not merely continental, consequence.

Walt Whitman's epic poem "Passage to India" portrayed the New World, suddenly "by its mighty railroad spann'd" and thereby "tying the Eastern to the Western sea / The road between Europe and Asia." In Whitman's understanding, the event carried an unmistakable message of providential purpose:

> *Lo, soul! Seest thou not God's purpose from the first?*
> *The earth to be spann'd, connected by net-work,*
> *The people to become brothers and sisters,*
> *The races, neighbors, to marry and be given in marriage,*

The oceans to be cross'd, the distant brought near,
The lands to be welded together.

One hundred fifty years later, it's difficult to appreciate the nineteenth-century certainty that a railroad built by an oddly assorted collection of deeply flawed human beings represented an unmistakable demonstration of divine power and purpose. Today, we view technological progress as inevitable, incremental, and natural, not miraculous.

Yes, a number of factors came together to enable the completion of the transcontinental line in 1869: the peerless vision and leadership of "Crazy" Theodore Judah; the astonishing survival of Grenville Dodge from his many war wounds; the unfailing advocacy of the sainted, martyred Lincoln; the timely secession of the southern states that allowed congressional approval. Above all, contemporary observers emphasized the importance of the recent Civil War in enabling the triumph at Promontory Summit. Historian Stephen Ambrose reflects that "Dodge and nearly everyone else involved in building the road later commented that it could not have been done without the Civil War veterans and their experience. It was the war that taught them how to think big, how to organize grand projects, how to persevere."

But even without these fateful factors, or the examples of good fortune and good judgment that characterized most of the process, a cross-continent link would have developed eventually. Canada completed its own east-to-west line in November 1885 and then celebrated the achievement with typically Canadian understatement. Twenty years later, and thirty-six years after the American achievement, czarist Russia finished the Trans-Siberian Railway connecting Moscow to Vladivostok over the perilous course of 9,289 miles—some three times the length of its Yankee counterpart.

Yet the Americans came first and the timing of their accomplishment meant everything to citizens of that era. The unspeakable slaughter of the Civil War had inspired the first serious public doubts about God's special aid in the rise of the Republic, and of America's status as "this favored land," in the phrase employed by Lincoln in his

First Inaugural Address (and by Andrew Jackson in his presidential farewell twenty-four years earlier). The most recent scientific estimates report that the four years of sectional conflict claimed at least 740,000 lives on both sides, all of them American, with another half million grievously wounded. How could anyone argue that providence uniquely nourished the American people when they had just experienced the bloodiest internal conflict in world history to that time? Inevitably, many citizens speculated that the unprecedented suffering signified a special curse, or at least a purposeful punishment, rather than the special blessing that their forebears consistently acknowledged.

Lincoln himself speculated on this chastisement in his last significant public utterance: the Second Inaugural Address, delivered just five weeks before his murder:

> If we shall suppose that American slavery is one of those offenses which, in the providence of God, must needs come, but which, having continued through His appointed time, He now wills to remove, and that He gives to both North and South this terrible war as the woe due to those by whom the offense came, shall we discern therein any departure from those divine attributes which the believers in a living God always ascribe to Him? Fondly do we hope, fervently do we pray, that this mighty scourge of war may speedily pass away. Yet, if God wills that it continue until all the wealth piled by the bondsman's two hundred and fifty years of unrequited toil shall be sunk, and until every drop of blood drawn with the lash shall be paid by another drawn with the sword, as was said three thousand years ago, so still it must be said "the judgments of the Lord are true and righteous altogether."

Coming just four years after the conclusion of that presumed war of atonement, and with Lincoln's own martyrdom still a vivid memory, the much-heralded completion of the transcontinental railroad seemed to signal forgiveness, rebirth, and America's return to its divinely ordained, world-leading status. Like many of his contemporaries, Walt Whitman saw the railroad as realization of "inscrutable purpose, some hidden prophetic intention," that had been America's fate from its beginnings:

> . . . thou born, America, (a hemisphere unborn,)
> For purpose vast, man's long probation fill'd,
> Thou, rondure of the world, at last accomplish'd.

As Ben Wright and Zachary W. Dresser conclude in their 2013 anthology *Apocalypse and the Millennium in the American Civil War Era:* "The railroad became an actor in God's divine drama, a supreme symbol of millennial destiny."

In other words, the transcontinental connection could not only carry Americans from the East Coast to the West but also transport the country from the guilt and mourning and sacrifice of the war to the manic growth of "the Confident Years" between the Civil War and World War I.

REDEMPTION BY RAILROAD

Theodore Dehone Judah had come early to that unshakable confidence in his relentless efforts to provide his stricken, divided country with redemption by railroad.

Though his ongoing surveying in the Sierra caused him to miss the formal groundbreaking for the Central Pacific Railroad that he had created, he still struggled to supervise every detail of the early work toward realization of his dream. Unfortunately, conflicts with his partners and investors increasingly intervened. To summarize a complicated series of disagreements that came to divide the principals, Judah wanted to build the best railroad the world had ever seen, while the Big Four sought to construct an adequate, functional road as quickly and profitably as possible. More and more annoyed by Ted's challenge to their authority, the all-powerful investors offered to buy him out of the company in return for a payment of $100,000; in response, "Crazy" Judah proposed buying *them* out and resolved to take one more trip to the East Coast in a desperate effort to raise the money to do so.

As usual, he was accompanied by his adoring wife, Anna; they sailed from San Francisco to the Isthmus of Panama, where they boarded the small, sputtering train to take them across the swamps and jungles to the Caribbean coast. By the time they arrived, a torrential tropical downpour had made it difficult to walk even the short distance to the steamship that awaited them, especially since Ted insisted on helping all of the women and children who also needed to make their way from the train to the docks.

Once in his stateroom, Judah began shivering and complained of a "terrible headache." Anna put him to bed and called the ship's doctor, who suggested that her thirty-six-year-old husband had contracted yellow fever. This meant that their quarters had to be quarantined and she never left his side as they steamed toward New York. Though others viewed the childless state of their marriage as a tragedy, Anna saw it as a disguised blessing that allowed her to travel at Theodore's side on frantic trips like this one and to savor their adventurous expeditions for surveying, and painting, the rugged mountains they loved.

On board the SS *St. Louis*, she held his hand, bathed his face with cool water, and occasionally dipped her fingertips in brandy so she could apply a few drops to his feverish lips. According to her recollections: "He was delirious and talked of nothing but 'my road.'"

They arrived at the New York wharf on October 26, 1863, and the ship's doctor helped carry Theodore to a waiting carriage. The Judahs traveled to their reserved rooms at the Metropolitan Hotel; a Manhattan doctor who also happened to be a family friend was summoned. "Anna, dear, it is yellow fever," he told the frightened wife as he put his arm on her shoulder.

She naturally protested that her husband was much too young to die and that he must recover to finish his grand work. Four days later, she knelt in prayer at his bedside and heard Theodore awake. "The road," he murmured. "Anna, we started the ball rolling . . . the road . . ."

He died at dawn on the second of November. Anna buried him in Greenfield, Massachusetts, in a quiet cemetery near her childhood home.

As a widow, she tried to follow the progress of both the Central Pacific and the Union Pacific over the next five and a half years, but amazingly, no one thought to invite her to Promontory Summit to honor her husband's enormous contribution to the epic triumph that inspired the nation.

That afternoon, she listened to the cheerful sound of pealing bells from local churches, after they received the telegraphic news of the final blow that struck the Golden Spike more than two thousand miles away, completing the vision that had consumed her late husband's brief life. She responded to the jubilation by putting on her hat and shawl and walking, alone, to the cemetery, acutely conscious that this great day—May 10, 1869—would have been their twenty-second wedding anniversary. After returning home on the spring evening, she wrote that "it seemed as though the spirit of my brave husband descended upon me, and together we were there."

Theodore Judah's legacy no doubt suffered from the absence of children or grandchildren who might have fought in later years for the recognition he deserved for initiating the awe-inspiring project that reignited the nation's faith in its role as an instrument of divine will. But his own ringing words in the introduction to his *Practical Plan for Building the Pacific Railroad* remain as testimony to his gift of foresight. "It connects these two great oceans," he enthused. "It is an indissoluble bond of union between the populous States of the East, and the undeveloped regions of the fruitful West. It is a highway which leads to peace and future prosperity. An iron bond for the perpetuation of the Union and independence which we now enjoy." His crowning declaration might stand as an appropriate summary of his own engineering plans along with the even greater experiment of America itself. "It is," he wrote, "the most magnificent project ever conceived."

UNCLE SAM AS "THE MODERN MOSES": Just eight months after the
assassination of Russia's czar, which provoked brutal massacres against the country's
Jewish population, the satirical magazine *Puck* depicted the United States as the favored
refuge for the oppressed masses. "To the immigrants themselves, and to the astonished
Americans who watched their mass arrival in amazement, the sudden explosion in the
American Jewish population seemed miraculous, inevitably suggesting biblical analogues."
OPPER & KEPPLER'S "THE MODERN MOSES" (1881)—CORNELL UNIVERSITY—PJ MODE
COLLECTION OF PERSUASIVE CARTOGRAPHY

4

The Abrahamic Advantage

A Young Nation Seeks an Ancient Blessing

Barely a decade after the Pacific railroad consolidated America's claim to a continental New World empire, old-world upheavals produced a sudden tidal wave of immigration that rooted that claim in biblical prophecy.

Starting in 1881, some two and a half million desperate, destitute eastern European Jews washed up on American shores to connect an ancient text to a young nation's sense of its own special destiny. For the implacably confident citizens of the surging United States, these exotic newcomers provided new perspective on three mystical Genesis verses that had resonated with their forebears since the earliest days of British settlement.

"Go for yourself from your land, from your relatives, and from your father's house to the land that I will show you," God commands Abraham (still called Abram at that point in the text). The Almighty reassures the puzzled patriarch by pledging a world-changing outcome to this directed journey into the unknown: "And I will make of you a great nation; I will bless you, and make your name great, and you shall be a blessing."

The Pilgrims and Puritans prayed for similar benedictions and connected their own "errand into the wilderness" with Abraham's fateful mission to build a new, godly life in a promised land he hadn't even seen. Proudly identifying themselves as "New Testament Hebrews," they also cherished the biblical idea that the other tribes of Earth would one day earn reward or punishment based on their treatment of the new nation God had decreed into existence. "I will bless those who bless you, and him who curses you I will curse," the Lord assures Abraham and, by implication, his descendants, far into the future. "And all the families of the earth shall bless themselves by you" (Genesis 12:1–3).

With this formulation in mind, many of the radical Protestant doers and dreamers who ultimately planted a new civilization in North America embraced the notion that their cosmic purpose involved the protection of the children of Abraham—an idea they expressed in sermons and scholarly treatises long before any actual Jews turned up in their struggling New World outposts.

"THE MOST HONORABLE NATION
OF THE WORLD"

In 1648, for instance, a long-serving member of Parliament named Sir Edward Nicholas penned an influential pamphlet that blamed England's present problems on "the strict and cruel laws now in force against the most honorable nation of the world, the nation of the Jews, a people chosen by God." This startling new attitude and Sir Edward's bold description of the Jews as "our brethren" represented a striking departure from the well-established medieval view that they constituted "the spawn of Satan," worthy of torture, genocide, and expulsion.

Nicholas and like-minded thinkers pressed their arguments as necessary atonement for the ghastly treatment of Jews by earlier generations of Englishmen, who expelled them from Britain in 1190 and barred their return for more than 350 years. According to the arguments of Puritan leaders, putting an end to such persecution could win for Britons the spiritual and material blessings explicitly promised to those who dealt kindly with descendants of the biblical patriarchs.

When English Puritans crossed the Atlantic with dreams of building holy refuges on a wild and desolate continent, they took these philosemitic attitudes with them. In New England, the influential theologian and charismatic pastor Roger Williams pleaded incessantly for acceptance, and even welcome, of the widely despised and persecuted Jews. When he found himself expelled from the Massachusetts Bay Colony in 1635 for his defiant insistence on congregational autonomy, he proceeded with his followers to found the new colony of Rhode Island with its capital pointedly designated as "Providence." During a visit to England in 1652, Williams petitioned Parliament on the issue of welcoming Jewish immigration to all corners of the British world: "I humbly conceive it to be the duty of the civil magistrate to break down that superstitious wall of separation (as to civil things) between us Gentiles and the Jews, and freely (without their asking) to make way for their free and peaceable habitation amongst us."

Four years later, Parliament made the fateful decision to accede to that request and to permit a reestablished Jewish presence in Britain; just two years after that, Roger Williams welcomed the first Jewish settlers to his own New England colony of Rhode Island. By the time of the American Revolution, the pioneering community in Newport, made up of the descendants of Sephardic Jewish refugees from Spain and Portugal, had grown to thirty families.

"DISGUST AND UNWILLINGNESS"

A similar group of exiles faced a far less gracious reception when they attempted to make a new home for themselves in the Dutch fur-trading settlement of New Amsterdam on the southern tip of heavily forested, wolf-infested Manhattan Island.

By most accounts, September 1654 marks the real beginning of American Jewish history with the arrival of twenty-three individuals who had escaped the town of Recife on the coast of Brazil. There, Sephardic traders and craftsmen had established a significant Jewish community that thrived for the twenty-four years that the Dutch West India Company controlled the territory, placing their priority on pursuit of profit rather than preservation of religious purity. When the Portuguese military recaptured the town in 1654, they encouraged the Jewish residents to find new homes elsewhere—a familiar process for the perennial refugees whose ancestors had been expelled from the Iberian Peninsula more than 150 years before.

The Recife Jewish community therefore made a sensible decision to pack what they could and to crowd onto sixteen ships for a trip across the Atlantic to Holland. Nearly all the vessels made it safely, except for a single ship that seemed to endure a consistent spate of improbably bad luck. This misbegotten craft wandered horribly off course, buffeted by uncooperative winds and tides and the incompetence or malfeasance of its hired navigators. According to other near-contemporary accounts, the frightened refugees were captured, detained, and ultimately ransomed by an especially ruthless band of real-life pirates of the Caribbean. In any event, after these ordeals the helpless, hapless passengers had little appetite for more months at sea and so sought a safe harbor somewhere, anywhere, in the Western Hemisphere that would allow them to maintain their cherished dreams of a new life in the New World.

When the exhausted group—consisting of four couples, two widows, and thirteen children—finally arrived at the site of today's New York, the local authorities promptly threw them into jail, since they lacked the money to pay their ship's captain what they owed him for their transportation. The local Dutch Reformed minister, Johannes Megapolensis, strongly supported the imprisonment of these "godless rascals," denouncing the children of Israel who "have no other God than the unrighteous Mammon, and no other aim than to get possession of Christian property." Peter Stuyvesant, the harsh-tempered, peg-legged director general of the struggling commercial outpost, also worried that "the very repugnant" Jews would fatally "infect" the already fragile colony, and wrote to his employers at the Dutch West India Company in Amsterdam to allow the immediate, permanent expulsion of the Hebraic newcomers.

As it turned out, the corporation denied the request on the pertinent basis "that many of the Jewish nation are principal shareholders in the company." This didn't stop Stuyvesant from persecuting the unwelcome arrivals by banning public synagogue services, limiting their ability to build homes or purchase property, and forbidding their practice of any crafts other than butchery. The governing council also forbade the males in the little group from serving in the local militia because of "disgust and unwillingness" on the part of respectable Christian burghers "to be fellow-soldiers with the aforesaid nation and to be on guard with them in the same guard house." In a perverse, seventeenth-century version of catch-22, the same bureaucrats who prevented the Jews from serving then penalized them with a special monthly tax to punish their avoidance of service.

Considering the inept and feckless quality of New Amsterdam's vaunted military forces, the reviled Jews may have actually gotten the best of the bargain. On a sultry August day in 1664, four English frigates sailed into New Amsterdam's harbor and demanded the town's immediate surrender. Stuyvesant, as usual, raged and stormed, tearing the invader's letter into bits. He might have been willing to sacrifice his one remaining leg rather than submit to the arrogant enemy, but the director general's subjects, already weary of his impetuosity, had no interest in losing either limb *or* life. The English took official possession of New Amsterdam in June 1665, reincorporating the village as New York, in honor of the king's younger brother, the Duke of York (and the future king James II).

Much to the relief of the long-suffering local Jews, the humiliated Peter Stuyvesant sailed back to old Amsterdam to report to his corporate bosses on his tumultuous term as director general and the disastrous loss of their entire colony of New Netherland. Shortly thereafter, he quietly returned to the remote northern end of Manhattan Island, far outside the little town he had once led, and lived out the remaining seven years of his life on an isolated sixty-two-acre farm surrounded by thick woods and gloomy swamps, near the site of current-day Harlem.

The ferocious hostility Peg Leg Pete displayed to his town's tiny Jewish community (as well as to any stray Catholics, Quakers, and even Lutherans who threatened to corrupt his colony) hardly qualifies him as an example of enlightened pluralism. But his historical role did serve to exemplify the workings of God's reputed promise to Abraham: having cursed the patriarch's children, he earned historic curses of his own.

Meanwhile, the British takeover of New Netherland brightened prospects for the struggling Jewish community almost immediately. They could now conduct religious services openly and by 1730 managed to build the city's first synagogue dedicated to that purpose. Within three centuries, the descendants of the fugitives once derided as "godless rascals" had managed to collect in New York the largest Jewish population of any city ever assembled in the history of the world.

"LIKE THE JEWS, AS LIKE AS LIKE CAN BE"

The New England colonies to the north and east never developed this sort of teeming Jewish presence, but their deeply religious leaders nevertheless displayed a consistent fascination with the Hebrew language and pored with reverent enthusiasm over the sacred texts of the children of Israel. Boston saw the first stirrings of an organized Jewish community (as opposed to a handful of wanderers, loners, and temporary visitors) only in 1840, but some 220 years before that settlers in Massachusetts cherished the philosophical arguments and even some of the ritual practices codified in the Talmud.

Cambridge-trained historian Nick Bunker notes that William Bradford, the longtime governor of Plymouth Colony, "fell under the influence of Judaism, its rabbis of the Middle Ages, and their manner of interpreting the Bible and the vagaries of human life." In *Making Haste from Babylon* (2010), Bunker affirms that "Hebrew possessed a special appeal for Puritans. They wished to swim back up the stream of learning and to absorb the wisdom of the Bible from as close to the source as possible, free from what they saw as Roman Catholic duplicity or errors in translation."

In the study of his rustic home at the edge of the forbidding American wilderness, Governor Bradford struggled to teach himself the language in which "God, and angels, spoke to the holy patriarchs of old time," as he put it. He used a book he had brought with him in the turbulent voyage across the Atlantic, and, amazingly, his painstaking Hebrew exercises have been preserved for nearly four hundred years, scribbled in his own hand on the blank spaces of many pages. Bunker even argues that Bradford and his colleagues based their celebration of the first Thanksgiving on the traditional Judaic practice of Birkat HaGomel: a prayerful expression of gratitude after a perilous journey or other life-threatening experience. The early New England settlers most certainly knew of that ancient formulation, and "A Blessing for Deliverance" would have seemed as natural to them as it is to observant Jews to this day.

In the next three generations of New England leadership, the most prominent scholars and magistrates brought even greater focus and passion to their obsessive identification with the children of Abraham. John Cotton (1585–1652), the preeminent theologian of the Massachusetts Bay Colony, believed that the residents of this model godly commonwealth should follow Old Testament law "because God, who was then bound up in covenant with [the Hebrews] to be their God, has put us in their stead and is become our God as well as theirs and hence we are much bound to their laws as well as themselves."

Cotton Mather, son of Increase Mather—who was the sixth president of Harvard College—became the most influential American Hebraist of his day. He quoted regularly from his encyclopedic knowledge of rabbinic literature, going beyond the Tanach and Talmud to include Maimonides, Nachmanides (his special favorite), Midrash, Rashi, and even mystical, Kabbalistic volumes like the Zohar. Several sources report that he adopted the habit of wearing a skullcap as he pursued these studies at home and even began calling himself "Rabbi" at age thirty-three in 1696. No wonder that Mather's contemporary Peter Folger, a Baptist missionary, a pioneer settler of Nantucket Island, and Benjamin Franklin's grandfather, proudly observed: "In New England they are like the Jews, as like as like can be."

Despite this intense identification with ancient Israel, few Americans ever got the chance to explore either the wisdom of the past or the prospects for the future with their Jewish contemporaries. One of the exceptions was Ezra Stiles (1727–1795), the seventh president of Yale and an influential minister and scholar. Before assuming his most celebrated position in New Haven, Connecticut, he spent twenty years pastoring a major church in Newport, Rhode Island. During that time, Stiles made a point of paying frequent visits to the small, struggling synagogue that had managed to survive for more than a hundred years despite the lack of meaningful growth in the Jewish population. At these services, Stiles made the acquaintance of an esteemed visiting rabbi from the Holy Land. Raphael Haim Isaac Carregal had been born in Hebron, not far from the reputed burial site of Abraham and the other patriarchs and matriarchs of Israel. He spoke at synagogues in Philadelphia and New York, but during his time in Newport he became close friends with Ezra Stiles. The Christian New Englander recorded the substance of each one of their twenty-eight extended meetings and after the rabbi's departure they maintained a lively correspondence in Hebrew. Unlike Cotton Mather, who expressed the hope that even the religious Jews he so passionately esteemed would ultimately find their way to Christ, Stiles expected Rabbi Carregal to remain fully Jewish and became excited by visions of what Jews and Christians might achieve together. He commissioned a portrait of his friend to display at Yale and encouraged publication of two of his sermons in English translations from the original Spanish. In particular, Stiles believed that the ultimate "return of the twelve tribes to the Holy Land" might well occur at any time, igniting an explosion of faith that would enable believers "to convert a world."

While praying for the prophesied redemption of an ancient people, Dr. Stiles played a prominent role in the miraculous birth of a new nation in North America. As a fearless advocate for the cause of independence, this patriot-preacher delivered a famous sermon after the Revolution's triumphant conclusion titled "The United States Elevated to Glory and Honour." Near the climax of his argument, the Christian scholar reasoned that part of the purpose for that elevation involved a presumed American role in efforts to "recover and gather" the children of Israel "from all the nations." At that point "the words of Moses . . . will be literally fulfilled; when the posterity of Abraham shall be nationally collected, and become a very distinguished and glorious people." George Washington himself kept a printed copy of this stirring oration among the cherished books of his personal library.

"SCATTER LIGHT AND NOT DARKNESS
IN OUR PATHS"

During the Revolutionary War, Jewish participation intensified the impulse of the founding generation to link the fate of America to that of Israel. Haym Salomon, a Polish-born financial broker, arrived in New York on the eve of the Revolution and immediately involved himself with the radical Sons of Liberty. Imprisoned by the British after they occupied the city in 1776, he managed to escape only to be arrested again for active support for the rebellion against the crown. He escaped one more time, after intense suffering in captivity, and made his way to Philadelphia, where he played a crucial role in selling the bonds and bills of exchange that kept the infant Republic's shaky finances afloat. At the end of eight years of toil and turbulence, the struggle for independence had broken his health, both physically and financially. When he was forty-four, he died of tuberculosis, just two years after the war's formal conclusion, and his generous, unsecured loans and outright bequests to leaders of the cause left him in poverty at the time of his demise.

The Jewish community never numbered more than 2,500 through the course of the war, representing less than one-tenth of 1 percent of the overall colonial population of nearly three million. Nevertheless, contemporaries looked with admiration on the overwhelming percentage of Jews who backed the fight for independence, in contrast to the bitter divisions in the population at large. More than one hundred Jews fought with Washington, including my wife's distant ancestor who qualified my own daughters for membership in the Daughters of the American Revolution.

With these contributions in mind, in the second year of his presidency under the new Constitution, Washington made a special point to honor and praise the Republic's tiny Jewish communities. In a celebrated letter to "The Hebrew Congregation of Newport, Rhode Island" (at the time the nation's largest, with nearly two hundred souls), the president declared: "It is now no more that toleration is spoken of, as if it was by the indulgence of one class of people, that another enjoyed the exercise of their inherent natural rights. For happily the

Government of the United States, which gives to bigotry no sanction, to persecution no assistance, requires only that they who live under its protection should demean themselves as good citizens, in giving it on all occasions their effectual support."

In 1790, the suggestion by the president of the Republic in a public proclamation that Jews might be considered "good citizens" in any sense would have struck other nations as shocking, radical, dangerous, and unprecedented.

In Great Britain, it took another sixty-eight years and a long, bitter, polarizing fight before Parliament at last agreed to eliminate the "civil disabilities" burdening the Jewish population and accepted a duly elected Jew as an MP. (Future prime minister Benjamin Disraeli had entered Westminster twenty years earlier, but he had been conveniently baptized a Christian at age twelve.) "Jewish emancipation" didn't arrive in France until 1806 (under Napoleon), reaching Austria-Hungary only in 1867, Brazil in 1890, Spain in 1910, and Russia (with the revolution) in 1917.

At the time that the august, revered George Washington wrote his remarkable message to the Newport congregation and through them to the Jews in the rest of the world, no other nation on Earth even came close to offering Jews equal access to citizenship and public office. Nevertheless, the first president concluded his missive with a hope for the future that read like a benediction, replete with references to Hebrew Scripture: "May the Children of the Stock of Abraham, who dwell in this land, continue to merit and enjoy the good will of the other Inhabitants; while every one shall sit in safety under his own vine and figtree, and there shall be none to make him afraid. May the father of all mercies scatter light and not darkness in our paths, and make us all in our several vocations useful here, and in his own due time and way everlastingly happy."

In another 1790 message to an even smaller Jewish community (the tiny, struggling synagogue in Savannah, Georgia), Washington expressed similar sentiments and explicitly linked the fate of the new Republic to the distinctive destiny of the children of Israel. He wrote, "May the same wonder-working Deity, who long since delivering the Hebrews from their Egyptian Oppressors planted them in the promised land—whose providential agency has lately been conspicuous in establishing these United States as an independent nation—still continue to water them with the dews of Heaven and to make the inhabitants of every denomination participate in the temporal and spiritual blessings of that people whose God is Jehovah."

"THE MOST ESSENTIAL INSTRUMENT
FOR CIVILIZING THE NATIONS"

As these comments indicate with their openhearted emotion, the early leaders of the United States identified the American experience with the story of the ancient Hebrews in the Bible, and they had done so since the days of the Pilgrims and Puritans. When Benjamin Franklin and Thomas Jefferson faced the task of designing the first official seal for the new nation in 1776, they each came up with images depicting the children of Israel escaping from Egyptian slavery under God's miraculous protection, as the Lord split the sea or guided them through the wilderness with pillars of cloud and flame.

As David Brooks wrote in 2017, "The story Americans told about themselves was a biblical story—an exodus story of various diverse peoples leaving oppression, crossing a wilderness and joining together to help create a promised land." The idea wasn't that Americans would replace the covenantal relationship between the Almighty and the Jewish people but might somehow replicate it, or join in it, to share the special blessings of heavenly favor.

John Adams, the second president of the United States, enthusiastically embraced that notion in a letter to one of the most prominent Jews in the country. In 1819, eighteen years after leaving the White House, the former chief executive decided "to let my imagination loose" in correspondence with Mordecai Manuel Noah, a tireless journalist, playwright, and diplomat who, as consul to the Kingdom of Tunis, became the first American Jew to win a notable federal appointment. While assuring Noah of his "respect and esteem," the "Atlas of Independence" mused: "I could find it in my heart to wish that you had been at the head of a hundred thousand Israelites indeed as well disciplin'd as a French army—& marching with them into

Judea & making a conquest of that country & restoring your nation to the dominion of it—For I really wish the Jews again in Judea an independent nation."

Eleven years earlier, Adams had already begun expressing the philosemitism so typical of the founders. "I will insist that the Hebrews have done more to civilize men than any other nation," he wrote. "If I were an atheist and believed in blind eternal fate, I should still believe that fate had ordained the Jews to be the most essential instrument for civilizing the nations. . . . They are the most glorious nation that ever inhabited this earth."

Encouraged by such attitudes on the part of some of the most revered figures in the Republic, Mordecai Noah launched a grandiose plan to prepare for Israel's restoration by establishing a designated refuge for persecuted Jews under the jurisdiction of the United States. He planned to build his colony on Grand Island in the Niagara River, not far from Buffalo. He began buying up land for that purpose (at $4.38 an acre) and designated the new settlement "Ararat"—just as the biblical Noah brought his ark to rest on Mount Ararat after a flood of suffering and horror, so the modern-day Noah would provide a safe haven on his Ararat for the masses of Jews threatened by persecution and deadly violence.

He also hoped to draw another afflicted segment of the population to his new "City of Refuge" by convincing Native American tribes that they, too, counted as children of Abraham. "The Indians of the American continent," he wrote, "being in all probability the descendants of the Lost Tribes of Israel, which were carried captive by the King of Assyria, measures will be adopted to make them sensible of . . . their condition and finally reunite them with their brethren, the chosen people."

His utopian plan drew far more enthusiastic support from sympathetic Christians than it ever did from his fellow Jews or local Indian tribes, and on September 2, 1825, a crowd of several thousand marched to St. Paul's Episcopal Church in Buffalo for the dedication of the new settlement. Though the building could barely handle the eager throngs, Noah managed to lead the crowd in singing psalms in Hebrew before presenting the ceremonial cornerstone he meant to plant on the island refuge over which he would preside as "by the grace of God, Governor and Judge of Israel." This four-hundred-pound rock had been inscribed with the Hebrew words of the biblical Shema ("Hear O Israel, the Lord our God, the Lord is One") and then the English proclamation: "Ararat, a City of Refuge for the Jews, founded by MORDECAI MANUEL NOAH in the Month of Tishri, 5586 (September, 1825) and in the Fiftieth Year of American Independence."

Unfortunately, this much-celebrated undertaking attracted such scant support from America's tiny, timid Jewish community that the island colony of Ararat never built anything more substantial than that massive foundation stone, the only remnant of an American dreamer's soaring scheme to draw vast hordes of Jewish refugees a full half century before those huddled masses actually began to arrive.

"HIS MANIA IS OF THE RELIGIOUS SPECIES": Warder Cresson
(1798–1860), first American consul in Jerusalem; a former Quaker, Shaker,
Mormon, and Campbellite; and ultimately, a convert to Orthodox Judaism.
He saw the fates of the Jewish people and the United States as inextricably
linked and argued with Herman Melville about the rebuilding of Zion.

"HIS MANIA IS OF THE RELIGIOUS SPECIES"

Mordecai Noah's failed but highly publicized plans to establish himself as "Governor and Judge of Israel" over a new Jewish commonwealth in the United States only added to his notoriety and influence. But another visionary of the antebellum era sacrificed his wealth, family, and reputation in his determination to use his own wildly eccentric life to link the recently arrived power of America to his dreams for a newly revived people of Israel. The strange, largely forgotten story of Warder Cresson, who became the first American consul to Jerusalem, provides a haunting demonstration of the spectral connection between the rise of the young Republic and the ancient Hebraic culture that had fascinated its founders.

Warder Cresson's Huguenot ancestors first came to the New World from Holland in 1657, settling in Delaware and New York. After some adventures in the West Indies, his grandfather Solomon found his way to Philadelphia, where he became an ardent member of the Society of Friends and part of the new city's Quaker establishment. As successful artisans and entrepreneurs, the Cressons owned prime real estate on Chestnut Street in the center of town as well as valuable agricultural properties in the surrounding countryside.

Born in 1798 as the second of eight children, Warder began working the family farms in nearby Darby and Chester counties at age seventeen, impressing relatives and neighbors with his business and leadership abilities. Married at twenty-three to another devout Quaker, he proceeded to raise six children of his own and to follow the clan's pattern of judicious investment and accumulation of wealth.

As he approached thirty, however, religious doubts began to torment him, and he published outspokenly radical religious tracts (including *Babylon the Great Is Falling!*) that questioned his Quaker faith, challenging its perceived emphasis on "an outward form, order of discipline" without proper attention to the "inward man." Cresson formally rejected the Society of Friends and affiliated himself with a series of unconventional sects that had arisen during America's second "Great Awakening," including, in turn, the Shakers, the Mormons, the Seventh-day Adventists, and the "Campbellites," who believed in restoring the united, purified Christianity of the apostles.

In the process, farmer Cresson developed a local reputation for sharing his insights and inspirations by "haranguing in the streets" of Philadelphia. With his flowing, Old Testament black beard and burning blue eyes, he cut a formidable, unforgettable figure, frightening unsuspecting passersby with stentorian warnings about God's wrath and the imminent apocalypse.

Inevitably, this agitated religious seeker found his way to Mikveh Israel, the city's leading Jewish congregation, where he received an unexpectedly warm reception from the ardent abolitionist and influential scholar Isaac Leeser. As the synagogue's leader, he patiently engaged Cresson in wide-ranging discussions on biblical interpretation and messianic redemption, while introducing him to the work of Mordecai Manuel Noah, the political operative and man of letters who had begun pushing for an American commitment to reestablish a Jewish homeland in the Middle East.

Cresson became instantly captivated by that idea and reached the conclusion that "there is no salvation for the Gentiles but by coming to Israel." He also reached the conclusion that God himself had created the United States for one purpose above all others: rescuing the Jews of the world from exile and oppression. He discerned profound significance in his young Republic's national symbol, since the prophet Isaiah had promised for the weary and fainthearted that "the Lord will renew their strength; they will soar on wings like *eagles*." He felt sure that the prophecy of a reborn Israel would be fulfilled by the soaring power of the American eagle that would "overshadow the land with his wings."

To assure his own role in these miraculous forthcoming events, he contacted a friendly Philadelphia congressman named E. Joy Morris to arrange his appointment as America's first consul to Jerusalem. At the time, the Holy City that loomed so large in religious imagery had degenerated into a run-down, isolated village of barely fifteen thousand souls (half of them Jewish) that hardly merited its own consulate by any conventional calculation. But Representative Morris wrote to Secretary of State John C. Calhoun that the American pilgrims and missionaries who visited Jerusalem in increasing numbers could benefit from a diplomatic outpost in that remote corner of the Ottoman Empire. More important, he made it clear that Warder Cresson, relying on his personal wealth, had volunteered to work for the government without compensation. This was an offer that the perennially cash-strapped State Department could hardly refuse, so the official appointment came through on May 17, 1844.

Cresson set out immediately, ready to make a decisive break with his past. He wrote in his diary at the time of his departure: "In the Spring of 1844 I left everything near and dear to me on earth. I left the wife of my youth and six lovely children (dearer to me than my natural life), and an excellent farm, with everything comfortable around me. I left all these in the pursuit of truth, and for the sake of Truth alone."

Almost immediately, protests arose over the suitability of the selection of this relentless truth seeker for a new diplomatic post. Samuel D. Ingham of New Hope, Pennsylvania, a former congressman and Treasury secretary under President Andrew Jackson, wrote to Secretary of State Calhoun: "The papers have recently announced the appointment of Warder Cresson, Consul to Jerusalem. This man . . . has been laboring under an aberration of mind for many years; his mania is of the religious species. He was born a Quaker, wanted to be a preacher . . . and has gone round the compass from one job to another, sometimes preaching about the church doors and in the streets; his passion is for religious controversy . . . but, in truth, he is withal a very weak-minded man and his mind, what there is of it, quite out of order. . . . His appointment is made a theme of ridicule by all who know him."

Calhoun responded to this alarming dispatch by writing to Cresson and announcing, in President John Tyler's name, that the government would not sponsor the establishment of a Jerusalem consulate after all. By that time, the idealistic emissary had already departed for the Holy Land, where he disembarked melodramatically from a British ship at the port of Jaffa, stepping ashore with an American flag in one hand and a caged dove of peace in the other.

Quickly establishing himself as the official representative of the United States, he created a new consular seal and issued a sweeping proclamation to all the Jews of the Holy City to assure them that they would henceforth enjoy the firm protection of the American government. But before Cresson could do much to give meaning to that promise, word finally reached him that his appointment had been canceled at the highest levels in Washington.

For Cresson, this news constituted only a minor inconvenience: he enjoyed the title of consul far too much to give it up and continued to present himself as the envoy of the American Republic, however dubious his claims. The bemused Turkish authorities mostly shrugged at his pretensions, while no other American officials bothered to travel to the remote region to raise uncomfortable questions about his status.

Meanwhile, Cresson took great satisfaction in hosting visiting dignitaries and startling them with his increasingly elaborate and grandiose plans for reconfiguring the Middle East and, ultimately, the rest of the globe. He welcomed the brilliant British novelist William Makepeace Thackeray and informed him that the United States would work closely with the United Kingdom to enlist the other powers of Europe in establishing a promising, prosperous new homeland for the Jewish people. The author of *Vanity Fair* remained singularly unimpressed by this preposterous scheme. "He has no other knowledge of Syria but what he derives from prophecy," reported Thackeray. "I doubt whether any government has received or appointed so queer an ambassador."

As if the conversational initiatives didn't count as queer enough, there were also his increasingly ebullient writings. Shortly after his arrival, Cresson hastily penned a glowing paean to his new hometown, describing in rapturous terms the ancient but squalid village that most other visitors viewed as dirty and decrepit. *Jerusalem, the Centre and Joy of the Whole Earth*, published in Philadelphia and London at Cresson's direction, failed to inspire a measurable upsurge in either emigrants or tourists but did draw enough attention so that he followed it with other book-length pamphlets combining reportage with religious argument.

Those arguments began drawing the peripatetic would-be consul far from his Christian roots, especially as he became personally engaged with the leading Sephardic rabbis in Jerusalem. At age forty-nine, after seven years of study and contemplation, after intoxicating exploration of the shrines and byways of the God-haunted Judean hills and the shores of the tranquil Sea of Galilee, Warder Cresson reached the most consequential decision of a turbulent life. "I remained in Jerusalem in my former faith until the 28th day of March, 1848," he wrote, "when I became fully satisfied that I never could obtain Strength and Rest, but by doing as Ruth did, and saying to her Mother-in-Law, or Naomi (The Jewish Church), 'Entreat me not to leave thee . . . for whither thou goest I will go. In short . . . I was circumcised, entered the Holy Covenant and became a Jew."

During the course of this transition, he'd been writing to his wife and children to keep them informed of his spiritual progress—and of his new name, Michael Boaz Israel ben Avraham. He had no desire to abandon the family that he "loved most dearly above anything else on earth" and felt certain that he could persuade them to share the satisfactions of his new faith and to return with him to his mystical mission in Zion.

"A MAN'S 'RELIGIOUS OPINIONS' NEVER CAN BE MADE THE TEST OF HIS SANITY"

Sailing back to Philadelphia just two months after completing his conversion, the former consul received a devastating reception from his nearest and dearest. His wife, Elizabeth, had taken sole possession of their property, selling off the family farm as well as Warder's personal effects. She ignored his appeals for a settlement and joined other family members in lodging a formal charge of "lunacy" against him. A "sheriff's jury" of six men quickly agreed with their arguments and issued its verdict of insanity, but Cresson, who never spent a day in an asylum, challenged their decision in court.

The resulting trial lasted for almost three years, included more than a hundred witnesses, and became a national sensation. Aside from the obvious attempt by a frustrated and embittered wife to seize what remained of her wandering husband's wealth, the dispute involved the government's power to stigmatize and punish a citizen's midlife decision to embrace an ancient faith. Cresson fiercely defended his right to select his own religious path, no matter how exotic or bizarre its practices might seem to his former neighbors. Esteemed physicians, theologians, and legal scholars gave testimony on both sides. While no one denied Cresson's reputation as "a strange bird" (in the words of one reporter), the leaders of the nation's small Jewish community testified on his behalf, resisting the notion that conversion to Judaism in any way constituted automatic evidence of insanity. Cresson's lawyer, the eminent Horatio Hubbell Jr., characterized the case as a crucial test of the religious liberty guaranteed by the First Amendment. His impassioned closing statement ended with a dramatic denunciation of the attempt to discredit an unconventional thinker based on his religious ideas alone. "The only charge left with which to accuse my client," he thundered, "is that he became a Jew."

By that time, the newspapers covering the trial had swung to support of Cresson's cause and they unanimously expressed their jubilation at his vindication. Philadelphia's *Public Ledger* saw the decision as "settling forever . . . the principle that a man's 'religious opinions' never can be made the test of his sanity."

Having overturned the prior verdict of lunacy, the court enabled the newly minted Michael Boaz Israel ben Avraham to continue worshipping at Philadelphia's Mikveh Israel Congregation, where he enjoyed the status of local hero and meticulously followed Jewish religious law. He used his last months in the United States to pen a spiritual autobiography filled with exultant, sometimes terrifying prophecies, predicting the imminent rebirth of the Land of Israel and the ingathering of the exiles, despite unimaginable trials and terrors. The cover for his publication showed a sketch of a human heart, consumed by flame, locked within the traditional six-pointed Star of David. The title proclaimed: "THE SHIELD OF DAVID: HOLO-CAUST TO THE UNITY OF GOD AND TO DAVID THE MESSIAH."

The peculiar use of the term "holocaust," more than eighty years before Hitler's rise to power, offers one more example of Cresson's haunting insights and premonitions, which became increasingly inseparable from his overwhelming weirdness and uncompromising oddity. Within a year of his trial's successful conclusion, he divorced his wife and returned to Jerusalem in 1852 with a new mission: to restore the Land of Israel by restoring the land itself. He used his background as a "practical farmer" to argue that the establishment of scientifically sophisticated agricultural settlements could remake the ancient earth of Judea at the same time that they reshaped the Jewish soul. Working the land, he averred, "is the one true foundation, the proper beginning and basis for all the other sciences and arts, the foundation for all of life's needs and living conditions."

His determination to plant model colonies amid the desolate landscape and to achieve national redemption through tireless farming not only anticipated future Zionist pioneers by nearly half a century, but seemed distinctly, decisively American in its ambitious, against-the-odds vision. He raised money to purchase a substantial empty tract of land near Jaffa (today's Tel Aviv) and another significant parcel known as Emek Refaim (Valley of the Healers) outside Jerusalem's Old City—which is today an elegant, cosmopolitan neighborhood that's home to numerous American immigrants to Israel, including my brother Jonathan.

"ONLY BY A MIRACLE"

In Cresson's era, on the other hand, visiting Yankees saw a far less appealing prospect. In 1856, a frustrated thirty-seven-year old novelist borrowed money and made his way to the Middle East, where he "looked to Palestine as the source of human experience and a possible hope for the future." As Michael Oren, onetime Israeli ambassador to the United States, points out in his captivating 2007 book *Power, Faith, and Fantasy*, the struggling writer may have been "despondent" over the meager sales of his recent novel *Moby-Dick*, and sensed grim and foreboding signs everywhere he traveled in the Holy Land. "In the emptiness of the lifeless antiquity of Jerusalem," Herman Melville wrote in his journal of the trip, "the migrant Jews are like flies that have taken up their abode in a skull."

He sought out one of those tenacious flies: the famous former

American Warder Cresson, now remarried to a Sephardic Jewish woman and raising their two young children in his devoutly observant Jerusalem home. Melville had been initially intrigued by the erstwhile consul's soaring Yankee schemes of establishing cooperative farms to transform physical and spiritual realities, but he dismissed those ideas when they actually met and engaged in extended conversations. "The idea of making farmers of the Jews is vain," Melville argued. "In the first place, Judea is a desert, with few exceptions. In the second place, the Jews hate farming . . . and besides the number of Jews in Palestine is comparatively small. And how are the hosts of them scattered in other lands to be brought here? Only by a miracle."

Cresson had long maintained that only the United States could serve as the anointed instrument for that miracle. He also came to believe that by re-creating a Jewish state to inspire the world, America could simultaneously save itself from approaching disunion over the tormenting issue of slavery. "God hath chosen Zion . . . *as the centre and joy of the whole world*," he wrote, and "there cannot be unity and harmony . . . without this concentration."

Melville left the Holy Land unconvinced and unimpressed, while the farming settlements Cresson dreamed of establishing never progressed beyond the planning stages. Nevertheless, subsequent generations rediscovered and praised the prescient nature of his schemes. "There are modern elements in Cresson's plans that only sprouted and came into being many years later," wrote Israeli professor Yaacov Shavit in 1988, hailing the nineteenth-century visionary for combining mystical, biblical insights with the earthy pragmatism of a Quaker Pennsylvania farmer—a mixture that seemed to presage some of the tensions of modern Zionism.

In 1860, on the verge of the American Civil War that Warder Cresson both dreaded and predicted, the always vigorous and outspoken Michael Boaz Israel ben Avraham took suddenly ill with an undiagnosed malady and, after twelve days of ebbing strength, passed on the Sabbath day at age sixty-two. The newspapers of the time reported the burial of the onetime diplomat as a significant civic occasion, with all the Jewish businesses in Jerusalem closed in his honor. The funeral procession drew one of the largest crowds anyone could remember for such an occasion. A long line of mourners trudged up the steep slope of the Mount of Olives in the autumn season of the High Holy Days to grant him "such honors as are paid only to a prominent rabbi." Unfortunately, neither of his two Jerusalem-born children—Avigail Ruth and David Ben-Zion—survived to adulthood, both dying within three years of their American father. Without descendants to tend to his grave site, its location, like memories of the consul's historic role, was lost to history for some five generations.

In 2013, however, renewed interest in the arguments and oddities of Warder Cresson's turbulent life led to the rediscovery of his damaged but still-identifiable gravestone. It turned up among the relics in the crowded and ancient cemetery on the Mount of Olives, and was suitably restored as a small memorial not long before his two homelands took the joint historic step of establishing the first American embassy in Cresson's holy capital of Jerusalem.

"IT IS TOO EARLY TO THANK GOD"

Cresson, Noah, John Adams, George Washington, Ezra Stiles, and other farsighted patriots during America's first hundred years of independence had been right to anticipate the way America would help to shape a new destiny for the Jewish people. But none of them predicted that the Jewish people would reciprocate in playing their own role in molding the modern United States, with a sudden mass migration that took both the wayfarers and their destination by surprise.

Beginning in 1881, the impoverished eastern European communities that had shown limited interest in relocating to the old promised land began migrating en masse to the new land of promise. On prior occasions, Jews abandoned their longtime homes, fleeing as desperate refugees from Spain in 1492, or from the German states in the Middle Ages, or from ancient Israel itself on several occasions. But each of these instances saw them scatter, dispersing to so many different new locations that their historical condition came to be known as the *diaspora*—the dispersion.

This time, the Jewish migrants moved in mostly the same direction and with a greater sense of purpose, sharing an ardent expectation that their new exodus could mean their redemption as well as their survival. In addition to running from death and danger, the journey to America also offered life and hope. Of the more than two and a half million Jews who fled disparate nations in a single generation, more than 80 percent went to the United States, with far smaller numbers finding their way to western Europe, South Africa, Canada, Argentina, and Australia; a few made it to the struggling settlements in Palestine that hoped to reclaim the ancient homeland in the Middle East.

This new exodus began with a single act of monstrous, senseless savagery that bore no apparent connection to either the downtrodden Jewish masses of eastern Europe or their new refuge in the New World.

On March 13, 1881, in wintry St. Petersburg, a small band of Russian radicals made the latest in a seemingly endless series of failed assassination attempts against Czar Alexander II.

Fifteen years before, a young apprentice pushed the emperor out of the line of fire and saved his life; the next year, another ferociously determined shooter attacked his carriage but a misfire meant the bullets struck only a horse. In 1878, an engineering student tried to affix a bomb to the hull of the czar's yacht on the Black Sea but he was apprehended and executed. The next year, in April, another enraged intellectual took his shots at the czar in a public parade ground, firing five times, but the nimble autocrat ran the equivalent of a broken-field pattern and dodged death each time.

Six months later, a more organized attempt involved a series of powerful bombs buried beneath train tracks to blow up the emperor's train. The first device never went off and the second, planted the next month, successfully exploded the wrong train; the czar's imperial car had passed, undamaged, ninety minutes earlier. The bombing continued with a devastating attack on the Winter Palace meant to murder the imperial family at dinner. The explosion did kill eleven guards and servants, wounding thirty others, but the royals had delayed their scheduled festive meal due to the late arrival of the czar's nephew, the Prince of Bulgaria.

Aside from the bloody results and the swift executions that inevitably followed, these ongoing efforts to hunt down the "Autocrat of All the Russias" had a slapstick, almost comical aspect: like the fortunate Road Runner endlessly thwarting the elaborate schemes of Wile E. Coyote in the classic Warner Bros. cartoons. The Russian public, however, saw all the thwarted assassination attempts as a sign of divine protection for their revered ruler, and contributed to lavish churches and monuments to commemorate his frequent but narrow escapes.

The 1881 assault seemed to follow the all-too-familiar pattern: Every Sunday the czar reviewed a military parade and traveled back to his palace along the narrow streets of St. Petersburg. One radical lobbed a bomb beneath the horses' hooves as the imperial carriage hurtled past him. The explosion killed one of the ruler's Cossack guards and an innocent bystander but did only minor damage to the steel-reinforced, bulletproof carriage, a gift from French emperor Napoleon III.

The czar emerged bruised and shaken but without serious injury, as usual. His aides and bodyguards pleaded with him to leave the scene and return to the palace, but he insisted on inspecting the site of mayhem, lending comfort and reassurance to the wounded. According to some reports, he declared his readiness to thank God for his deliverance.

At precisely that moment, a second assassin from People's Will (Narodnaya Volya) shouted back "It is too early to thank God!" and rolled a second bomb directly toward the czar's boots. It exploded beneath him, blowing away his lower legs, so that blood poured out of both shattered thighs. A member of the imperial party recalled that "twenty people, with wounds of varying degree, lay on the sidewalk and on the street. . . . Through the snow, debris, and blood you could see fragments of clothing, epaulets, sabers, and bloody chunks of human flesh."

Taken by sleigh to the Winter Palace, sixty-two-year-old Alexander bled to death by three in the afternoon.

Jews had almost nothing to do with this hideous crime. Neither of the assassins was Jewish; among the plotters later apprehended and sentenced to death, only one, a pregnant advocate of "free love" who passionately protested her innocence, came from a Jewish family. The People's Will terrorist movement, which had ostentatiously sentenced the czar to death several years earlier as revenge for the execution of prior would-be assassins, did have a scattering of Jewish participants. But historians estimate they never amounted to more than 15 percent of the total membership.

Nevertheless, the rage and bloodlust that erupted following Alexander's assassination fell almost immediately on the hapless heads of the empire's seven million sorely oppressed Jews. In Ukraine alone, pogroms broke out in 166 towns and cities, with thousands of Jewish homes, shops, and synagogues looted and burned, while numerous adults and children were beaten, raped, and murdered. Anti-Jewish riots spread through the rest of the empire, with 1,500 homes utterly destroyed in Warsaw alone. Instead of protecting its Jewish population, the czarist government actively and openly encouraged the ongoing violence: it provided a convenient release for the unrest that inevitably followed the beloved czar's murder. Meanwhile, most of the desperate radicals who dreamed of overthrowing the regime also applauded the wave of anti-Jewish brutality: even those militants of Jewish ancestry hailed the uprising as the first stirrings of authentic revolutionary consciousness.

The pogroms reinforced the reputed proclamation of Konstantin Pobedonostsev, advisor to three czars and a powerful leader of the Orthodox Church, that the only solution to Russia's stubborn Jewish problem would involve "one third Christianization, one third emigration, and one third starvation." Under Pobedonostsev's influence, the dedicated anti-Semite Alexander III, son and successor to the murdered czar, promulgated the draconian May Laws, forcing half a million Jews to vacate their homes in small towns and rural areas while sharply curtailing their access to education and livelihoods. These measures produced one of the most massive and consequential population transfers in human history. Within a single generation, nearly a third of the Russian Jewish population left their communities to resettle overseas. The great bulk of them found their way to America.

"THE MODERN MOSES"

The specific timing of the czar's assassination helped make this mass migration possible, even logical: had earlier attempts succeeded in felling the emperor, American conditions after the devastation of the Civil War would have provided a far less compelling lure than the booming, rapidly industrializing economy of the 1880s and '90s. The rocketing rise of commerce and manufacturing also helped to bury the nativist, anti-immigrant sentiment that had played such a potent role in American politics and culture before the war for the Union. The concerns for ethnic and religious purity that had once allowed the Know-Nothing, or American, Party to become a national political force ran up against the insatiable appetite of factories, workshops, and railroads for more manpower. The Jews and other migrants who jammed the transatlantic ships of the period faced little discouragement from complicated paperwork or bigoted bureaucrats: if they could pass rudimentary Ellis Island health exams (concerned primarily with communicable diseases), they could take their place in the "Goldene Medinah"—the Golden Province.

To the immigrants themselves, and to the unprepared Americans who watched their mass arrival in amazement, the sudden explosion in the American Jewish population seemed miraculous, inevitably suggesting biblical analogues. In December 1881, just as desperate Jewish refugees began to pour into New York and other cities on the eastern seaboard, the satirical magazine *Puck* ran a striking cartoon depicting Uncle Sam as "The Modern Moses." In the image, the smiling national symbol, with rays of light extending from his top hat, stands atop a rock, extending a rod labeled "Liberty." Below him, a crowd of destitute Jewish families, most of them depicted with stereotypical beards and hook noses, carry their children and meager possessions through a blessedly parted Red Sea toward safety in their new promised land. The walls of water threatening to engulf them, held back by Uncle Sam's genial but supernatural power, have been labeled "Oppression" and "Intolerance."

The fateful arrival of hordes of eastern European Jews transformed the United States just as dramatically, and even more instantaneously, than it changed the immigrants themselves. In 1881, the year of the czar's death, the Jewish population of New York City stood at 80,000. Twenty years later, the number had risen to 510,000—an increase of more than 600 percent. The crowded tenement district of the Lower East Side, where the bulk of the newcomers lived and worked, occupied barely two square miles and constituted for several decades the most densely populated spot on the planet.

The sheer number of eastern Europeans immediately overwhelmed, and occasionally alarmed, the small, discreet, and cautiously respectable communities of mostly German Jews who had previously populated New York and other cities. As the late British historian Paul Johnson eloquently described this development in his superb *A History of the Jews*: "The immigrants gave the kiss of life to American Jewry. They transformed it from an exercise in gentility, doomed to mortify, into a vibrant creature of an entirely new kind—a free people, cradled in a tolerant republic, but shouting their faith and their nature from the rooftops of a city they turned into the greatest Jewish metropolis in the world. Here was a true City of Refuge, and more than that—the nucleus of a power which in time would exert itself effectively on behalf of Jews throughout the world."

"MOTHER OF EXILES"

In one of those strange coincidences that so often illuminate our nation's history, the final stages of construction and fundraising for a gigantic statue of "Liberty Enlightening the World" unfolded at virtually the same moment that the massive Jewish emigration from eastern Europe captured international attention.

Originally, the huge figure in the harbor had nothing to do with immigration of any kind. An ardent French abolitionist proposed the statue to commemorate Union victory in the Civil War, the end of American slavery, and the common commitment of the United States and France to the cause of liberty. Plans for the monument gathered force with the exhibition of the enormous right forearm with its uplifted torch at the 1876 Centennial celebration in Philadelphia, where awed crowds gaped at the vast scale of the undertaking. The finished

"FROM HER BEACON-HAND / GLOWS WORLD-WIDE
WELCOME": Emma Lazarus (1849–1887). Praised and promoted
by Ralph Waldo Emerson and other icons of American literature,
the brilliant, tragically short-lived poet and translator organized
emergency assistance for arriving Jewish refugees and helped raise
money for the new Statue of Liberty. Her sonnet "The New
Colossus" is inscribed on the monument's base.

work, more than 150 feet tall from her sandaled toes to the topmost
flame in her torch, finally took its place on Bedloe's Island (later Liberty Island) in 1886 at the very moment that the flood of Jewish humanity toward the United States was reaching its high tide. One
ardently Jewish poet, who advanced the idea of a preordained American role in the rescue and redemption of her people, gave passionate
voice to the great lady of the "silent lips."

Emma Lazarus was raised in a cultivated Sephardic Jewish family that had prospered as New York merchants for nearly two hundred years. At age eighteen, she published her first book of poems,
and her work quickly attracted encouragement and friendship
from the New England eminence Ralph Waldo Emerson. Fluent in

French, Italian, and especially German, Lazarus also published masterful translations of poetry by Goethe, Heine, Victor Hugo, and many others, placing her work in prestigious magazines in all the world's capitals.

While establishing a truly international reputation, Lazarus focused scant attention on her own Jewish heritage, but when she was thirty-one, the vicious pogroms following the assassination of the czar sparked a passion for self-discovery. She translated the zealous Hebrew lyrics of the medieval mystic Yehuda Halevi, who wrote of his yearning to journey to Israel and participate in its miraculous rebirth. She also organized charitable efforts to aid the penniless Russian hordes who began washing into New York City, providing them with relief and survival supplies, while teaching the basics of American history and culture and defending them, fiercely, from anti-Semitic taunts in the public press. Her contact with these destitute dreamers fueled her pride in the Jewish past and her visions for a grandiose future, as her poetry suddenly burned with exhortation and purpose:

> *Wake, Israel, wake! Recall to-day*
> *The glorious Maccabean rage*
>
> . . . .
>
> *Oh, for Jerusalem's trumpet now,*
> *To blow a blast of shattering power,*
> *To wake the sleepers high and low,*
> *And rouse them to the urgent hour!*
>
> . . . .
>
> *Oh deem not dead that martial fire*
> *Say not the mystic flame is spent!*
> *With Moses' law and David's lyre,*
> *Your ancient strength remains unbent.*
> *Let but an Ezra rise anew,*
> *To Lift the BANNER OF THE JEW!*

She raised the banner herself by founding the Society for the Improvement and Colonization of East European Jews with the goal of inspiring a mass exodus from Europe and, ultimately, the United States, to take possession of the ancient homeland. She wrote to a friend that the prospect of a reconstituted Israel "opens up such enormous vistas in the past & future, & is so palpitatingly alive at the moment, that it has about driven out of my thoughts all other subjects."

Even so, she managed to make a contribution to an auction of art and manuscripts in 1883 that would raise money for the final stages of the construction and installation of the Statue of Liberty. The resulting handwritten sonnet simultaneously expressed her tenderness for the desperate new arrivals fleeing starvation and the czar, while exulting in the epochal role of America as refuge and redeemer. The Jewish view of the United States as a supernatural sanctuary in a harsh, hostile world has never been expressed more movingly or memorably:

The New Colossus

Not like the brazen giant of Greek fame,
With conquering limbs astride from land to land;
Here at our sea-washed, sunset gates shall stand
A mighty woman with a torch, whose flame
Is the imprisoned lightning, and her name
Mother of Exiles. From her beacon-hand
Glows world-wide welcome; her mild eyes command
The air-bridged harbor that twin cities frame.
"Keep ancient lands, your storied pomp!" cries she
With silent lips. "Give me your tired, your poor,
Your huddled masses yearning to breathe free,
The wretched refuse of your teeming shore.
Send these, the homeless, tempest-tost to me,
I lift my lamp beside the golden door!"

The haunting phrase "Mother of Exiles" seemed particularly resonant for Russian Jewish immigrants who, more than the other new arrivals from literally a hundred other nations, had been deliberately driven from their longtime homes. Twenty years after its composition, Emma's poem was inscribed on a burnished plaque at the base of the statue whose meaning she had defined, forever, with her words.

By that time, Emma Lazarus had been dead for fifteen years. She became seriously ill during an exhausting 1887 tour of Europe, where the leading lights of Continental culture welcomed her as an exotic literary celebrity. Upon her return to New York, doctors diagnosed an unspecified but virulent form of cancer and the never-married thirty-eight-year-old poet died just two months later. Sadly, the aid and re-settlement organizations she had assembled during her last crowded years promptly died with her, even as the larger cause of enlisting American power on behalf of a reborn Israel drew fresh life from a strikingly different source.

"GOD'S LITTLE ERRAND BOY"

Meanwhile, in upstate New York, an ecstatic, boisterous, and rustic revival meeting inspired an eleven-year-old Methodist boy to give his life to Christ and to commit himself to hastening the Savior's prom-ised return. That devoted and unfailingly cheerful child, William Eu-gene Blackstone, became one of the most influential religious figures of the nineteenth and early twentieth centuries and won unexpected recognition from the nation's most prominent Jewish leader as the true "Father of Zionism."

Until middle age, Blackstone combined his fervent religiosity with the joys of raising a family and the demands of a commercial career. Settling in Oak Park, Illinois (the leafy Chicago suburb that later produced Ernest Hemingway), a young Blackstone, with his genial temperament, helped achieve conspicuous success in "the business of building and property investments"—as a developer, in other words. But after one fateful night of anguished spiritual struggle, he became certain that Christ's return was real—and imminent. Renouncing material pursuits, he used his peerless persuasive powers to prepare the world for the epochal events to come.

With no college education or formal theological training, the self-schooled businessman nonetheless published *Jesus Is Coming* in 1878, which quickly sold more than a million copies, earned translation into forty-seven languages, and became one of the most influential religious tomes of the nineteenth century. The book elucidated the promised pattern of dramatic transformations for the world's last days, and insisted in chapter 15 for "Israel to Be Restored." Unlike other evangelists who pitied the Jews as stubbornly clinging to an ancient but incomplete faith, Blackstone wrote admiringly of their faithfulness. "Do you wonder that the great mass of Jews, at the present time, have an abiding faith that they are to be returned to Canaan?" he asked. "And shall we, who have accepted so much greater light, refuse this overwhelming testimony of the Word? God forbid."

A mere three years after he wrote those words, literally millions of Jews in the Russian Empire responded to savage persecution by uprooting themselves to find safety and new life in the United States. Blackstone welcomed this development as a fulfillment of prophecy and a precious opportunity. He felt a new determination to unite Christians and Jews in America, to return control of the Holy Land to Abraham's children, and to bless the Jewish people and secure God's blessings on American Christians in return.

Traveling to Palestine with his daughter, Flora, in 1888, Blackstone returned with the conviction that a massive resettlement in the desert wastes of the ancient homeland was not only possible but also urgently necessary. It was the only way to rescue suffering Russian Jews from annihilation, the only way to make a desolate tract of underdeveloped real estate fruitful and productive again.

Two years later, Blackstone convened a Thanksgiving week "Conference of Israelites and Christians Regarding Their Mutual Relations and Welfare" that drew many prominent ministers as well as a sprinkling of leading rabbis. That gathering birthed a "Memorial," or petition, demanding that the rising Republic in the New World should lead other great powers to restore the Jews to full control of their homeland.

Amazingly enough, the resulting "Blackstone Memorial" won the endorsement of 437 distinguished and well-known Americans, including figures of truly dazzling power and prominence. John D. Rockefeller signed, as did J. P. Morgan, Cyrus McCormick Jr., and Charles Scribner II. Chief Justice Melville Fuller attached his name, along with Speaker of the House Thomas Brackett Reed, future president William McKinley, and the mayors of Philadelphia and Chicago. Editors of ninety-three newspapers also pledged their support to Blackstone's cause, representing all the major publications in Boston, Baltimore, Philadelphia, New York, and Chicago.

While Blackstone humbly persisted in describing himself, well into his eighties, as nothing more than "God's Little Errand Boy," he won the right to present his plea in person at the White House, during a well-publicized meeting in March 1891. His document began with a series of pressing questions. "What shall be done for the Russian Jews? . . . Why not give Palestine back to them again? According to God's distribution of nations it is their home, an inalienable possession from which they were expelled by force."

As someone who had recently spent months touring the Holy Land, Blackstone insisted that a new Israel would benefit not only the Jews but the land itself. "Under their cultivation it was a remarkably fruitful land, sustaining millions of Israelites, who industrially tilled its hillsides and valleys. They were agriculturalists and producers . . . the center of civilization and religion."

In an accompanying note that Blackstone presented at the White House to President Benjamin Harrison and Secretary of State James G. Blaine, God's Little Errand Boy made a starkly personal plea:

> Not for twenty-four centuries, since the days of Cyrus, King of Persia, has there been offered to any mortal such a privileged opportunity to further the purposes of God concerning His ancient people. May it be the high privilege of your Excellency, and the Honorable Secretary, to take a personal interest in this great matter, and secure through the Conference, a home for these wandering millions of Israel, and thereby receive to yourselves the promise of Him, who said to Abraham, "I will bless them that bless thee," Genesis 12:3.

Despite his visitor's eloquent arguments, President Harrison failed to seize the "privileged opportunity" of the centuries to become a New Cyrus to lead the Jews home. He included a sentence in his annual message to Congress protesting the czar's cruelty to his Jewish subjects, but failed to mention anything about the radiant dream of providential return.

And so history moved on without President Harrison. Six years later, in the balmy summer of 1897, Austrian drama critic and pamphleteer Theodor Herzl called the First Zionist Congress in Basel, Switzerland, that led to the official recognition of the new Jewish state fifty-one years later.

William Eugene Blackstone watched these events with mounting excitement. He announced his unqualified support for Herzl's efforts and sent him a personal Bible, with carefully highlighted verses that applied to the restoration of Israel. For years, the leader of modern Zionism displayed that gift prominently on his desk.

In 1916, the aging Blackstone (then seventy-five) received another encouraging sign from the most famous of all American Jews: Louis Brandeis, recently appointed by President Wilson as the first Jewish justice on the Supreme Court of the United States. Nathan Straus, the noted philanthropist and owner of the Macy's department store, wrote to Blackstone at the judge's behest, declaring that "Mr. Brandeis is perfectly infatuated with the work that you have done along the lines of Zionism. It would have done your heart good to have heard him assert what a valuable contribution to the cause your document is. In fact he agrees with me that you are the Father of Zionism, as your work antedates Herzl."

At the urging of Brandeis, Blackstone submitted a second "Memorial" to President Wilson, urging him to shape the upheaval of the Great War to fulfill the ancient dream of a reborn Israel. The next year, America's British allies issued the Balfour Declaration, expressing support for a "national home" for the Jewish people in Palestine, and English general Edmund Allenby entered Jerusalem as its conqueror and liberator.

Blackstone lived for eighteen years more, watching with satisfaction and amazement as hundreds of thousands of idealistic *halutzim* (pioneers) settled in the Middle East, founding the first new Jewish metropolis (Tel Aviv) in more than two thousand years, while even more Jewish migrants continued to make their way to the United States. He spent his final years in Los Angeles, where, despite his status as an almost entirely self-educated scholar, he had served as the founding dean of the Bible Institute of Los Angeles (now, using the acronym of its title, known as Biola University). By the time of his passing at age ninety-four in 1935, the apocalyptic expectations of God's Little Errand Boy seemed close to fulfillment—with both Hitler's hideous persecutions and Israel's ultimate emergence looking increasingly inevitable.

"I AM CYRUS!"

William Eugene Blackstone's visions and arguments have continued to influence the history of both the United States and the Jewish people. When the modern state of Israel proclaimed its independence on May 14, 1948, American recognition came a mere twelve minutes later, with President Harry Truman overriding key advisors to make the decision. In so doing, the president risked a serious split with his esteemed secretary of state, General George C. Marshall, who told Truman that instant recognition of the new Jewish state would make it impossible for him to even vote for the president he served in the upcoming election. Yes, Truman hoped to compensate for that lost ballot by winning added support from Jewish voters in key states, but his biographers agree that a deeper calculation played a role. In his Baptist Sunday school and his parents' fervently religious home, Truman learned the same lesson that Blackstone proudly preached—that regardless of electoral consequences, alliance with the chosen people of the Bible brought cosmic benefits.

Some five years later, in the months after President Truman left the White House, his World War I army buddy and onetime Missouri business partner Eddie Jacobson helped arrange a meeting with eminent scholars at the Jewish Theological Seminary in New York City. Jacobson beamingly introduced the former president to the assembled Jewish dignitaries. "This is the man who helped create the State of Israel," Jacobson proudly announced.

"What do you mean, 'helped to create'?" Truman sharply shot back. "I am Cyrus. I am Cyrus!"

In other words, Truman had taken up the opportunity that Benjamin Harrison had declined some fifty-seven years earlier—to imitate the Persian ruler Cyrus the Great, who conquered the Babylonians in 539 B.C. and dispatched the Jewish exiles back to Jerusalem to rebuild their ruined Temple. In Truman's case, the new Cyrus won his underdog presidential race just six months after recognizing Israel, thereby scoring one of the most startling upsets in political history.

The same calculus has influenced Christian leaders even in recent years. In 1967, as Israel faced potential annihilation in the run-up to the Six-Day War, Billy Graham reminded his American audience that "Jews are God's chosen people" and that "we cannot place ourselves in opposition to Israel without detriment to ourselves." In 1981, the influential evangelist Jerry Falwell made an even more explicit case for the Abrahamic imperative of siding with the Jews. In *Listen America!* he declared: "If this nation wants her fields to remain white with grain, her scientific achievements to remain notable, and her freedom to remain intact, America must continue to stand with Israel." In answering reporters' questions, he explained that "history supports the premise that God deals with nations as they deal with Israel."

Though the wars and genocides of the twentieth century are now fading in the public's consciousness, it shouldn't be impossible to apply this premise—based on the "bless those who bless/curse those who curse" promise in the Book of Genesis—to the historical record. Since medieval times, Germany and Russia emerged as the two nations that, in simple mathematical terms, slaughtered the most Jews. Germany suffered catastrophic destruction and loss of life by the end of the Second World War, with its Nazi regime a permanent byword for evil, while Russia endured unimaginable suffering with bloody defeat in the First World War, massacres of the Bolshevik Revolution and civil war, and then another twenty million civilian deaths (at least) through Stalin's depredations and World War II.

In the United States, the Jewish population remained so minuscule during the country's first hundred years of independence that it never made much difference, either practically or mystically. But it's intriguing to note that the years of massive Jewish immigration—1881to 1924—coincided almost precisely with the years of the nation's most rapid economic growth, the emergence of America's dominant role in industry and invention, and an unequivocal rise to world power status. Of course, the correlation of peak immigration makes sense, since seekers will feel most powerfully attracted to dynamic societies. Yes, Jews swarmed to America because of the nation's rise, but it's also true that the nation rose more quickly because the Jews came.

The interlude that followed, from 1924 to 1941, brought the most troubling period of anti-Semitic attitudes, beginning with a draconian immigration bill, specifically designed to halt or drastically curtail immigration by Jews (and other "less desirable elements" such as Italians), that blocked the entry of desperate refugees just as they fled Hitler's Europe in fear for their lives. The "Roaring Twenties" also saw the roaring return, nationwide, of the revitalized Ku Klux Klan, with traditional racism now proudly combined with hatred of Catholic immigrants and a special fear and resentment of Jews. The strident priest Charles Coughlin developed one of the largest radio broadcast audiences in the country's history in the early 1930s—said to be second in popularity only to the blackface comedy show *Amos 'n' Andy*—with his fulminations against "Jew bankers" and war profiteers, and his bristling condemnations of "Franklin Delano Rosenfeld" as a tool of Hebraic power. Finally, lavishly admired national heroes like Henry Ford and Charles A. Lindbergh maintained great popularity despite their shameless expressions of classical anti-Semitism.

This period brought some of the darkest years in our history, with the Depression imposing unprecedented levels of poverty, unemployment, and dislocation, while the Dust Bowl showed nature itself seeming to rise up against a landscape that previously brought prodigious blessings to its inhabitants. Then came the ugly catastrophe at Pearl Harbor and entry into worldwide war, when the country's unequivocal determination to defeat evil enemies brought about an instant change in the national psyche and American circumstances.

"PROTECTING WINGS FOR THEM"

The long-term trajectory of American history has always arced upward, and the overall treatment of Abraham's children has remained inarguably exceptional. The idea of the United States specially "blessing" the children of Abraham doesn't mean that the nation extended special privileges or unusual solicitude to Jews that no other immigrants received. It suggests, rather, that the treatment Jewish arrivals enjoyed at the hands of Americans differed dramatically, and consistently, from the reception they experienced anywhere else on Earth.

From the beginning of mass emigration from eastern Europe to the United States in the 1880s, most Jews and many Americans could plausibly conclude that the newcomers and the new country had been made for each other. In his wonderfully insightful 1977 book *The Jews*, British writer Chaim Bermant observes:

> Until a generation ago—or even less—no one was more inclined to share America's exalted view of itself than the Jew. He really did believe that it was God's own country, opened up just as the position of European Jewry was becoming untenable, whose very creed might have been laid down by the Prophets, a new world without the phobias and dogmas of the old, where past histories were written off and each individual could advance on his own merits. In Europe, the Jew, anxious to integrate within the host society, was subject to rebuffs. . . . The Jew could, however, be an American without presumption or abasement and he gloried in the role. America had no more eager proselytes than the Jews who had found prosperity and acceptance.

And those proselytes played a disproportionate role in creating the very notion of "Americanism" in art and entertainment. In the world of music, Jewish composers have played a conspicuous, occasionally dominant role in creating a distinctive American sound that stirred the country and fascinated the world. Our "Second National Anthem," "God Bless America," was an eve-of-war contribution with words and music by Irving Berlin, a Russian-born cantor's son originally known as Israel Beilin. Berlin also wrote "White Christmas," of course, as well as a deeply moving, richly harmonized choral setting of "Give Me Your Tired, Your Poor," based on the Emma Lazarus words on the base of the Statue of Liberty.

In classical music, no one has done more to crystallize the ineffable essence of Great Plains or Appalachian homesteads than Aaron Copland. The Brooklyn-born son of Lithuanian immigrants used the evocative title *The Tender Land* to designate his only full-length opera and to express his abiding love for the landscape and the figures who inhabit it. When it came to Broadway musicals, all the greatest collaborations—George and Ira Gershwin, Rodgers and Hammerstein, Rodgers and Hart, Kern and Hammerstein, Lerner and Loewe, and Bernstein, Sondheim, and Laurents (on *West Side Story*)—featured the collaboration of two (or more) Jewish talents.

Jews played such an overwhelmingly dominant role in compiling the cherished Great American Songbook that a revealing story centers on the most significant non-Jewish songwriter of the golden age of Tin Pan Alley, the Episcopalian, Indiana-born, Yale-educated son of privilege Cole Porter. After ten years of frustration in looking for his creative breakthrough, he reportedly confided to Richard Rodgers: "I think I've found the key to success. I'm going to write Jewish tunes." Musicologist Albert Evans recently suggested that "Porter was on to something. Musical theater songs had undergone a striking change since the influx of Jewish composers. Consciously or not, Jews had brought the flavor of temple chants and klezmer tunes to Broadway melodies: modal scales, 'bent' notes and major/minor ambiguities."

Few ambiguities tainted the benevolent, irresistibly compelling vision of America provided by another Jewish industry in the 1930s, '40s, and '50s, when seven of the eight dominant motion picture studios were Jewish-owned family businesses. Hollywood historian Neal Gabler and others have argued that these Jewish moguls crafted a glowing, nostalgic image of a paragon nation that never quite existed, in a bid to win acceptance that they never quite succeeded in securing. But their efforts bolstered the world's century-long love affair with the United States, while enabling the Hollywood "Dream Factory" to become the planet's principal source of popular entertainment.

In a sense, Hollywood blessed talented Jewish refugees from war-torn Europe, and the newcomers blessed Hollywood right back by creating an industry that all but obliterated its international competition. In the same way, the United States blessed Jewish refugees (like Albert Einstein, Edward Teller, and the ancestors of J. Robert Oppenheimer) and those researchers blessed America back by developing the weapon that won the war—and beating the Nazis to possession of the awesome power of the atom. As it turned out, there's nothing too mysterious or supernatural about this blessing business; it's transactional, not mystical: America's been good to the Jews and (for the most part) the Jews have been good for America.

And still, it's impossible to examine this history without some sense of wonder. First, there's the peculiar notion that early English settlers identified with the Jews long before more than a few dozen of them had even arrived on these shores. When the crazed revolutionaries finally blew up the czar after a dozen failed attempts, and incidentally drove Jewish multitudes to a new life, it's almost as if they arrived in a country that was waiting for them, filling some vacuum that no one had previously identified but that made for a fateful fit. In his moving book *1939: The Lost World of the Fair,* Yale computer scientist David Gelernter describes the wildly disproportionate prominence of Jewish American politicians, scientists, artists, businesspeople, and even athletes on the eve of World War II: "We tend not to teach our schoolchildren a fact that every one of them, Jew and gentile, ought to know—that America's willingness to stand aside and let Jews go wild in the 1930s, to attend and even politely applaud that dazzling fireworks display of pent-up genius, is an extraordinary achievement in the history of toleration. We are fools not to credit this country with an awe-inspiring feat—a feat that few nations in all history could even have contemplated, much less carried off."

Even after the thrill of that achievement, after the intoxicating romance of the immigrant generation and its children had begun to dissipate, there remained a sense of what Jews call *bashert*—destiny, fate, a preordained outcome—about the sudden influx of families who made their way here and found their path forward after they got here.

Even in the cynical 1970s, with communal leaders worrying that assimilation had begun to push distinctive Jewish identity toward a long, slow fade, Chaim Bermant observed that "Jews still believed in the concept of America as something uniquely wholesome and that if it did not quite represent the Millennium it could serve as one until the real thing came along."

And what if that "something uniquely wholesome" had come into existence for the sake of just these wanderers, and their descendants, and specially for their benefit?

After all, as early as 1798, Elias Boudinot, a former president of the Continental Congress and a founder of the American Bible Society, openly associated America's providential progress with its mission to bless the children of Abraham. "America has been greatly favoured by God, in all her concerns, both civil and religious," he wrote. "She has been raised up in the course of divine Providence, at a very important crisis, and for no very inconsiderable purposes. She stands on a pinnacle—She cannot act a trifling or undecided part. . . . Who knows but God has raised up these United States, in these latter days, for the very purpose of accomplishing his will in bringing his beloved people to their own land."

America has fulfilled this purpose so miraculously that most Jews see the United States, as much or more than Israel, as "their own land." There's been a generous quality to the American experience that evokes the biblical description of a land "flowing with milk and honey," offering not just acceptance and encouragement, but nourishment.

For three centuries, an array of American Christian leaders proclaimed not only an obligation to welcome the Jews but a duty to protect them, wherever they traveled. Ethan Smith, a Revolutionary War veteran and an influential pastor in the remote village of Poultney, Vermont (not exactly a traditional center of Jewish learning), published *A View of the Hebrews* in 1823, advocating unconditional kindness for the children of Abraham under "the protecting wings of a great Eagle . . . a land that, when all other lands shall be found to have trampled on the Jews, shall be found to have protecting wings for them; free from such cruelty, and ready to aid them."

"KINGDOM OF KINDNESS"

One of the beneficiaries of that protection went on to become the most influential and consequential Chassidic rabbi in the world. Menachem Mendel Schneerson (the Lubavitcher Rebbe) arrived in New York in 1941, escaping the war and genocide consuming the European continent. Over the next fifty-three years of his long life, Schneerson frequently referred to the United States as the Malchus shel Chesed—the "Kingdom of Kindness." That kindness he praised, the open and generous spirit that so easily overrides the insanities and inanities of American life, enabled him to build a Brooklyn-based Jewish revival movement that now boasts more than 3,500 thriving outposts in all corners of America and around the world.

For Jews, and most other immigrant arrivals, the Kingdom of Kindness has delivered opportunities for adventure and advancement, while still providing refuge beneath the eagle's mighty wings.

Herman Melville, who had argued with Warder Cresson in Jerusalem over prospects of a Jewish return to the Holy Land, still saw America's future in distinctly biblical terms as "the Israel of our time," destined for its own Mosaic mission. "Escaped from the house of bondage, Israel of old did not follow after the ways of the Egyptians," he wrote in his novel *White-Jacket* in 1850. "To her was given an express dispensation; to her were given new things under the sun. And we Americans are the peculiar, chosen people—the Israel of our time; we bear the ark of the liberties of the world. . . . God has predestinated, mankind expects, great things from our race; and great things we feel in our souls. The rest of the nations must soon be in our rear. We are the pioneers of the world; the advance-guard, sent on through the wilderness of untried things, to break a new path in the New World that is ours."

"BATTLING FOR THE LORD": Theodore Roosevelt turned every significant endeavor of his life into a sacred cause and a grand crusade—especially his impossible drive to return to the presidency in 1912. That "Bull Moose" campaign reached its melodramatic climax when the candidate received a bullet in his chest less than a month before the election.

5

The Reaper and the Bull Moose

Theodore Roosevelt Duels Death

The most dramatic and disturbing campaign speech in American political history began innocently enough, with the on-time arrival of a private rail car bearing a celebrity candidate to address an eager, adoring throng.

In October 1912, former president Theodore Roosevelt roared into Milwaukee in the final stages of his exhausting, insurgent "Bull Moose" campaign. Progressive Wisconsin represented one of his best hopes of capturing electoral votes in that year's complicated, four-way contest. Three weeks before Election Day, the indomitable warrior planned "a great series of sledge hammer speeches upon every vital issue in the campaign" that would take him "to the very close of the fight." Despite the long odds against his victory, Roosevelt hoped that his "sledge hammer speeches" could make him competitive in the final tally.

"IT MAY BE THE LAST ONE I EVER DELIVER"

Roosevelt's train pulled into the station as the damp autumn twilight descended on Milwaukee. The local organizers of his hastily assembled Progressive Party had turned out big crowds to welcome him to town, and planned a lavish civic feast in his honor. But TR's nervous aides wanted him to dine quietly in his private train car, the Mayflower, to rest his vocal cords before the eight o'clock rally. After nearly two months of whistle-stop, coast-to-coast touring in which he delivered up to a dozen rousing and impassioned speeches every day, TR's piercing, commanding tenor had been reduced to a reedy rasp. Dr. Scurry Terrell, a Dallas throat specialist who had begun traveling with the campaign, insisted that the candidate limit himself to brief words of greeting when he faced the ten thousand wildly energized supporters who already awaited him in the recently constructed Milwaukee Auditorium. After that, a designated replacement could deliver the hour-long policy speech he had prepared as a capstone of his campaign.

This notion sparked indignant alarm from the civic committee of volunteers who jammed into the train car and protested this plan, and Roosevelt's instincts pushed him, predictably, to take their side. After all, to those who knew him—and the whole country felt that they knew him—Theodore Roosevelt counted as the last man on Earth who could sit silently onstage as a lesser mortal read aloud the words he had carefully crafted for the occasion.

Overriding his associates, he insisted on attending the scheduled dinner at a nearby hotel and presenting his lengthy prepared oration. Riding in an open seven-seater automobile past the thousands who lined the streets on both sides for more than a mile from the train station, he waved his hat over his head in acknowledgment as they cheered their glimpse of passing greatness.

By the time his entourage bustled into the Gilpatrick Hotel, Roosevelt already felt exhausted. Before his dinner in a hospitality suite, he sat down for a moment in a rocking chair and promptly fell asleep—an uncharacteristic development for an outspoken advocate of "the strenuous life" who had become legendary for his inexhaustible energy. Shortly before eight o'clock, he took the fifty pages of typed text for his oration, folded it over twice, and stuffed it into the inside pocket of his suit jacket. He then descended the stairs and walked out into the poorly lit street, where a police detail had cleared a path to his waiting vehicle.

When he clambered into his topless touring car and settled onto its leather backseat, the cheers erupted once again, and the crowd surged forward to press closer to the candidate. TR stood up and turned around to face the rear of the vehicle, raising his right arm and waving his hat above his head as the applause continued. In the darkness, Roosevelt could hear the cheers but he couldn't see the broad-faced stranger who lifted a revolver and took aim at him from close range.

Several witnesses say they caught the flash and heard the percussive pop associated with its discharge. The gunman fired his recently purchased .38 Colt, striking the former president in the chest. Roosevelt collapsed instantly onto the seat of the car, falling without a sound.

Elbert Martin, one of TR's private secretaries and a former college football star, immediately leapt out of the vehicle and tackled the gunman. Joined by other aides and bodyguards, he wrestled for control of the weapon and began pummeling the assailant, making a serious effort to break his neck. Amid the screams and panic, the wounded candidate managed to raise himself into a seated position and tried to make sense of what had happened. While the shooter struggled with his captors, TR began bellowing orders. "Don't hurt him!" he shouted. "Bring him here. I want to see him."

They pulled the disheveled would-be assassin to his feet and brought him to the door of the car. Roosevelt reached out with both hands and grabbed the man's face between his palms to get a look at him in the dim light from a streetlamp. He wanted to see if he recognized that face, or could discern any purpose in the wide eyes that stared blankly back at him.

"What did you do it for?" the former president demanded. He got no response beyond a dull, disoriented, silent stare. "Oh, what's the use," Roosevelt declared. "Turn him over to the police."

Harry Cochems, a local campaign leader, remembered:

The crowd had quickly cleared from in front of the automobile, and we drove through, Col. Roosevelt waving a hand, the crowd now half-hysterical with frenzied excitement.... Mr. McGrath, one of the Colonel's secretaries riding at his right side, said: "Why Colonel, you have a hole in your overcoat. He has shot you."

The Colonel said: "I know it," and opened his overcoat, which disclosed his white linen, shirt, coat and vest saturated with blood. We all instantly implored and pleaded with the Colonel to drive with the automobile to a hospital, but he turned to me with a characteristic smile and said:

"I know I am good now; I don't know how long I may be. This may be my last talk in this cause to our people, and while I am good I am going to drive to the hall and deliver my speech."

Dr. Terrell, riding along in the seven-seater, disregarded his famous patient and ordered the driver to speed to the hospital as quickly as he knew how to drive. This time the colonel responded angrily. "You get me to that speech," he told the desperately confused driver. "It may be the last one I ever deliver, but I am going to deliver this one."

By the time they arrived, already close to a half hour late, the candidate's face had turned pale and his customary clenched-teeth smiles had disappeared, but his determination remained undiminished. He walked unaided to the waiting room backstage at the cavernous Milwaukee Auditorium, where two doctors from the audience joined Dr. Terrell in opening the colonel's shirt and examining his wound; just below the nipple of his right breast they saw a gaping hole that was still oozing blood and looked to be the size of a fist. Under no circumstances, the physicians declared, could the candidate be allowed to speak. He ignored them, of course, and politely inquired, "Has any one a clean handkerchief?" He placed the proffered square of cloth over his wound, buttoned up his clothes, and walked out onto the stage.

"IT TAKES MORE THAN ONE BULLET
TO KILL A BULL MOOSE"

Harry Cochems tried to calm the restless audience that, in an age before electronic broadcasting and instant news bulletins, had no idea what had just happened a few blocks away. While introducing the crowd's favorite, Cochems explained in a wavering voice that "there was no occasion for undue excitement" but that "an attempt to assassinate Col. Roosevelt had taken place; that the bullet was still in his body, and that he would attempt to make his speech as promised."

When Roosevelt came to the podium to thunderous applause, one cynic in the audience yelled out in clearly audible disrespect: "Fake! Fake!"

The taunt gave the former president a chance to flash his famous teeth, and he opened his vest where "the blood-red stain upon his linen was clearly visible."

Gasps and cries swept over the jammed hall, with many rising to their feet in horror and disbelief, but the candidate raised his hands and tried to calm them. "It takes more than one bullet to kill a Bull Moose," he announced. "I'm all right, no occasion for any sympathy whatever, but I want to take this occasion within five minutes after having been shot to say some things to our people which I hope no one will question the profound sincerity of."

Trying to make himself heard above the continuing murmurs and the protests, he asked for the rapt attention of the audience, and received it.

"Friends, I shall ask you to be as quiet as possible," he began. "The bullet is in me now, so that I cannot make a very long speech. But I will try my best."

As TR had demonstrated throughout the grueling campaign, his idea of a brief speech still ran for well over an hour, punctuated by frequent pleas from aides and audience to conclude his ardent but rambling remarks and make his way to the hospital. "I have altogether too important things to think of to feel any concern over my own death," he assured the crowd. "I am ahead of the game, anyway. No man has had a happier life than I have led; a happier life in every way."

A white-haired lady near the front of the hall could stand the ordeal no longer and pleaded with the colonel in a clearly audible voice to attend to his wound and stop the gathered thousands from suffering along with him. He thanked her but plowed forward. "I give you my word, I do not care a rap about being shot; not a rap. . . . I am all right and you cannot escape listening to the speech either."

He spoke at length against discrimination based on creed or national origin, praising immigrant comrades in arms from various nations and religious traditions who served and bled alongside him in his fabled Rough Riders regiment in the Spanish-American War fourteen years before.

Meanwhile, aides gathered in front of the stage, behind the footlights, to catch TR if he collapsed and fell forward. Noting their scuttling into position beneath him, he again affirmed his determination to continue talking. "I am all right—I am a little sore. Anybody has a right to be sore with a bullet in him. You would find that if I was in battle now I would be leading my men just the same. Just the same way I am going to make this speech."

He charged, indomitable and unstoppable, though his delivery grew steadily weaker, as he wandered back and forth between the extemporaneous expression of his passing thoughts and the fifty pages of prepared remarks that he had unfolded in front of him. Those remarks had been pierced by the bullet that entered his chest, and he proudly displayed the pages to his audience. As his biographer H. W. Brands appropriately noted: "During the previous weeks, Roosevelt's long-windedness had worn down his voice, which grew hoarser at each campaign stop; now it may have saved his life. The bullet plowed through the folded speech manuscript in the breast pocket of his coat before hitting his metal eyeglass case; together the bulky manuscript and case slowed the slug sufficiently that it did no lasting harm."

The doctors didn't know that, and they continued to hover just behind him, trying to halt the address as it reached the one-hour mark. "I know these doctors when they get hold of me they will never let me go back and there are just a few things more that I want to say to you."

Those "few things more" kept him going, as he contrasted his own aggressive record of trust-busting and supervision of big business with the pallid "states' rights" emphasis of his chief electoral rival, the Democrat Woodrow Wilson. Though he never attained the emotional crescendo he so ardently desired, his own exhaustion, combined with the tumultuous applause of the similarly drained audience, led him to conclude at last. As Dr. Terrell came up to help him off the stage, he told him: "Now I am ready to go with you and do what you want."

He turned down offers of support or assistance, of course, and walked briskly and unaided to the waiting car that sped him to Johnston Emergency Hospital, where the staff dressed his wound and X-rayed his chest. Rather than probe for the bullet that night, the local doctors decided to transport the former president to the far superior facilities in nearby Chicago, where he could be treated by the famous surgeon John B. Murphy.

With his private railcar hooked up to a special train, TR and his party left Milwaukee shortly after midnight. The two physicians who traveled with him wanted the patient to retire to his bunk immediately and to manage as much healing sleep as possible, but Roosevelt waved away their pleas: it was his habit to shave before bed, he crisply explained, and he saw no reason to vary his routine. Humming audibly and, his companions thought, contentedly, he passed the razor over his lathered cheeks and throat, then changed his bloody shirt to prepare for his arrival in the morning.

By the time the train chugged into Chicago's North Western Station at 4:00 a.m., Roosevelt had at last fallen asleep. Informed that an ambulance waited at the station to speed him to Mercy Hospital, TR angrily declined, declaring that he wasn't "a weakling to be crippled by a flesh wound" and that he had no intention of traveling through the city while "lying in that thing."

A crowd of four hundred reporters and well-wishers had gathered to greet him in the predawn darkness; when they recognized the former president, the cameras flashed and popped from every angle. "My gosh!" he roared. "Shot again!" He then waved and smiled to signify his hearty survival, calling out a preternaturally cheery "Good morning!" to all.

At the hospital, Dr. Murphy took additional X-rays and determined that the bullet had broken apart, with its fragments lodged in TR's fourth rib. He resolved not to try to extract it, unless infection made it necessary. He also concluded that Roosevelt's eyeglass case had slowed the bullet, but it was the folded sheets of his grand speech that had deflected the shot upward and into the rib. Had it not been for those fifty heavy papers, the bullet would have gone between the ribs and directly into his heart.

Roosevelt remained in the Chicago hospital for six full days until "the crisis passed," in the language of the day. His wife, Edith, had rushed from New York to help her restless husband receive an endless stream of visitors, nearly all of them eager to talk politics.

The candidate returned to his Long Island home, Sagamore Hill, on October 22, and five days later celebrated his fifty-fourth birthday with family and friends. He went back to campaigning the day before Halloween, addressing sixteen thousand admirers at Madison Square Garden, where more than thirty thousand supporters were turned away.

"GOD HAS CALLED ME TO BE HIS INSTRUMENT"

As Theodore Roosevelt gradually recovered from his wound, police and medical authorities back in Wisconsin struggled to understand the motive and mental processes of the thirty-six-year-old drifter who had shot the former president.

Born in Bavaria, John Flammang Schrank was nine years old when he came to America with his parents. They died shortly thereafter, leaving the quiet but earnest boy in the care of an uncle who owned a small tavern in the German neighborhood of lower Manhattan. When that uncle died, young Schrank tried to run the business himself but seemed to fall apart as a result of another personal tragedy. In June 1904, his sweetheart, Emily, died in a fire on a Hudson River excursion boat that killed a thousand members of a German Lutheran congregation on their way to a church picnic.

After her loss, he gave up his business and wandered from city to city along the East Coast, studying the Bible intently, trying to discern why God had surrounded him with death. He spent most nights in cheap rooming houses, brooding over his losses and writing mournful poetry. Schrank became especially obsessed with the death of William McKinley: the assassinated president appeared to him in vivid dreams, invariably rising from his coffin and demanding revenge on his successor—Theodore Roosevelt.

September 14, 1912, marked the eleventh anniversary of McKinley's murder, and at 1:30 in the morning Schrank solemnly penned a formal declaration of his intentions grandly addressed "To the People of the United States." It concluded with the words: "Never let a third term party emblem appear on an official ballot. I am willing to die for my country. God has called me to be his instrument. So help me God . . . INNOCENT—GUILTY."

He carried this letter in his pocket for the next four weeks, as he stalked the candidate through at least six states before arriving in Milwaukee for TR's big speech. In his first appearance in court a month later, Schrank insisted he was perfectly sane and wanted to take the consequences of his action. "I want to say now that I am sane, and know what I am doing all the time," he unequivocally declared.

A week later, the five doctors who had been assigned to evaluate Schrank's mental state unanimously disagreed, declaring him insane and paranoiac, with delusions they characterized as "grandiose in character." He spent the rest of his life in state hospitals for the criminally insane and died from pneumonia at age sixty-seven in 1943.

He outlived Roosevelt by more than two decades, but in all his thirty-one years in state asylums he received not a single visitor, nor a personal letter of any kind. Reporters did contact him for a reaction to TR's sudden death in 1919, since, as many of the obituaries noted, the former president died with Schrank's bullet still lodged in his chest. "A good man gone," he anomalously responded. "Personally, I admired his greatness."

"YOU MUST *MAKE* YOUR BODY. . . . I KNOW
YOU WILL DO IT"

And part of that greatness, for most of TR's legions of admirers, involved precisely the sort of sheer, mad recklessness he displayed on the painful night that his fate collided with Schrank's.

The spectacle of a fifty-three-year-old presidential candidate speaking for an hour and a half to an uneasy audience of ten thousand with an undiagnosed wound and a bullet in his chest reflected more than physical stamina and strength. It demonstrated a foolhardy, wildly irresponsible, and characteristic eagerness to court death, or at least to risk serious damage to his already battered body. Ostensibly, Roosevelt did so to deliver a verbose, mostly pedestrian address in a failing campaign for an election that he already acknowledged he seemed likely to lose. But a deeper purpose involved the former president's need to test the proposition on which he had staked his remarkable career in the first place: that a providential power protected and sustained him in every dangerous endeavor, beyond all reason and expectation, to serve the cause of America's rise to a righteous destiny. In the very midst of his life's greatest disappointment—a doomed, ill-considered presidential campaign—he wanted proof that fate still cherished him as one of fortune's favorites.

From earliest childhood, it seemed, Theodore Roosevelt gained strength every time he defeated death. Though he expressed only contempt for Friedrich Nietzsche's philosophy, his early years seemed to demonstrate the Nietzschean principle that "what doesn't kill us makes us stronger."

For TR, a host of childhood maladies very nearly did kill him, leaving a permanent mark on his personality. He suffered almost constantly as an infant before he could even describe his pain; then, as he learned to talk, he immediately began describing constant headaches, fevers, stomach discomfort, and intestinal distress. Asthma emerged as his chief affliction, blocking his breathing passages and bringing him close to suffocation on multiple occasions. His mother, a Georgia belle noted for her elegant taste and gracious manner, suffered from a frail constitution of her own and so proved for the most part unable to nurse her elder son through these frequent ordeals.

It was his father, Theodore Roosevelt Sr., who took it upon himself to keep the struggling young "Teedie" alive.

A scion of a genteel and prosperous family with roots in the Dutch New Amsterdam of the 1640s, the senior Theodore toiled in the family business of importing window glass but poured much of his passion into charitable and political endeavors. He also took great pride in his two boys and two girls, though Teedie, as the oldest male and most fragile of the bunch, received disproportionate attention. Nothing worked consistently to relieve his coughing and gasping fits, but fresh air sometimes seemed to help. When the danger struck at night, the father tried to make an adventure of it, bundling his elder boy in heavy blankets and taking him for a brisk carriage ride through sleeping Manhattan, with the horses' hooves clip-clopping over the dark and empty streets. As TR later recalled: "I could breathe, I could sleep when he had me in his arms. My father—he got me breath, he got me lungs, strength—life."

Theodore senior gave the struggling Teedie a new direction for living nearly as important as this gift of life. Taking note of the boy's bristling intelligence, he warned him against undermining his brain-power with feeble health. Once Teedie had survived to the age of twelve, "Great Heart" (as he was hailed by his children) took his son aside with an assignment to transform himself. "You have the mind but not the body," he declared, "and without the help of the body the mind cannot go as far as it should. You must *make* your body. . . . I know you will do it."

To begin this process, the father presented his older son with a punching bag, barbells, horizontal bars, and other gymnastic equipment. The lad began working assiduously to build his muscles and to pack new power onto his slight frame. A bullying incident when he was thirteen marred his experience at summer camp, and he began boxing lessons as soon as he returned to New York.

As a boxer at Harvard, he became known for endurance and grit under the punishing blows of his opponents rather than for skill or power. Despite the determination to add muscle mass to his five-foot-eight-inch frame, he weighed only 135 pounds and boxed as a light-weight.

He was still boxing at age fifty as president of the United States, staging sparring matches with young collegiate or military fighters and, occasionally, with professional boxers. In one of these sessions near the end of his term, a young artillery officer landed a blow that smashed the president's left eye, bursting a blood vessel, detaching his retina, and leaving him blind in that eye for the rest of his life. Roosevelt and his aides kept his injury a complete secret, not only to preserve his image of indestructibility but also, they said, to protect the other fighter from the ignominy of partially blinding the president.

Vision, in fact, had always been a problem. When Theodore was fourteen, his father bought him his first gun for hunting. Unfortunately, not only did the boy fail to hit his targets, but in many cases he couldn't even see them. Once Great Heart recognized the problem, he purchased a first set of spectacles for his son. Theodore's aim improved almost immediately, and the pince-nez spectacles became such a necessity in all his pursuits, and such a recognizable feature of his public image, that he ordered twelve specially made spares before he traveled to the front in the Spanish-American War. He stored the glasses inside the lining of his uniform, so they could be replaced even in the heat of battle.

The contrast between Theodore's fragility as a child and the heedless risk-taking that began in adolescence and persisted for the rest of his life helped define his personality. Once he felt that he had conquered his boyhood ailments, he ignored any sensible restraint on his frenetic activity; he came to believe that a higher power and grand destiny, combined with the sheer force of his will, would always prevent death or injury. His father worried about his energy—it "seems so superabundant that I fear it may get the better of him in one way or another."

His doting parents, in fact, believed that he remained too fragile and vulnerable for any conventional school and chose instead to prepare the brilliant boy through rigorous home schooling. The Roosevelts hired accomplished tutors to give Theodore a solid grounding in history, science, languages, writing, and philosophy. They judged him ready for Harvard at eighteen, but it remains unclear whether Harvard was ready for him. One of his classmates, Reverend Sherrard Billings, recalled that "when it was not considered good form to move at more than a walk, Roosevelt was always running."

Not even solid medical advice could slow the young man down. When Dr. Dudley Sargent warned Theodore that he should limit himself to a calm and tranquil life to avoid fatal consequences from his "weak heart," he replied, "Doctor, I'm going to do all the things you tell me *not* to do. If I've got to live the sort of life you have described, I don't care how short it is."

"TOO SACRED TO BE WRITTEN ABOUT"

He cared deeply, however, when a more painful reminder of mortality struck the home front.

As a leader of the reformist faction of New York Republicans, the senior Theodore Roosevelt won an 1877 appointment as Collector of Customs at the Port of New York. His nomination amounted to a transparent bid by the newly elected president, Rutherford B. Hayes, to clean up the corrupt patronage politics of both parties. Naturally, the GOP establishment angrily opposed that idea and fought to block Great Heart's confirmation by the U.S. Senate. The all-out political assault that followed weighed on his spirit and broke his health; many of his friends reported that he aged visibly in the ten weeks of the battle. Within six days of the Senate's rejection (by a vote of thirty-one to twenty-five), Roosevelt, then forty-six, collapsed and took to his bed with severe digestive distress and internal bleeding.

The stricken patriarch rallied briefly when his nineteen-year-old son came home from Harvard for the Christmas holiday. The proud father presented young Theodore with a double-barreled shotgun as a Christmas gift to encourage his passion for hunting and insisted he return to Cambridge to continue his successful studies. After his son's departure, Great Heart's condition deteriorated rapidly, but he instructed other family members to downplay his daily agonies and the grave diagnosis of intestinal cancer.

Summoned at the last moment, the younger Roosevelt arrived too late to see his father alive and mourned in his diary over losing "the finest man I ever knew" and "the only human being to whom I told everything." Weeks later, still finding it difficult to overcome his grief, he wrote: "I often feel badly that such a wonderful man as Father should have had a son of so little worth as I."

Despite this passing gloom concerning his own value, Theodore recovered enough self-confidence within eight months of his father's death to recklessly and ruthlessly pursue a seventeen-year-old beauty he met at the home of a friend from Harvard. Celebrated for her "blue-gray eyes and long, wavy golden hair," as well as a disposition so cheerful that she earned the family nickname "Sunshine," Alice Hath-away Lee resisted Roosevelt's obsessive insistence on matrimony for the better part of a year before she finally surrendered. They married on his twenty-second birthday, just four months after his Harvard graduation, when she was still nineteen. A few days after the wedding, he wrote in his diary: "Our intense happiness is too sacred to be writ-ten about."

But he did find an abundance of other topics worth writing about, as the words and pages poured forth in the opening chapters of his lifelong passion for producing books. Over the next thirty-eight years, he generated an astonishing total of thirty-eight volumes on history, zoology, hunting, travel, adventure, memoirs, biography, and more. He had begun his first project while still a Harvard senior and fin-ished *The Naval War of 1812* while living in Manhattan with Alice and attending Columbia Law School.

By that time, Theodore had resolved to spend more time waging war than he did writing about it, but the battlefield he chose appalled the privileged New York social circle in which he'd been raised. As he wrote in his autobiography: "The men I knew best were the men in the clubs of social pretension and the men of cultivated taste and easy life." When he discussed his growing interest in politics, they dis-missed it as a grubby business, dominated by "saloon-keepers, horse-car conductors, and the like." When they described politics as "low," he had a ready reply: "I answered that if this were so it merely meant that the people I knew did not belong to the governing class, and that the other people did—and that I intended to be one of the governing class."

Selected as something of a novelty candidate by his Manhattan district's Republican organization, he won election shortly after his twenty-third birthday in 1881 and just months before the publication of his first book. "I rose like a rocket," he immodestly recalled years later, reaching the status of minority leader of the New York State Assembly at the absurdly tender age of twenty-four.

From the beginning, he saw even the most mundane partisan bat-tles in apocalyptic terms, viewing himself as a lonely paladin for righ-teousness and honor. Above all, he despised the powerful Tammany

Hall machine that had long dominated New York City Democratic politics. "There are some twenty-five Irish Democrats in the House," he complained to his diary. "They are a stupid, sodden vicious lot, most of them being equally deficient in brains and virtue."

"THERE IS A CURSE ON THIS HOUSE"

After three years in the legislature, he began to develop friendships, or at least cordial working relationships, with some of those Democratic colleagues he had once described as "low, venal, corrupt and unintelligent brute[s]." When he received a telegram on the assembly floor announcing that Alice had just delivered their first child, a baby girl, he handed out cigars that he had secured for the occasion.

A terse second telegram put an end to the jubilation and back-slapping. It urged Theodore to speed as quickly as possible to New York City, where both his wife and his mother lay gravely ill. He embarked immediately, but the normal five-hour journey from Albany to Manhattan had been slowed by a thick, freezing February fog that shrouded the world in gauzy gray.

He arrived at Grand Central Depot at 10:30 p.m. and then rode in a hired carriage that made its agonizingly slow way through the otherworldly, mist-clogged streets to the elegant home at 6 West Fifty-seventh Street that his late father had had built for the family when TR was fourteen. The house looked forbiddingly dark, except for the gaslights on the third floor. His younger brother, Elliott, opened the door with a solemn pronouncement. "There is a curse on this house," he said, with an edge that mixed grief and anger. "Mother is dying, and Alice is dying too."

TR rushed upstairs to his wife first, finding her only semiconscious as he held her in his arms. The doctors explained that she had experienced kidney failure brought on by Bright's disease, which had gone undiagnosed during her pregnancy. Theodore hovered at her bedside for several hours, uncertain if she even recognized him, but trying somehow to revive her through the sheer force of his love. Bells from Fifth Avenue churches rang out to announce midnight, and the arrival of St. Valentine's Day—February 14, 1884—the fourth anniversary of the day they announced their engagement. Shortly after the chimes had finished, a message arrived in the sickroom from downstairs: Theodore must come immediately if he wanted to say goodbye to his mother.

She expired at 3:00 a.m., stricken by the typhoid fever that had been sweeping the city. Theodore ran back upstairs in the hours before dawn, hoping to will Alice back to consciousness and back to his life through the power of his embraces. The fog outside the third-story windows piled higher, more oppressively, on the wakening streets; the Roosevelts kept the lights burning through Valentine's Day. At two in the afternoon, Alice died, while her healthy newborn daughter cried for attention elsewhere in the house.

During these years of young manhood, TR left florid, vivid, excited entries in his diary, but on Valentine's Day he could find no words. Instead, he marked the blank page with a large, thick, black **X**. Beneath it he scrawled only eight words: "The light has gone out of my life."

Certainly, his fellow legislators never expected him to speedily rejoin their windy debates and parliamentary gamesmanship, their tedious committee meetings and investigations and drafting of comprehensive reports, mixed with frequent late nights of hearty meals and occasional carousing. But just two days after the joint funeral for his wife and his mother, he rushed back to Albany on the morning train, leaving his newborn daughter in the care of his older (and unmarried) sister, Anna (known universally as "Bamie").

"I have never believed it did any good to flinch or yield for any blow," TR wrote to a friend. "Indeed, I think I should go mad if I were not employed."

Or, as he put it more poetically a few months later: "Black care rarely sits behind a rider whose pace is fast enough."

"AMERICANS THROUGH TO THE VERY
HEART'S CORE"

He continued to toil at his post and got his first real taste of national politics as a delegate to the hotly contested Republican National Convention of 1884, where a "morally compromised" candidate he ardently opposed went on to win the nomination. Frustrated with the outcome, weary from the daily grind of the legislature, Roosevelt turned down the nomination for a fourth term in Albany.

Instead, he yearned to pursue wealth and adventure on the frontier by establishing cattle ranches in the rugged Badlands of Dakota Territory. In the summer before the death of his wife, he had indulged himself with a hunting trip to the sparsely settled region where he not only bagged bison and other beasts but also invested a significant portion of his inheritance from his father in buying the sprawling Maltese Cross Ranch. He ultimately pumped some $80,000 into his Dakota ventures, the equivalent of nearly $2 million today. Like other intrepid entrepreneurs at the edge of civilization, he hoped to make a quick killing in return for this bold investment.

But he also meant to do his share of more primal sorts of killing and prepared himself by designing his own "hunting costume." He wrote proudly to his sister Bamie, who was raising Theodore's baby daughter back in Manhattan: "I wear a sombrero, silk neckerchief, fringed buckskin shirt, sealskin chaparajos or riding trousers; alligator hide boots." He also carried a sheathed, silver Bowie knife from Tiffany's. "With my pearl-hilted revolver and beautifully finished Winchester rifle, I shall feel able to face anything," he confidently announced.

Given Roosevelt's fancy dress, thick spectacles (his ranch hands dubbed him "Old Four Eyes"), and free spending, it took him some time to earn the respect of the hard-bitten locals who lived on widely separated spreads near the tiny town of Medora. The Democrats of the New York legislature, once characterized by Roosevelt as "a stupid, sodden vicious lot," looked like paragons of refinement in comparison to some of the rough customers who rode the Badlands. Roosevelt damaged his own cause during one roundup when, at the top of his voice, with his distinctive, clipped, Gatling gun delivery, he barked out an oddly worded command to his cowboys: "Hasten forward quickly there!" They tried to obey, while stifling the inevitable snickers and guffaws.

Despite his big-city quirks, Roosevelt managed to lead a successful, month-long cattle drive that spanned nearly a thousand miles and to win general respect through his fearlessness and stubborn endurance. His prairie partners could even look past his suspect refusal—as a matter of principle—to join them in drinking, smoking, or cursing. Meanwhile, he came to admire the cattlemen around him as representative of an eternal archetype—"the herdsman of history"—who possesses "few of the emasculated, milk-and-water moralities admired by the pseudo-philanthropists; but he does possess, to a very high degree, the stern, manly qualities that are invaluable to a nation."

To develop his own "stern, manly qualities," he indulged himself in wilderness hunting expeditions that brought home prodigious quantities of game, ranging from small birds to huge bears. One especially productive jaunt to the Bighorn Mountains generated 175 carcasses in a single week. He wrote about these experiences in vivid, often lyrical prose and sent the pages east to popular magazines. A colorful collection of such dispatches comprised his second successful book: *Hunting Trips of a Ranchman* (1885).

In the biography that followed (*Thomas Hart Benton*, 1887), Roosevelt again stressed his irrepressible affection for the spirit of the frontier and the men who had conquered it. "They were a race of masterful spirit," he wrote, "and accustomed to regard with easy tolerance any but the most flagrant violations of law. They prized highly such qualities as courage, loyalty, truth, and patriotism, but they were, as a whole, poor, and not over-scrupulous of the rights of others."

A politician of another century might have described such individuals as "deplorables" but TR unequivocally admired them: "There was little that was soft or outwardly attractive in their character: it was stern, rude, and hard, like the lives they led; but it was the character of those who were every inch men, and were Americans through to the very heart's core."

"HOMESICKNESS AND LONGING FOR THE PAST"

His extended sojourns in the West amounted to a total of less than twelve months of Roosevelt's life between the years 1883 and 1887, since he regularly interrupted his time on the range to ride the rails east to attend to political and family business, and to one brief but consequential meeting in September 1885.

Roosevelt's preeminent biographer Edmund Morris speculates that his sister Bamie may have deliberately arranged the encounter at her home on Madison Avenue, where she was raising his daughter, Alice, but scant evidence exists because of Theodore's unmistakable reluctance to provide details in his diary. In any event, nineteen months after the death of his wife, the grieving widower who had recently transformed himself into a sunburned cowpuncher from the Badlands reconnected with one of the most cherished playmates of his childhood—a significant figure in his upbringing with whom he'd had scant contact for several years.

Edith Kermit Carow had literally grown up with the Roosevelts as a close friend of Theodore's younger sister, Corinne, and she spent much of her time during the summer months at the Roosevelt country home on Long Island. Nine-year-old Theodore developed a "puppy love" fixation on Edith, who was six; when given his own rowboat for adventures on Long Island Sound, he promptly christened it the *Edith* and asked its young namesake to design a flag for the formidable craft.

When Theodore departed for Europe at age ten for an extended tour with his family, he confided to his diary that he found it "very hard" to face separation from the little girl he adored. On November 22, 1869, shortly after his eleventh birthday, Theodore wrote in his diary: "Mama showed me the portrait of Edith Carow and her face stirred in me homesickness and longing for the past which will come again never, alack, never."

But sixteen years later, that past came rushing back at him full force, when he glimpsed Edith as a grown woman. At age twenty-four, she approached the dreaded status of "spinster" by remaining unmarried in the Victorian society in which they both functioned. During his years at Harvard, the two childhood friends had apparently experienced some unresolved argument; nevertheless, Edith had attended TR's wedding to Alice and, with manic and overflowing gaiety, outdanced all of the other guests "until the soles of my shoes fell off."

The athletic Miss Carow qualified as one of those society women described as "handsome" rather than dainty or beautiful, with her wide-set gray eyes and strong jaw; when TR glimpsed her at his sister's home, she was already older than the adored, departed Alice would ever be.

And yet that passing encounter produced an instant spark and a renewed connection inspired, perhaps, by the same "homesickness and longing for the past" that Theodore had described as a boy. Among her other unmistakable virtues, Edith offered a path back to a lost, cherished world of innocence, security, and ardent yearning. Little Theodore's rowboat of twenty years before, the *Edith*, represented just the sort of vessel that another writer who frequented Long Island Sound might have had in mind when he penned *The Great Gatsby* some fifty years later. "So we beat on, boats against the current," wrote F. Scott Fitzgerald, "borne back ceaselessly into the past."

For Edith, the timing of her renewed relationship with her childhood friend also served an important practical purpose: blocking her plans to relocate to Italy, where her recently widowed mother and younger sister found it more affordable to live a genteel life and wanted her to join them there. Instead, she found herself caught up in the whirlwind of Theodore's crowded, multifaceted existence: in addition to his ranching adventures, his book projects and magazine assignments, and his rekindled (but carefully concealed) romantic life, he agreed to run as the 1886 Republican nominee for mayor of New York City.

He ultimately finished third in his gallant but hopeless race (behind both the Democratic nominee and a radical independent candidate, philosopher Henry George), but the demands of the campaign pushed Theodore and Edith to keep their revived connection a complete secret from family and friends. Much to TR's consternation, some newspapers caught wind of the forthcoming nuptials and forced him to confess to his family. "I utterly disbelieve in and disapprove of second marriages. I have always considered that they argued weakness in a man's character," he wrote to his sister Bamie. "You could not reproach me one half as bitterly for my inconstancy and unfaithfulness as I reproach myself."

He overcame these reproaches with the public announcement of his engagement shortly after the election and a discreet ceremony in a London church on December 2, followed by an extended honeymoon of several months on the Continent.

"DEAD SQUARE, WAS ROOSEVELT, AND WE NEEDED HIM IN THE BUSINESS"

While the Roosevelts traveled through European capitals, the winter of 1886–87 proved to be the coldest season in North America's recorded history and became an unprecedented catastrophe for the open-range cattle industry of the Great Plains. Temperatures frequently reached forty or fifty degrees below zero and most of the livestock ultimately froze to death—including nearly all of Roosevelt's herd.

In April, after his honeymoon, Theodore traveled through the blighted landscape and rode for three days without seeing a living cow, while every gully and riverbed offered piles of emaciated, half-frozen, rotting carcasses. He stubbornly held on to his Dakota properties for another ten years but resigned himself to huge financial losses, abandoning hope of building a future on the frontier.

Instead, he established his new family on more familiar ground: a plot of family land near Oyster Bay, Long Island, where he completed Sagamore Hill, a rambling country home he had originally planned for Alice. There, the Roosevelts welcomed their four boys and a new daughter, to join the child of his first marriage, "Princess Alice" (as she later came to be known), who was barely two at the time of her father's remarriage.

Literary projects and political posts followed in quick succession: *The Winning of the West,* a four-volume historical series that proved both popular and profitable; appointment to the U.S. Civil Service Commission, his first job in Washington, D.C.; selection as the president of the New York Board of Police Commissioners, reestablishing his prominence in the teeming metropolis by cracking down on corruption and greatly enhancing morale in the ranks. Despite his popularity with the officers, Roosevelt ran into trouble with powerful saloon interests when he insisted on enforcing often-evaded laws limiting the sale of liquor on Sundays. As it became obvious that Roosevelt had no long-term future with the police board, one patrolman confided to the press that his departure was "tough on the force.... He was dead square, was Roosevelt, and we needed him in the business."

"HE DID NOT CARE WHOM WE FOUGHT
AS LONG AS THERE WAS A SCRAP"

Meanwhile, TR maneuvered for a position in a more prestigious business: an appointment to the administration of the newly elected Republican president, William McKinley. Given a successful book of history focusing on warfare at sea, he particularly coveted a post at the Department of the Navy. Still only thirty-seven years old, he had at various times urged American attacks on Mexico, Germany, England, Spain, and Chile. Once TR had established himself as assistant secretary of the navy in 1897, a Republican congressman from Pennsylvania, Thomas Stalker Butler, wryly observed: "Roosevelt came down here looking for war. He did not care whom we fought as long as there was a scrap."

While it's easy to deride Roosevelt's unabashed enthusiasm for combat long before he'd ever experienced it personally, it's also impossible to deny the prophetic nature of some of his strategic obsessions. He was an early advocate for an American takeover of the Hawaiian Islands as a necessary step to project power into the Pacific, and he warned of the need to contain the rising, imperialistic naval ambitions of Japan and Germany. Long before he became president and personally oversaw the digging of "the Big Ditch," he pushed tirelessly for construction of a canal on the Isthmus of Panama to connect our fleets in the Atlantic and the Pacific and to cement American dominance of both of the world's great oceans.

Once installed on his perch at the Navy Department under McKinley, TR took meaningful strides toward all of these ambitious goals and exerted an influence on both military and foreign policy that was outrageously inappropriate for a mere "assistant secretary."

It was Roosevelt, for instance, not President McKinley or Secre-

tary of the Navy John Davis Long, who crucially replaced the dodder-
ing and ineffective commander of the "Asiatic Fleet" with a tough,
no-nonsense, white-haired, and walrus-mustachioed man of action
more to TR's taste: Admiral George Dewey. On February 25, 1898,
after a mysterious explosion on the USS *Maine* killed 250 sailors in
Havana Harbor, TR took advantage of the secretary's absence to send
a fateful telegram to Dewey in Hong Kong:

> Keep full of coal. In the event of declaration of war [on] Spain
> your duty will be to see that the Spanish squadron does not leave
> the Asiatic coast and then offensive operations in Philippine Is-
> lands. . . . Roosevelt

In other words, an assistant secretary took it upon himself to
order invasion and occupation of a major, heavily populated, highly
strategic island chain that had been colonized by the Spanish for
nearly four hundred years.

Less than eight weeks after these audacious orders, immediately
after the declaration of war, Dewey followed his instructions to per-
fection: fighting the lopsided Battle of Manila Bay, resulting in the
destruction of the entire Spanish fleet without the loss of a single
American sailor or significant damage to any U.S. ship.

"I REALLY THINK HE IS GOING MAD"

Roosevelt took unabashed pride in such success but had no intention
whatever of spending the duration of the Spanish-American War at a
desk in the Navy Department. He had already indicated to the president that in the event of war he meant to resign as assistant secretary
and to organize an elite regiment that he would lead into battle.
McKinley didn't turn him down but didn't take his insistence seriously, either: TR was thirty-nine years old; his wife, Edith, had recently given birth to his sixth child, and she faced grave problems in
her feverish, painful recovery. Meanwhile, Theodore's eldest boy—
nine-year-old Theodore III—battled a mysterious illness. Most pertinent of all, Roosevelt had read and written extensively about warfare,

but had no meaningful military experience (aside from brief training with the New York National Guard); moreover, his notoriously weak vision and thick pince-nez spectacles made him an unlikely candidate for battlefield command.

His friend Henry Adams seriously suggested that TR had lost his mind. "Is his wife dead? Has he quarreled with everybody? Is he quite mad?" the great historian wrote to a mutual friend. Winthrop Chanler, an artist and designer the Roosevelts had befriended, wrote his wife: "I really think he is going mad. The President has asked him twice as a personal favor to stay in the Navy Dept., but Theodore is wild to fight and hack and hew. It is really sad. Of course this ends his political career for good."

Secretary of the Navy Long tried his best to dissuade his headstrong assistant, all but ordering him to remain at his job. When Long failed in this effort, he penned an anguished but prophetic entry in his diary:

> He has lost his head to this unutterable folly of deserting the post where he is of most service and running off to ride a horse and, probably, brush mosquitoes from his neck on the Florida sands. His heart is right, and he means well, but it is one of those cases of aberration—desertion—vainglory; of which he is utterly unaware. He thinks he is following his highest ideal, whereas, in fact, as without exception every one of his friends advises him, he is acting like a fool. And, yet, how absurd all this will sound, if by some turn of fortune, he should accomplish some great thing and strike a very high mark.

Only his immediate family rallied in support of his rash determination to rush into battle, ignoring this sound advice from his intimate circle of companions and colleagues. His six children, ranging from the aloof, headstrong fourteen-year-old Alice to the infant Quentin, didn't fully grasp the issues behind the war—in fact, few adults could articulate the precise American interests that impelled a major war against the fading Spanish Empire. But the "Bunnies" (as Theodore called his offspring) fed off the excitement that "Big Bear" (as they called him) fairly radiated as he began recruiting and organizing the volunteers for his new cavalry regiment.

"ROUGH, TOUGH, WE'RE THE STUFF!"

The first entry in his war diary, a week before his formal resignation as assistant secretary of the navy, proudly declared: "I have the Navy in good shape. But the army is awful. The War Dept. is in utter confusion."

Somehow, he couldn't shake the idea that the best antidote to that "utter confusion" would be to recruit and command his own cavalry regiment, imbued with the ruthless, frontier "fighting spirit" he always admired.

From its inception, this unconventional unit bore the ingenious designation of "the Rough Riders," borrowing the name of a troupe of agile performers in Buffalo Bill Cody's celebrated Wild West Show. The new regiment also featured Native Americans from the reservations who took pride in their war whoops; a philosophical sheriff from New Mexico famous for facing down gunslingers; tough New York cops who admired TR's work as police commissioner; professional boxers and yachtsmen and explorers; painters, prospectors, poets, polo players, marksmen, and doctors; and, inescapably, members of his own elite world of drawing rooms and private clubs. To the left-leaning reporter Lincoln Steffens, Roosevelt proudly pointed to "Harvard and Yale men going as troopers, to be exactly on a level with the cowboys." The mix of saddle-sore frontiersmen and foxhunting "swells" inspired glowing press accounts that described the Rough Riders as unmistakably and uniquely American for uniting volunteers from every stratum of society.

Despite his utter lack of battlefield experience, Roosevelt claimed the rank of lieutenant colonel of volunteers, making him second-in-command to his close Washington pal Leonard Wood, who had collaborated in conceiving and organizing the regiment. Colonel (soon to be General) Leonard Wood, a well-respected physician and another Harvard man, had served for more than a decade as an officer in the regular army, fighting Indians in the Arizona desert.

With the need for haste in mind, the battle-hungry TR rushed his men through their rudimentary training in San Antonio, Texas, where they drilled, donned uniforms, and familiarized themselves with their government-issue weapons and horses. They also developed enough unit cohesion to compose a regimental cheer:

> *Rough, tough, we're the stuff!*
> *We want to fight and we can't get enough!*
> *Whoopee!*

This chant reflected the sporting spirit of collegiate football far more than it expressed the stoic determination of a formidable fighting force facing deadly battle, which made some sense for a unit that contained a sprinkling of past and present Ivy League gridiron stars.

After their quick weeks of Texas training, the Rough Riders (with their 1,258 horses and mules riding in their own cars) rejoiced at boarding the Southern Pacific Railroad to make the four-day trek to Tampa for embarkation to the front. Unfortunately, when they got there the ships available to transport the army to Cuba could handle barely half of the thirty thousand troops who camped around the harbor. Roosevelt dreaded the possibility of missing the thrill of combat far more than he ever feared enemy fire, and he proceeded with ruthless (and unauthorized) maneuvers to outflank other units in pushing his "fine fellows" to the front of the line.

Despite his success in these efforts, the rusting tramp steamer he had commandeered for his men hardly seemed worthy of the "We're the Stuff" troopers and couldn't possibly accommodate all of the men with their horses and equipment. Ultimately, the dashing cavalry regiment had to leave behind nearly all its mounts in Florida—along with a third of its comrades in arms who couldn't possibly be jammed onto the *Yucatan*. Only officers got to bring their sixty horses; TR chose to transport two, reflecting his status as a wealthy celebrity and his leadership position among the volunteers.

Whatever his frustrations in the process of transporting his fighters to the front, the former assistant secretary of the navy felt exultant once he and his men set sail as part of the American convoy carrying them to their destiny. "We are steaming southward through a sapphire sea, wind-rippled, under an almost cloudless sky," he recorded in a strikingly poetic passage. "There are some forty-eight craft in all, in three columns, the black hulls of the transports setting off the gray hulls of the men-of-war. Last evening we stood up on the bridge and watched the red sun sink and the lights blaze up on the ships, for miles ahead and astern, while the band played piece after piece, from the 'Star Spangled Banner' at which we all rose and stood uncovered, to 'The Girl I Left Behind Me.'"

Even before his first taste of actual combat, he wrote to his sister that he sensed his place in a grand master plan. "It is a great historical expedition, and I thrill to feel that I am part of it. If we fail, of course we share the fate of all who do fail, but if we are allowed to succeed (for we certainly shall succeed, if allowed) we have scored the first great triumph in what will be a world movement."

"A CERTAIN FEELING OF UNEASY EXCITEMENT"

That great triumph began inauspiciously with the bungled landing at Daiquirí Beach: nearly all sixty horses that crossed the Caribbean ended up drowning in the chaotic unloading process. One of the casualties was TR's chosen horse, the large and powerful Rain-in-the-Face; he had been lowered by winch from the deck of the ship but perished under a crushing wave while unable to escape from his harness. Fortunately, the smaller, more agile of Roosevelt's two horses, the fearless chestnut gelding Little Texas, managed to survive and, ultimately, to gallop his way into equine immortality.

Before confronting the enemy, the Rough Riders had to move themselves into position on foot. Their orders called for dislodging the Spaniards from Santiago de Cuba, the fortified port city near the southeastern end of the long, narrow island. There, a Spanish fleet of six warships occupied the harbor, and the guns in local forts discouraged the U.S. Navy from challenging them. In addition, more than twelve thousand troops clustered in and around the town to defend against an attack by land. On the ridges and hills above the bay, the Spaniards dug extensive trenches from which their well-trained snipers could mow down the Yankee invaders.

To challenge these defenses, the American volunteers and regulars had to walk fifteen miles on primitive roads that snaked their way through steamy jungles before reaching the outskirts of the town. For the fabled horsemen of TR's cavalry regiment, this tropical hike added insult to exhaustion. Trying to maintain a sense of humor about their situation, "Roosevelt's Rough Riders" ironically rechristened themselves "Wood's Weary Walkers."

At the insistence of Roosevelt and Wood, the Rough Riders led the American column and bore the brunt of an enemy ambush in the first land battle of the Spanish-American War.

Near a place known as "Las Guásimas," the Spaniards had deployed two pieces of artillery and 1,500 well-armed men behind a curtain of dense jungle through which they could fire down on the startled Americans who were jammed along the road. A reporter on the scene noted the unsettling noise of hundreds of bullets cutting through the foliage and tearing the air with a hissing sound, then striking human flesh with a sickening "chug." Sergeant Hamilton Fish, one of the first to fall, was a twenty-four-year-old former captain of the Columbia University crew team and a grandson of Grant's secretary of state; shot through the heart, he was dead within a minute.

Colonel Leonard Wood, a combat veteran whose cool temperament had already earned him the nickname "Old Icebox" from his men, calmly ordered the troopers to stop swearing and start shooting. In contrast, TR could barely contain his boyish and explosive energy. Edward Marshall, a correspondent for Hearst's ardently prowar newspaper the *New York Journal*, reported that "Colonel Roosevelt, on the contrary, jumped up and down, literally, I mean, with emotions evidently divided between joy and a tendency to run." In Theodore's case, that tendency impelled him to run *toward* the enemy, not in the other direction. But as he rallied his men and lunged forward into the rain forest, his sword got caught between his legs so that he staggered and nearly fell, before righting himself and leading a successful charge that helped drive the Spaniards back toward Santiago de Cuba.

That night, he wrote to his sister with obvious satisfaction at his own success in leading his men under hostile fire for the first time. "We lost a dozen men killed or mortally wounded, and sixty severely or slightly wounded.... One man was killed as he stood beside a tree with me. Another bullet went through a tree behind which I stood and filled my eyes with bark. The last charge I led on the left using a rifle I took from a wounded man.... The fire was very hot at one or two points where the men around me went down like ninepins." As always, after one of his frequent, unlikely escapes from deadly danger, Roosevelt took his personal survival largely for granted.

In this case, as in so many others, that survival seemed to serve a larger purpose: Two of the senior officers were suddenly incapacitated with one of the tropical fevers that ultimately killed far more Americans than Spanish bullets, claiming more than two thousand lives among the troops—some eight times more than the 281 officially killed in action. Leonard Wood received an immediate promotion to brigadier general and Old Icebox moved up the chain of command. This meant that Roosevelt, to his "intense delight . . . got my regiment." He would now exert sole command over the Rough Riders.

In that capacity, he marched them till well after dark on the last night of June. He finally let the Weary Walkers set up their camp and bed down, knowing that when the sun came up they would be in sight of the chief Spanish trenches defending the San Juan heights that overlooked Santiago de Cuba. As usual, the Rough Riders would be expected to play the lead role the next day, along with the Ninth and Tenth Cavalry from the regular army, all-black units made up of the famous "Buffalo Soldiers" who had distinguished themselves in the Indian wars of the far West. In fact, black warriors accounted for an estimated one-fourth of all troops in the American expeditionary forces, chosen for this mission in the mistaken belief that their African ancestry would provide them with natural protection from the ravages of the tropical climate and the many diseases associated with it.

Unlike other commanders, Roosevelt took few precautions to

avoid illness for himself or his men. The night before the concerted assault he slept in a uniform he hadn't changed in days, now drenched with hot sweat and warm rain after a brief, intense downpour. He relied on his soiled saddle blanket to keep him above the mud, while he huddled under a rain slicker that protected him from further soaking. The jungle that loomed on all sides was a palpable presence in the dark, loud with insects. He tried to rest but later recalled that "there is always a certain feeling of uneasy excitement the night before a battle." He had already decided that July 1, 1898, would be "the great day of my life," and maintained that designation in all of the twenty years remaining to him.

"ONE CROWDED HOUR OF GLORIOUS LIFE"

Arising at 4:00 a.m., well before dawn, he reveled in his expectations for the new day. Bugle calls greeted the first light, rising from American encampments in the fields and hillsides all around him, connecting to a bit of poetry he had cherished in his youth and that came to mind that morning:

> Sound, sound the clarion, fill the fife,
> To all the sensual world proclaim,
> One crowded hour of glorious life
> Is worth an age without a name.

That idea—the notion that a fleeting moment of sublime martial glory counted for more than a long life of peaceful, uneventful plodding—had brought Roosevelt to Cuba in the first place. The lines came from "The Call," rousing stanzas by a warrior-poet named Thomas Osbert Mordaunt who served as a British officer in the Seven Years' War (1756–63). That was the same worldwide conflict that gave TR's hero, a young George Washington, his first taste of battle when he faced the French and Indians at the Battle of the Monongahela, emerging from the enemy's withering fire miraculously unscathed. TR could only hope that like the Father of His Country, he might be providentially protected.

"It was a very lovely morning," he wrote, "the sky of cloudless blue, while the level, shimmering rays from the just-risen sun brought into fine relief the splendid palms which here and there towered above the lower growth. The lofty and beautiful mountains hemmed in the Santiago plain, making it an amphitheater for battle."

As the sun rose in the sky and the temperature approached one hundred degrees, both officers and enlisted men knew they had come to this picturesque location not to enjoy the scenery but to storm the enemy's defenses near the top of the ridge, and they waited nervously for the orders that would tell them how to do it. Meanwhile, the Spaniards rained sheets of bullets down on the U.S. troops from their powerful Mauser rifles as the Americans tried (with mixed success) to dodge their fire. William Rufus Shafter, the sixty-three-year-old Civil War veteran in overall command of the American forces, suffered intensely from gout, the tropical heat, and the formidable challenges of maneuvering his huge, sweating, obese (well over three hundred pounds), and aching body anywhere near the front. On the morning of July 1, his personal indisposition added substantially to the paralyzing delay.

Even under the best of circumstances, Theodore Roosevelt seldom displayed the virtue of patience, and under these conditions, watching his men hiding behind trees and brush, occasionally wounded or killed by the ceaseless Spanish fire, he felt ready to disregard the chain of command. He suggested to some of his fellow officers that he might slip his leash and lead his men in a headlong charge into the enemy guns, when a lieutenant colonel showed up with the order "to move forward and support the regulars in the assault on the hills in the front."

As he recalled in his bestselling memoir, *The Rough Riders*: "The instant I received the order I sprang on my horse and then my 'crowded hour' began." He had originally made the sensible decision to walk toward danger along with his men but the urge to gallop ahead of the rest, astride the fast, edgy horse Little Texas, struck him with a force he couldn't resist.

In rational terms, this impulse made no sense at all: he knew the Spaniards had been specially trained to aim at American officers, and as the only man on horseback in the entire regiment he offered an ir-resistible target. To place himself even more at risk, or more likely to show his utter disregard to the very notion of risk, he took his blue-and-white checkered handkerchief out of his pocket and tied it around his floppy, broad-brimmed western hat. The piece of cloth would trail behind him like a pennant, making it easier, he said, for the men to follow his lead—and, of course, for the snipers to find their mark.

He also knew that the books on strategy and the science of war that he had eagerly devoured while training in Texas declared that infantry must never—never!—make frontal assaults over open terri-tory against well-prepared defenses. But as Roosevelt later wrote: "All men who feel any power of joy in battle know what it is like when the wolf rises in the heart."

"VERY GALLANT, BUT VERY FOOLISH"

With that wolf howling, TR spurred Little Texas directly toward danger, then rode back and forth along the advancing line of his men, urging them onward and upward. They paused in the tall grass at the foot of the rise known as Kettle Hill. The Spaniards waited in trenches, at an elevation more than one hundred feet above them. Theodore's orders had called for him to support the regulars, but the only regulars he could find were the black veterans of the Ninth Cav-alry, lying in the grass to hide themselves from enemy fire while await-ing further commands. Unable to find any officer above the rank of captain, Roosevelt brusquely declared: "I am the ranking officer here, and I give the order to charge!"

The uncertain captain blinked back at him without responding, and told Roosevelt to keep his men in place until he received further orders. Aboard his fidgety horse, Theodore registered the man's con-fusion and fear, and lost patience with the situation. "Then let my men through, sir," he snapped.

From that point, the slope rose at an angle of about forty-five de-grees. TR rushed ahead, waving his hat with its trailing blue-and-white handkerchief through the air, wildly yelling to his men to follow.

The gentlemen of the press watched from a facing hillside in skeptical amazement. "By God, there go our boys up the hill," yelled one of them. Richard Harding Davis, the celebrity novelist and reporter for Hearst's *New York Journal*, saw this doomed and ill-considered mission unfolding before him and fought the powerful impulse to call them back from certain death. "No one who saw Roosevelt take that ride expected him to finish it alive," he reported.

At the front of that slow-moving, implacable blue line with five hundred Rough Riders, Roosevelt felt a bullet grazing the skin off his elbow while another nicked Little Texas without slowing him. He also lost the spectacles he needed to see even a few feet ahead of him, but without slowing down he fumbled in his pockets for one of the abundant extra pairs he carried with him.

He rode up to a wire fence about forty yards from the top, jumped off his horse, and crawled through. Only a single trooper accompanied him—an Arizona miner named Bradshar—who shot two Spaniards as they scuttled out of their trench. The rest, perhaps more than a hundred of them, had already escaped, running at full speed away from the arriving Americans, with men of several other units joining the Rough Riders, who massed behind Roosevelt in dazed, glorious possession of Kettle Hill.

But with the wolf heart throbbing and imposing its own imperatives, TR wouldn't pause to savor the moment of victory. Surveying the battlefield from the commanding height he and his men had secured, he saw a line of American troops slowly advancing on higher Spanish positions on another hill along the ridgeline, less than half a mile away. On foot now, Roosevelt yelled for the assembled and breathless soldiers to follow him as he began running downhill before beginning a new ascent on the enemy rifle pits on the heights. As he leapt over another wire fence, he realized that "the troopers were so excited, what with shooting and being shot, and shouting and cheering, that they did not hear, or did not heed me; and after running about a hundred yards I found I had only five men along with me. Bullets were ripping the grass all around us." Those bullets immediately struck two members of his tiny band, wounding one of them mortally.

"I REALLY BELIEVE FIRMLY NOW THEY CAN'T KILL HIM": In leading his unmounted Rough Riders in their charge up Kettle Hill, Theodore Roosevelt provided the perfect target to Spanish sharpshooters as the sole officer on horseback. Frederic Remington, celebrated painter of the American West, witnessed the battle and captured Roosevelt's "one crowded hour of glorious life" for posterity.

"IT WAS A MIRACLE HE WASN'T KILLED"

Still on his feet, but looking around and realizing he was utterly exposed, Roosevelt ordered the uninjured men to drop down in an effort to hide themselves in the tall grass and to keep firing at the Spaniards while awaiting his return. Meanwhile, he rushed back to the other slope to bellow insults at his confused and waiting men ("What, are you cowards?"), who now pledged to follow him without question or delay. Shouting an unmistakable "Forward March!," the troops responded this time with shouts of their own, signaling their determination for another advance. The impromptu force that formed behind Colonel Roosevelt now included scores, perhaps hundreds, who had joined the Rough Riders from other regiments, with white and black troops marching side by side. They fell into an excited trot behind their yelling, gesturing colonel, rushing to the base of the new hill and then ascending sharp slopes toward the Spanish rifle pits. Again, the enemy fled, running headlong from their trenches and turning their backs, well before the Americans got close enough for hand-to-hand combat.

Nevertheless, the enemy sharpshooters with their state-of-the-art rifles inflicted a heavy toll. In the course of the day, the 490 Rough Riders who participated in the various assaults suffered 89 losses, killed or wounded. Roosevelt took solemn pride in the idea that this casualty rate—nearly one in five—amounted to the heaviest sacrifice of any unit in any engagement of the war. At least a dozen of these men fell within mere feet, or even inches, of their seemingly invulnerable commander, who escaped with only minor scratches and one broken set of spectacles. Even his gallant galloper, Little Texas, managed to survive the battle with mere flesh wounds and made the trip home with his famous rider. At TR's insistence, the little horse found a new home at his Sagamore Hill estate, where he lived out his days (five more years) as the beloved playmate of the six Roosevelt children.

As a hinge of history, TR's "crowded hour" produced a crowd of consequences. By nightfall, the Spanish had abandoned all their guard towers, trenches, and snipers' nests along the ridgeline of the San Juan heights, melting away before the general American assault. Just two days after the against-the-odds, uphill charge by the Rough Riders, the Spanish fleet in the harbor tried to evacuate in the face of the nearby U.S. Navy; the resulting encounter saw the utter destruction of all six Spanish ships, with 494 men killed or wounded and 1,889 captured. The war effectively ended there, less than three months and three weeks after it started.

The conflict also transformed Theodore Roosevelt from a colorful, incurably eccentric public figure on the fringes of power to an irresistible national hero, instantly discussed as a future president. He seemed to bear the unmistakable indicators of fate's favor: as the only horseback fighter on the field of fire on Kettle Hill, clearly designated as a significant officer by the blue-and-white handkerchief fearlessly, flamboyantly decorating his sombrero, he should have been killed, or at least seriously injured. His survival made no more sense than his manic, irrational courage. "Holy Godfrey, what fun!" he proclaimed to his men in the midst of the fighting.

An old family friend, and new Rough Rider, eloquently described Roosevelt's state of mind. Bob Ferguson had tramped along on several hunting trips with TR and related the day's achievements to the exhilarations of sport. "Dear Mrs. Theodore," he wrote to Edith. "No hunting trip so far has ever equaled it in Theodore's eyes. . . . T. was just reveling in victory and gore." More soberly, Ferguson reflected. "I really believe firmly now they can't kill him."

Sixty-three years later, students of the battle still marveled at Roosevelt's role. In an afterword to the 1961 edition of TR's *The Rough Riders*, the distinguished UCLA historian Lawrence Clark Powell summarized the amazing outcome: "It was inevitable that Colonel Roosevelt, came galloping home, with toothy grin, glasses and sombrero, straight into the hearts of the American voters. . . . It was a miracle he wasn't killed."

"THE COMING AMERICAN OF THE
TWENTIETH CENTURY"

More miracles paved his path to the presidency, allowing him to ascend to the White House barely three years after his wartime heroics. In the process, the specter of untimely death, the cruel adversary that threatened his childhood and claimed both parents and an adored first wife, suddenly became an unexpected ally. The reaper didn't cooperate by clearing implacable enemies from TR's road to Rushmore, but it did remove two prominent obstacles to his destined role as the first new president of the new "American Century."

Even before TR's return from Cuba in August 1898, prominent Republican leaders in New York State had begun promoting him as a candidate for governor in the elections just barely three months ahead. The GOP incumbent, Frank Black, looked vulnerable due to a major scandal involving one of his appointees to the Erie Canal Commission, who wasted more than $1 million in public funds. With his reformist, good-government credentials, the dashing Roosevelt seemed a far more promising candidate. To force the hand of the party machine, Theodore tentatively maneuvered toward an independent candidacy on the "Citizen Union" ticket—a prospect that would have spelled disaster for GOP officeholders up and down the ballot.

After receiving the Republican nomination, Roosevelt began barnstorming the state with his customary energy and verve. He addressed as many as a half-dozen rallies a day, always surrounded by some of his recent comrades in arms dressed in full Rough Rider regalia. Each event began with military bugle calls, giving the festive crowds a chance to celebrate the nation's sweeping victory of just a few weeks before. One Republican leader put Roosevelt's oratorical skills in balanced perspective. "The speech was nothing," he remembered, "but the man's presence was everything, it was electrical, magnetic.... I looked in the faces of hundreds and saw only pleasure and satisfaction."

Despite that magnetism, TR won the governorship by a margin of only 1 percent, or less than twenty thousand votes. That didn't stop him from seizing his new opportunity in Albany with an ambitious program of reform that aimed to curb the power and influence of giant corporations for the benefit of small businesses and ordinary citizens. He also developed a determined desire to personalize the governorship, holding two press briefings every day. As the *New York Times* approvingly observed: "He has torn down the curtain that shut in the governor and taken the public into his confidence ... beyond what was ever known before."

Roosevelt's new national profile caught the attention of influential journalists who began touting him as a future leader of the Republican Party and the nation. The esteemed Kansas editor William Allen White explicitly connected TR to America's destiny for a glorious future. "He is the coming American of the Twentieth Century," he declared.

No one thought that he'd earn a place on a national ticket until some point after President McKinley had won and finished his second term. In fact, Roosevelt expressed some interest to his friends and family in possibly rejoining the McKinley administration—this time as secretary of war rather than assistant secretary of the navy. But before such plans could take on a life of their own, and weeks before he'd even completed his first year as governor of New York, a shocking development in Washington profoundly altered TR's prospects.

Like most Republicans, Theodore respected the unassuming vice president, Garret Hobart, who had expanded the influence of his much-derided office due to his deep friendship with McKinley. A wealthy corporate lawyer with a weak chin but a mighty walrus mustache, Hobart had been selected for the national ticket despite never holding public office higher than a seat in the New Jersey state legislature. McKinley trusted him and the two men grew so close that the president and vice president often dined together in Washington and vacationed together in the summer months.

Late in 1898, however, this trusted advisor began to develop heart problems that he carefully concealed from the press and most of his colleagues. The next year, the doctors prescribed complete rest and quiet, so the vice president retreated to the Jersey Shore resort of Long Branch, where he spent his time communing with two pet fish—a gold one named McKinley and a silver one named Bryan. After a last vacation to Lake Champlain with the president, Hobart returned to New Jersey, where he died on November 21, at age fifty-five. An overflow crowd of fifty thousand attended his funeral, and the president told Hobart's wife and children, "No one outside of this home feels this loss more deeply than I do."

"ONLY ONE LIFE BETWEEN THIS MADMAN
AND THE PRESIDENCY"

The Republican leadership also felt the loss deeply. McKinley's bid for reelection loomed in less than a year, and they needed a high-profile replacement for the fallen vice president. They came to see the Rough Rider governor of New York as the most promising possibility.

But TR hated the idea. He thought of the vice presidency as a powerless, ceremonial office with no assigned duties other than occasionally presiding over the Senate. He wrote to his close friend Senator Henry Cabot Lodge: "I would greatly rather be anything, say a professor of history, than Vice President."

In February 1900, he publicly declared his unequivocal rejection of a place on the ticket that appeared in Albany papers under the headline: "ROOSEVELT'S EMPHATIC NO!" The governor declared: "It is proper for me to state definitely that under no circumstances could I, or would I, accept the nomination for the Vice-Presidency."

In spite of TR's apparently unshakable determination, the boss of New York's well-oiled Republican machine very much wanted the governor to reconsider. Senator Tom Platt, known as "the Easy Boss" because of his elegant manners and wardrobe, thought that the party establishment would benefit if they managed to dispense with the fiercely independent governor by "kicking him upstairs" and placing him in a harmless position like the vice presidency. He applied pressure by telling Roosevelt if he shunned the vice presidency and sought another term as governor, he might well face significant opposition in the primary.

When Platt arrived in Philadelphia for the Republican convention in June, he confidently announced to the press: "Roosevelt might as well stand under Niagara Falls and try to spit water back as to stop his nomination." The president's chief political advisor, Senator Mark Hanna of Ohio, remained adamantly opposed, distrusting TR's unpredictable instincts and flamboyant public persona. Behind closed doors, he told delegates: "Don't any of you realize that there's only one life between this madman and the presidency?"

These considerations persuaded no one—even Hanna reconciled himself to the inevitable when the vice presidential nomination came to the convention floor and the delegates roared their near-unanimous approval; TR himself cast the single dissenting vote. After leaving Philadelphia, the disappointed Senator Hanna grumbled to some of his closest associates: "The best we can do is pray fervently for the continued health of the president."

Fortunately, both candidates on the Republican ticket enjoyed excellent health during the campaign of 1900 as they dutifully performed their assigned roles. McKinley went about his White House business, assuming the incumbent's traditional above-the-fray pose, while his running mate frantically rode the rails and addressed adoring crowds in 567 towns in twenty-four states.

On election night, Roosevelt waited for returns at the family home in Sagamore Hill in the presence of a small crowd of journalists assigned to report his reaction. When the results clearly showed a landslide victory for the McKinley-Roosevelt ticket, some members of the press (never truly objective when it came to their favorite, TR) applauded and offered congratulations.

"Please don't!" responded the vice president–elect, and then offered an off-the-record obituary for his own career. "This election tonight means my political death."

"ABSOLUTELY NO HOPE"

After the inauguration, Theodore's service as vice president proved to be nearly as undemanding and inconsequential as he had feared. "The Vice Presidency . . . ought to be abolished," he wrote to his Rough Rider compadre Leonard Wood. "I do not think that the President wants me to take any part in affairs, or give him any advice."

In fact, Roosevelt began to spend most of his time outside of Washington, offering a special seminar for Harvard and Yale undergraduates at Sagamore Hill, speaking to the Long Island Bible Society, and making plans to finish the law school studies he had left incomplete some twenty years before. He also arranged an expedition to hunt bears and wolves in Colorado, declaring enthusiastically that he hoped to "kill a big grizzly or silver-tip with our knives, which would be great sport."

For his family, he devised a less ferocious excursion into the wilds. In early September, after six months as vice president, he planned a trip with Edith and their six children to a rustic lodge in New York's Adirondack Mountains.

On the way to meeting them there, he traveled to a series of New England speeches, including a luncheon address to the Vermont Fish and Game League on September 6. A crowd of more than a thousand gathered to meet the vice president at a former governor's spectacular estate on an island in the middle of Lake Champlain. After the meal, TR lingered to shake hands and chat with admirers, but they were interrupted by an insistently ringing telephone inside the mansion.

The call turned out to be for Roosevelt and he disappeared into a private room.

When he returned a few minutes later, shortly after four o'clock on that Friday afternoon, he told the assemblage the shocking news he had just received: President McKinley, while visiting the Pan-American Exposition in Buffalo, had been shot and gravely wounded.

The vice president would secure the fastest available transportation to rush to the side of his stricken chief.

TR boarded a special train and the railroad cleared the tracks to speed his progress. On the way, he reviewed the available facts about the attempted assassination. The president and the First Lady had been touring the same wildly popular exposition that Theodore and Edith had visited earlier in the summer—a 350-acre world's fair noted for its dazzling display of electric lights that "obliterated the darkness." On Friday afternoon, McKinley greeted well-wishers in a receiving line in the Temple of Music, one of the signature buildings at the fair. A young anarchist, determined to strike a fierce blow against capitalism, waited his turn with a pistol concealed by a handkerchief. When the president extended his hand, Leon Czolgosz extended his gun, shooting McKinley twice in the abdomen.

By the time Roosevelt arrived on the scene, the doctors had stabilized the president's condition. They had performed emergency surgery to repair the wounds to the stomach walls, front and back, and tried to locate the bullet that remained in McKinley's body. For that purpose, they considered making use of the newly invented X-ray machine that had been displayed with much fanfare at the nearby world's fair, but they worried needlessly about potential side effects that could have harmed the wounded president, and decided to leave the bullet lodged in his flesh.

Nevertheless, McKinley seemed to make dramatic steps toward recovery: his fever fell and his spirits rose. The physicians still limited the flow of visitors in order to conserve the president's strength but he affably pleaded for company. "It's mighty lonesome in here," he complained, but the many officials who hovered near the wounded leader received only brief, fleeting authorization to satisfy this craving for social interaction. In a sense, the scene in Buffalo only intensified Theodore's abiding discomfort with the vice presidency itself: the world seemed to expect his presence but the situation left him with nothing to do beyond waiting for the president to recover or die. For TR, the best part of the president's apparent recovery involved his pending release from bondage and boredom in an inherently awkward role. "With a light heart" he departed from Buffalo on September 10 in order to join his wife and children at the rustic mountain lodge where they had already begun the family's planned vacation.

Two days later, Edith joined him in leading a party of nearly a dozen for an ascent of Mount Marcy, at 5,300 feet the tallest peak in the Adirondacks. They spent the night in cabins surrounding a small lake halfway up the slope, but rain the next morning led Mrs. Roosevelt to take the children back to the lodge. TR characteristically refused to surrender to the discouragement of the elements, and insisted on finishing the climb with one of the guides in the party. They reached the summit with their clothes drenched by the rain, then paused for lunch on the way down. As they ate, Roosevelt spotted a stranger hiking purposefully out of the woods, carrying a message for the vice president. The telegram declared:

The president is critically ill. His condition is grave. Oxygen is being given. Absolutely no hope.

The message was dated September 13, 1901—Friday the thirteenth.

"A MAN OF DESTINY"

Theodore Roosevelt officially became the twenty-sixth president of the United States after midnight, several hours before he learned of his change in status. McKinley passed away at 2:15 in the morning due to an infection that had spread quickly, implacably, through his body. At the time, TR was bouncing on a buckboard down muddy mountain roads in the rainy darkness, trying to travel the four hundred miles back to Buffalo as quickly as possible. He connected to a rail line just as the first dim light of that damp dawn began to bring the world back into focus, and Roosevelt received word that the president had died.

This unexpected tragedy transformed his life even more decisively and completely than the untimely passing of Vice President Hobart a mere twenty-two months before. Had death not taken both of these political leaders, who occupied the two most prominent of all federal offices, TR's path to the presidency, if there were any, would have been very different.

As it was, after his return to Buffalo he stood beside McKinley's body in the private home where it rested, tried to comfort the dead president's inconsolable widow, and took the formal oath of office before several members of the cabinet who had gathered for that purpose.

He assumed power fourteen weeks before the end of the first year of the new century. Americans had already begun sensing the hand of fate pressing him forward; on election night in 1900, one of the leaders gathered at the victorious Republican headquarters had reportedly declared: "I feel sorry for McKinley. He has a man of destiny behind him."

TR clearly associated his own ascent with the glorious destiny he foresaw for the United States—the destiny he hailed with memorable grandiosity in the nominating speech he had delivered for McKinley at the Republican National Convention in Philadelphia.

"We stand on the threshold of a new century big with the fate of mighty nations," he began. "It rests with us now to decide whether in the opening years of that century we shall march forward to fresh triumphs or whether at the outset we shall cripple ourselves for the contest. Is America a weakling, to shrink from the world-work of the great world-powers? No. The young giant of the West stands on a continent and clasps the crest of an ocean in either hand. Our nation, glorious in youth and strength, looks into the future with eager eyes and rejoices as a strong man to run a race."

Suddenly, chance, luck, fate, or providence had given the nation a leader who exemplified the traits TR ascribed to America itself: "glorious in youth and strength" while rejoicing "as a strong man to run a race" while looking "into the future with eager eyes"—even if those eyes might be severely nearsighted, blinking behind pince-nez.

Senator Mark Hanna, who had counseled against the dangerous expedient of nominating the "madman" Roosevelt for the vice presidency, might angrily protest to his Republican colleagues: "Look now! That damned cowboy is president of the United States!"

But the bulk of the populace embraced the new chief executive precisely because of his cowboy characteristics. The English parliamentarian and biographer Lord Morley, who befriended Theodore Roosevelt, definitively declared to the socialite Lady Harcourt: "He is not an American, you know, he *is America*." As historian Paul Johnson observed, tens of millions came to see TR as "the archetypal American 'good guy,' combining the best of the inherited English tradition of gentlemanly honor with a rip-roaring taste for adventure which is quintessentially American."

That taste for adventure combined with a relentless work ethic to produce two presidential terms that bristled with notable achievements—construction of the Panama Canal; doubling the size of the U.S. Navy and deploying the new fleet in an awe-inspiring round-the-world cruise; presidential intervention to settle a polarizing, paralyzing coal miners' strike; a Nobel Prize (the first for any American) for settling a destructive war between Japan and Russia; the beginning of federal regulation to provide greater safety of the food supply and the industrial workplace; a tripling of the acreage under federal protection by the National Forest Service; huge strides for national parks and monuments; and much more.

But no policy achievements could overshadow or even explain the profound, visceral manner in which Roosevelt's personality captured the imagination of the American people and, ultimately, the people of the world.

"The infectiousness of his exuberant vitality made the country realize there was a new man in the White House, indeed a new kind of man," observed the muckraking reporter Mark Sullivan, an initially skeptical progressive Republican. "His high spirits, his enormous capacity for work, his tirelessness, his forthrightness, his many striking qualities, gave a lift of the spirits to millions of average men." Another reporter, J. W. Bennett, noted: "While he is in the neighborhood, the public can no more look the other way than the small boy can turn his head away from a circus parade followed by a steam calliope."

The president made an even stronger impression on visitors to the White House. "His personality so crowds the room that the walls are worn thin and threaten to burst outward," one of them recalled. "You go to the White House, you shake hands with Roosevelt and hear him talk—and then go home to wring the personality out of your clothes."

Since he couldn't invite the whole country into the White House, he also maintained an unquenchable appetite for touring the country, savoring its natural wonders (many of which he worked to preserve and protect) while giving literally hundreds of thousands of ordinary Americans the chance to catch a glimpse of him. In this context, he became the first president ever to travel beyond the borders of the United States, touring the Isthmus of Panama to inspect progress on "the Big Ditch": the canal he had initiated to connect Atlantic to Pacific, thereby cementing American naval power in both of the globe's great oceans.

"WONDERFUL ESCAPE FROM DEATH"

Not all of his excursions worked out so well. In the late summer of 1902, not yet a year into his presidency, Roosevelt faced the challenge of House and Senate campaigns, with Democrats hoping to make significant gains at the expense of the rookie chief executive. To shore up GOP strength, and to affirm his leadership of a divided party, TR planned a tour of New England.

On the final day of the tour—Wednesday, September 3—the crisp morning air delighted the president with its autumnal hints as he got off the train. Roosevelt boarded an open carriage drawn by four horses into Pittsfield, Massachusetts. Singing schoolchildren greeted the presidential party, which included the state's Republican governor. The carriage with its load of dignitaries then made its way to the local country club for the most important speech of the morning.

At the same time, a trolley car hurtled down the track at top speed, full of excited citizens who wanted to get to the location in time to find seats for the president's speech. With the two vehicles moving too fast to break or turn, the streetcar slammed into the carriage at full force, sending it skidding forty feet to the other side of the road. All the passengers—the president, the governor, the president's secretary, and his Secret Service bodyguard—went flying into the air, landing at scattered points of the accident scene.

The president hit the ground face-first, cutting his mouth and suffering heavy bruising and scratches on one cheek and the side of his neck. More seriously, he received a blow to his shin, which he felt immediately when he struggled to his feet. The Massachusetts governor and the presidential secretary were more fortunate, having been badly shaken up but somehow uninjured.

As Roosevelt tried to take command of the situation, he searched for his bodyguard, "Big Bill" Craig, a six-foot-four giant and a veteran of the British military who, since McKinley's assassination a year before, had obsessively protected the president in every waking moment. To his horror, TR found Big Bill's body: it had been thrown under the wheels of the trolley, which cut through him at three different points, killing him instantly. Bill Craig became the first agent of the Secret Service ever killed in the line of duty.

In the aftermath of the horrifying accident, Secretary of State John Hay, next in line to the presidency in the absence of a vice president, calculated that TR had escaped death by only two inches. "Had the trolley car struck the rear hub instead of just grazing it, and crashing into the front wheel . . . the President would have been tossed to the left and under the car just as poor Craig was," he wrote.

The newspapers the next morning all hailed the president's "Wonderful Escape from Death," concentrating on his stubborn insistence on delivering his scheduled speech and showing up for his other planned events, despite his purplish, unsightly, and severely swollen face and the badly injured limb. He shook hands with assembled multitudes, pronouncing his customary exclamation "Dee-lighted!" with each new citizen he greeted. Novelist Edith Wharton, a distant relative of Edith Roosevelt's and a resident of the area, found herself dumbstruck at the determination with which he delivered his address. "I think if you could have seen the President here the other day, all bleeding and swollen from that hideous accident," she wrote, "and could have heard the very few quiet and fitting words he said to the crowd gathered to receive him, you would have agreed that he is not all—or nearly all—bronco-buster."

Despite his gallantry and stoicism, the injury to his shin refused to heal. A sizable knob, resembling a large walnut, rose nearly two inches above the skin. Interrupting another campaign tour, eighteen days after the accident, TR consulted four surgeons in Indianapolis, who decided on an immediate operation. The president refused anesthetic, and they drained the fluid from his shin. A week later, back in Washington, another surgery cut directly to the bone, stripping away infected flesh. The possibility of amputation, or death, remained real, not only to the surgeons but to the president himself, who spoke with his secretary of war, Elihu Root, about the need to supervise an orderly transition of power if the worst occurred.

Even with the forty-three-year-old president confined to a wheelchair for more than two weeks, the general public learned little of the gravity of the situation. Moreover, despite the near-death experience limiting his campaign activities, Roosevelt's Republicans gained two seats in the Senate and nine in the House, reflecting the bond he had already established with the electorate.

The Pittsfield horror, and the president's determination to transcend his pain and continue with his plans as if nothing had happened, obviously presaged the far more publicized assassination attempt that left a bullet in his chest in October 1912, almost exactly ten years later.

But it also echoed another potentially fatal experience in October 1885, the day before his twenty-seventh birthday.

Recently returned to Long Island from his ranches in Dakota Territory, he delighted to participate in a foxhunt with some of the expert riders on the fashionable North Shore. His horse, Frank, proved less energetic and nimble than the mounts assigned to the other horsemen, but Theodore pressed him so hard that he rode ahead of the pack for most of the first five miles. At that point, after vaulting many fences, Frank tripped over the top rail of a barrier nearly five feet high, pitching his rider onto rocks and gravel on the ground, then rolling over him and breaking his arm.

Roosevelt knew he had suffered a serious fracture, but rather than lying where he fell and waiting for rescue, or limping to a nearby farm for immediate assistance, he stubbornly pulled his mount to its feet and managed, with his one functional arm, to drag himself back into the saddle. TR continued to ride in pursuit of the fox, with the broken arm hanging uselessly to one side and his face and clothes that "looked pretty gay . . . like the walls of a slaughterhouse." Later that evening, with his arm secured into splints and his severely cut face covered with plasters and bandages, he attended the Hunt Ball in elegant dress and prepared to celebrate his birthday at midnight.

"I viewed the affair from the first as mainly comic in character," he wrote to his best friend Henry Cabot Lodge. "All I minded was missing the rest of the hunting season. . . . My face will not be scarred except across the nose—which, however, will not be handsome. . . . I don't grudge the broken arm a bit; I would willingly pay it for the fun I have had on Frank. . . . I am always willing to pay the piper when I have had a good dance; and every now and then I like to drink the wine of life with brandy in it."

"IF YOU DON'T STOP, I'LL CALL YOU 'TEDDY'"

Throughout his life, pain and injury scared him less than defeat and humiliation, and he initially approached his campaign for reelection in 1904 with some trepidation and uncertainty. As a historian, he knew the record of vice presidents who had assumed office on the death of their predecessors, and all four of them who preceded him in that role (John Tyler, Millard Fillmore, Andrew Johnson, and Chester Arthur) had failed to win election in their own right; in fact, all four had been defeated in their efforts to win their own party's nomination.

TR also faced a formidable potential challenger with dreams of his own nomination: Senator Mark Hanna, the wealthy and profoundly influential Ohio industrialist who had warned McKinley and other party stalwarts of the danger of choosing "that madman" Roosevelt as a nominee for vice president.

After the assassination, TR reached out to ask for Hanna's support in the Senate, which he agreed to provide under two conditions: First, Roosevelt must work to complete the fallen McKinley's political agenda. Second, he must promise to avoid addressing Hanna (twenty-one years Roosevelt's senior) with the annoying sobriquet "Old Man." The new president cheerfully agreed on both points, but Hanna warned him of the dire consequences if he ever reverted to the informal designation he despised. "If you don't stop, I'll call you 'Teddy,'" he warned, establishing a balance of terror between them.

Despite such good-natured banter and several instances of political cooperation, Hanna remained hugely popular with the big-business elements in the Republican Party that deeply distrusted Theodore's "trust-busting" rhetoric. Throughout 1903, the Ohio senator addressed crowds that lustily chanted "Hanna in 1904!" J. P. Morgan, the uncrowned king of Wall Street, hosted Hanna and his wife for Thanksgiving dinner and pledged his limitless wealth to supporting a Hanna for President campaign if he agreed to run. The Ohio senator listened with interest but remained noncommittal.

The first month of 1904 saw serious maneuvering in preparation for the forthcoming presidential race; Hanna attended the jocular Gridiron Dinner but fell ill shortly thereafter, reportedly from typhoid fever. He remained immobilized in his rooms at the Arlington Hotel, where President Roosevelt came to visit him on February 15, but by that time he was too sick for callers. Hanna passed away later that same day at age sixty-six, bumping Theodore Roosevelt's chances of winning the Republican nomination from highly likely to absolutely certain.

For the third time in just five years, an unexpected but eerily convenient death had intervened to secure Roosevelt's claim to the presidency, with the perfectly timed passings of Vice President Garret Hobart, President William McKinley, and Senator Mark Hanna.

In the general election campaign that followed, TR's Democratic opponent managed to stay alive in a physical sense even though his candidacy displayed few vital signs.

The bland, bald jurist Alton Brooks Parker wore a heavily waxed handlebar mustache and cloaked himself in a stodgy formalism that contrasted mightily with Theodore's hearty, explosive spontaneity. Parker, who had never held public office aside from a series of judicial posts in upstate New York, captured the Democratic nomination when better-known possibilities (former president Grover Cleveland; former nominee William Jennings Bryan) declined to run against the popular Roosevelt.

At the height of the campaign, Judge Parker developed the curious strategy of lashing out at the Roosevelt administration for providing too much excitement and entertainment value for the American electorate. In desperation at his inability to generate traction, the Democratic standard-bearer and his campaign team indulged an eager appetite for undigested adjectives to express their contempt, describing the president in a single sentence as "spasmodic, erratic, sensational, spectacular and arbitrary." They also sniffed haughtily at their opponent's "shameless exhibition of a willingness to make compromise with dignity."

In the end, it surprised no one that voters preferred a candidate who might seem "sensational" and "spectacular" to a dreary, reliably dull alternative; in the whole history of presidential politics, the public has rarely selected boredom over thrills and fun. The results on election night gave TR a record victory margin of more than two and a half million votes, as he carried every state outside the one-party territory of the Democratic South and earned more than 70 percent of the Electoral College.

Just after 9:00 p.m., the president received a concession statement from Judge Parker and an hour later he welcomed a crowd of reporters in his executive office. After some impromptu discussion about the encouraging results, with rapid-fire answers to the questions thrown at him, he demanded quiet, leaned back in his chair, and dictated a history-bending statement to the assembled correspondents and his own startled secretary.

"I am deeply sensible of the honor done me by the American people in thus expressing their confidence in what I have done and have tried to do," he began. "On the 4th of March next I shall have served three and one half years, and the three and one-half years constitute my first term. The wise custom which limits the President to two terms regards the substance and not the form. Under no circumstances will I be a candidate for or accept another nomination."

Eyewitnesses recalled that as he finished his dictation, barking out his words with an emphatic sense of satisfaction and significance, his wife, Edith, and oldest daughter, Alice, both visibly winced. He had discussed the dramatic statement with no one, though he later insisted he hadn't acted on impulse. He sincerely viewed the decision as noble, selfless, and patriotic, and he cared deeply that his countrymen should see it in the same light.

But as the election night glow began to fade, and the speculation began about the president's likely successors, Roosevelt quickly understood that he'd damaged himself by foreclosing future options with his self-imposed status as a lame duck. Regarding the declaration that he had so proudly dictated to stunned reporters, he confided to a friend, "I would cut my hand off right there if I could recall that written statement."

"A LOT HARDER FOR YOU, THEODORE, TO BE AN EX-PRESIDENT"

His closest associates understood more readily than he did how much it went against his nature and instincts for Theodore to walk away, willingly, from the "strenuous life" he relished at the center of power. In 1901, shortly after TR assumed the presidency, Nicholas Murray Butler assured him, "I do not fear for you in the presidency, Theodore." Butler, who had just taken over his own presidency as head of Columbia University, went on with prophetic insight: "Your most difficult task will come when you finally leave the White House.... It will be a lot harder for you, Theodore, to be an ex-President than President."

According to the publicly announced timetable, TR would leave the White House at age fifty: younger than most prospective presidents when they first contemplate a candidacy. In the last year of his tenure, fifty-five newspapers across the country asked their readers whether they wanted President Roosevelt to reconsider his pledge and become a candidate for a third term; 21,475 people responded, and an astonishing 69 percent wanted him to run again.

Instead, TR honored his pledge and the traditional two-term limit established by Washington. He made a point of selecting a worthy, well-qualified successor: the genial, incorruptible, dependably competent William Howard Taft, a three-hundred-pound walrus of a man who had served as TR's secretary of war and governor-general of the Philippines, after a distinguished career in both the federal and the Ohio judiciary.

To give Taft every chance to escape from his predecessor's looming shadow in the first months of the new presidency, Roosevelt left the country just nineteen days after his friend's inauguration and stayed away for a full fifteen months.

He used the time for an extended safari in Africa with his twenty-year-old son Kermit, accompanied by scores of porters, guides, naturalists, and taxidermists, who helped them bag 512 animals and large birds as "scientific samples" for the Smithsonian, including seventeen lions, twenty rhinos, eleven elephants, and nine giraffes. After that, Mrs. Roosevelt reunited with the mighty hunter and they proceeded to tour the glittering capitals of Europe, where the youthful ex-president met with the most significant crowned heads and political leaders, and delivered well-regarded university lectures.

When he finally returned to New York Harbor on June 16, 1910, an armada of literally hundreds of private craft joined six navy battleships to welcome the former president with the ecstatic firing of guns, honking of horns, blaring of sirens, ringing of bells, and lusty shouts of "Huzzah!" In a parade route that ran five miles from the Battery up Broadway, a collection of mounted Rough Riders, along with a hundred-piece military band, escorted TR's carriage, as hundreds of thousands lined the streets to give Roosevelt the most ecstatic reception of his career.

The nation had missed their *dee-lighted* former leader in part because the easygoing President Taft had proven to be something of a disappointment. At the time of Roosevelt's return, the Republicans faced an upcoming midterm election that threatened the worst drubbing in the party's history: in November, the GOP lost a crushing total of fifty-seven seats in the House and ten in the Senate, reflecting the dispiriting division in the ranks between the increasingly restive "progressives" (who looked to Roosevelt as their savior) and the Taft-loyalist Old Guard.

THE "HONEYFUGLER" VS. THE "GUINEA PIG"

Even before TR's triumphal return, Taft already faced the certainty of a progressive contest for the Republican nomination, expecting to fend off a furious challenge from the Wisconsin "Insurgent," Senator Robert La Follette. As his state's reformist governor, and after 1906 as one of the most prominent, outspoken senators in Washington, La Follette displayed such an aggressive appetite for political combat that he earned the nicknames "Fighting Bob" and "Battle Bob." But despite his determination to make a run, La Follette's battle against Taft and the Old Guard couldn't begin while most of his potential backers kept dreaming that Roosevelt would enter the fray and pose a more meaningful threat to the incumbent.

TR repeatedly reaffirmed his official commitment to support the nominee of the Republican Party, which meant, for all practical purposes, that he stood behind his old friend Taft. But at the same time, the former president began dropping broad hints that he'd be available for an "honest draft" if the party's rank and file demanded it. In mid-February 1912, less than six months before the election, he received a public letter—which he had secretly solicited—from seven Republican governors who shared his progressive leanings. In it, these GOP state leaders flatly declared that "a large majority of the Republican voters of the country favor your nomination, and a large majority of the people favor your election as the next President of the United States."

Soon thereafter, TR set out to prove them right by waging active campaigns under the new system of "preference primaries" that had recently been adopted by thirteen states. In the earliest contests, Battle Bob La Follette prevailed in his home state of Wisconsin and in sparsely populated North Dakota, while President Taft easily won New York, where Wall Street interests and most of the major newspapers despised Roosevelt. After that, the terrain proved more hospitable to the Rough Rider, who gained momentum and swept the field, winning nine of the ten remaining primaries, mostly by landslide margins. This culminated with an embarrassing loss for President Taft in his home state of Ohio, where Roosevelt outpolled him by more than fifteen points and demonstrated that only a minority of grassroots Republicans supported another term for President Taft.

But the party machinery remained firmly in the hands of the Old Guard, and Taft racked up delegates wherever Republicans relied on state conventions, caucuses, or state committees rather than primaries to decide which prospective delegates to send to the national convention in Chicago. The two candidates, once closely aligned, now competed for the most colorful invective to hurl at each other.

President Taft called his onetime sponsor "the greatest menace to our institutions that we have had in a long time . . . because of his hold upon the least intelligent voters and the discontented."

Taft also surmised that "such extremists are not progressives—they are political emotionalists or neurotics." Finally, to top it off, the president of the United States flung the ultimate arcane insult at the former president, condemning Roosevelt as a notorious "honeyfugler." For those who bothered to consult their dictionaries on that designation, they would have discovered an old-fashioned term denoting "an individual who entices or hoodwinks through the use of flattery."

TR himself used more down-to-earth insults to blast the president, calling him a "fathead" (an obvious jab at Taft's now 330-pound girth) and a "puzzle wit" while suggesting that "his intellect falls slightly shy of a guinea pig's"—this despite Taft's position as salutatorian (second-highest honors) in his class of 1878 at Yale. (How else could he have come up with the term "honeyfugler"?)

At the end of the long, brutal campaign, Roosevelt held 411 committed delegates, while Taft counted 367, and minor candidates claimed 46. Unfortunately for TR, the Old Guard dominated the credentials committee that was supposed to decide how to distribute more than 254 hotly disputed delegates—if TR won only half of them he would easily become the nominee. But in the end, the Republican National Committee awarded 235 of the disputed delegates to Taft, and only 19 to Roosevelt—acknowledging that they worried more about losing control of their party than they did about losing to the Democrat Woodrow Wilson in November.

To TR, this amounted to something much worse than an ill-considered if typical political maneuver by the entrenched power brokers of the Republican Party; it represented a crime of cosmic consequence.

Breaking the tradition that kept candidates for the presidency from attending conventions in person, he boarded a train for Chicago. During a rousing address at the Chicago Auditorium, he urged his followers to leave the crooked convention and inflamed their passions. "It is not a partisan issue; it is more than a political issue; it is a great moral issue," he declared. He denounced the "great crime" that Taft and his henchmen had perpetrated and averred that it jeopardized "not merely our Democratic form of government but our civilization itself."

The conclusion of his speech became famous for its soaring (some might say heretical) rhetorical flourish, combined with an apocalyptic biblical reference: "Fearless of the future; unheeding of our individual fates; with unflinching hearts and undimmed eyes; we stand at Armageddon, and we battle for the Lord!"

"BATTLING FOR THE LORD"

He returned to Chicago and repeated this end-of-the-world proclamation at the Progressive Party National Convention, with two thousand delegates hastily assembled just five weeks after the contentious Republican conclave broke up at the end of June, amid recriminations and foreboding over the November prospects for the GOP.

The Progressives, mostly disillusioned former Republicans like

Roosevelt, adopted a platform so detailed and ambitious that it must be described as visionary or prophetic or deeply delusional. It called for women's suffrage, a shortened workweek, limitations on campaign contributions, registration of all lobbyists, a national health service, prohibition of child labor, and an easier amendment process for the Constitution. TR made the case for these sweeping reforms in a truly remarkable (and remarkably long) speech after he won the new party's unanimous nomination for the presidency. The Bull Moose became the enduring symbol of the movement, based on TR's boast that he felt "strong as a Bull Moose" and fully prepared for the rigors of the long-shot campaign ahead.

But the tone of the convention evoked an ecstatic revival meeting, with its missionary zeal and religious uplift, more than a wilderness retreat with antlers, head-butting, and survival of the fittest. After all, the official title of TR's inspiring but exhausting acceptance speech was "A Confession of Faith," and at its conclusion he repeated the popular line about "standing at Armageddon and battling for the Lord."

In that spirit, the Progressive conventioneers adapted the hymn "Onward, Christian Soldiers" as their unofficial anthem and belted out its challenging verses at every opportunity. With music by Sir Arthur Sullivan (of "Gilbert and Sullivan" fame), the second verse in particular provided a clear indication of how the Progressives viewed their uncompromisingly righteous position in the political universe:

> At the name of Jesus
> Satan's host doth flee;
> On then, Christian soldiers,
> On to victory!
> Hell's foundations quiver
> At the shout of praise:
> Brothers, lift your voices,
> Loud your anthems raise!

Today, it might be difficult to understand how even the most enthusiastic TR true believer could see the staid Republican backers of the bland, benign William Howard Taft as part of "Satan's host." But the Christian soldiers of the new Progressive army, shaken by their sense of monumental wrong over the "stolen" nomination, chanting a biblical commandment ("Thou Shalt Not Steal!") as one of their persistent cheers, and excited by the militantly reformist platform of their Bull Moose candidate, proudly exulted in the apocalyptic potential of their moment. Just as Moses descended the mountain and shattered the tablets of the law when he saw the worship of the Golden Calf, they felt ready to shatter their party to protest the heathen revels of their opponents.

Even if the astonishingly complicated electoral contest of 1912 didn't exactly equate to the end of the world, it did mean the end of the Republican Party as it had existed since its founding, exploding the long-standing balance between its conservative and "progressive" wings. The messianic ardor of Roosevelt's devoted new followers left little room for compromise or doubt. Near the end of the gathering, a mocking handbill from an unidentified source mysteriously appeared on the chairs of most convention delegates, announcing "At Three o'Clock Thursday Afternoon, Theodore Roosevelt Will Walk on the Waters of Lake Michigan."

To some of TR's former friends and colleagues in the GOP establishment, his seemingly sudden shift to faith-fueled fanaticism seemed suspect and insincere. Elihu Root, the corporate lawyer who served TR as both secretary of war and secretary of state, later becoming a senator from New York and a crucial supporter of Taft's reelection, decried his former chief for having "gone off upon a perfectly wild program," which he tried to explain to another former associate of Roosevelt's. "He is essentially a fighter and when he gets into a fight he is completely dominated by the desire to destroy his adversary," Root noted. "He instinctively lays hold of every weapon which can be used for that end. Accordingly he is saying a lot of things and taking a lot of positions which are inspired by the desire to win. I have no doubt he thinks he believes what he says, but he doesn't. He has merely picked up certain popular ideas which were at hand as one might pick up a poker or chair with which to strike."

"SUNDAY SCHOOL IN THE WOODS"

Skeptics like Secretary Root might have written off TR's policy prescriptions as shallow and self-serving, but even many Taft loyalists generally acknowledged that the new religious emphasis with which he presented those policies amounted to more than a convenient cudgel: Roosevelt had long stressed the pursuit of righteousness as both a personal and a national imperative.

A fervent, weekly churchgoer all his life, Theodore scribbled childhood diary entries that describe his father conducting "Sunday School in the woods," taking his offspring to the Great Outdoors for prayer and Bible study. At Harvard, Theodore himself taught Sunday school for three years, hoping to inspire disadvantaged youth as a volunteer for a Boston mission. As vice president and then as president, he worshipped at the modest, unassuming Grace Reformed Church, with its brisk, no-frills Calvinist style in liturgy and learning connecting him to his family's Dutch Reformed roots. "I take sentimental satisfaction in worshipping in the church of my fathers," he explained.

He made it a habit to walk to Sunday services in every sort of weather, a hike of three miles round-trip, setting an aggressive pace that left the two Secret Service agents who always accompanied him puffing and scurrying to keep up. A few of the six White House children also made the trek, with the others joining their mother at the more elaborate and elegant Episcopal services she preferred. Inside his church, the president sang along lustily with his favorite hymns and listened intently to the scholarly sermons, jotting down notes and challenges to take up with the minister.

In this comfortably religious context, TR had seen himself as "battling for the Lord" long before the Armageddon of the 1912 GOP convention. As a reformist legislator in Albany, a tireless police commissioner in New York, a fearless cavalry commander in Cuba, and then as an incomparably energetic, activist president of the United States, he had always viewed himself as a battler for light, truth, and American grandeur, defeating the dark forces of doubt and denial.

In that context, TR's audacious, messianic Bull Moose campaign didn't produce some new sense of himself as a providential, protected leader; rather, that well-established self-image generated the all-but-hopeless campaign.

Others might look at the daunting task of organizing a new party and conducting a competitive race in just ninety days and conclude that Roosevelt's doomed Progressive campaign defied all logical calculations, but the candidate himself could reflect on a history of success and survival that already made no rational sense.

By the fall of 1912, he had escaped from so many dangerous, near-death encounters that he had begun to count on his own apparent invincibility. After overcoming the frailty and grave illness of his childhood and the perils of an inexperienced cowboy on the Dakota frontier, he had emerged relatively intact after the 1885 fox-hunting accident that scarred his face and broke his arm when his mount pitched him onto the ground and then rolled over him. In Cuba, as nearly a fifth of his regiment became casualties, he rode ahead of them all as a prime target, the only battlefield figure on horseback, and escaped with minor cuts and scratches. Even as president, he survived a gruesome trolley accident that killed the huge and hearty Secret Service protector who had been riding right beside him.

The other deaths surrounding his ascent—of his father, of his wife and his mother on the same horrid day, and of the vice president and then the president of the United States, securing his path to the White House—seemed to indicate that destiny had marked him as a necessary survivor.

No wonder that the assassin who shot him in the chest in the last days of the campaign not only failed to stop his race for the presidency but, due to the candidate's reckless insistence, even failed to stop the speech he had planned for that night. The story of how his bulky, folded speech text and his metal eyeglass case managed to slow the bullet and save his life, allowing the bleeding campaigner to stagger to the public podium and speak for an hour, could reassure Roosevelt's admirers, if not his detractors, that he remained a man of destiny.

But the startling circumstances of the attempted assassination failed to persuade a thoroughly divided electorate to give the Rough

Rider a plurality of their votes. After recovering from his wound, the former president managed to return to active campaigning just a week before Election Day, but he knew the outcome would be grim.

At least he managed to best Taft—which he told friends had become his chief goal—by winning 27 percent of the popular vote to the incumbent's 23 percent. With the Republican vote hopelessly split, the Democrat, Woodrow Wilson, easily prevailed (with 42 percent of the popular vote and 435 electoral votes). Roosevelt won 88 electoral votes, the best showing ever for a third-party candidate—an achievement that provided small comfort.

Another curious coincidence seemed to continue a peculiar pattern that had haunted TR's strange career. On the very day that the seriously wounded Roosevelt returned to active campaigning, just six days before the election, one of the multiple opponents arrayed against him and featured prominently on national ballots dropped dead.

Fifty-seven-year-old James Schoolcraft Sherman, vice president of the United States and President Taft's running mate, passed away quietly on October 30 from Bright's disease—the same kidney malady that had claimed TR's first wife, Alice, some twenty-eight years before. Poor Vice President Sherman didn't live long enough to receive the meager eight electoral votes that the Taft-Sherman ticket, carrying only Utah and Vermont, won.

"I THINK THAT THE AMERICAN PEOPLE FEEL
A LITTLE TIRED OF ME"

After the apocalyptic, public passion of the Bull Moose campaign, Roosevelt, still only fifty-four years old, searched for a project or purpose that wouldn't amount to an anticlimax. During a tour of South America that combined lectures and hunting, he seemed to find the sort of challenge he wanted: hearing of a huge river in the Amazon rain forest that had never been explored or mapped, Roosevelt became fascinated by the prospect of tracing its entire course of perhaps a thousand miles, collecting specimens, and writing his conclusions along the way. The Brazilian government felt grateful for the interest of the famous American and mounted a major expedition under the joint command of TR and a colonel in their army who had already achieved considerable acclaim for his scientific explorations of the Amazon region.

As on his African safari of three years before, Roosevelt invited his son Kermit, now twenty-three, to accompany him, but on this trip it wasn't just the animals they hunted that became endangered. From the beginning of their expedition, forty-eight days passed before they saw another human being. Five of the seven well-equipped dugout canoes were smashed by rapids and roiling water of the appropriately named "River of Doubt." The entire team, including all the scientists and military officers and paddlers, contracted tropical fevers that seriously incapacitated them. One Brazilian officer drowned and a paddler, crazed with fever, killed his supervisor and disappeared into the rain forest.

After a month of hardship and illness, with food supplies running short, Roosevelt seriously injured his leg when he jumped into the river in an effort to save one of the remaining canoes. He opened a new gash on the same spot below the knee that had been seriously injured, requiring two surgeries, in the Massachusetts streetcar collision twelve years earlier. Under the jungle conditions, his wound refused to heal and became seriously infected.

Roosevelt's temperature rose to 105 degrees and he became delirious, repeating the same verses of poetry (from "Kubla Khan" by Samuel Taylor Coleridge) again and again. He couldn't be moved in that state and in brief moments of lucidity he urged the others to save themselves and go on without him. He told his son that he would take a deadly dose of morphine to end the suffering, but Kermit refused to abandon him. In one final deliverance from death, he survived because the younger Roosevelt helped lead the struggling expedition, and transport his stricken father, to a juncture with the Amazon River that carried them to rubber plantations at the edge of the jungle.

TR lost fifty-seven pounds on the trip (a fourth of his prior body weight) and walked with a cane that he jauntily described as his "big stick." His health never fully returned, but he continued to ponder yet another bid for the presidency. In 1916, the remaining loyalists of the Bull Moose Party scheduled their national convention at the same time and in the same city as the Republicans, with a dream of reunification behind TR's candidacy. Republican conservatives remained staunchly opposed, but they accepted the "moderately progressive" Supreme Court justice Charles Evans Hughes. The Progressives still tried to nominate Roosevelt, but he sent a telegram refusing to run and expressing his endorsement of Justice Hughes.

In so doing, he restored and rescued the two-party system; had he perished in Milwaukee at the end of the Bull Moose campaign, or during his disease- and dementia-ridden experience on the River of Doubt, the Progressives would have doubtless continued their fledgling party "in his memory" and presidential politics may have taken an entirely different course over the next century.

He also played a crucial and decidedly controversial role in the most significant issue of the day: America's posture toward the Great War, which broke out just three months after his return from Brazil. While President Wilson insisted on neutrality and noninvolvement, Roosevelt believed that the cause of righteousness required American support for Britain and France: "More and more, I come to the view that in a really tremendous world struggle, with a great moral issue involved, neutrality does not serve righteousness; for to be neutral between right and wrong is to serve wrong."

More consistently and conspicuously than any other public figure, he campaigned for the ethical necessity of America's entry into the war and for the immediate military preparations that would make that possible. His determination stemmed in part from his old insistence that the United States must move boldly and decisively to assume what he always considered its proper, predestined role: as military, moral, and political leader of the world.

He persisted in his impassioned appeals despite his private acknowledgment that public opinion leaned in the other direction. "I think that the American people feel a little tired of me," he confided in 1915. "I have spoken out as strongly and as clearly as possible, and I do not think it has had any effect beyond making people think that I am a truculent and bloodthirsty person, endeavoring futilely to thwart able, dignified, humane Mr. Wilson in his noble plan to bring peace everywhere by excellently written letters sent to persons who care nothing whatever for any letter that is not backed up by force!"

In his campaign for reelection, Wilson infuriated Roosevelt by running on the slogan "He Kept Us Out of War"; TR maintained that American participation in the war counted as inevitable, necessary, and imminent. He derided the president as "a Byzantine logothete backed by flubdubs and mollycoddles"—an even more contemptuous (and incomprehensible) insult than his own prior designation as a "honeyfugler."

"YOU CAN'T RESIST THE MAN"

When Wilson won reelection (very narrowly) over Charles Evans Hughes, and finally, reluctantly, declared war just a month after his second inauguration, Roosevelt immediately resolved to change his tone. He did so for the sake of national unity and to secure the fulfillment of his fondest wish: to return to battle as commander of a division of volunteers that he would rush to the front far more quickly than the regular army could deploy its forces.

His letters show him nearly giddy at the prospect of once more risking his life in a noble cause, nearly two decades after his "crowded hour" in Cuba. At fifty-eight, he knew he was younger, and more capable of the "strenuous life," than some of the senior generals in the army, even though he'd never fully recaptured his health since his journey on the River of Doubt. As always, he felt ready, even eager, to face down death. "It would have mattered very little whether or not I personally cracked—from pneumonia in the trenches, or shell fire, or exhaustion or anything else," he wrote. "If I should die tomorrow, I would be more than content to have as my epitaph, and my only epitaph, 'Roosevelt to France.'"

In correspondence with the War Department, the responsible officials respectfully declined the former president's offer, even after TR raised the ante and began talking of recruiting and leading eight divisions (two hundred thousand men) and not just one. Nevertheless, President Wilson agreed to meet with him personally on April 10,

1917, just four days after Congress granted the declaration of war that Wilson had requested and Roosevelt had long demanded.

Riding the train to Washington from Oyster Bay, Roosevelt stepped into the White House and found himself exhilarated by the atmosphere and memories of the executive mansion he had ruled so memorably for nearly eight years. He complimented the current president on his war declaration speech and explained that his plan for recruitment and instant deployment would put those noble words into action. Wilson listened respectfully but refused to commit himself, and TR left their meeting in high spirits.

When Roosevelt had gone, and the burst of energy that always surrounded him had begun to dissipate, Wilson asked his secretary Joe Tumulty what he thought of his frequent critic and onetime opponent, Theodore Roosevelt. "I told the President of the very favorable impression the Colonel had made upon me by his buoyancy, charm of manner, and his great good nature."

Wilson, amazingly, agreed. "Yes, he is a great big boy. I was, as formerly, charmed by his personality. There is a sweetness about him that is very compelling. You can't resist the man. I can easily understand why his followers are so fond of him."

"OBLIGED TO DO THE JOB ALL OVER AGAIN"

Of course, the president felt no eagerness to multiply those followers by giving Roosevelt the chance to win new heights of battlefield glory. To Roosevelt's profound disappointment, the War Department definitively declined his offer to lead new recruits to France, leaving TR to focus instead on arranging prominent (and dangerous) military postings for his four sons and his son-in-law.

During their absence, TR wrote loving, eloquent, regular letters to all of the boys and to the three daughters-in-law they left behind. "I hate to feel that I am out of it," he wrote to Kermit, "especially because I so strongly believe that where physical conditions will permit it is the old, the men ... who have drained the cup of joy and sorrow, of achievement and failure, who should be in the danger line, for the little sooner or the little later matters little to them."

He felt especially close to Kermit, a decorated artillery officer under Pershing, because of the hunting and exploring adventures they had shared in the past. "Well, old side partner, your letters are perfectly delightful and surely you must know how my heart thrills with pride whenever I think of you," he wrote. "I don't believe in all the United States there is any father who has quite the same right that I have to be proud of his four sons."

All of the boys displayed conspicuous valor, winning medals for their courage and competence, while Ted junior and Archie survived serious wounds.

Twenty-year-old Quentin, the youngest, best-liked, and most dashing of all the boys, dropped out of Harvard to go to war, at the same time becoming engaged to Flora Payne Whitney, the granddaughter of Cornelius Vanderbilt, a beautiful artist who helped to found the Whitney Museum of Art after the war. Quentin crashed one plane during his flight training but survived with minor injuries and his enthusiasm for aerial combat undiminished. He wrote home jubilantly about his first dogfight, in which he shot down one German plane and escaped two others. Less than a week later, on July 9, 1918, just four months before war's end, he and three other American pilots engaged seven German planes behind enemy lines; in their maneuvering to escape, Quentin drew machine gun fire from a plane behind him and took two bullets in the back of his head.

The Germans recovered Quentin's body after the plane went down, identified it as the son of the former president, and buried young Roosevelt with full military honors.

Remarkably, all three of the surviving Roosevelt boys insisted on returning to frontline combat in World War II more than two decades later, despite the fact that the youngest of them, Archie, was forty-nine before he saw action. His two older brothers died in uniform: Brigadier General Theodore Roosevelt Jr., of a heart attack, after earning a Medal of Honor at Normandy; Major Kermit Roosevelt, of a self-inflicted gunshot wound at Fort Richardson, Alaska, after losing battles with alcoholism and depression.

In 1918, TR and Edith knew nothing of the tragedies that would befall their older boys in another world war, but the former president did foresee that cataclysmic conflict with prophetic accuracy. He warned against an inconclusive peace, bitterly condemning President Wilson's determination to negotiate a truce rather than crush the German war machine and win an unconditional surrender. "Let us dictate peace by the hammering guns and not chat about peace to the accompaniment of the clicking of typewriters," he wrote.

He had long held that Germany's imperialist ambitions represented a mortal threat to the United States. As early as 1914, he wrote that if Germany prevailed in the confrontation against Britain and France it would be "quite on the cards to see Germany and Japan cynically forget the past and join together against the United States and any other power that stood in their way."

In an editorial in October 1918, just three weeks before the armistice, he decried Germany as "the outlaw among nations" that required isolation and punishment. "It is a much worse thing to quit now and have the children now growing up obliged to do the job all over again, with ten times as much bloodshed and suffering, when their turn comes," he declared.

Roosevelt felt such visceral contempt for Wilson's apparent willingness to accept an indecisive outcome to the war that he transformed his profound, debilitating grief over Quentin's heroic death into a relentless determination to change the nation's course. Just four months after the Roosevelt family's devastating loss, the nation went to the polls in congressional elections that President Wilson explicitly framed as a referendum on his conduct of the conflict.

Though hobbled by health problems (including new surgery on the same leg that had been seriously damaged by the streetcar accident and reinjured in Brazil), TR took the leading role in making the case for the GOP. "The Republicans, feeling rather hopeless, are turning towards me to act as their leader in opposition," he noted with no small satisfaction. Most significantly, the old bitterness surrounding his Bull Moose campaign had faded into irrelevance. Days before the election, he climaxed the campaign with a triumphant address to a packed audience in Carnegie Hall. "We must make the Republican Party forward-looking and not let Wilson appear as the progressive champion," he roared.

To the surprise of nearly all seasoned observers, Roosevelt's Republicans prevailed in the election, winning enough seats in both the House and the Senate to take unequivocal control of Congress and, most important, reinstalling Theodore's best friend, Henry Cabot Lodge, as chairman of the Senate Foreign Relations Committee. Just days after the balloting, Wilson and the war-weary Allies accepted German pleas for an armistice, before a single Allied soldier had penetrated German territory.

"THERE IS ONLY ONE FIGHT LEFT IN ME"

With the fighting concluded across the Atlantic, the attention of the political class shifted to the upcoming struggle for control of the White House in 1920. Following their surprising congressional victories, odds heavily favored the Republicans—especially with Roosevelt as their obvious consensus candidate. For once, TR faced no significant political obstacles on his path to the nomination and his robust advocacy for preparedness and enthusiastic prosecution of the war made him look prophetic. As it happened, the eventual Republican nominee for president, the little-known senator Warren G. Harding of Ohio (a Roosevelt critic and a Taft loyalist), won one of the greatest landslides of all time with more than 60 percent of the popular vote. Had TR been the nominee, as most Americans expected at the end of 1918, he might have won an even more resounding victory.

Meanwhile, the aging Rough Rider faced a more formidable foe than any Democrat or Republican rival. The decline in his health and energy became apparent in the days after Quentin's death and led him to turn down the offer of a gubernatorial nomination in New York as preparation for his next presidential campaign. He told his younger sister that he had no choice but to walk away from the race. "Corinne, I have only one fight left in me and I think I should reserve my strength in case I am needed in 1920." He assured her this didn't mean he felt too seriously ill to consider a return to the presidency but that "I am not what I was and there is only one fight left in me."

Even before he celebrated his sixtieth birthday with family on October 27, he had sardonically described himself as "an elderly literary gentleman of quiet tastes and an interesting group of grandchildren" and added that he had become "Methuselah's understudy." Following the quiet celebration, his daughter Ethel reported that he grew dizzy if he moved too quickly and that he reported "queer feelings" in his head.

As New York City lustily celebrated the end of the war, the most prominent advocate for America's participation in that conflict quietly entered Manhattan's Roosevelt Hospital for an extended stay. The staff of the prominent medical institution (named for a third cousin of TR's grandfather who had endowed it in 1871) gave the press varying reasons for the former president's admission: they cited lumbago, sciatica, gout, or, most often, inflammatory rheumatism as the basis for his hospitalization. Edith moved into an adjoining room to monitor his progress, and he remained there, with considerable pain eased by frequent doses of painkillers, for seven weeks.

Most modern medical authorities believe that his condition was related to the infections that had afflicted him since his Amazon expedition, or perhaps to the malaria he briefly suffered in Cuba more than two decades before. His biographer H. W. Brand notes: "Quite likely he harbored parasites that were undetectable by contemporary medical tests." It's also probable that he had never properly healed from his hospitalization ten months earlier when surgeons again scraped infected flesh from his badly injured leg.

Despite feeling frequently feverish, TR saw a constant stream of visitors and dictated numerous letters and columns to Flora Whitney, Quentin's grieving fiancée, who had temporarily taken up a job as Theodore's stenographer.

To many, Roosevelt seemed ambivalent about the future. One old friend held his hand but found him listless, lacking the explosive energy that had always defined him. "I am pretty low now, but I shall get better," he promised. "I cannot go without having done something to that old gray skunk in the White House."

Above all, he refused to become the object of pity. When another old friend tried to comfort him over the loss of Quentin and his lingering illness, he snapped back: "Do not sympathize with me. Have you ever known any man who has gotten so much out of life as I have?" The sentiments precisely echoed those he expressed, repeatedly, in the long, rambling speech he delivered six years before, after Schrank had wounded him in the chest.

When his doctors acknowledged that Roosevelt's condition had improved, or at least stabilized, they heeded the pleas of Theodore and Edith and let them return to Sagamore Hill to celebrate Christmas. Roosevelt reveled in his grandchildren and their excitement at opening their presents, but failed to devour the holiday meal with his customary gusto. New Year's Day brought a new attack of rheumatism, with intense pain to his right wrist. Nevertheless, he continued to dictate articles and columns on the issues of the day, questioning Wilson's plan for a League of Nations that might compromise American sovereignty, and enthusiastically endorsing a constitutional amendment to guarantee the vote for women.

With Roosevelt still in pain, Edith placed an urgent call to James E. Amos, who had been TR's trusted valet and confidant during his White House years, to ask for his help on an emergency basis. Amos temporarily left his new position at the William J. Burns International Detective Agency to provide service to his "beloved boss."

On the night of Sunday, January 5, Theodore stayed up with Edith till ten o'clock watching the "dancing flames" in the fireplace and spoke of his satisfaction at being home. Asking her to help him sit up, he reported that he felt as if his heart and lungs were about to give in. "I know it is not going to happen, but it is such a strange feeling," he said. Edith called the doctor, who recorded his heartbeat as steady and his lungs clear. He also agreed to Edith's suggestion of a shot of morphine to help him sleep.

James Amos eased him into his bed and then turned him on his side so he could watch the fire. Theodore Roosevelt, who had spoken and written literally millions of words, then pronounced his last, brief request. "James, will you please put out the light?"

"DO YOU REMEMBER THE FUN OF HIM . . . ?"

The death certificate recorded the time of his passing as 4:15 a.m. on Monday, January 6, 1919. Amos had been sitting outside the bedroom, listening to TR's labored breathing, which became irregular and then quietly ceased in the small hours of the morning. The official cause of death was an embolism of the lung, with "multiple arthritis" listed as a contributing factor.

The nation and the world reacted with surprise and disbelief at the gentle passing of a rugged figure who had always seemed indestructible. The banner headline in the *New York Times* summarized the general response: "THEODORE ROOSEVELT DIES SUDDENLY AT OYSTER BAY HOME; NATION SHOCKED, PAYS TRIBUTE TO FORMER PRESIDENT; OUR FLAG ON ALL SEAS AND IN ALL LANDS AT HALF MAST."

At his direction, the funeral that brought him to rest near his beloved Long Island home remained spare, with no military or musical elements; his favorite hymn, "How Firm a Foundation," was recited rather than sung. The officiating minister, Reverend George Talmadge, mentioned the former president's name only once, saying: "Theodore, the Lord bless thee and keep thee. The Lord make his face to shine upon thee, and be generous to thee."

No remarks mentioned Roosevelt's part in shaping the nation he loved, or his major role in leading its entry into the twentieth century. No one spoke about his uncanny rise to power, his illogical survival through countless perils, or his standing as a "man of destiny."

Roosevelt himself always shied away from such ruminations, preferring to credit extraordinary "luck" rather than heroic exertions or supernatural anointing. As he settled into his first year as governor of New York in 1899, he wrote: "Last year luck favored me in every way. . . . If I hadn't happened to return from the war in a year when we had a gubernatorial election in New York I should probably not now be governor." Later, he amplified the same theme: "I can entirely assure you that there is not a particle of genius or of any unusual talent in anything I have ever done. By a combination of accidents, I am where I am."

Near the end of his life, however, he referred to the potential role of a higher power sparing him for some important purpose. TR several times mused over his role in fulfilling an unseen plan in intimate conversations with Reverend Ferdinand C. Iglehart, a leader of New York's Anti-Saloon League who had befriended him during his days as police commissioner. On occasion, Iglehart visited Washington and spoke with the president as he hiked back and forth from the modest church he invariably attended.

Two weeks after Roosevelt's death, Iglehart recalled their final conversation, presumably during a visit at Roosevelt Hospital. Referring to their previous talks about divine protection, TR reportedly said: "He did spare me and I thank Him. But I thank Him most for sparing me to take a part in the settlement of the great world war. . . . I thank God that I have lived to see the victory which places the United States in the forefront of the free peoples of the world."

In seconding these sentiments, Reverend Iglehart concluded, "I believe that God was in him and back of him in his miraculously great personality and service for his country and the world."

In more modest terms, a New York City police captain came to the funeral at Oyster Bay to mourn the leader he had served during TR's early days as commissioner. Watching the pallbearers carry the oak casket to its hillside resting place, he commented to the president's sister Corinne: "Do you remember the fun of him . . . ? It was not only that he was a great man, but, oh, there was such fun in being led by him."

Vice President Thomas Marshall, deputized by Woodrow Wilson to attend the funeral of the president's archrival, also invoked TR's distinctive brand of combative vitality. "Death had to take him sleeping," Marshall told the press, "for if Roosevelt had been awake, there would have been a fight."

There *was* a fight, all his life. He couldn't defeat death, of course, but he spent sixty years defying it.

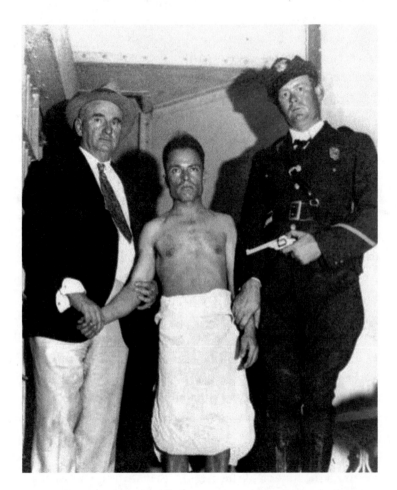

"I WANT TO MAKE EVEN WITH THE CAPITALISTS BY KILLING
THE PRESIDENT": Diminutive and demented Giuseppe ("Joe") Zangara
in police custody, shortly after mortally wounding the mayor of Chicago and
nearly murdering President-elect Franklin Roosevelt (February 15, 1933).

6

Two Close Calls

Franklin and Winston Dodge Disaster

Within the span of fourteen months in the early 1930s, two bloody American encounters nearly killed both individuals most essential for the Allies to prevail in World War II.

Had either of the disconnected incidents produced different results, the impact would have been catastrophic. Instead, these close calls affirmed the old idea advanced by George Washington in his First Inaugural Address: that an "Invisible Hand which conducts the affairs of men" consistently protected and sustained the interests of the United States.

"DOOM MARCHING FORWARD STEP BY STEP"

The first episode struck Winston Churchill (quite literally) in the streets of New York City, shortly before Christmas in 1931.

He wasn't American, obviously, but his mother was. The Brooklyn-born socialite Jennie Jerome entitled young Churchill to feel special kinship with his hundred million cousins across the sea. Andrew Roberts, author of the superb biography *Churchill: Walking with Destiny* (2018), argues that the contemptuous reaction to Winston by so many of his fellow aristocrats stemmed, in part, from their anti-

American instincts: In the brash, perpetually pushy parliamentarian they saw the same vulgar characteristics associated with the crude former colony on the other side of the pond. The posh poet and essayist Hilaire Belloc, for instance, dismissed Winston as a "Yankee careerist."

By 1931, however, Churchill's once promising career had detoured into frustrating "Wilderness Years" of parliamentary isolation and political irrelevance. At age fifty-seven, the onetime chancellor of the exchequer and first lord of the Admiralty found himself banished from his Tory Party's front bench, consigned to writing provocative articles for the popular press and making well-paid lecture tours to reduce his debts after devastating losses in the stock market crash of 1929.

Churchill's latest expedition to the New World featured forty speaking engagements across North America. The first talk, in Worcester, Massachusetts, drew an enthusiastic Saturday night crowd, and by Sunday afternoon the Churchills had settled into the Waldorf Astoria on Park Avenue in New York City. After dinner with his wife, Clementine, and daughter Diana, Winston received a call from his friend, financier and presidential advisor Bernard Baruch, who invited him to his Fifth Avenue home to meet other influential Americans for chat, cigars, and, no doubt, liquid refreshment (despite the prevailing strictures of Prohibition).

Given the late hour (nearly 9:30 when he got the call), Churchill immediately fortified himself against the wintry weather with a heavy, fur-lined overcoat, and bundled into a cab for the drive up Fifth Avenue. Unfortunately, he had neglected to jot down his friend's address but felt confident that the taxi driver would surely know the residence of such a famous figure. If not, Churchill assumed he himself would recognize the building's distinctive and elegant front, having visited Baruch two years before.

The cabbie dutifully crept along Fifth Avenue, hoping to spot a familiar landmark. Finally, between Seventy-sixth and Seventy-seventh Streets, Churchill thought he spotted the right apartment building, or at least identified the appropriate neighborhood. He paid his fare and, conscious of his own tardy arrival (already 10:30), he took a few steps along the sidewalk before concluding he had gotten out on the wrong side of the street.

Recalling these embarrassing miscalculations a few days later, Churchill wrote of a stage play in which "an impressive effect is given of doom marching forward step by step and of every human preventive slipping silently out of the path."

Sad to say, Winston Churchill never indulged the simple "human preventive" of checking the busy Fifth Avenue traffic before boldly crossing the boulevard and stepping directly into the path of an onrushing car. "Suddenly upon my right I was aware of something utterly unexpected and boding mortal peril," he wrote. "I turned my head sharply. Right upon me, scarcely its own length away, was what seemed a long dark car rushing forward at full speed."

The police and eyewitnesses estimated that speed as thirty-five miles an hour, giving the driver scant chance to brake or slow down. "There was one moment—I cannot measure it in time—of a world aglare, of a man aghast. I certainly thought quickly enough to achieve the idea, 'I am going to be run down and probably killed.' Then came the blow.

"I felt it on my forehead and across the thighs. But besides the blow there was an impact, a shock, a concussion indescribably violent. . . . In my case it blotted out everything except thought. . . . The car shuddered, and after skidding somewhat under the brakes, came to rest in probably a few lengths. Three or four feet from the right-hand wheel lay a black, shapeless mass."

Conscious, but too stunned to move, Churchill sensed a loud outcry as bystanders ran up to try to help. "A man has been killed!" he heard someone shout, and ardently hoped that they were wrong.

"I DO NOT UNDERSTAND WHY I WAS NOT BROKEN LIKE AN EGG-SHELL"

He later reflected, "I do not understand why I was not broken like an egg-shell or squashed like a gooseberry. . . . I certainly must be very tough or very lucky, or both.

"Meanwhile, I had not lost consciousness for an instant. Somewhere in the black bundle towards which the passers-by are running there is a small chamber or sanctum wherein all is orderly and undisturbed. . . . This mind is in possession of the following conclusion:

"I have been run over by a motorcar in America. All those worries about being late are now swept away. They do not matter any more. Here is a real catastrophe. Perhaps it is the end."

In time to disabuse him of that notion, another taxi volunteered to transport the gravely injured victim to nearby Lenox Hill Hospital. There, the physicians treated him for a concussion, severe contusions requiring sutures on his forehead and nose, two cracked ribs, and heavy bruising on his leg, right arm, and chest. He remained hospitalized for more than a week, taking advantage of the situation to lie in bed, writing a report for the London press under the headline "MY NEW YORK MISADVENTURE."

To his immense delight, he sold the piece as a two-part exclusive to the *Daily Mail* for $2,500—the equivalent of nearly $40,000 today—offering some consolation for the lucrative lecture dates he had been forced to miss. As he wrote to his old friend Archie Sinclair nearly three weeks after the accident: "I had a terrible bump, and how I was not squashed or shattered I cannot imagine. I was also very lucky in escaping the wheels, which only went over and broke the tips of my toes."

After his release from the hospital, Churchill traveled with his wife and daughter to the Bahamas for further recuperation and to celebrate New Year's Day, using the funds from his newspaper account of the ordeal to finance the jaunt. When they returned to the United States, he managed to complete thirty-six of his forty scheduled lectures.

At the first of them, in Brooklyn, the unemployed twenty-six-year-old who had been driving the car that nearly killed him listened respectfully. Mario Contasino lived with his elderly immigrant father in Yonkers, and felt so horrified for having nearly killed a visiting dignitary on Fifth Avenue that he visited Churchill several times in the hospital. He apologized repeatedly and profusely, even though the Englishman always insisted that he alone deserved the blame for stepping in front of the oncoming car. After the Brooklyn lecture, Churchill greeted the nervous young man like an old friend and presented him with a signed copy of his recently published book, *The Unknown War*.

In surviving the ardors of his six weeks of touring and talking, Churchill received special encouragement and assistance from the doctors who treated him at Lenox Hill Hospital. A prescription from O. C. Pickhardt, MD, recommended regular doses of his patient's favorite sort of medicine: "This is to certify that the post-accident convalescence of the Hon. Winston S. Churchill necessitates the use of alcoholic spirits especially at meal times," the good doctor wrote. "The quantity is naturally indefinite but the minimum requirements would be 250 cubic centimeters." That authorization enjoyed special significance in America during Prohibition; no wonder that Churchill, at the top of the precious prescription, scrawled out three words: "Keep on hand."

Through the entire experience, Churchill lost neither his sense of humor nor the certainty that the fates meant him to gain from this ordeal. Of course, he shared that lesson in his reflective article in the *Daily Mail*. He wrote:

> The message I bring back from these dark places is one of encouragement, I certainly suffered every pang, mental and physical, that a street accident or, I suppose, a shell wound can produce. None is unendurable. There is no room for remorse or fears. There is neither time nor the strength for self-pity. If at any moment in this long series of sensations a grey veil deepening into blackness had descended upon the sanctum I should have felt or feared nothing additional. Nature is merciful and does not try her children, man or beast, beyond their compass. It is only when the cruelty of man intervenes that hellish torments appear. For the rest—live dangerously, take things as they come; dread naught, all will be well.

"IT IS A GOOD THING TO KEEP THE NAME
IN THE FAMILY"

That same attitude characterized Franklin Roosevelt, who suffered his own near-death experience just a year and two months after Churchill's "New York Misadventure." Like his British colleague, Roosevelt seemed to enjoy fateful protection or illogical luck.

The two men had met only briefly at a crowded, glittering London dinner party in May 1918. At the time, Churchill was already a national celebrity, having been a popular journalist and prominent minister in British governments for more than ten years. Roosevelt, on the other hand, occupied the far less exalted post of assistant secretary of the navy under President Woodrow Wilson, and seemed to resent the fact that Churchill hardly noticed him. He later recalled to Joseph P. Kennedy that the boisterous British politico had "acted like a stinker" when they first met, "lording it over all of us."

By 1933, however, their situations had dramatically reversed. Churchill had become a curmudgeonly outcast in British politics, while Roosevelt rose to the very pinnacle of American power.

FDR accomplished this through a series of conscious choices and convenient coincidences that allowed him to replicate the step-by-step ascendance of his distant relative President Theodore Roosevelt. As fifth cousins, Franklin and Theodore shared a great-great-great-great-grandfather: the onetime fur trader Nicholas Roosevelt, who was born in 1658. His two sons, Johannes and Jacobus, set up competing branches of the family in the Hudson Valley and on Long Island Sound. The country squire Roosevelts of Hyde Park on the Hudson established themselves as conservative Democrats, while the mercantile Oyster Bay Roosevelts embraced the Republican cause. These geographical and political differences kept the two Roosevelt breeds distinct but didn't prevent them from taking satisfaction in the achievements of their intra-family rivals. In June 1900, young Franklin rose several notches in the estimation of his prep school classmates when Governor Theodore Roosevelt delivered a speech for his graduating class at Groton School.

Five years later, the two Roosevelts met again at an even more significant life cycle event: the wedding of Franklin and Eleanor Roosevelt, where President Theodore Roosevelt gave away the bride. The tall, shy, and sensitive Eleanor had lost her socialite mother to diphtheria when she was eight and her father—the charming, charismatic younger brother of Theodore—died of chronic alcoholism before she turned ten.

Though absorbed with his political career, Theodore tried when possible to function as a substitute father for his orphaned niece. At her lavishly publicized wedding, the press asked the ever-quotable chief executive for his opinion of the Roosevelt-Roosevelt match. "It is a good thing to keep the name in the family," he boomed.

Franklin felt similarly gratified to cement the connection with a relative who had made their family name famous: since boyhood, he had followed Cousin Theodore's relentless rise with avid interest, making occasionally conscious efforts to retrace his path.

He followed TR to Harvard, for instance, and then to Columbia Law School. There, both Roosevelts interrupted their legal training before graduation to pursue political opportunities. Both men also won election to the New York legislature in their twenties.

The two Roosevelts ended up with strikingly similar families: just as Theodore and his second wife, Edith, produced four boys and a girl, so, too, Franklin and Eleanor raised four boys and a girl (after their second son died as an infant). As they rose in prominence and power, both men won appointment as assistant secretary of the navy while in their thirties, and then secured their respective party's vice presidential nominations.

But unlike Cousin Theodore, thirty-eight-year-old FDR lost his vice presidential race. Despite the young candidate's ardent efforts, the massive Republican tidal wave that carried Warren G. Harding in triumph to the White House in 1920 swamped the doomed Democratic ticket.

Even so, FDR made a powerful impression on both party bosses and the public with his tireless campaigning and ebullient personality. Barnstorming around the country, he managed to deliver nearly a thousand speeches in just four months, averaging more than eight a day—a prodigious accomplishment considering the limitations of rail travel in the early twentieth century.

This exuberant energy, even in a losing cause, recalled the "strenuous life" famously advocated by Franklin's presidential cousin. In fact, TR's sudden, untimely death in 1919 helped fuel the public hunger for a new Roosevelt in the next year's campaign.

"NOTHING BUT AN ACCIDENT COULD KEEP HIM FROM BECOMING PRESIDENT"

Inevitably, an air of destiny, even anointing, settled around the tall, aristocratic FDR, who began talking openly of his own presidential aspirations as soon as his vice presidential loss became apparent. A mostly adoring press helped encourage these dreams, as did the two most important figures in Roosevelt's life and career: his wife, Eleanor, and his fanatically devoted chief aide and advisor, Louis Howe.

Eleven years older than FDR, and more than a foot shorter, the sickly, pockmarked, chain-smoking, but politically savvy Howe first attached himself to his dream candidate when Franklin was a rising young member of the New York State Senate. A fellow reporter described him as a "medieval gnome," and Howe relished that description, confessing that "children take one look at me on the street and run."

Quite naturally, these characteristics impelled the gnome himself to run *toward* Roosevelt, the self-confident aristocrat who possessed every quality he lacked—grace, breeding, good looks, athleticism, and inherited wealth. The two men first met when Howe conducted a newspaper interview at the Albany home of Senator Roosevelt, then twenty-nine, who strode into the room and stood before a crackling fire below the family coat of arms carved into the fireplace. "Almost at that very first meeting," Howe recalled, "I made up my mind that nothing but an accident could keep him from becoming president."

A few months later, in one of his early letters to FDR, he teasingly addressed his new friend as "Beloved and Revered Future President." In a sense, Eleanor's similarly unwavering devotion to Franklin's career displayed a more puzzling aspect: thirteen years and five children into their marriage, she discovered a bundle of love letters between her husband and her own social secretary, Lucy Mercer, a glamorous

SMOOTH SAILING: Franklin Delano Roosevelt at age twenty-six, just three
years away from his election to the New York State Senate. He always enjoyed
sailing with his family from his summer home on Campobello Island off the coast
of New Brunswick, Canada, where he fell victim to paralyzing polio in 1921.

young socialite. Despite discussions of divorce in that turbulent year
of 1918, Eleanor at no time abandoned her unfailing belief in her
husband's fate as a future president; though they never again shared a
bed, she consistently shouldered her role as a ceaseless, reliable pro-
moter of his pursuit of higher office.

For both Howe and Eleanor, along with others who felt irresistibly inspired by the prospect of another President Roosevelt, this commitment had little or nothing to do with ideology and everything to do with force of personality, producing an instinctive, quasi-mystical faith that the smooth political operator they admired would fulfill a fated role as the nation's predestined deliverer.

Until he became president, Roosevelt never embraced a coherent political philosophy or associated himself with a particular faction in the Democratic Party. He invoked vague platitudes of "reform" and "good government" but made his peace with the Tammany Hall Democratic machine, offering support to their candidates and causes when it served his purposes to do so. As late as 1932, he railed against high taxes and meddlesome, unnecessary government programs, while extolling the old-fashioned virtues of balanced budgets.

FDR's most devoted acolytes cared far more about the aura of inevitability that seemed to surround the man than they did about new ideas or bold agendas. This explains their horror and disbelief when a devastating illness interrupted his seemingly preordained presidential progress in 1921—precisely the sort of appalling "accident" that Howe had uncannily anticipated.

ABANDONED AS "A CHOSEN INSTRUMENT OF GOD"

Immediately following his vice presidential race, Roosevelt accepted a different sort of vice presidency—as an executive with the Fidelity and Deposit Company on Wall Street. That summer, he looked forward to joining his wife and five children at the family's longtime vacation home on the rustic Canadian island of Campobello, off the coast of Maine. On the way there, he stopped for a well-publicized, politically minded appearance at a Boy Scout jamboree held in the recently established Bear Mountain State Park in the Hudson River valley. According to many of his later biographers and the medical professionals who have studied his case, that brief visit with thousands of youngsters camping and eating in close quarters may well have exposed him to the polio virus that altered his life.

After leaving Bear Mountain, Franklin sailed aboard a private yacht that took him northeast to join his vacationing family. In high spirits over their reunion, he immediately led the children in a whirl-wind of frenetic activity: sailing along the scenic, rocky shoreline of Campobello Island, racing his brood for nearly two miles to plunge into a freshwater pond for a quick swim, even organizing an im-promptu bucket brigade to extinguish the beginnings of a potential forest fire. Through all this, he felt exhilarated rather than exhausted.

Later that evening, after dining quickly and going to bed earlier than usual, Franklin became weak and feverish. The most alarming symptom involved the numbness in his legs; when he tried to get out of bed, he couldn't stand. The first doctors called for consultation rec-ommended a deep massage of his long legs to try to restore their proper function, but when Eleanor and Louis Howe took turns trying to rub the life back into his suddenly useless limbs, Roosevelt found their efforts agonizingly painful. His temperature eventually reached 102, and he fell into delirium.

At one point, he reportedly screamed from his sickbed, feeling betrayed by the protective Deity who had persistently favored him. As Jonathan Alter summarized this reaction in his moving book *The Defining Moment,* Franklin "had always believed in himself as a cho-sen instrument of God and now felt abandoned."

It took four doctors and three harrowing weeks to diagnose Franklin's desperate condition: infantile paralysis, or poliomyelitis, which left him scant hope of regaining the normal use of his now fully paralyzed legs. At that point, the family resolved to transport him from the remote Canadian island to New York Presbyterian Hospital in Manhattan. At Howe's direction, all those involved in Roosevelt's treatment took extraordinary steps to conceal the severity of his con-dition from the prying press. He realized that if local townspeople saw FDR carried away on a stretcher, they would reach dire conclu-sions. To avoid such embarrassment, six men collaborated in moving the onetime vice presidential candidate: like a large slab of valuable but secret cargo, he was concealed on the floorboards of a small boat to make the choppy crossing from the island to the mainland.

When the *New York Times* reported on the celebrity politician's sudden illness and his arrival back in the city, it featured the misleading sub-headline "Recovering, Doctor Says," assuring the worried public that "it was said that the attack was very mild and that Mr. Roosevelt would not be permanently crippled." None of FDR's physicians appear to have offered any such assurances, but his political handlers, led by the obsessed and determined Louis Howe, almost certainly did. At this point, Howe largely abandoned his own family and the routines of normal life to move in with the Roosevelts. Many nights he slept in an extra bed in FDR's sickroom, or on a cot right outside his door. Having already spent seven years of his own life patiently fanning his patron's ambitions for presidential glory, Howe refused to allow Franklin or Eleanor to give up these dreams of another national campaign, even though the potential candidate could neither walk nor stand unaided.

IT PROTECTED HIS PRESIDENTIAL PROSPECTS

In retrospect, it could be argued that Franklin's incapacitating illness not only failed to shatter his White House ambitions but illogically, implacably sustained and advanced them. Polio may have wrecked his body, but in three significant ways it protected his presidential prospects.

On the first and most obvious level, the timing of his suddenly grave condition worked perfectly to kill a lurid scandal that might otherwise have ruined any chance of his holding future office. On July 20, 1921, a mere three weeks before the crisis at Campobello, a front-page story in the *New York Times* gave him the harshest press treatment he had yet received, attacking both FDR and his boss, Navy Secretary Josephus Daniels:

LAY NAVY SCANDAL TO F.D. ROOSEVELT

SENATE NAVAL SUB-COMMITTEE ACCUSES HIM AND DANIELS IN NEWPORT INQUIRY

DETAILS ARE UNPRINTABLE

The newspaper's forbearance in publishing those "unprintable details" granted Roosevelt only a temporary reprieve, since the facts had enjoyed enough circulation among Washington insiders to be sure to resurface when he sought the presidency. The "Newport Inquiry" involved FDR's apparent approval of an outrageous undercover operation to root out rampant homosexuality at the Newport Naval and Training Station. FDR told investigating senators he had no recollection of this misbegotten mission and certainly knew nothing about its most shocking element: orders to enlisted men chosen for the project to perform oral sex on suspected homosexuals (and a prominent clergyman who consorted with them), a twisted attempt to disgrace the participants and discharge them from the service. The public in 1921 felt such profound disgust over the navy's involvement in any of the "unnatural acts" described in the investigation that respectable news outlets felt some relief when FDR's suddenly tragic situation allowed the press to drop the sordid story with its "unprintable details."

Aside from its role in deflecting scandal, Roosevelt's affliction also spared him from what would have been political suicide: his planned presidential race in 1924. No Democrat, not even a candidate with the charisma and charm of Franklin Roosevelt, could have prevailed in that year's battle to wrest the White House from GOP control. The incumbent, Calvin Coolidge, had assumed the presidency when Warren Harding expired suddenly in 1923, and proved extraordinarily popular with the public, which credited Coolidge with cleaning up his predecessor's scandals and blessing the nation with a booming economy.

In the end, Coolidge won a solid majority, nearly doubling the 29 percent for the forlorn Democrat, John W. Davis—the lowest popular vote percentage for a Democratic nominee in nearly two hundred years of party history. Had FDR followed his prior vice presidential loss with a presidential wipeout, it would have ruined him: no first term for Franklin, let alone four of them. Only the intervention of devastating illness preserved him from the disaster.

"TWICE BORN MAN"

Finally, his battle with paralysis and the courage he displayed in minimizing its impact gave him a character-forming backstory that made him stand out as someone more substantive, more sympathetic, than a pampered, shallow, preternaturally cheerful son of privilege. The idea that Roosevelt's physical brokenness allowed him to connect with the wounds and afflictions of the common man amounts to a convenient, reductionist explanation of his complex character, but it also connects to time-honored Christian themes of a messianic figure ennobled by suffering.

Louis Howe inevitably summarized the transformation, or transfiguration, of his hero from that perspective. In Franklin's pre-polio days, "You couldn't pin him down," Howe once explained to his secretary, Lela Stiles. "He rode, he swam, he played golf, tennis, he sailed, he collected stamps, he did about every damn thing under the sun a man could think of doing. Then suddenly there he was flat on his back with nothing to do but think. He began to read, he began to think, he talked, he gathered people around him—his thoughts widened, his horizons widened. He began to see the other fellow's point of view. He thought of others who were ill and afflicted and in want. He dwelt on many things which had not bothered him much before. Lying there, he grew bigger day by day."

Whether or not polio actually enriched and elevated FDR's character, his suffering most certainly changed the way that others perceived him. William Phillips, for instance, who served in Wilson's State Department while FDR toiled at Navy, visited him for the first time in a decade and found "a different person from the charming and at times irresponsible young man of the old Wilson days. The two-year fight against the dread disease had evidently given him new moral and physical strength."

His uncle, Frederic A. Delano, summarized the transformation with an emphasis on the spiritual dimension, noting that Franklin's "severest test was the 'Polio,' and to my mind that is what really made him what he is—a 'twice born man.'"

However, an early biographer of FDR, Arthur M. Schlesinger Jr., downplayed any religious aspect to his ultimate triumph over his disability. "Even religion provided only conventional and unexamined consolation," he wrote in *The Crisis of the Old Order*. "He believed in being a good Episcopalian as he believed in being a good American; but he did not like to reflect on sin and salvation. As he once told Eleanor, 'I think it is just as well not to think about things like that too much!'"

Some doubters found his sunny disposition somewhat forced and false, almost compensatory, fulfilling some deep need to prove his victory over physical limitations. To these skeptics, "Roosevelt must always be a little less than glamorous," wrote Milton MacKaye in the *New Yorker* during the campaign for his first term as president. "The reason is that his outlook on life is perennially optimistic, that he pushes ahead with full speed, always with a confidence that every story has a happy ending. . . . He is all light and no darkness; all faith and no skepticism; all bright hope and no black despair. One expects shadow and depth in a great man."

Winston Churchill, however, came to see FDR's celebration of each moment as the irresistible essence of the man. After he got to know Roosevelt during the early years of World War II, the British leader observed that meeting Roosevelt, "with all his buoyant sparkle, his iridescence," was like "opening a bottle of champagne."

FDR himself always preferred a down-to-earth explanation when admirers asked about his unshakably optimistic disposition: "If you had spent two years in bed trying to wiggle your big toe, after that anything else would seem easy!"

In that context, FDR's disability served to magnify even the most prosaic activities and most pedestrian performances, elevating them into heroic achievements that captivated the public and sent him on his way toward the White House.

"HE'LL TAKE SOME OF THE CURSE OFF YOU"

In 1924, the year he had once selected for a presidential run, FDR resolved to make his formal return to the world of politics. He still couldn't maneuver himself from place to place without risking embarrassment or the accentuation of his helplessness. But fitted with steel braces that weighed fourteen pounds and attached with a broad belt around his waist, he could stand up when two men lifted him to his feet and allowed the catches at his knees to lock into place. With crutches under each arm, he could then move forward, swinging one leg at a time like dead weight in a semicircular movement to sway in the direction he needed to go. He practiced this painful, impractical method of locomotion with intense and exhausting dedication as he prepared for an appearance on the largest possible stage.

Governor Al Smith of New York, while planning his first campaign for president, remembered Roosevelt from the days they spent together in the state senate and asked him to become titular head of "Citizens for Smith." They had never been close, but Smith knew that Roosevelt's reputation as an idealistic reformer would counteract the governor's association with the seamy Tammany Hall machine.

As the Democratic National Convention prepared to convene at Madison Square Garden, FDR benefited from one of those sudden, inexplicable, profoundly convenient deaths that so often boosted the rise of his cousin Theodore in the prior generation. The New York worthy chosen to give the nominating speech suddenly died, and the campaign needed a quick replacement. When Governor Smith asked who should stand in for the deceased orator, an aide instantly replied, "Roosevelt, you're a Bowery mick and he's a Protestant patrician and he'll take some of the curse off you."

Roosevelt and Howe instantly grasped the magnitude of the opportunity and began practicing for the big moment. This had less to do with writing or practicing lines—Roosevelt, with his smooth, resonant baritone and aristocratic accent, could read the phone book and make it sound lyrical—and more to do with Roosevelt rehearsing a dramatic, essential walk to the podium without tripping or hesitating.

The convention took on added importance because it became the first such gathering to be broadcast to most of the country, live, on radio. Graham McNamee, who had become famous the year before for originating play-by-play coverage of baseball games, promised to bring the same skill at descriptive narrative to his vivid accounts of the action at the convention. Roosevelt also drew strength from this innovation: his commanding voice seemed nearly as well suited for the new broadcast medium as the operatic tones of McNamee.

Even before he took the podium, FDR became a center of attention. As floor manager for the Smith forces, he always made something of a grand entrance: during the intensive two weeks that the convention met, his aides brought his car as close as possible to Madison Square Garden, then helped him into a wheelchair. They pushed him to the entrance nearest the New York delegation, where Roosevelt then grabbed the arm of his tall, athletic sixteen-year-old son, Jimmy, who helped install a crutch under his father's right arm. Clanking his braces, swinging his legs forward as he lurched toward his seat, grabbing his son's bicep with a ferocious grip, Franklin never failed to flash a jaunty smile to all who watched his tortured progress. In the sweltering summer heat in that era before air-conditioning, Roosevelt's grinning countenance diverted all attention from his struggling, sweaty body as he made his way to the New York standard—the brightly lettered pole that marked the location of the convention's largest delegation.

At first, the crowds in the galleries viewed this difficult process as an inspiring distraction and watched in respectful silence, but after two days they began applauding, even cheering, every time they saw FDR enter the convention floor. That reaction, in turn, caught the attention of Graham McNamee, who sonorously and elaborately treated Roosevelt's comings and goings as episodes of cosmic significance, with a dramatic grandeur suitable for the seventh game of the World Series. To the national radio audience, FDR became a star of the occasion even before he delivered his scheduled speech nominating Al Smith for the presidency.

"THE TREMENDOUS, ROARING OVATION"

That moment arrived at noon on June 26, as Jimmy pushed his father's wheelchair from the convention floor up a ramp to the rear of the platform, where FDR waited and sweated before his big moment. Approximately two minutes before his introduction, his son helped him to his feet and asked for breathing room on the crowded platform. James Roosevelt later remembered: "His fingers dug into my arm like pincers." As FDR listened to a lavish and extended introduction, he asked one of the dignitaries nearby to check the rostrum to make sure he could lean on it; if it pitched forward under his weight and he fell on his face in front of twelve thousand delegates and spectators, his short-lived comeback would be prematurely terminated.

When the time finally came for the long-winded lead-in preceding his speech, Franklin took the second crutch from his son and stared down the fifteen feet that separated him from the podium. Thirty-five years later, Jimmy recalled the moment: "As he slowly swung himself forward, he saluted the crowd—since he could not lift his arms—with his big smile. Then, as he reached the rostrum came the tremendous, roaring ovation. At that moment I was so damned proud of him that it was with difficulty that I kept myself from bursting into tears."

He spoke for thirty-four minutes, delivering a steady stream of competently crafted partisan platitudes—extolling the Democrats as the party of the people and shredding the Republicans as tools of plutocrats and special interests. The speech contained none of the drums and trumpets that would echo through his most celebrated presidential addresses, perhaps because FDR wrote virtually none of it. In fact, he tried to remove the only phrase that anyone remembered from the talk—a reference to Al Smith as "the happy warrior of the political battlefield"; Roosevelt thought that the allusion to a Wordsworth poem wouldn't work with the down-to-earth political operatives on the floor.

Instead, it was Roosevelt's presence, his visible triumph over adversity, and not his words, that moved the conventioneers. Elmer Davis of the *New York Times* wrote that he "placed both hands on the speaker's desk and stood with head erect, a vigorous and healthful figure except for his lameness." He remained on the platform for seventy-five minutes longer while Smith's delirious loyalists staged an explosive and seemingly endless demonstration.

Tom Pendergast, the tough and ruthless Kansas City boss who later shaped Harry Truman's political career, watched in amazement. "Had Mr. Roosevelt ... been physically able to have withstood the campaign, he would have been named by acclamation," he told a friend. "He has the most magnetic personality of any individual I have ever met." The *New York World* offered similar effusions, describing Roosevelt as "the real hero" of the hour who emerged as "the one leader commanding the respect and admiration of delegates from all sections of the land."

Even the skeptical journalist Walter Lippmann declared himself uncharacteristically impressed. He wrote privately to Roosevelt that he considered the "Happy Warrior" speech "a moving and distinguished thing. I am utterly hard-boiled about speeches, but yours seems to me perfect in temper and manner and most eloquent in its effect."

Despite all the accolades for Franklin's magical moment, the candidate he placed in nomination failed to become the party's standard-bearer, falling short after an exhausting 104-ballot deadlock, as the Democrats went on to lose the presidency and both houses of Congress by landslide margins. Four years later, Al Smith tried again, and after capturing the nomination asked FDR to run to replace him as governor of New York. In part, the Happy Warrior believed that with the popular Roosevelt's name on the ballot he stood a better chance of carrying his home state in the presidential battle. As it turned out, Smith lost to Herbert Hoover by one hundred thousand votes in the Empire State, but Roosevelt prevailed by the narrowest of margins, seizing yet another exalted post previously occupied by Cousin Theodore on his path to the presidency.

COUNTERING "CACTUS JACK"

At that point, FDR's White House candidacy became all but inevitable, especially when his governorship mobilized an energetic, activist response to the suffering of the Great Depression that offered a compelling contrast to the flailing gestures and pervasive gloom that emanated from Herbert Hoover's White House. As Secretary of State Henry L. Stimson confided to one of his close friends, "a private meeting with Hoover is like sitting in a bath of ink."

In the primary campaign that followed in 1932, Roosevelt proved the most consistent winner but still arrived at the Chicago convention well shy of the two-thirds of delegate votes needed for nomination. Roosevelt's former ally Al Smith became his most implacable rival, but FDR also faced a challenge from the Speaker of the House, John Nance Garner of Texas.

Affectionately known as "Cactus Jack," Garner had spent thirty years as a congressional representative of the vast, empty stretches of "brush country" in southwest Texas. He relished the political game and reveled in entertaining members of both parties for after-hours sessions of what he designated "the Board of Education." At these regular gatherings for poker and fine cigars, the Speaker, conservative though he was, dispensed liberal servings of bourbon and branch water, encouraging his guests to "strike a blow for liberty" at the height of Prohibition. Standing just over five feet tall, even with his western boots and cowboy headgear, Garner made frequent fun of his single most notable feature: two unruly eyebrows that he described as looking like "two caterpillars 'rasslin.'"

Time magazine later sketched him in more dignified terms as "a hickory conservative who does not represent the Old South of magnolias, hoopskirts, pillared verandas, but the New South: moneymaking, industrial, hardboiled, still expanding too rapidly to brood over social problems. He stands for oil derricks, sheriffs who use airplanes, prairie skyscrapers, mechanized farms, $100 Stetson hats."

In that context, Cactus Jack bore little connection to his party's progressive, pro-labor, Wilsonian elites and actually took bipartisan pride in another of his nicknames: "the Texas Coolidge." He described his own philosophy as classically Jeffersonian, and looked askance at reformist do-gooders who meant to expand government. Even at the depths of the Depression in 1931, he declared that "the great trouble we have today is that we have too many laws. I believe that primarily a government has but two functions—to protect the lives and property rights of citizens. When it goes further than that it becomes a burden."

With the influential support of press baron William Randolph Hearst, who distrusted internationalists and warmed to Garner's use of the slogan "America First," Cactus Jack beat both Roosevelt and

Smith in the California primary and came to Chicago with a substantial block of delegates. On each of the first three ballots, FDR led the pack but couldn't reach the two-thirds majority the rules required. In a break in the balloting for bonhomie and booze (the party platform called for quick repeal of Prohibition), FDR's indefatigable lieutenants met with members of Garner's high command. Both sides agreed that they wanted to avoid another deadlocked convention that could damage the party's chances in November. William G. McAdoo, chairman of the California delegation and Woodrow Wilson's son-in-law, suggested that Garner might release his delegates if Roosevelt promised to pick Cactus Jack for the vice presidency.

As FDR awaited news of the negotiations at the governor's mansion in Albany, his deputies placed the difficult long-distance call and, over a crackling connection, got the decisive okay from their chief. According to the traditions of the time, presidential candidates never appeared at conventions, and instead waited until a delegation of dignitaries showed up at their homes to present formal notification of nomination. With the Garner-McAdoo deal all but assuring his nomination, Roosevelt began plotting a masterstroke to shatter that tradition.

"I HAVE NO CONTROL OVER THE WINDS OF HEAVEN"

After waiting until midnight to listen to his official nomination on the radio, the governor of New York made hurried and risky arrangements to fly to Chicago early the next morning in order to address the Democrats in person before they departed. As his biographer Jean Edward Smith (*FDR*, 2007) points out, passengers were two hundred times more likely to die in plane crashes in 1932 than passengers forty years later. Smith writes: "By smashing precedent and going to Chicago, Roosevelt was demonstrating a spirit of urgency that a dispirited country could embrace."

American Airlines offered only a single flight out of Albany each day, but they made special arrangements for the candidate, reassigning a Ford 5-AT Tri-Motor from its scheduled Dallas to Los Angeles run. "People were afraid to fly," an airline spokesman later explained. "To get a governor on a plane might help spread a little confidence. That's why we were willing to go to so much trouble."

Thirteen passengers, mostly the bulk of the Roosevelt clan and key staff, jammed into the ungainly little plane noted for its puffy appearance and dismissive nickname, "the Tin Goose." With its three propellers making a mighty growl, the Goose could travel no faster than 110 miles an hour.

Nonetheless, they headed west, with scheduled refueling stops in Buffalo and Cleveland. "There were storms all around us," remembered one of the pilots. With the nervous passengers bouncing wildly in the crowded cabin, the crew prepared for an emergency landing in Rochester before a sudden gap in the clouds and gusts allowed them to keep going.

When FDR finally arrived at the convention around 6:00 p.m., the assembled multitudes greeted his arrival with a mighty roar: their newly anointed redeemer had descended literally, miraculously, from the sky, as he parted the ominous clouds. Of course, he seized the moment and amplified its dramatic and symbolic value:

I regret that I am late, but I have no control over the winds of Heaven. . . .

I have started out on the tasks that lie ahead by breaking the absurd traditions that the candidate should remain in professed ignorance of what has happened for weeks until he is formally notified of that event many weeks later. . . .

Let it be from now on the task of our Party to break foolish traditions. We will break foolish traditions and leave it to the Republican leadership, far more skilled in that art, to break promises.

Let us now and here highly resolve to resume the country's interrupted march along the path of real progress, of real justice, of real equality for all our citizens, great and small.

He went on in similarly stirring style, leaving the convention-goers delirious with joy and confidence, commanding a vast radio audience in which millions heard his voice for the first time. The ringing conclusion provided the name for both his campaign agenda and his new administration:

> I pledge you, I pledge myself, to a new deal for the American people. Let us all here assembled constitute ourselves prophets of a new order of competence and courage. This is more than a political campaign; it is a call to arms. Give me your help, not to win votes alone, but to win this crusade to restore America to its own people.

Even without such rousing rhetoric, Roosevelt would have been an easy winner in Depression-racked America. Unemployment stood at 25 percent, farm foreclosures reached twenty-five thousand a month, and foreign trade had plummeted by almost 80 percent from its levels three years before. Under these conditions, Brooklyn's hard-bitten boss John McCooey tartly observed: "Roosevelt could have spent the entire summer and fall in Europe and been elected just the same."

Despite the widespread expectation that he'd win in November, prominent intellectuals from both left and right continued to underestimate the obvious front-runner. After the convention, H. L. Mencken declared that FDR labored under "the burden of his own limitations. He is one of the most charming of men, but like many another very charming man he leaves on the beholder the impression that he is also somewhat shallow and futile."

Even Walter Lippmann, who heard the "Happy Warrior" speech eight years earlier and felt moved to write FDR a letter of private praise, now dismissed him as an affable airhead lacking in substance or passion. In an infamous column, he ripped his fellow Harvard graduate as a "highly impressionable person without a firm grasp of public affairs and without very strong convictions. . . . He is an amiable man with many philanthropic impulses but he is not the dangerous enemy of anything . . . a pleasant man who, without any important qualifications for the office, would very much like to be president."

His seemingly effortless landslide, beating Hoover by seven million votes and carrying forty-two of the forty-eight states, only served to intensify the doubts about his substance and seriousness. The *New Republic* contemptuously reported that "all informed observers agree that the country did not vote for Roosevelt; it voted against Hoover."

"GETTING A MARVELOUS REST"

In the nearly four months between Election Day and inauguration, Roosevelt hardly helped his own cause by largely disappearing from public view. The battered incumbent asked for FDR's collaboration in formulating an emergency response to the darkening economic crisis, but the president-elect shunned any involvement in a new round of Hoover-linked failures. Instead, he met privately with advisors and operatives to organize a cabinet, or indulged in extended vacations at Warm Springs, Georgia (where he had established a national research and treatment center for polio victims), or toured with his family and an array of wealthy, well-born friends.

A particularly lavish escape involved two weeks of Caribbean sailing and fishing on board the *Nourmahal*—at 263 feet long one of the largest and grandest luxury yachts in the world. Organized by the great craft's proud owner, *Newsweek* publisher Vincent Astor, the jolly all-male excursion provided a balmy February escape from the dreariest month of winter. The guest list drew exclusively on alumni of Harvard's toniest clubs, including TR's adventurous son, Kermit, and FDR's eldest boy, Jimmy. "Getting a marvelous rest—lots of air and sun," the president-elect wrote to his always protective mother, Sara Delano Roosevelt.

When the *Nourmahal* majestically cruised into Miami's Biscayne Bay, Astor staged a sentimental and stylish farewell dinner for his happy crew, with reporters allowed on board only during dessert to pester the president-elect. Roosevelt exulted over his "perfectly grand" two weeks of fishing, swimming, and conviviality, taking considerable pride in the fact that he "didn't even open a briefcase!"

But that very night, February 15, the looming pressures of the presidency called him away from festivities and friends. Leaving the dock at nine o'clock, FDR got into a green Buick convertible for a short ride to Bayfront Park. He had agreed to address the American Legion's annual encampment, which swelled with curious locals to a throng of more than twenty-five thousand—reportedly the largest crowd in Miami history to that time. They waited nearly three hours for the famous guest's arrival before the little motorcade of three cars began parting the crowds and crawling toward the illuminated bandstand, where festive strands of red, white, and blue lights had been arranged to honor the man of the hour.

In the vehicle right behind Roosevelt's open car, Ray Moley, the Columbia professor who led his "Brains Trust" of academic advisors, rode with Vincent Astor. Both remembered speaking about how easy it would be for some maniac to take a shot at the president-elect in the dark, tropical night in this crowded, chaotic situation. An American Legion drum-and-bugle corps played patriotic favorites while the spectators sang and cheered. Then Gus Gennerich, the big, burly New York City cop who'd been Roosevelt's personal bodyguard for the four years since he took over as governor, lifted his boss to a perch on top of the backseat. From that position, more of his eager admirers could watch his spotlit smile when he spoke.

To the disappointment of the crowd, the president-elect offered only brief, forgettable remarks, lasting less than two minutes. He shared his pride and delight over all the fish he'd reeled in during his Caribbean vacation, and expressed some chagrin over the weight he gained in the process. He also pledged that "one of my first official duties will be taking the ten pounds off" while promising to make a return visit to Florida during his first year as president and earning polite applause from the crowd.

Considering the late hour and Roosevelt's plan to take an overnight train to New York, he didn't want the occasion to drag on, but his aides found it impossible to whisk him away from the people who had waited to get a glimpse of the nation's new leader. The mayor of Chicago, Anton "Tony" Cermak, enjoying his own Florida vacation, sidled up to the Buick and made a special point of trying to talk to Governor Roosevelt. For one thing, he wanted to make peace after having ardently opposed FDR's nomination at the Chicago convention. He also meant to plead for federal aid for the collapsing Windy City schools.

But before His Honor could make his case, a newsreel crew pushed through the milling crowd, and the lead reporter clambered onto the trunk to approach Roosevelt, who remained immobile on his perch behind the backseat. The insistent newsman pleaded that his film crew had missed recording the president-elect's brief remarks because of some equipment problems, and now wanted FDR to repeat them, on camera. Despite anguished pleas about traveling a thousand miles to get those few precious seconds of footage, FDR turned them down, with mounting irritation. He looked over to his bodyguard to help facilitate a timely escape, and the loyal Gus Gennerich tenderly, expertly grabbed the governor's arms and helped him slide down into place in the backseat—and in the process very probably saved his life.

Instead of his whole upper body offering a large target when sitting on top of the car, now only the leonine head was barely visible, mostly obscured by the press of bystanders surging close to the Buick. This included Mayor Cermak, who finally finished his quick chat with the president-elect and turned to begin walking away. Another Democratic Party official had just launched an attempt to hand Roosevelt a six-foot-long scroll with signatures of local supporters and wishes for success to the nation's new leader.

At precisely that moment, a loud popping sound caused all heads to turn. Roosevelt himself initially assumed someone had lit a firecracker in the midst of the celebratory occasion; others suspected that one of the magnesium flashbulbs commonly used in 1933 had just exploded with louder-than-normal force.

A brief pause followed that first blast before four more gunshots rang out in quick succession. Mayor Cermak staggered forward a few steps, as friends tried to steady him; by the time he fell to the ground, the blood on the right side of his chest had already soaked through his white shirt. Within seconds, the pressing crowd had ducked or run for cover. The screams started closer to the car and then spread through the thousands in the park like a rolling wave of panic. One woman shrieked over the melee: "Don't let him kill Roosevelt!"

At the center of confusion, Roosevelt's unmistakable voice rose above the din. "I'm all right," he shouted, to reassure the bystanders. "I'm all right!"

Nevertheless, Gus Gennerich threw his beefy form as a human shield over FDR's body and yelled for the driver, a Miami police officer, to push the car into gear and "get him out of here!" But the president-elect quickly countermanded the order. "I called to the chauffeur to stop. He did—about fifteen feet from where we started," FDR told the *New York Times* shortly after the incident. "Looking back, I saw Mayor Cermak being carried. I motioned to have him put in the back of the car.... He was alive but I didn't think he was going to last. I put my left arm around him and my hand on his pulse, but I couldn't find any pulse.... For three blocks I believed his heart had stopped. After we had gone another block, Mayor Cermak straightened up and I got his pulse. I held him all the way to the hospital and his pulse constantly improved. I talked to him all the way. I remember I said, 'Tony, keep quiet—don't move. It won't hurt if you keep quiet.'"

At Jackson Memorial Hospital, the doctors praised Roosevelt for keeping the wounded mayor from going into shock. The five bullets directed at the president-elect had wounded six people all together, one of them ricocheting off the trunk of the car where Roosevelt had been seated moments before. Most grievously injured were Mabel Gill, the wife of a local power company executive, and Cermak.

FDR waited at the hospital until the doctors wheeled Cermak out of the emergency room, with assurances for his ultimate recovery. According to a story in the *New York Tribune*, an unnamed witness heard Cermak tell Roosevelt: "I'm glad it was me and not you, Mr. President." Later historians have concluded that the wounded mayor's press aide planted the story, to make his boss sound noble and selfless; in any event, Cermak still faced excruciating pain from the bullet that penetrated his rib cage and a desperate struggle to survive. The night of the shooting, Roosevelt visited the other wounded victims, expressing concern and encouragement, before returning to his luxury berth on the yacht *Nourmahal* near midnight, then boarding a morning train, unscathed and unshaken, for his trip north and his own "rendezvous with destiny."

"PUSHA DA BUTTON!"

The shooter who perpetrated the horrors of that bloody Florida night was a diminutive thirty-two-year-old unemployed bricklayer and anarchist named Giuseppe "Joe" Zangara.

Born in Ferruzzano, Italy, he lost his mother at age two and suffered brutal abuse from a perpetually angry father. The regular beatings may have contributed to the chronic, burning abdominal pain that afflicted him from childhood and became the source of constant complaint after he turned twenty. Never growing to more than five feet in stature, he immigrated to the United States with his uncle at age twenty-three and worked as a bricklayer in New Jersey. Determined to save every dollar he earned, he managed to accumulate $3,000 and moved to California and then Florida, hoping the warmer climates would improve his health and relieve his constant pain.

With the advent of the Depression, Joe Zangara could find no work and began gambling away his savings—losing $200 on horse races in just two days. In February 1933, he read an announcement of Roosevelt's planned appearance at Bayfront Park two days later and bought a silver .32-caliber pistol for $8 at a North Miami Avenue pawnshop. With the new gun concealed in the pocket of his loose-fitting pants, he arrived early at Bayfront Park and tried to slither and slide his way to the front of the crowd, drawing as close as possible to the side of the bandstand where the spotlights awaited the president-elect.

As he tried to push to the very front, a tourist from Iowa named H. L. Edmunds blocked his way, reminding Zangara that the front seats were reserved for women and children and that he was showing bad manners. The would-be assassin had to settle for a position no more than ten yards from the back of Roosevelt's Buick. After the president-elect arrived, Zangara tried to scout out a clear line of fire, but two or three rows of adults, virtually all of them taller than he was, blocked his view. In desperation, as FDR finished his brief words, Zangara stood up on a rickety chair, looking over the large hat of a doctor's wife who stood just in front of him. That woman, Lillian Cross, saw the strange and unkempt little man teetering on the chair and drawing his gun; she apparently deflected his arm with her handbag and became an instant national hero. In his numerous jailhouse confessions, however, the foiled assassin refused to credit her: "When I fired the first shot, the chair I was standing on moved and the result was it caused me to spoil my aim."

At that point, a middle-aged carpenter from Miami, Thomas Armour, reached up and began struggling with the gunman, making sure that the last four shots never found their intended target. He also helped wrestle the little man to the ground, with the crowd yelling to "Lynch him!" or "Cut his throat." Three policemen handcuffed the suspect to the outside rack on one of the cars in FDR's motorcade; by the time he arrived at the station, most of his clothing had been ripped away.

In jail, Zangara proudly admitted his crimes, and claimed that he had purchased another pistol ten years before in an attempt to kill Italy's king Victor Emmanuel. "I have always hated the rich and powerful," he said. "I do not hate Mr. Roosevelt personally. . . . I hate all officials and everybody who is rich. . . . Since my stomach hurt I get even with capitalists by kill the president. My stomach hurt a long time."

Since he never contested his guilt, no trial was necessary, and the defiant anarchist received a sentence of eighty years of hard labor, the maximum for multiple counts of attempted murder. On the way out of the courtroom, he shouted to the bench: "Oh judge, don't be stingy. Give me a hundred years." Judge E. C. Collins replied, "Maybe there will be more later."

Mayor Anton Cermak's deteriorating condition made those words prophetic. On March 4, FDR took the oath of office as president of the United States and told the economically paralyzed nation: "The only thing we have to fear is fear itself." Immediately after the ceremony, the new chief executive called Cermak to check on his recovery. "Tell Chicago I'll pull through," the mayor reportedly said from his hospital bed. "This is a tough old body of mine and a mere bullet isn't going to pull me down." Less than forty-eight hours later, at the very dawn of the New Deal, the Chicago pol who took a bullet meant for Roosevelt succumbed to his infected wounds.

The very next day, Zangara returned to his Miami courtroom for resentencing, this time based on the charge of murder. The sentence of "death by electrocution" was pronounced three days later. On hearing his fate, the killer yelled back at the judge: "You give me electric chair. I no afraid of that chair! You're one of the capitalists. You is crook man too. Put me in electric chair. I no care!"

On Monday morning, March 20, Zangara walked into the death chamber at Florida State Prison that housed "Old Sparky," the electric chair used for the state's executions between 1924 and 2000. He angrily refused the services of an attending Catholic priest meant to ready him for death. "Get the hell out of here, you son of a bitch!" he yelled. "I go sit down all by myself."

When the guards placed a black hood over his face, he shouted: "Viva Italia! Goodbye to all poor peoples everywhere."

The sheriff asked if the killer had any last words for history. "Pusha da button!" he yelled. "Pusha da button!"

The officials pronounced him dead at 9:27 a.m.—just thirty-five days after he came close to murdering the president-elect of the United States.

"I HAVE NEVER IN MY LIFE SEEN ANYTHING MORE MAGNIFICENT"

FDR himself seldom spoke of his close brush with death in Miami, but his aides and associates more than made up for him.

Ray Moley, the Brains Trust boss who had ridden in the car right behind Roosevelt on the way to the band shell at Bayfront Park, described his astonishment at his chief's display of courage and calm. They tried to relax with him back on Vincent Astor's yacht after the shock and menace of a bloody night. "All of us were prepared, sympathetically, for any reaction that might come from Roosevelt now that the tension was over and he was alone with us," he wrote years later. "There was nothing. Not so much as the twitching of a muscle to indicate that it wasn't any other evening in any other place. Roosevelt was simply himself—easy, confident, poised, to all appearances unmoved."

Seven years later, Moley broke sharply with the New Deal, becoming an outspoken conservative and, eventually, a prominent contributor to William F. Buckley's *National Review*. But despite his second thoughts on policy issues, he remained an unabashed admirer of FDR's character, especially in the face of danger, adversity, and trial. "FDR had talked to me once or twice during the campaign about the possibility that someone would try to assassinate him. But it is one thing to talk philosophically about assassination and another thing to face it. I confess that I have never in my life seen anything more magnificent than Roosevelt's calm that night on the *Nourmahal*."

Perhaps FDR's courage and calm in the face of physical danger related to his deep connection with his cousin Theodore. They shared many milestones—state legislator, assistant secretary of the navy, governor of New York, vice presidential candidate, and president—but now came a connection that seemed stranger still: narrowly surviving serious murder attempts within weeks of the climax of a presidential campaign. The experience also linked FDR to his future friend Winston Churchill, who unforgettably declared: "Nothing in life is so exhilarating as to be shot at without result."

The Miami events sent FDR to the inauguration platform with an intensified sense of providential purpose. As his biographer Jean Edward Smith summarized the national reaction, FDR's "cheerful contempt for danger brought forth a national surge of confidence. It was abundantly clear that FDR lacked physical fear, and his courage rallied the country behind him. It provided a tonic on the eve of the inauguration; a vital pickup for a nation grappling with unprecedented unemployment, widespread hunger and need, and a banking system that teetered on the brink of collapse."

Letters poured in to Roosevelt, discerning God's Hand in the protection of the new president. Joseph Williams wrote: "Just as God made You the President of the American people, as He preserved You at Miami, I feel sure that he has destined You to be the Saviour of Our Country." From New Haven, Anne Bodek rejoiced that "God saved you, not only the dear God above, but that little lady Mrs. Cross. Now you'll be one of our greatest presidents in history."

Around the country, press and public marveled at the tiny twists that enabled FDR's survival.

Had FDR grudgingly agreed to go along with the newsreel crew and repeated his brief speech for their cameras, he would have exposed himself to fatal fire. If Gus Gennerich hadn't lowered his boss into the Buick's backseat just when he did, moments before the shots began; if a tourist from Iowa hadn't blocked Zangara's push to the front rows, scolding the odd stranger on his bad manners; if Lillian Cross hadn't deflected his arm with her handbag as he began shooting; if the gunman hadn't teetered on his flimsy wooden chair . . . If all this intricate choreography hadn't fallen so precisely into place, Cactus Jack Garner might well have taken the oath of office seventeen days later on the East Portico of the Capitol.

And the very question of Garner's potential succession to the presidency in FDR's place comes with its own inescapable aura of eerie and mysterious coincidence: the Twentieth Amendment to the Constitution won final ratification just twenty-four days before Zangara drew his silver pistol and fired into the darkness at Bayfront Park. That newly ratified amendment established for the first time in the Republic's history a clear procedure on what to do if a president-elect perishes after his selection by the Electoral College but before inauguration day. In that case the vice president–elect takes the place of the fallen leader and serves out his term. Had the Miami incident occurred just four weeks before, and proven fatal to FDR, confusion over the proper presidential succession could have added constitutional chaos to the nation's woes before inauguration day.

"HINGE OF FATE"

But even if Congress and the judiciary would have known what to do thanks to the amendment's timely passage, it is hard to imagine that John Nance Garner would have known how to handle the presidency with anything like Roosevelt's assurance, charisma, and flexibility.

In direct contrast to FDR's determination to expand the reach of the federal government and the presidency, the Texas Coolidge had a visceral distrust of Washington's intrusion into personal affairs. He gave only three stump speeches during the campaign of 1932 and those went so badly that Democratic Party officials sent him home to

Uvalde for the duration. There, he complained to all who would listen about the indignities of a vice presidential nomination and the uselessness of the office itself.

At the end of two terms as the long-suffering veep, Garner made a doomed attempt to challenge FDR for the presidential nomination when Roosevelt won his third term in 1940, but after that Cactus Jack enjoyed a long, healthy, and wealthy retirement, finally expiring just two weeks shy of his ninety-ninth birthday. In 1960, he was still spry and opinionated enough to advise his fellow Texan Lyndon Johnson to turn down John Kennedy's offer of the vice presidency. Being VP, he declared, "isn't worth a pitcher of warm piss." Reporters of the time thoughtfully cleaned up this salty remark by substituting "bucket of warm spit" for Garner's original language—a slightly more genteel, if less emphatic, way of making the same point.

Meanwhile, Garner's presidency-that-never-was plays a significant role in the brilliant 1962 novel *The Man in the High Castle* by the tormented mystic and science fiction writer Philip K. Dick. Adapted in 2016 as a wildly popular and critically acclaimed television series, the story conjures an alternate reality following total victory by Nazi Germany and Imperial Japan in World War II. The pivotal event that determines this dire outcome is the assassination of Franklin D. Roosevelt by Giuseppe Zangara.

The characters in the book struggle against the oppressive Japanese regime that rules the western United States and the German overlords who dominate the East Coast and Midwest. One of the few meager sources of hope in occupied America is an underground novel that sketches an alternate reality to the alternate reality—a sequence of events in which America actually prevailed in the devastating global conflict.

How? In Philip K. Dick's fantasies, the future of all humanity hinged on the brief encounter between Roosevelt and Zangara in a Miami park. "If Joe Zangara had missed him, he would have pulled America out of the Depression and armed it," explains one of his most sympathetic characters while chafing under her Japanese rulers. "Roosevelt would have been a terribly strong President. As strong as Lincoln . . . The book is fiction. I mean, it's in novel form. Roosevelt isn't assassinated in Miami; he goes on and is reelected in 1936, so he's President until 1940, until during the war. Don't you see? He's still President when Germany attacks England and France and Poland. And he sees all that. He makes America strong. Garner was a really awful President. A lot of what happened was his fault."

It doesn't take a science fiction writer to surmise that Cactus Jack, with his mildly isolationist streak and his background in cheerfully corrupt backroom politics, might well have become "a really awful President." One of the leading historians of the twentieth century, Arthur M. Schlesinger Jr., reached much the same conclusion. In a memorable presentation to the International Churchill Society he concluded: "It is true enough that personalities do play a role in history. . . . Would the next two decades have been the same had the automobile killed Winston Churchill in 1931 and the bullet killed Franklin Roosevelt in 1933? Would Neville Chamberlain or Lord Halifax have rallied Britain in 1940? Would John N. Garner have produced the New Deal and the Four Freedoms?"

In 1950, Churchill published the fourth volume of his magisterial history of World War II. He called it *The Hinge of Fate* because it described the turning point in the worldwide struggle to save Western civilization. Yet those fourteen anxious Depression months between Winston's "New York Misadventure" and Franklin's deliverance from the five close-range bullets fired in his direction represented a no less significant turning point, a more intimate, altogether unplanned "hinge of fate."

In describing his sudden selection as prime minister of the realm in May 1940, Churchill famously wrote: "I felt as if I were walking with destiny, and that all my past life had been but a preparation for this hour and for this trial."

No doubt he and his great collaborator, Franklin Roosevelt, already walked with destiny nine years before. Yet their experience clearly indicates that even great men should check oncoming traffic before they decide to cross the street.

"A BEAUTIFUL SILVER WATERFALL, THESE DIVE
BOMBERS COMING DOWN": The simultaneous attack
on the Japanese carriers *Akagi* and *Kaga* at the Battle of
Midway, June 4, 1942. Charcoal-and-chalk sketch by
Commander Griffith Bailey Coale, official U.S. Navy
combat artist.

7

The Five-Minute Miracle

The Midway Marvel Alters Everything

Any honest description of the Midway Atoll inevitably resorts to the word "desolate."

Lost in the vast emptiness of the North Pacific, these windblown specks of coral, rock, and sand amount to a combined landmass of just 2.4 square miles. But for three frantic days in 1942, three insignificant islands became the focus of one of history's most consequential confrontations. The outcome, which reversed the tide of war between America and Japan, hinged on five minutes of miracles: a concentrated cascade of coincidence and luck that still confounds analysts today.

The pattern of strange connections began long before the Second World War, when a Yankee sea captain pushed his seal-hunting expedition into uncharted waters. In 1859, N. C. Middlebrooks stumbled upon tiny islands clustered behind a coral reef and proceeded to claim them for himself and his country. Though later officially designated as the westernmost component of the Hawaiian Islands chain, the new discovery lay more than 1,200 miles from Honolulu and shared none of Hawaii's lush greenery or history of human habitation. Instead, Captain Middlebrooks found lonely dunes lightly covered with struggling grasses and shrubs that offered a convenient way station for thousands of ferociously cackling migratory birds.

Those birds, in turn, provided a convenient pretext for American conquest: the recently passed Guano Islands Act authorized that any American citizen chancing upon previously unclaimed territory with a significant accumulation of bird droppings could take official possession of the site under U.S. law. Neither Captain Middlebrooks nor any subsequent entrepreneur ever attempted to exploit the vital guano resources of the newly mapped atoll, but in August 1867, the secretary of state decided to add the undeveloped islets to the growing American empire. In the midst of arduous negotiations over the purchase of an exponentially larger tract of land (later called Alaska), William Henry Seward took time to secure congressional approval for the annexation of the atoll, already designated "Midway" because of its geographic location roughly halfway between California and the mainland of Asia.

Noting this advantageous position, a private company got money from Congress in 1871 to dredge through the reefs and establish a mid-Pacific coaling station, but the effort proved a total failure. A handful of other workers turned up in 1903 and planted some nonnative trees as they toiled to lay cable for a transpacific telegraph; that same year, the navy opened its own radio station on the islands.

As tension mounted with Japan in the late 1930s, Franklin Roosevelt ordered construction of airstrips, gun emplacements, and a seaplane base, covering nearly the entire surface of the unlovely islands. In response, the population of this remote American outpost exploded to 437.

Today, residents of the islands number no more than sixty, most of them engaged in operating the Midway Atoll National Wildlife Refuge and Battle of Midway National Memorial. There, a few modest plaques and displays quietly commemorate the three days in June 1942 when some 250 ships, carrying one hundred thousand military personnel, American and Japanese, collided in mortal combat to decide control of Midway's desolation and with it, the fate of the world.

"I SHALL RUN WILD FOR THE FIRST SIX MONTHS"

For Admiral Isoroku Yamamoto, the charismatic naval commander who became a national icon after his brilliantly executed sneak attack on Pearl Harbor, the remote enemy outpost on Midway Atoll never represented an especially tempting conquest to add to Japan's burgeoning colonial empire. His purpose in targeting the island base in the spring of 1942 wasn't to add real estate but rather to lure the still-crippled and ill-prepared American fleet into a desperate attempt to defend Midway. In open ocean, with his vastly superior and better-trained forces, Yamamoto felt certain that he could destroy the Yankee fleet, sending its few surviving big ships to the bottom of the ocean while any battered survivors limped back to Pearl Harbor. At that point, he could assemble his massive fleet to surge eastward, launching a virtually uncontested assault on Hawaii, with plenty of seasoned troops for landing and occupation. From there, according to the thinking of Yamamoto's colleagues in the Imperial High Command, the menace of bombing raids on California's aircraft- and ship-building industries, or even the destruction of the Panama Canal, could push the beaten Americans to cut their losses and sue for peace.

But Admiral Yamamoto knew better: he had spent more than five years in the United States as an economics student at Harvard and with two postings as a naval attaché in Washington. The descendant of a venerable samurai family and the adopted son of another, he learned to speak fluent English, traveled across the continent, and made extensive studies of American business and culture. In the process, he also developed a strong taste for American whiskey and gambling, favoring serious games of poker and bridge while occasionally joking he might leave the military to run a casino in Monaco. He once told a secretary at the Japanese embassy in Washington: "People who don't gamble aren't worth talking to."

In this context, he understood that a war with the Americans would amount to a long-shot bet with potentially dire consequences for Japan. He contemptuously disagreed with other military planners who chronically underestimated the Americans, dismissing the materialistic Yankees as soft, spoiled, and utterly lacking in the fierce warrior spirit that animated their own disciplined, dedicated armed forces.

Yamamoto had personally explored the prodigious productive power of the U.S. economy and the indescribable vastness of the North American landmass and warned against expectations of any quick or easy victory against the empire's Pacific Ocean rival. "Should hostilities once break out between Japan and the United States," he wrote, "it would not be enough that we take Guam and the Philippines, nor even Hawaii and San Francisco. To make victory certain, we would have to march into Washington and dictate the terms of peace in the White House."

Since he disregarded the idea of capturing the White House as preposterous and inconceivable, he saw no prospect of final victory in a Japanese-American war. Just half a year before Pearl Harbor, Prime Minister Fumimaro Konoe asked Yamamoto whether the world-class naval resources he had assembled could prevail against the unready Americans. His famous reply proved uncannily prophetic: "If I am told to fight regardless of the consequences, I shall run wild for the first six months or a year, but I have utterly no confidence for the second and third years of the fighting," he responded. The Battle of Midway concluded on June 7, 1942—exactly six months after the attack on Pearl Harbor brought the outraged American colossus into the war.

But first came Admiral Yamamoto's promised half year of running wild.

Victor Davis Hanson describes the results in his provocative book *The Second World Wars*, noting the weeks immediately following Pearl Harbor, with the mighty Imperial fleet "easily erasing the old European colonial and American spheres of influence. Naval superiority meant virtually unopposed landings at the Philippines, Thailand, Malaysia, the Dutch East Indies, Wake Island, New Britain, the Gilbert Islands, Guam, and Hong Kong. . . . In just four early naval battles preceding the Battle of the Coral Sea—at Pearl Harbor, Singapore, in the Indian Ocean and the Java Sea—they sank or grounded six Allied battleships, one carrier, one battle cruiser, six cruisers, and five destroyers, and killed over six thousand British, Dutch, Commonwealth, and American seamen, all without suffering a single ship lost and fewer than two hundred dead."

"AS GOOD AS LOST"

With that casualty ratio of thirty to one, the empire's formidable propaganda machine promoted the Imperial Navy's triumphs so effectively that even Western war correspondents began to believe the claims of Japanese invincibility. After the Battle of the Coral Sea in the first days of May, Emperor Hirohito publicly congratulated his navy on another splendid victory and Tokyo gloated over the sinking of both American and British battleships. Actually, no Allied battleships had even been in the area, let alone sunk, and the Americans fought the Imperial Navy to a draw that turned back, or at least delayed, their relentless push toward Australia.

Nevertheless, Adolf Hitler himself gloated over the reported results in the Coral Sea and hailed the devastation of the common enemy. The Führer wrote: "After this new defeat, the United States warships will hardly dare to face the Japanese fleet again, since any United States warship which accepts action with the Japanese naval forces is as good as lost."

The losses had been appalling on the American side, particularly at Pearl Harbor, of course. There, eight battleships had been sunk or severely damaged, with 188 aircraft totally destroyed, and another 159 planes knocked out of commission. At the Battle of the Coral Sea, off the northeast coast of Australia, the mighty carrier *Lexington* went down and the *Yorktown* appeared to be fatally damaged. According to Japanese intelligence estimates in May, before they set out on their Midway expedition, the entire remaining strength of the U.S. Pacific Fleet included no more than three carriers (and probably just two), perhaps two battleships, thirteen cruisers, and fourteen destroyers—no more than forty fighting ships in all.

Against this underwhelming force, Admiral Yamamoto put to sea with the largest armada ever seen in the Pacific—and perhaps the largest naval force gathered for a single mission in the history of the world: 190 ships, including 8 carriers, 11 battleships, 23 cruisers, 65 destroyers, and nearly 700 planes. This enormous fleet planned to consume more fuel in this one decisive operation than the entire peacetime navy used in a full year. Pounding eastward across the Pacific, the ships stretched out into an enormous arc covering 1,800 miles.

At the center of this display of unparalleled nautical power, Admiral Yamamoto exercised personal command from the bridge of his behemoth flagship, the *Yamato*—the largest battleship ever built. Weighing more than seventy thousand tons, the seagoing monster boasted steel armor in many places that ran to sixteen inches thick, along with the most powerful guns ever employed in naval warfare, with barrels nearly seventy feet long. The elite crew ran to 2,800.

The *Yamato* and its supporting vessels, known as "the Main Body," rode four hundred miles behind the Kido Butai, the carrier striking force, led by the four finest aircraft carriers in the Imperial Japanese Navy, with 261 planes between them. The plan called for using these planes to bomb and strafe the American base on the Midway Atoll, followed by marines in landing craft to occupy the little islands. That, in turn, would lure the remaining American fleet out of Pearl Harbor in a doomed, belated effort to defend or recapture the outpost. While fully engaged with the superior Japanese forces of the Kido Butai, the Main Body would arrive with its awesome firepower to finish the job—the total destruction of the U.S. Navy in the Pacific.

On board his gigantic flagship, Admiral Yamamoto meant to supervise that destruction personally as the natural conclusion of his six months of "running wild" against the British and the Americans. The decisive battle would also echo his first triumphant experience of combat some thirty-seven years before. In 1905, as a freshly minted twenty-one-year-old officer, he lost two fingers of his left hand in the Battle of Tsushima Strait, where the Russian czar lost virtually his entire navy in the lopsided victory that dramatized Japan's glorious emergence as a world power.

Like most inveterate gamblers, Yamamoto relied on superstition to improve his odds: in order to reprise the victorious heroics of his youth, he selected the precise anniversary of Tsushima—May 27—to launch his strike on Midway and American possessions that lay beyond.

In fact, Seward's other acquisition—the immense, forbidding, lightly guarded Territory of Alaska—became a secondary target of the Japanese armada. Many military historians believe that Yamamoto ordered a simultaneous attack on the Aleutian Islands as a diversion, to force the already overmatched Americans to divide and weaken their defensive forces. Others argue that he envisioned a potential pincers movement, with the victorious Japanese sweeping south and east from Alaska while the bulk of their forces surged north and east from Hawaii, converging on the mainland to devastate California at both ends, and to end the war.

On June 2, President Franklin Delano Roosevelt sent a blunt warning to General Douglas MacArthur in Australia, who had only recently evacuated the Philippines: "It looks, at this moment, as if the Japanese Fleet is heading toward the Aleutian Islands or Midway and Hawaii, with a remote possibility it may attack Southern California or Seattle by air."

"ON THE VERGE BETWEEN BRILLIANCE AND BEING CRAZY"

FDR knew of those dire possibilities not through spy planes or satellites (which didn't exist during World War II), but from brilliant, indefatigable code breakers (who very fortunately did). Joseph Rochefort dropped out of high school and lied about his age to enlist in the navy at the end of World War I; his passion for crossword puzzles led a friend to recommend him for training in the emerging science of cryptography. In the interwar period, the navy sent him to Asia to learn the Japanese language and to apply his talents to monitoring the aggressive rising power in the Pacific. Earning the rank of commander, he won assignment to "Station HYPO," the crowded, top secret, below-ground bunker down a flight of stairs and behind a guarded steel door in a hidden corner of the Pearl Harbor base, where Rochefort toiled tirelessly to penetrate the heavily encrypted codes that the

Imperial Japanese Navy used to communicate with its far-flung forces. Empowered to fill the fluorescent-lit "dungeon" with handpicked obsessives and eccentrics, Rochefort slept on a cot beside his perpetually cluttered desk. He became notorious for wearing slippers and a bright red smoking jacket over his rumpled khaki uniform, a costume that provided plenty of pockets for his pipe and tobacco pouch; the blue clouds of fragrant smoke that surrounded him day and night aided his concentration. A sign on a colleague's nearby desk proclaimed YOU DON'T HAVE TO BE CRAZY TO WORK HERE BUT IT HELPS A HELL OF A LOT, and Rochefort himself later recalled that his most valuable associates lived "on the verge between brilliance and being crazy."

Despite the persistent skepticism of top navy brass, and especially on the part of intelligence chiefs nearly five thousand miles away in Washington, the unorthodox puzzle solvers in the cramped chaos of the dungeon produced remarkable results. They managed to decipher the most important Japanese codes at least two months before Yamamoto launched his strike on Midway and the Aleutians, but the authorities in the Navy Department in the nation's capital refused to accept their conclusions. The chief of naval operations, Admiral Ernest King, naturally worried that the oddballs at HYPO had reached illogical or unreliable interpretations of the decoded data, or that the Japanese had sent false signals intended for interception, misleading the Americans as to the enemy's intentions and battle plans. The idea that a bold commander like Yamamoto would deploy nearly all of his overwhelming resources against a minor target like Midway seemed to make no sense, and King hesitated to launch a preemptive response to a threat that hadn't yet materialized.

Fortunately for Rochefort, his commanding officer at Pearl Harbor had developed enough respect for his resident mad genius to challenge the Washington higher-ups on his behalf. Admiral Chester Nimitz, commander in chief of the U.S. Pacific Fleet (or CINCPAC, in navy lingo), was as businesslike, unflappable, and by-the-book as Joe Rochefort was impulsive and unconventional. Known as "the Blue-Eyed Man" for his penetrating, Bunsen-burner gaze, Nimitz allowed the dungeon boys to stage a cunning ruse to validate their translation of hundreds of coded enemy messages. They ordered the local commander on Midway to send out a plain-language radio message falsely reporting that the atoll's desalinization plant had stopped working and the outpost faced an acute shortage of freshwater. Sure enough, the Japanese picked up the erroneous report and broadcast an encrypted transmission to the entire fleet that an important destination designated only as "AF" faced a lack of drinking water and the ships should prepare accordingly. This left no reasonable doubt that "AF" could only be Midway, and that the bulk of the Imperial Japanese Navy would be headed that way.

Nimitz moved decisively to get there ahead of them and to prepare a deadly surprise.

"WITH A FLY SWATTER AND A PRAYER"

But the first challenge to achieve that ambush involved repairing a precious, badly damaged carrier that the Japanese thought they had already sunk. In the Battle of the Coral Sea, the *Yorktown* managed to dodge seven enemy torpedoes but took a single bomb that penetrated her flight deck, exploding below and killing or wounding some sixty sailors almost immediately. The survivors battled desperately against the resulting flames, which raged long enough to threaten the big ship's survival. Taking on water, the *Yorktown* still managed to limp back toward Pearl Harbor, leaving a streak of leaking oil that extended for nearly a mile behind her like an ugly tail.

Navy inspectors checked the damage in dry dock and initially wanted two to three months to make the crippled craft seaworthy and battle ready. Under pressure from Nimitz, and with round-the-clock work schedules, they revised the timetable to two weeks. But the CINCPAC scalded them with his burning blue eyes and ordered that the *Yorktown*, in whatever state of readiness, must sail in three days or not at all. Nimitz demanded Band-Aids and patches that could get the carrier to Midway, not a thorough restoration. Rather than try to restitch every ruptured seam, the frantic repair crews installed one huge steel plate that would serve to cover the most gaping wounds.

The navy secured every available worker in Honolulu, about 1,400 of them, toiling with no breaks or lapses. At night, giant flood-

LIKE A PRESUMED-DEAD ADVERSARY SUDDENLY REEMERGING FROM
THE GRAVE: The aircraft carrier *Yorktown*, severely damaged at the Battle of the
Coral Sea, in dry dock to receive emergency repairs, May 29, 1942. The next day,
she left Pearl Harbor to play a fateful role in the Battle of Midway.

lights illuminated the work, defying the blackout meant to protect the islands against potential Japanese bombers. Hundreds from the ship's crew joined the craftsmen who swarmed over the crippled carrier, some of whom worked twenty-four or even thirty-six hours at a time. After three days of hysterical but exhilarating intensity, the flattop left the dry dock and put out to sea. Just six years after its initial launch, the battered war machine didn't look or feel like new, but its mere presence might unsettle the overconfident Japanese, like a presumed-dead adversary suddenly reemerging from the grave.

The *Yorktown*, along with the other two available aircraft carriers, the *Enterprise* and the newly commissioned *Hornet*, and their task forces, proceeded to their meeting point, about three hundred miles northeast of where HYPO's intelligence led them to expect the Japanese striking force. The Americans designated the site of their rendez-vous "Point Luck," because all personnel knew they would need outrageous good fortune to stand any chance of prevailing, or even surviving, the coming confrontation with the far superior Japanese forces.

Robert Casey, a civilian reporter assigned to the heavy cruiser *Salt Lake City*, wrote in his diary: "As usual, we seem to be holding the short end of the stick, this time shorter than usual. We muster carriers, cruisers, and about half a dozen destroyers to face one of the biggest fleets ever turned loose on the Pacific. An armada that rates as a good half of the Jap fleet and we're meeting it as usual with a fly swatter and a prayer."

Fighter pilot Scott McCuskey experienced a similar sense of foreboding. He later recalled "a profound feeling of doom. This whole situation looked desperate. Admiral Nimitz was throwing everything he had against the superior Japanese force approaching Midway Island—including the battle-damaged *Yorktown*."

On board the destroyer *Aylwin*, Lieutenant Burdick Brittin expressed similar anxiety after the ship's sealed orders had been opened. "Lord! This IS the real thing," he wrote in his diary. "We have history in the palm of our hands during the next week or so. If we are able to keep our presence unknown to the enemy and surprise them with a vicious attack on their carriers, the U.S. Navy should once more be supreme in the Pacific. But if the Japs see us first and attack us with their overwhelming number of planes, knock us out of the picture, and then walk in to take Midway, Pearl will be almost neutralized and in dire danger—I can say no more—there is too much tension within me—the fate of our nation is in our hands."

On the Japanese side, officers likewise understood that their complex, coordinated strike against the already reeling Americans would decide the outcome of the war. Before setting sail from the crowded, humming naval base at Kure near Hiroshima, Admiral Yamamoto risked public scandal by sending for the celebrated geisha Chiyoko Kawai, who had been his adored companion for nearly a decade. While devoted to his wife, Reiko, and their four children, Yamamoto, the gambler, treated Chiyoko as an even higher priority; he spent four idyllic days with her at a rustic mountain inn before launching the cross-Pacific attack he had so meticulously planned. "I myself will devote all my energy to fulfill my duty to my country to the very end," he wrote to her from the bridge of his colossal flagship, the *Yamato*, "and then I want us to abandon everything and escape from the world to be really alone together."

Meanwhile, the men under his command felt none of the uncertainty that afflicted the Americans. As the Kido Butai steamed toward Midway, Commander Magataro Koga of the guard destroyer *Nowaki* noted: "Our hearts burn with the conviction of sure victory."

The first step toward achieving that sure victory involved the destruction of Midway's air base and its quick subjugation by the Midway Occupation Force of fifty-one thousand men available for that purpose. At 4:30 in the morning of June 4, Admiral Chuichi Nagumo, the aristocratic, hotheaded commander of the carrier striking force, dispatched 108 planes to launch the attack. The mix of dive-bombers, torpedo bombers, and their protective fighters reached their target on schedule at dawn but not before the land-based American planes, alerted by radar and the superior U.S. intelligence, scrambled to meet them.

With aid from accurate antiaircraft fire from the base, the Americans managed to destroy eleven of the Japanese attackers while heavily damaging fourteen more. Nevertheless, the dawn raid inflicted widespread destruction, despite leaving the only runway virtually untouched. Nagumo meant to use it for his own aircraft after occupation, so the American bombers could still use it to refuel and attack the Japanese invasion force. Returning to their carriers with fuel running low, the surviving aircraft of the Kido Butai informed their commanders that Midway couldn't be neutralized without a second-wave attack.

Meanwhile, some thirty American bombers launched from the base in the darkness before the first Japanese strike found their way to the Japanese carriers at 7:10 in the morning and launched their own attack. The enemy's fast and maneuverable Zero fighter planes made relatively short work of the American intruders, but a single B-26, after serious damage from flight-deck antiaircraft fire, made an apparent suicide run at Nagumo's flagship, the *Akagi*. Making no effort to alter its trajectory, the doomed aircraft aimed directly toward the carrier's deck and barely missed crashing directly into its bridge and almost certainly killing Admiral Nagumo and his entire command staff.

This narrow escape may have persuaded the admiral to disregard his explicit order from Yamamoto to keep half of his aircraft in reserve, armed for antiship operations, in case the American fleet got close enough to threaten the Kido Butai.

Instead, moments after his close call on the bridge, he ordered his reserve aircraft rearmed with contact-fused general-purpose bombs for use against land targets: Nagumo had decided to finish off the already battered base at Midway before worrying about American carriers that might, or might not, be lurking in some still-undisclosed location. With that began "a fantastic chapter of accidents and blunders," described thirteen years later by two of Nagumo's most capable and decorated subordinates in their retroactive analysis of the battle.

The process of refitting the planes, loading them with their new bombs, and preparing them for launch normally took more than an hour. But after less than thirty minutes, at 7:40, came a radio report from a scout plane of a sizable American fleet to the east. The chain of command delayed some twenty minutes before confronting the admiral with this disturbing news, perhaps fearing his volcanic reaction.

When the already rattled Nagumo finally received the report, he immediately reversed his recent order to rearm the bombers with land-based ordnance to prepare them for a second attack on Midway. The American warships offered a higher-priority target. He demanded that the scout plane determine the specific composition of the American force before he decided how to deploy his aircraft, and asked the already exhausted crews to go back to the original plan of equipping the planes with torpedoes and armor-piercing shells for use against enemy ships. As a decorated veteran of the engagement, Mitsuo Fuchida summed up the situation on the flight decks that frantic morning: it was "order; counter order; disorder." Another crucial half hour elapsed before the *Akagi* received signals that the American ships included a single carrier, with the one reconnaissance aircraft somehow failing to sight the other two.

The timing could hardly have been less propitious, because all four Japanese carriers now had to clear their decks to receive the incoming planes from the first Midway attack. If they failed to move aside or to stow the waiting aircraft belowdecks, the low-on-fuel returning pilots would be forced to ditch in the ocean, losing their planes if not their lives.

In the midst of this confusion, Nagumo ordered a change of course for the entire striking force, turning ninety degrees east-northeast to draw closer to the Americans. Minutes later, between 9:25 and 10:00, a wave of torpedo bombers from each of the American carriers, totaling forty-one planes, found their quarry and flew in low to drop their payloads among the Japanese flattops.

"A FEAST FOR CONDEMNED MEN"

The pilots of these American planes knew they had signed up for perhaps the most dangerous job in the military, especially on a run like this one with no accompanying fighters to protect them. On board the *Yorktown*, the torpedo pilots received a special breakfast of steak and eggs and one of them grimly described it as "a feast for condemned men." The night before, Torpedo Squadron Eight listened to a pre-battle briefing on board the *Hornet* from Lieutenant Commander John C. Waldron, a popular, forty-one-year-old officer who told his fliers to prepare for "the biggest battle of the war" that "may well be the turning point also." An Oglala Sioux on his mother's side, he graduated from the Naval Academy but supplemented his military career by studying law; he passed the bar and was raising a family. "My greatest hope," he told his men, "is that we encounter a favorable tactical situation, but if we don't and worse comes to worst, I want each one of us to do his utmost to destroy our enemies. If there is only one plane left to make a final run-in, I want that man to go in and get a hit. May God be with us all. Good luck, happy landings, and give 'em hell."

They did just that as they swarmed around the huge Japanese ships, but their slow-moving, lightly armed Douglas Devastators proved no match for the battle-tested Mitsubishi Zeros that immediately rose to counter them. Though the fliers managed to come in low and close, surrounding the carriers as they'd been instructed, their notoriously ineffective Mark 13 torpedoes meant that even the most skillful, daring delivery of their precious payloads posed no major threat to the Japanese ships. In several cases the torpedoes actually hit the armor of the enemy craft with an audible, sickening *clang*, but somehow failed to explode. Designed to travel below the sea's surface to mask their trajectory from the enemy, the self-propelled weapons sank gradually as they traveled; occasionally they passed directly *underneath* their intended targets, then dropped harmlessly to the ocean floor.

Despite a brutal cost in both human and material resources, the fearless waves of torpedo bombers scored not a single meaningful hit, while thirty-five of the forty-one planes either fell to enemy fire or ran out of fuel, forcing their pilots to splash down in the ocean rather than returning to the American fleet. As he seemed to have anticipated in his final briefing on board the *Hornet*, the capable, eloquent Lieutenant Commander Waldron perished in aerial combat, along with nearly his entire squadron.

As the few surviving Devastators scurried away from death and danger to seek the safety of familiar flight decks, the Japanese pilots and crew aboard their great carriers felt a moment of exultation and fury that recalled the glory of all their prior victories. They continued to run across the crowded decks, rushing to complete the complicated job of preparing and launching those long-delayed new waves of bombers and fighters. They had a right to expect that these superbly well-trained airmen, part of a vastly larger force, would deal a final, decisive blow against the vulnerable American fleet. Perhaps they already had.

Since well before dawn, the emperor's elite forces had been engaged in ceaseless combat. Some of the men checked their watches, which read 10:24—a time to savor what had turned out to be a morning of brilliant blue skies reflected in the sparkling Pacific, all elegantly ornamented by low-hanging, picturesque patches of gleaming white clouds at three thousand feet. Concerning this pregnant, pivotal moment, Rear Admiral Samuel Eliot Morison, a Harvard scholar and the official historian of the U.S. Navy, summarized its significance:

"For about 100 seconds," he wrote, "the Japanese were certain they had won the Battle of Midway, and the war."

And then the sky opened: those fluffy clouds had provided perfect cover for high-flying American dive-bombers.

"A BEAUTIFUL SILVER WATERFALL,
THESE DIVE BOMBERS COMING DOWN"

At first, the Japanese officers failed to spot them, including Mitsuo Fuchida, the expert aviator who had flawlessly led Yamamoto's attack on Pearl Harbor. Unable to fly at Midway because of his recent appendectomy, he paced and fretted on the deck of Nagumo's flagship, the *Akagi*, uneasy over the frustrating delays at dispatching planes to strike the American ships. "At 10.20, Admiral Nagumo gave the order to launch when ready," he recalled. "On *Akagi's* flight deck all planes were in position with engines warming up. The big ship began turning into the wind. Within five minutes all her planes would be launched. . . . At 10:24 the order to start launching came from the bridge by voice-tube. The air officer flapped a white flag and the first Zero fighter gathered speed and whizzed off the deck.

"At that instant, a lookout screamed, 'Hell-divers!' I looked up to see three black enemy planes plummeting towards our ship. Some of our machine guns managed to fire a few frantic bursts at them, but it was too late. The plump silhouettes of the American Dauntless dive-bombers quickly grew larger, and then a number of black objects suddenly floated eerily from their wings. Bombs! Down they came straight at me."

A total of forty-seven bombers from the various American carriers had arrived at the precise moment of the enemy's greatest vulnerability, just as the last of the doomed torpedo bombers had been shot down and chased away.

Even more remarkably, the Dauntless bombers had left their different flight decks at different times (with departures separated by more than an hour) and had all flown more than 170 miles on dramatically different routes, searching the open ocean for the Japanese fleet, and then, after more than two hours in the air, they chanced upon the Kido Butai—and each other—at exactly the same time.

Gordon Prange, professor of history at the University of Maryland and onetime chief historian on Douglas MacArthur's staff, described these coincidences with a touch of awe in his posthumously published book *Miracle at Midway* (1982). He observed with wonder that for the Japanese "the final debacle was due to a stroke of good luck on the United States side—the uncoordinated coordination of the dive bombers hitting three carriers at once while the torpedo strikes were still in progress. Except for those six short minutes, Nagumo would have been the victor, and all his decisions would have been accounted to him for righteousness."

An American admiral received those plaudits instead, and the battle-day decisions of Raymond Spruance proved not only righteous but wise. Another quirk of fate and inexplicable stroke of luck placed him in command of the *Enterprise* and the *Hornet* just days before the ships left Pearl Harbor for Midway. Their previous commander, Admiral William "Bull" Halsey, had contracted a painful case of shingles that forced him to spend the most crucial days of the war in the hospital rather than on the bridge. He recommended Spruance to take his place and Nimitz agreed, despite the new commander's lack of experience in naval aviation. The bookish, even-tempered officer, known for walking miles on his flight decks for exercise and meditation, later earned the nickname "the Quiet Admiral"—a sharp contrast to the impulsive, and sometimes explosive, temperament of Halsey. In reference to the movie stars of the day, Spruance reflected none of the macho swagger of John Wayne, and no trace of the dashing charisma of Errol Flynn, but instead embodied the quiet strength of Gary Cooper, with a touch of Jimmy Stewart's "aw shucks" humility. In *Pacific Crucible* (2012), an authoritative and hugely satisfying account of the first two years of the war against Japan, naval historian Ian W. Toll declares flatly: "In Raymond Spruance, Nimitz had discovered the most valuable American seagoing commander of the Second World War."

Ordered to attack the Japanese striking force as soon as he possessed even a remote chance of success, Spruance made the single most crucial decision of June 4. Though the range might have been extreme, with no assurance of his pilots' safe return, he decided in the predawn hours that they could conceivably find the lurking enemy and do some meaningful damage to their carriers. Rather than following the established protocols for naval aviation and directing the various squadrons to waste time assembling in the air in order to fly together toward the target, Spruance told each of them to proceed immediately on their missions without reference to the others. The different speeds and characteristics of the various planes (fighters, dive-bombers, and torpedo bombers) would have been tough to synchronize in any event, and the Quiet Admiral dispatched them on separate attacks with the hope that these sorties would continue over a long period to delay or eliminate the Imperial Japanese Navy's ability to launch a counterstrike.

Watching from the deck of an American cruiser in "the dawn's early light" of June 4, reporter Robert Casey saw the American planes depart, in wave after wave, rising into the sky and then heading in different directions. "It would seem that the carriers are sending up all they've got," he wrote. "The sky over toward the starboard horizon is filling up with little black crosses. . . . It's all spectacular and beginning to be thrilling. Few men, after all, have had a chance to look upon a spectacle like this. In the nature of things, few will look on anything like it again."

Each air group took its own course and followed an independent schedule, based on its leader's distinct (and widely diverging) solutions to the navigational challenges. The main strike force from *Hornet* missed the enemy entirely, going too far in the wrong direction before heading home with fuel running low. The ten fighter planes accompanying those squadrons all ran out of gas and ditched in the ocean, hoping for rescue that never came for most of them.

The pilots from the *Enterprise* faced similar frustrations, finding no trace of the enemy as they crisscrossed the skies above the empty ocean. Group Commander C. Wade "Mac" McClusky refused to abandon the search, even though he knew that emptying fuel tanks, enemy fire, or a combination of the two might make this a one-way trip for most of his fliers. At the very point of giving up, he felt a sudden, electrifying thrill of possibility and relief when he suddenly spotted a lone Japanese destroyer, the *Arashi*, far below. The fast-moving craft steamed at full speed to the north, while trailing a long, frothy white wake, which appeared from the skies like a sign carved onto the ocean's smooth surface.

Two hours earlier, Robert Casey had watched the planes take off and seen the symbol of crosses rising in the sky; now McClusky saw an arrow on the sea, pointing the way for his planes to follow. The single destroyer had separated from the Kido Butai in an unsuccessful attempt to drop a depth charge on an annoying American submarine. The small ship then struggled to rejoin its mighty carriers as quickly as possible, never spotting the Yankee planes that soared overhead, traveling above the cloud cover at a much faster rate of speed.

"As they approached a break in the clouds," Ian Toll writes, "the entire enemy fleet came into view beneath them, like a collection of toy boats on a pond." Bomber pilot Clarence Dickinson recalled the panoramic vision that spread below him. "Among those ships, I could see two long, narrow, yellow rectangles, the flight decks of carriers. Apparently, they leave the decks either the natural wood color or possibly they paint them a light yellow. But that yellow stood out on the dark blue sea like nothing you have ever seen. Then farther off I saw a third carrier."

And at the same time, McClusky spotted something even more important: additional American planes, from the two other carriers, arriving from different directions, unexpectedly, inexplicably, and displaying the "uncoordinated coordination" that seemed to point to victory as clearly as the wake-arrow in the ocean.

McClusky led his planes to attack with the sun behind them, to conceal their approach and blind the antiaircraft gunners who tried to shoot them down. They dived steeply, at a seventy-degree angle. Events unfolded so quickly, so unexpectedly, that it remains unclear which planes hit which ships, but all the bombers took pride in their work. Lieutenant Dickinson recalled, "I was making the best dive I had ever made. The people who came back said it was the best dive they had ever made. We were coming from all directions on the port side of the carrier, beautifully spaced."

To counteract any Zeros that might try to disrupt the "beautifully spaced" attacks, the Americans relied on the redoubtable Jimmy Thach, a crack fighter pilot from Arkansas who later rose to the rank of four-star admiral. From his cockpit, he watched and wondered as the magical five minutes unfolded, moved to an uncharacteristically poetic description. He noted "this glint in the sun, and it just looked like a beautiful silver waterfall, these dive bombers coming down. . . . I'd never seen such superb dive-bombing."

At the receiving end of the U.S. bombs, Fuchida watched the same scene with a very different reaction that mixed horror with disgust. He noted that the Japanese fighter planes had been busy finishing off the doomed American torpedo bombers so that they had no chance to build altitude to confront the cascade of dive-bombers who seemed to swoop down from above, magically, from all directions at once. "It may be said," he wrote years later, "that the American dive bombers' success was made possible by the earlier martyrdom of their torpedo planes."

"IT ALL HAPPENED SO QUICKLY"

The crowded condition of the flight decks contributed to the devastating results for the Japanese carriers: as harried crews were still working to fuel planes and to switch their armaments, much of the available space was filled with bombs, torpedoes, and gasoline tanks, dangerously exposed to the Dauntless bombers that plunged directly toward their targets. Even though the *Akagi* seems to have received only one direct hit, that single thousand-pound bomb did catastrophic damage. Crashing through the center of the flight deck, it penetrated into the upper hangar deck before exploding, triggering secondary explosions from fueled planes and stored ordnance. Admiral Nagumo's chief of staff, Ryunusuke Kusaka, reported "a terrific fire . . . bodies all over the place. . . . Planes stood tail up, belching livid flame and jet-black smoke . . . making it impossible to bring the fires under control."

Kaname Shimoyama, assigned to the hangar, remembered a feeling of utter helplessness on the part of the crew. "It all happened so quickly. The hangar was very dark, but engulfed in a sea of fire. . . . I thought that our carrier would sink at any moment." Some desperate sailors, terrified by the leaping flames, made doomed attempts to save themselves by jumping overboard.

Two other carriers in the striking force met similar, simultaneous fates: by 10:26 in the morning, the dive-bombers had also hit the *Kaga* and the *Soryu* with multiple strikes, lighting both great ships from stem to stern. "It all happened so quickly," as Shimoyama observed—so quickly that not even the returning American fliers knew for certain which diving planes had struck which particular targets.

The *Soryu*, which had taken three hits from thirteen planes in the course of three minutes, suffered an appalling 711 crew killed. Six hours later, crippled but still afloat, the stricken craft took a torpedo from a Japanese destroyer so it would never fall into enemy hands. The captain, Ryusaku Yanagimoto, refused pleas for his safe evacuation, and instead insisted on going down with his ship; he did so while lustily singing the Japanese national anthem as the carrier slipped beneath the waves.

An hour after that, at dusk, a second wave of American dive-bombers found the *Hiryu*, the only previously undamaged Japanese carrier, and struck her four times: the *Hiryu* sank at nine the next morning, with the bodies of 389 men still aboard.

All told, the Japanese lost 3,057 men—including many of the most valued and experienced pilots of the First Air Fleet. Their killed in action exceeded the 307 dead Americans by a ratio of almost ten to one. In addition to the destruction of all four carriers of Nagumo's Kido Butai, the Imperial Japanese Navy lost a heavy cruiser, with serious damage to another cruiser and to three destroyers. The 275 lost Japanese planes corresponded to the American sacrifice of 132, while the United States lost only two ships: the battered, heroic, hastily repaired carrier *Yorktown* and one escorting destroyer, both torpedoed by a Japanese submarine on their way back to Pearl Harbor.

In a matter of moments, the era of Japanese naval superiority in the Pacific had come to an abrupt, fiery, bloody, catastrophic conclusion. Steaming west to reunite with the powerful Main Body of the Imperial Navy's armada, and unready to face the wrath of his superior, Yamamoto, Admiral Nagumo announced his intention to take his own life and many of his staff officers shouted their readiness to join him. Chief of Staff Kusaka angrily rebuked them: "You are just like hysterical women," he declared. "First, you get excited over easy victories, and now you are worked up to commit suicide because of a defeat! This is no time for Japan for you to say such a thing."

Twenty-five months later, the arrogant and irascible admiral did take his own life, after another abject failure in the attempted defense of Saipan. Nagumo opted to place a bullet through his head rather than follow the traditional samurai method of seppuku by cutting open his belly.

In Tokyo, the Japanese government responded to the Midway debacle in a distinctly more modern fashion: with lies and laughably distorted propaganda. On June 6, Radio Tokyo broadcast an English-language announcement proclaiming that "six carriers of the United States Navy, which is very deficient in carriers, were sunk in a single smashing blow. Our fleet broke down the pitiful opposition of the United States fleet, bombarded the defenses of Midway and captured the islands with insignificant losses on our part. An attack has been started on Pearl Harbor and Honolulu."

Days later, Rear Admiral Tanetsugu Sosa wrote in one of Tokyo's popular newspapers: "Now that America's northern attack route against our country and the most important enemy base in the Pacific Ocean have been crushed by the Imperial Navy in the recent battles of Dutch Harbor and Midway, Japan can now concentrate on attacking the mainland of the United States. With its east coast constantly menaced by German and Italian warcraft and its west coast fully exposed to the possible attack by Japan, the United States has been driven between the devil and the deep sea."

It's unclear whether any responsible parties in the government or military actually believed such grotesque distortions but Admiral Isoroku Yamamoto most certainly did not. He continued to direct the empire's naval operations with his customary competence but with fading confidence in the ten months after Midway. In April 1943, after the bloody Japanese defeat on Guadalcanal, Yamamoto planned an inspection tour of Pacific facilities to boost morale. U.S. naval intelligence intercepted dispatches with the details of his schedule and successfully decoded the contents. President Franklin Roosevelt personally authorized a mission to remove the enemy's most capable officer from the field of battle: eighteen American planes ambushed his transport flight and shot it down over the jungle. Yamamoto never did get the chance to spend quiet time with his beloved geisha, or to indulge his fantasy of operating a casino in Monaco. But he did receive a state funeral, with many posthumous decorations, including Nazi Germany's Knight's Cross of the Iron Cross with Oak Leaves and Swords—the highest honor Adolf Hitler ever bestowed upon a foreigner.

"GOD'S SAMURAI"

For another Japanese hero, his nation's epic defeat at Midway carried not just strategic significance but deep spiritual meaning as well. Mitsuo Fuchida became a national symbol of courage and competence as the chief aviator at Pearl Harbor, personally transmitting the famous order "Tora! Tora! Tora!" to command his fellow pilots to follow his lead in the flawlessly executed sneak attack. Returning home in triumph, he received the supreme honor of a personal audience with the emperor. He meticulously prepared to lead the attacks on Midway, but suffered a life-threatening bout of appendicitis six days before the battle. Refusing an emergency flight to a Japanese hospital, he endured a shipboard appendectomy that forced him to view the aerial fight from the bridge of the *Akagi* rather than from the combat cockpit he preferred.

When American dive-bombers turned the flagship into a blazing wreck, leaping flames surrounded the bridge, and the surviving officers attempted to evacuate down a dangling rope. As Fuchida descended, a sudden explosion threw him down onto the burning deck, shattering both his ankles. After several months of hospitalization and recovery, he received a promotion to captain and took a post as a staff officer on Tinian, an island near Japanese-occupied Guam. Or-

"GOD'S SAMURAI": Captain Mitsuo Fuchida
(1902–1976), the highly decorated aviator in the
Imperial Japanese Navy, personally honored by the
emperor for leading the devastating attack on Pearl
Harbor. After suffering severe wounds at Midway and
witnessing the miraculous U.S. victory, he played a
prominent postwar role as an outspoken admirer of
America and celebrated Christian evangelist who
appeared on several occasions with Billy Graham.

dered to Tokyo just two weeks before the American invasion, he escaped the fate of all the other staff officers—who ritually disemboweled
themselves in a mass suicide after the enemy prevailed.

In the war's final days, he attended a military conference in Hiroshima so he could organize aerial defenses for a glorious last stand
against the invader. On the evening of August 5, 1945, he received
urgent orders to return to Tokyo, where, at breakfast the next morning, he heard the horrifying news: all the colleagues with whom he'd
interacted the day before, along with nearly one hundred thousand
more of their fellow citizens, perished in the world's first atom bomb
attack.

Retiring to the countryside, he resolved to set aside his military
honors and decorations and to pursue the onetime family business of
chicken farming. "It was a rainy day in my life," he later recalled, and
his inner landscape felt as damaged and devastated as the physical
scenery around him. "Life had no taste or meaning. . . . I had missed
death so many times and for what? What did it all mean?"

He got his answer in 1947, after General Douglas MacArthur

summoned him to testify in trials of Japanese war criminals. Fuchida had never been implicated in crimes of any kind, but he felt determined to defend his accused comrades in arms. "War is war," he reasoned, and planned to collect evidence to prove that Americans treated their prisoners of war with the same ferocious cruelty for which the Japanese officers now stood trial. Greeting more than a hundred returning POWs at Uraga Harbor, Fuchida reconnected with his former flight engineer, who had been presumed dead at the Battle of Midway. The survivor not only denied that the Americans practiced torture or abuse but spoke warmly of a young woman named Peggy Covell who cared for the captured Japanese "as a sister would treat a relative." Amazingly, her own parents, Christian missionaries in the Philippines, had been beheaded by soldiers of the Imperial Japanese Army just moments after praying that God should forgive their own executioners.

These stories, and the account of another American POW who had experienced his own "awakening to God" during his nearly four years of brutal captivity, helped Fuchida find a new purpose in his life. "That's when I met Jesus," he told *Stars and Stripes*, the military's official newspaper, in 1971. "Looking back, I can see now that the Lord had laid his hand upon me so that I might serve him."

From that realization in 1949 until his death at seventy-three in 1976, he devoted his life to Christian evangelism, working with Billy Graham and other famous preachers of the Gospel to tell his story to rapt audiences throughout the United States and Europe. He wrote several books and pamphlets, including *From Pearl Harbor to Calvary* and, for a broader audience, *Midway: The Battle That Doomed Japan*. A brief and admiring biography of Fuchida designated him as "God's Samurai."

He remained acutely aware of the way a few fateful seconds on June 4, 1942, utterly transformed both his own life and the life of his nation. "Five minutes!" he wrote. "Who would have believed that the tide of battle would shift in that brief interval of time?"

Even without undergoing religious conversions, other Japanese officers looked back on the miracle minutes that wrecked their hopes with similar awe and the same sense that the outcome reflected more than chance or miscalculation. Admiral Kusaka discerned in the Midway debacle "God's punishment for the sin of Hubris." After the war, a consensus emerged that the all-conquering Japanese military had been fatally infected by the dangerous "victory disease"—an assumption that no earthly power could overcome the empire's combination of skill and might. According to most postwar analysis, this defiant arrogance virtually assured humiliation. Commander Masataka Chihiya insisted that "there was nothing to wonder about" in the disastrous setback for the emperor's forces. "That defeat was . . . something pre-ordained."

"EVENTS DO NOT JUST HAPPEN"

More than two thousand years before the epic struggle in the Pacific, the Greek tragedian Sophocles concluded: "Fate has terrible power. . . . No fort will keep it out, no ships outrun it."

Immediately after the battle, Americans expressed a combination of wonderment, relief, and profound gratitude. Robert Casey reported: "It turns out that we have fought a major engagement—one of the biggest naval battles of all time. And miracle of miracles, we have won. It was too stupendous to contemplate as we lolled in a mist of nervous exhaustion, mumbling to one another in senseless monosyllables, falling to sleep over our coffee."

In Honolulu, Admiral Nimitz hesitated to credit himself for the victory. "We were shot with luck on the morning of June 4, when the fate of the operation was decided. . . . All that I can claim credit for, myself, is a very keen sense of the urgent need for surprise and a strong desire to hit the enemy carriers with our full strength as early as we could reach them." No one needed a reminder that the navy task forces had assembled at an open ocean rendezvous optimistically designated "Point Luck."

In a 2011 review in the journal *Naval History*, Robert J. Mrazek concludes: "Fate played an important role in achieving this critical victory. There was no planned coordination of the courageous attacks by the three torpedo squadrons that came in one by one and helped buy the battle time that allowed the dive bombers to arrive from the Yorktown and Enterprise under optimum battle conditions."

Many of those who experienced the battle firsthand felt less hesitation in acknowledging a force beyond luck or fate, and seeing some knowing guidance, an organizing principle, behind the "uncoordinated coordination" that altered everything.

Captain Stanford E. Linzey, a naval chaplain rooted in the Pentecostal Assemblies of God denomination, survived the sinking of the *Yorktown* in the last stages of the battle. After the war, he wrote a deeply touching little book called, simply, *God Was at Midway*. "Divine providence is as relevant today as it was in Bible times," he wrote. "Events do not 'just happen.'... We did not win those battles by our wits alone. The odds were stacked against us at Midway, but in answer to the prayers going on back home in our great nation, the enemy forces made crucial mistakes at Midway. Those errors cost them the loss of ships and men, which resulted in their defeat and the turning of the tide in the war." Captain Linzey survived to tell the story again and again, until he passed at age eighty-nine in 2010. He and his wife, Verna, enjoyed nearly seventy years of marriage and raised ten children, half of whom followed their father into the military chaplaincy.

Another notable veteran of the battle, Ensign Lee McCleary, passed peacefully a year after Captain Linzey, in 2011. Shot down at the height of the battle, he clung to life for sixty hours in a bullet-riddled raft while pursued by hungry sharks. He concluded, reasonably enough, that "it was only through God's mercy that I survived and was rescued." Recuperating in his hospital bed at Pearl Harbor, he recalled a visit from Admiral Chester Nimitz himself. "He said to me that it was by the providence of God that we won the battle," McCleary recalled. "That was exactly the conclusion I had come to."

In the weeks and years that followed, less devout observers followed the lead of Linzey and McCleary and openly acknowledged Midway's illogical elements and cosmic importance.

Army Chief of Staff George C. Marshall responded to news of the battle by calling it "the closest squeak and the greatest victory." Gordon Prange, the eminent University of Maryland historian who had previously penned the Pearl Harbor bestseller *At Dawn We Slept,* called his own account of the mid-Pacific confrontation *Miracle at Midway.* And the eminent British military historian John Keegan unequivocally anointed Midway as "the most stunning and decisive blow in the history of naval warfare."

No one reveled in the triumph more gleefully than Winston Churchill, who marveled over Midway in his memoir of the global struggle. "The annals of war at sea present no more intense, heartshaking shock," the former prime minister exulted. "The novel and hitherto utterly unmeasured conditions which air warfare had created made the speed of action and the twists of fortune more intense than has ever been witnessed before. . . . As the Japanese Fleet withdrew to their far-off home ports their commanders knew not only that their aircraft-carrier strength was irretrievably broken, but that they were confronted with a will-power and passion in the foe they had challenged equal to the highest traditions of their Samurai ancestors, and backed with a development of power, numbers, and science to which no limit could be set."

"ONLY THE DARK GODS KNOW"

Detractors of the United States and her enduring delusions of grandeur, and even skeptics among its own citizens, may groan at Churchill's effusions. And yet something about the odd, illogical story of Midway compels grudging wonderment, even among embittered enemies.

In his great novel *War and Remembrance* (1978), the late Herman Wouk evoked the point of view of a fictional German general and military historian, Armin von Roon, who declares:

The annals of military conflict, from their dim origins in Chinese and Egyptian accounts to the present era, show no equal to . . . the Five Minutes of Midway. . . . In that mere instant of combat time, three Japanese carriers, with their full complements of aircraft, were reduced to smoking flotsam. These giant victims embodied the national strength and treasure of Japan, the culmination of half a century of heroic effort to become a first-class military power. In those five explosive minutes, Japan's world status, laboriously built up from Tsushima Strait to Singapore, Manila, and Burma, was shattered; though she had yet to suffer three years of defeat and final atomic-blast horror before accepting this fact. . . .

The United States of America has been a lucky nation, and this luck held remarkably on June 4, 1942. How long it will hold in the future, only the dark gods know who bestowed on this crass mercantile nation of mongrelized blood and cowboy culture a virgin continent with almost infinite natural resources.

Those same gods—or God—preserved the illogical American claim to the three islets at Midway Atoll, though those forlorn scraps of land hardly represented the ultimate prize of the struggle. No ghosts cling to this meager territory, unlike other legendary battlefields; the fight here concerned huge ships that never even sailed within sight of one another, dispatching their intrepid swarms of little planes to attack the opposing fleet from hundreds of miles away. The modest memorials left behind to mark their heroic deeds offer little basis for contemplation, but the vast, encircling, empty ocean surely does, even at a remove of eighty years.

William Henry Seward's largest land deal, for Alaska, surely changed the destiny of the United States. But his smallest acquisition, in terms of acreage, altered the fate of the whole great globe and saw the decisive battle in history's greatest war.

"HE LOOKS LIKE A HAYSEED, TALKS LIKE A
PROPHET, AND ACTS LIKE AN EMBARRASSED
SCHOOLBOY": Henry A. Wallace, vice president of the
United States (1941–1945). Leaders of the Democratic Party
considered his pro-Soviet sympathies so dangerous that they
organized "the Conspiracy of the Pure of Heart"
to dump him from the ticket.

8

The Right Vice

A Switch in Time Saves the American Century

"Nobody knew the president was sick. For a lot of us, we didn't even know he was mortal."

That's what my late father told me, recalling one of the darkest days of his young life. On April 12, 1945, he got the news that Franklin Delano Roosevelt had suddenly passed into eternity. A nineteen-year-old draftee stationed in California, awaiting navy deployment as part of the final, bloody push against the Japanese home islands, my father felt suddenly lost, vulnerable, devastated after the president's death. He was six years old when FDR first took charge in the White House; he couldn't remember another name attached to the title "president." As a boy, he watched his Russian immigrant parents—my grandparents—celebrate their newly earned citizenship by clipping a magazine image of President Roosevelt, encasing it in a gilt-and-glass dime-store frame, and patriotically installing it in a place of honor on the wall of their South Philadelphia living room.

No other figure in the nation's history ever served as long in the highest office, or struck his countrymen as so irreplaceable. Even his detractors readily conceded that Roosevelt's life contained aspects of the miraculous—including his triumph over polio and permanent disability, and his narrow escape from the Miami assassination attempt that threatened to kill him before he even took the oath of office. As president, he managed a nearly seamless transition from the long, frustrating battle against the Depression to taking charge of an all-out global war.

But before that war reached its victorious conclusion, the circumstances surrounding Roosevelt's death began to look every bit as strange, illogical, and purposefully preordained as the achievements of his life. Had fate altered the timing of his departure from the scene, or dictated a different outcome to a secondary political skirmish just months before his demise, the course of world history and the survival of American ideals might easily have taken a catastrophic turn for the worse.

Often, providence proves its power through the unexpected elevation of some unlikely aspirant for high office: take Lincoln's startling nomination and election as president in 1860, after just a single, contentious two-year term in the House of Representatives, and two failed efforts to win a Senate seat.

On other occasions, fate may turn aside the wrong man, an even more important process than installing the right one—protecting the Republic by blocking a presumed president with every reason to anticipate his own installation.

"AN IMPRESSIONABLE KOOK"

At the beginning of 1944, Americans who followed politics looked to Vice President Henry Wallace as the obvious, inevitable successor to FDR.

As Roosevelt completed his unprecedented third term and continued to steer the nation to wartime victory, the main question provoking pundits and politicos was whether he would run for a fourth. If he did, then Wallace could wait another four years before taking his turn at the top of the ticket; if not, "the Oddball from Iowa," always associated with quirks and question marks, might immediately ascend to the pinnacle of power he so clearly coveted.

One of FDR's first authoritative biographers, James MacGregor Burns, dismissed Wallace in 1970 as a would-be philosopher-king, "a baffling combination of agrarian progressive, administrative politician, scientific agriculturalist, and philosophical mystic." Forty years later, another biographer, Conrad Black, mocked the onetime New Deal favorite as "an obscurantist leftist mystic" who "was clearly a hazardous occupant of the vice presidency" let alone a plausible chief executive. "The facts are that Roosevelt, once he got a good look at Wallace, thought him an impressionable kook," wrote Black, "too naïve and gullible for the highest offices."

Some of the deepest skepticism about Wallace came from his fellow true believers on the American left, who always expressed concern over his weak character and bad judgment despite their shared ideological orientation. Norman Thomas, the former Presbyterian minister who ran for president six times as the nominee of the Socialist Party, told the United Press in 1948 that "Wallace is using Franklin Roosevelt's name.... His campaign is emotion with very clever manipulation underneath.... But the group who are manipulating his campaign are Communists, or Communist sympathizers. And you cannot work with Communists and escape getting burned." Another revered American socialist, the writer and theorist Irving Howe, pilloried Wallace as "a completely contrived creature of Stalin."

Oddly enough, he began his career as a midwestern Republican, not as a Bolshevik of any kind. His grandfather, the first well-known Henry Wallace, started his career as a Presbyterian preacher. Pastor Wallace, widely and affectionately known as "Uncle Henry," later began two publications that spread the family name throughout the rural heartland—*Iowa Homestead* and *Wallaces' Farmer*. The second Henry Wallace expanded this folksy informational enterprise and won appointment as secretary of agriculture in the conservative Republican administrations of Warren Harding and Calvin Coolidge.

When he went away to Washington, Henry Wallace Jr. left his son, Henry Agard Wallace, in charge of the thriving dynastic empire. The young man quickly gave *Wallaces' Farmer* and the family's other published products an up-to-date, scientific sheen, based on his own advanced studies of crop genetics and hybridization at Iowa State.

Eventually, this youngest Henry founded groundbreaking companies of his own, most notably Pioneer Hi-Bred, based on his personal breakthroughs on crossbreeding the first commercially viable hybrid corn. Whatever the ups and downs of the national economy or the detours of the founder's political career, these enterprises continued to prosper and helped make Henry Wallace "perhaps the greatest socialist capitalist of the 20th century" in the estimation of Daniel Gross at *Slate*. When Wallace's children ultimately sold their shares of Pioneer Hi-Bred to DuPont in 1997, the stock delivered $770 million to the former vice president's daughter, and another $573 million to his fortunate son—an impressive haul for the family of a left-leaning idealist who expressed nothing but contempt for Wall Street machinations and corporate greed.

With those progressive perspectives in mind, Wallace abruptly abandoned his family's ancestral commitment to the GOP, due as much to personal grudges as to ideological divergence. The Republicans nominated Herbert Hoover for president in 1928, who, as commerce secretary, had feuded with Henry's father in the Harding-Coolidge cabinet. The younger Wallace came to believe that this soul-killing strife hastened his dad's death in office, so he fiercely opposed Hoover in both his first race for the White House and his doomed drive for reelection in 1932, lending energetic support instead to the campaign of Franklin Delano Roosevelt. To express gratitude for this influential farm state backing, FDR named Wallace as one of the two nominal Republicans in his new cabinet, assigning him the same position his father had once occupied with distinction. Honoring this family heritage, the new secretary of agriculture conducted much of his work at the Department of Agriculture on a massive table, below a huge, grim, and looming portrait of the fondly remembered former secretary, watching over the innovations of the New Deal with a furrowed-brow gaze of vague but unmistakable discomfort.

"IT IS ALWAYS GOING TO SEEM
FAINTLY RIDICULOUS"

In Washington, this new addition to the Roosevelt team looked slightly out of place from the beginning. The savvy reporter Allen Drury (who later wrote the bestselling 1950s novel about senatorial shenanigans *Advise and Consent*) described Wallace in vivid terms: "A shock of silver-graying hair sweeps over to the right of his head in a great shaggy arc. He looks like a hayseed, talks like a prophet, and acts like an embarrassed schoolboy," Drury observed. "No matter what he does, it is always going to seem faintly ridiculous, and no matter how he acts, it is always going to seem faintly pathetic—at least to the cold-eyed judgments of the Hill." Another insider pointedly observed: "Henry's the sort that keeps you guessing as to whether he's going to deliver a sermon or wet the bed."

As a perpetually earnest, self-described "truth seeker," Wallace neither drank, smoked, nor gossiped, and disliked Washington social gatherings, where most of the participants did plenty of all three. His wife, Ilo, shared his preference for a quiet, frugal home life, despite the substantial earnings of their burgeoning corn companies, and they enjoyed fifty-one years of a respectful, stable marriage. As historian Arthur M. Schlesinger Jr. aptly summarized their durable relationship: "No one saw them kiss, nor did anyone see them fight."

Henry saved his fighting spirit for the office, and for the cabinet room. As Schlesinger concluded: "Wallace was a great secretary of agriculture. In 1933 a quarter of the American people still lived on farms, and agricultural policy was a matter of high political and economic significance." The new secretary aimed "to give farmers the same chance to raise income by controlling output that manufacturing concerns already possessed." He also launched visionary programs for soil conservation, land use planning, free milk, food stamps, innovative strategies against livestock and crop diseases, and hybrid seeds (based on his prior scientific success in Iowa) to enhance production.

Somehow, he also found time for spiritual explorations. He had left the Presbyterian church of his youth when local elders objected to his teaching William James's *Varieties of Religious Experience* to his adult Sunday school class. At that point, his biographers John Culver and John Hyde suggest that Henry "engaged upon a fantastic spiritual voyage, a quest for religious understanding that took him from the pews of mainstream Protestantism to the esoteric fringes of Eastern occultism." In the midst of that journey, he wrote to a friend: "Fundamentally, I am neither a corn breeder nor an editor but a searcher for methods of bringing the 'inner light' to outward manifestation."

To further that ambition, he completed correspondence courses in the occult that promised "the opportunity of entering and placing your feet on the Path that leads to Eternal Light and Life." He dabbled in astrology and meditation, while developing an abiding disdain for "the wishy-washy goodygoodness" and "the infantile irrelevancy" he saw in most of American Christianity.

Shortly before his appointment as secretary of agriculture, Wallace fell under the spell of a Russian mystic famous for his dreamlike paintings of mountains, caves, and medieval scenes, and for his unrivaled, magical ability to communicate with the "spirit sphere." With his eyes covered, Nicholas Roerich would let another world dictate insights and commands through "automatic writings" over which he said he exercised no conscious control. One of those orders from the Great Beyond told him to accept donations to build a museum in New York to display his masterworks. Duly impressed, one wealthy stockbroker provided the money to erect a twenty-nine-story edifice on Riverside Drive that housed apartments near the top while devoting the bottom floors to a thousand of Roerich's dazzling canvases.

Aside from the paintings, Roerich pursued both theatrical and political goals—designing the stunning sets and costumes for the premiere production of Stravinsky's *Rite of Spring* ballet, which provoked a major riot on its opening night in Paris for its invocation of prehistoric Russian fertility rites and human sacrifice.

As a political operator, Roerich put himself forward as the chief "Guardian of World Peace and Culture" and tried to persuade all nations to sign onto his "International Treaty for the Protection of Cultural Treasures" as well as to accept the "Banner of Peace" he had personally designed for that purpose. Eventually, the influence of Henry Wallace overcame the angry resistance of the State Department and resulted in twenty-nine Western Hemisphere nations—including the United States—formally signing the "Roerich Pact." In all of this wide-ranging work, Roerich benefited from the aid of his glamorous wife, Helena, an aristocratic Russian beauty who became the author of many books on Buddhism and Hinduism, while translating the works of her fellow Russian spiritualist Madame Helena Blavatsky.

During a brief visit in New York, Wallace got a glimpse of the powerfully hypnotic paintings and fell instantly under the spell of the eccentric and charismatic couple. The future secretary of agriculture had already begun explorations in which he identified himself with the spiritualist handles "Cornplanter," "Chief Standing Corn," and "Galahad." Now, he designated Roerich simply but respectfully as "Guru" in a notorious series of private letters in 1933 and '34, right after joining the Roosevelt administration.

In one, Cornplanter compares himself to a "Young Saul or David to whom a Samuel had appeared. But instead of oil there is musk and rose from the sacred heights ... of the crystal soul behind the living eyes above the cleft of beard."

In another soulful outpouring, Wallace dedicated himself to "the Search, whether it be for the Lost Word of Masonry or the Holy Chalice or the potentialities of the age to come—is the one supremely worth while objective. All else is karmic duty. Here is life. But surely every one is a potential Galahad, a Parsifal incurring the utmost peril insofar as his energy is in this search in terms of the outer world."

"Long have I been aware of the occasional fragrance from that other world which is the real world," the secretary of agriculture mused. "But now I must live in the outer world and at the same time make over my mind and body to serve as fit instruments for the Lord of Justice."

The entire correspondence fairly reeked with the "occasional fragrance" of fatuity and gullibility, especially after the crafty Roerich found a way to use the Wallace connection to arrange a handsome government salary and U.S. military support for his crackbrained scheme to establish a new, independent republic between Russia and Manchuria, with Guru himself as its enlightened ruler.

"SOME EXTRAORDINARY PHANTASY
OF ASIATIC POWER"

In May 1934, Nicholas Roerich left the United States to search for exotic, drought-resistant grasses in the remote plains of Central Asia. The Department of Agriculture sponsored the expedition in hopes of finding hardy new plants to prevent continued soil erosion in the badly stricken Dust Bowl of the American Midwest. Knowles A. Ryerson, chief of the Bureau of Plant Industry, insisted on well-trained scientists to head the expensive, high-priority mission but Wallace, his boss, overruled him. Galahad cited Roerich's deep immersion in various Asian cultures and his status as a spiritual leader "revered in Japan, China and Russia." In fact, Roerich's previous travels in the East had generated so much controversy that the British Foreign Office officially designated him an "unbalanced individual" after his purported discovery in a Tibetan monastery of conclusive proof that Christ conducted his first messianic ministry in India.

None of this seemed to shake the secretary of agriculture's certainty that his personal guru qualified as the perfect choice to lead a bold, complicated scientific mission to one of the most troubled regions on Earth where three empires—Japan, China, and Soviet Russia—contended for supremacy. In fact, Henry Wallace found taxpayer money to pay Roerich's thirty-two-year-old son, George, as second-in-command of the USDA grass-gathering expedition. Wallace also ordered the General Accounting Office to provide speedy approval of necessary items of scientific equipment, including a housecoat, trousers, rolling pin, and stockings for Guru's supremely stylish wife, Helena.

When the "researchers" landed in Tokyo with their elaborate equipment, the Japanese authorities looked askance at the strange, long-bearded Russian with the piercing eyes and hawk nose, dressed in the linen robes and sandals of a mad monk affiliated with no recognizable order. He planned to take his oddly assorted crew to Manchukuo, the puppet state the Japanese had set up in Manchuria after their invasion and occupation. Unfortunately for him, the U.S. government never recognized Manchukuo, but that didn't stop Henry Wallace from contacting local authorities to force better press coverage of the visitors from America. As Roerich wrote back to his sponsor in the Roosevelt cabinet: "We are battling with the dark forces but as always are moving valiantly forward."

Amazingly, more than a year passed before Wallace—beset with complaints about Roerich from every foreign government in the vicinity, botanists on the expedition staff, international journalists, and his own State Department—began to question his unwavering confidence in the flamboyant Guru. By that time, the swelling group had acquired a menacing cadre of armed Cossack guards, as well as trucks, motorcars, and military tents, all at government expense. Wallace had once again intervened with the Fifteenth U.S. Army Infantry unit in Tientsin to secure rifles, revolvers, and plentiful ammunition for the botanical mission that began to look much more like an invading army.

The jittery Russians also began to worry: Roerich had been writing and speaking for years of his obsession with founding an autonomous utopia somewhere in the vast emptiness of Siberia. In his writing, he had even given the project a code name—"Kansas"—perhaps in a clumsy attempt to appeal to the agriculture secretary's midwestern sensibilities. In Moscow, the American military attaché remained distinctly unimpressed, warning in an official communiqué of an "armed party . . . making its way toward the Soviet Union, ostensibly as a scientific expedition, but actually to rally former White elements and discontented Mongols."

The discontent back home only amplified when the *Chicago Tribune* ran a front-page story under the headline: "JAPANESE EXPEL EXPLORERS SENT BY SEC. WALLACE." The article described an eccentric Russian painter traveling like royalty under the American flag, surrounded by "armed White Russian Cossack guards" and causing "embarrassment to American diplomatic and military officials."

That embarrassment at last reached the office of Henry Wallace and in September 1935 he informed Helena Roerich: "I desire that there be no communication, direct or indirect, by letter or otherwise between the Roerichs (father, mother, and sons) on the one side and myself on the other." He also wrote to others that he now recognized his former mentor as "a megalomaniac" with disciples "determined to stop at nothing in helping him to work out some extraordinary phantasy of Asiatic power." While indulging that "phantasy" for more than two years of wandering on Uncle Sam's dime, Guru delivered not a single plant sample—not one—suitable for use in replanting the Dust Bowl.

This bizarre episode bears recounting because it helps to explain the public's intense indignation when, instead of firing Wallace over his bureaucratic bungling, mystical malfeasance, and the grotesque waste of government money, President Roosevelt proposed elevating the wayward agronomist to the vice presidency of the United States.

"THE VOICE FROM THE SEWERS"

That strange notion arose amid the confusion surrounding FDR's personal plans for the upcoming election of 1940. According to an unwritten but near-sacred rule going back to Washington and Jefferson, no president had ever served more than two terms. Only after Roosevelt's death did Congress and the state legislatures formally incorporate that rule into the Constitution as the Twenty-second Amendment. In fact, as he neared the completion of eight years in office, the president gave every indication he meant to follow the example of his illustrious predecessors.

For one thing, Roosevelt did nothing to discourage his two-term vice president, John Nance Garner, from making his own run at the top job, or to keep him from speaking out publicly against the idea of any president seeking a third term. But with cataclysmic war raging overseas, and with embattled Britain relying on American help to survive the Nazi onslaught, some in Roosevelt's inner circle worried about relinquishing power to an unprepared or even isolationist new commander in chief. Even as the Chicago convention opened in July, the president refused to rule out another run and thereby paralyzed the campaigns of all his potential Democratic rivals. To make matters worse, he also refused to travel to the convention, insisting that critical world events demanded his full attention at the White House;

France had surrendered to the invading Germans less than four weeks before, leaving Hitler in unchallenged control of western Europe.

In sweaty Chicago Stadium, the Democratic delegates felt surly, anxious, and resentful, awaiting some signal from the White House as the nomination process began. Finally, when taking over as permanent chairman of the convention, Senate majority leader Alben Barkley dramatically announced a personal message from the president. Reportedly, Roosevelt had dictated the contents over a phone call.

"The President has never had, and has not today, any desire or purpose to continue in the office of the President, to be a candidate for that office, or to be nominated by the convention for that office," Barkley read from his notes to the suddenly hushed crowd. "He wishes in all earnestness and sincerity to make it clear that all the delegates to this convention are free to vote for any candidate."

The confused silence continued for a moment before speakers throughout the hall began broadcasting a chant that seemed to come from nowhere and everywhere. "We want Roosevelt! We want Roosevelt!" bellowed the disembodied voice, part of a prearranged plan by the Democratic machine of Chicago's mayor, Ed Kelly. The voice that continued to repeat the magical three words, like an incantation, belonged to Superintendent Thomas D. Garry, head of Chicago's Sewer Department, who had been awaiting a signal in a little room beneath the stadium floor. Other city employees, strategically placed throughout the crowd inside Chicago Stadium, took up the pleading cry. Inevitably, even dubious delegates joined in with the hypnotic, pro-Roosevelt frenzy. The rumbling baritone of the unseen sanitation bureaucrat would go down in history as "the Voice from the Sewers."

The next day, the anti-Roosevelt candidates collected more than 150 votes among them, but the president won an easy majority with 86 percent of the delegates. He did not, however, immediately accept the nomination: he meant to select his own running mate before he agreed to run. Breaking with another long-standing tradition that gave conventions the final say on selecting a vice presidential nominee, Roosevelt insisted that the delegates ratify his choice.

And his choice, he let it be known, was Henry Wallace—despite the fact that the secretary of agriculture had never run for public office of any kind; had impressed all who encountered him as off-kilter and spooky; had been a registered Republican as recently as four years before; and struck the party's moderates and conservatives, especially its congressional barons from the South, as dangerously liberal, even radical.

In defense of the controversial selection, Roosevelt's ground troops at the convention tried to make the case for his eccentric selection. For one thing, the Democrats couldn't possibly renominate the sitting VP, Cactus Jack Garner, because he'd already gone on record with his opposition to Roosevelt—or anyone else—ever seeking a third term.

Wallace appealed to Roosevelt precisely because he bore so little resemblance to the incumbent he would replace. Garner savored the grit and sweat of old-fashioned patronage politics; Wallace sniffed the "occasional fragrance" of "musk and rose from the sacred heights"; Cactus Jack kept the "Board of Education" in his Capitol Hill office well stocked with fine bourbon, even during Prohibition; Chief Standing Corn remained a resolute teetotaler and his favorite form of exercise involved walking alone along the banks of the Potomac, throwing an aboriginal boomerang high into the air and then managing to catch it upon its return. Unlike the crusty Garner, a former Speaker of the House, Wallace possessed no political base and could function as a loyal "Deputy President," entirely beholden to his chief, rather than a ticket balancer with his own cadre of supporters.

The convention delegates, disproportionately selected from big-city machines, industrial labor unions, and country backwaters of the South and Midwest, found Wallace and his quirks more appalling than appealing. They would have disliked him even more had they learned the exotic details of the Roerich mess, but to that point the press had largely ignored the convoluted story of the conniving Russian guru and his eager Iowa acolyte.

As the nomination process began, podium invocations of the name "Henry Agard Wallace" produced far more boos, groans, and jeers than lusty cheers or even respectful applause. Listening to the proceedings on the radio at the White House, the president of the United States felt annoyed and insulted by the rude show of defiance from the restive convention crowd. "Damn it to hell!" he reportedly yelled. "They will go for Wallace or I won't run."

The word went out by telephone to loyalist cadres in the convention hall to begin working the delegations to make sure that the party faithful bent to the nominee's will. In case those efforts failed, Roosevelt began writing out a brief, dramatic speech turning down his third-term nomination. "It would be best not to straddle ideals," he wrote. "Therefore, I give the Democratic party the opportunity to make that historic decision by declining the honor of the nomination for the presidency." He handed the notes to his veteran speechwriter Sam Rosenman. "Sam, take this inside and go to work on it. . . . I may have to deliver it very quickly so please hurry it up." In the convention hall a thousand miles away, Eleanor Roosevelt caused a stir when she took her seat beside Wallace's nervous wife, Ilo, in an ostentatious show of support. When the rowdy nominations concluded, an expectant hush fell over the proceedings before the voting began. Everyone knew that the outcome remained uncertain—with the main challenge to the president's choice coming from Speaker of the House William Bankhead of Alabama—perhaps best known at the time (and for long afterward) as the father of the sultry, scandalous Hollywood star Tallulah Bankhead.

A very different sort of star put an end to Speaker Bankhead's hopes when Eleanor Roosevelt strode briskly to the podium—the first president's wife ever to address a national convention. She never mentioned the name Henry Wallace—that moniker had already been booed enough—but her sturdy platitudes stressed the need to put aside bickering and petty differences. "You must know that this is the time when all good men and women give every bit of service and strength to their country that they have to give," she pleaded.

Despite her efforts, the first roll call showed William Bankhead two votes ahead, before some of the previously abstaining states fell into line for Wallace and others switched their votes. After the Speaker's brother, Senator John Bankhead of Alabama, followed the courteous tradition of moving to make the vote for Wallace unanimous, the "noes" easily outshouted the "ayes," but Henry Wallace had won the nomination nonetheless.

"THE CENTURY OF THE COMMON MAN"

In the campaign that followed, the new vice presidential candidate barnstormed energetically across the country, and the Democratic ticket prevailed by a comfortable margin, but without the epic landslides FDR had won in his two previous campaigns. Running against the Indiana-born Wendell Willkie, Roosevelt and Wallace actually lost the crucial farmer vote by a fourteen-point margin—a disappointing performance blamed in part on the ticket's controversial new addition, Chief Standing Corn, who had always been more popular among activists and academics than among the ordinary country folk he had been meant to attract.

Like other vice presidents before him, Wallace felt quickly bored by the meager duties of his office and took no satisfaction in presiding over a Senate in which he had never served. He much preferred to give high-toned, high-profile speeches across the United States and around the world.

The most celebrated of these utterances came in response to an editorial in *Life* magazine in which the publisher of *Time* and *Life*, Henry Luce, proclaimed an "American Century" early in 1941. "[We must] accept whole-heartedly our duty and our opportunity as the most powerful and vital nation in the world," Luce declared, "and in consequence to exert upon the world the full impact of our influence, for such purposes as we see fit and by such means as we see fit."

Vice President Wallace responded to this fabled proclamation in May 1942, after Pearl Harbor and shortly before Midway, rejecting the notion of American dominance after the war. "Some have spoken of the 'American Century,'" he declared to a gathering of foreign and domestic dignitaries in New York (the Free World Association) and to a worldwide radio audience that listened to the live broadcast. "I say that the century on which we are entering—the century which will come into being after this war—can be and must be the century of the common man."

To him, America's battle against Japan and Germany represented just the latest stage of a world-changing revolutionary struggle. "The march of freedom of the past 150 years has been a long-drawn-out people's revolution. In this Great Revolution of the people, there were the American Revolution of 1775, the French Revolution of 1792, the Latin-American Revolutions of the Bolivarian era, the German Revolution of 1848 and the Russian Revolution of 1918."

The prominent inclusion of the Russian Revolution on his honor roll of enlightened uprisings that constituted "the march of freedom" counted as outrageously audacious—especially at a time when the heir to that revolution, Joseph Stalin, had already slaughtered at least six hundred thousand of his fellow citizens in the Great Purge of 1936–38. Nevertheless, Wallace found common elements in the cited rebellions, emphasizing that "the significant thing is that the people groped their way to the light. More of them learned to think and work together."

His remarks drew enthusiastic applause from many quarters and inspired Pine-Thomas Productions, a division of Paramount Pictures, to release its own version of the famous speech. The introductory crawl, backed by a stirring score typical of that Hollywood era, proudly announced: "Recording some of the many highlights of this remarkable address, we have the honor to present the Vice President of the United States."

Highlighted by more rousing music, along with heroic imagery meant to illustrate "freedom on the march," the speech even inspired the great American composer Aaron Copland to write one of his most memorable compositions: the perennially popular "Fanfare for the Common Man," with its thundering drums and blaring brass, deliberately evoked Wallace's title and his ideas.

The idealistic Iowan naturally relished this adoring attention and in 1943 he departed on a forty-day, seven-nation "good will" tour of Latin America. He had been studying Spanish and spoke fluently, with an authentic accent, displaying those skills before monumental and worshipful crowds everywhere he went. In Costa Rica, an astonishing sixty-five thousand greeted his arrival—some 15 percent of the nation's population. The *New York Times* flatly declared: "The reception accorded Mr. Wallace was the greatest in the history of Costa Rica." In Chile, more than a million lined the streets of Santiago to catch a glimpse of the distinguished visitor, and more than one hundred thousand jammed into the national stadium to hear his words. The American ambassador reported back to the State Department: "Never in Chilean history has any foreigner been received with such extravagance and evidently sincere enthusiasm," noting that "the masses . . . responded almost hysterically."

Back home, most Americans seemed to share the enthusiastic response to Wallace and his globe-trotting diplomacy, as he made history as the first vice president ever to undertake such well-publicized and extensive foreign travels. As 1944 began, Gallup polled Democratic voters to ask their presidential preferences in the event that FDR declined to run for a fourth term. A clear majority (57 percent) chose Wallace, more than double the support for his closest competitor.

"I HOPE IT WILL BE THE SAME OLD TEAM"

Wallace's political position looked so secure, in fact, that FDR sent him on an even more arduous and ambitious overseas trip that would keep him abroad until the Democratic National Convention—a gathering widely expected to renominate both of them. This time, Wallace would travel to the Soviet Union and China, with the crucial wartime mission of pushing Chiang Kai-shek's Nationalists and Mao Zedong's Communists into closer cooperation to defeat the common Japanese enemy.

Excited by the prospect, Galahad made a determined effort to learn some rudimentary Russian and insisted on giving a substantial address in that unfamiliar language in Irkutsk, shortly after he arrived in Siberia. Naturally, the Russians provided a carefully orchestrated, polite response, regardless of their difficulties in comprehending what the earnest visitor attempted to say. During the remaining Soviet segments of his closely supervised tour, they also showed off some of their utopian, productive, idyllic, and up-to-date collective farms, full of happy peasants who only interrupted their performances of lusty folksongs to sing the praises of America's "Great Ally," Comrade Stalin, lavishly enumerating his heroic achievements. Later, the vice president made enthusiastic remarks to the press comparing the warmhearted, industrious Russians he met on his travels to the hardworking midwestern farm families of his Iowa boyhood.

Amazingly, throughout his journey, Wallace appeared altogether oblivious to Russia's long tradition of "Potemkin villages"—cunningly contrived showplaces designed to impress (and mislead) gullible foreigners. The vice president showed no interest whatever in the numerous forced labor camps that brutally and lethally imprisoned literally hundreds of thousands of political prisoners in the very regions through which he traveled. He also expended no effort in finally locating those elusive "drought resistant grasses" of Central Asia he had dispatched his former guru, Nicholas Roerich, to find a decade earlier.

He returned home on July 10, 1944, a month and four days after D-Day, following fifty-one days and twenty-seven thousand miles of grueling travel. When the vice president landed at National Airport after an all-night flight from Seattle, a gaggle of reporters besieged him with questions about the upcoming Democratic National Convention and his plans for another campaign as FDR's running mate. "I am seeing the president at four-thirty," Wallace gruffly announced. "I have a report to make on a mission to China. I do not want to talk politics."

Later that afternoon, however, he allowed FDR to steer their conversation and the subject turned inevitably to the convention and the campaign. The president reaffirmed his intention to win a fourth term, which he planned as "really progressive." He also expressed his clear preference for Wallace to serve once more as his vice president, though warning darkly of unnamed "professional politicians" who believed that the repeat presence of such an unabashed liberal would cost the ticket two to three million votes in the more moderate regions of the country. Roosevelt also warned Wallace of the painful certainty of "catcalls and jeers" at the Chicago convention from those opposing his renomination and expressed his concern for potential wounded feelings for the vice president's family.

Three days later, after Wallace managed to recover from the exhaustion of his travels and to catch up with the paperwork in his office, he returned to the White House for a private lunch with Roosevelt. There, the vice president proudly displayed results of a new Gallup Poll asking Democratic voters for preferences for the vice presidential nomination. A full 65 percent chose Wallace, with only 17 percent preferring Senator Alben Barkley—a candidate Roosevelt considered unacceptable because his status as a recognizable southerner would hurt the ticket in the industrial battlegrounds of the Northeast and Midwest. Meanwhile, a largely unknown Missouri senator named Harry Truman drew only 2 percent of the voters polled—less than one-thirtieth of the backing for Henry Wallace.

Nevertheless, Roosevelt surprised an alarmed vice president by revealing that some influential party bosses wanted Truman—"the only one who had no enemies and might add a little independent strength to the ticket." He still assured Wallace of his personal support and, when questioned, agreed to express that support in a personal letter to the chairman of the convention. When the vice president asked if Roosevelt would offer any alternative names, he promised that he would not.

When Wallace stood up to go, the president drew him closer for a surprisingly vigorous handshake and one of his famous confident smiles. "While I cannot put it just that way in public," he said, beaming, "I hope it will be the same old team."

"THE INTERESTING THING IS THE WORLD DIDN'T HANG"

If Franklin Roosevelt truly wanted that same old team's return, he easily could have settled the matter in advance of the convention: four years before, he had boldly declared he wouldn't run himself without Wallace at his side, and the delegates, after some grumbling, inevitably fell into line. Now, in the final stages of an epochal world war, it hardly seemed credible that they would mutiny against their gallant commander in chief.

Nevertheless, FDR's chief advisors and most of the Democratic establishment had become painfully aware of secret information that made this vice presidential nomination uniquely sensitive and profoundly important: the president was dying, with scant chance of completing his new term.

In December 1943, when he returned from his historic strategy meeting with Churchill and Stalin in Tehran, the president looked ashen, fragile, and distracted. His personal physician, Vice Admiral Ross T. McIntire, assured press and public that his patient suffered from a mild case of the flu and would quickly return to normal. But his condition failed to improve in the weeks that followed, and alarmed visitors to the White House saw his hands shaking so badly he couldn't light his own cigarettes, or watched him spill liquor when mixing the drinks he loved to serve each evening.

At the end of March 1944, his daughter Anna demanded that her father receive more intensive medical attention and he allowed himself to be wheeled into Bethesda Naval Hospital for a top secret, thorough examination by Lieutenant Commander Howard Bruenn, chief of cardiology.

The results, later confirmed by three more senior physicians, brought grim news that Roosevelt and his closest associates determined to hide from the public, his cabinet, and even most of his family. The president suffered from congestive heart failure and severe hypertension. His heart had already become "markedly enlarged" and he experienced almost constant exhaustion. Bruenn's notes at the time described the president of the United States as "a drawn, gray, and exhausted individual, who became short of breath on the very slightest exertion. The examination of his eyes revealed some changes due to arteriosclerosis and hypertension."

From that time forward, Dr. Bruenn received orders to ignore all other responsibilities, to accompany Roosevelt at all times, and to concentrate on a single assignment: keeping the president alive as long as possible. To ease the strain on the heart, the medical team pre-scribed digitalis and put the president on a strict diet. They ordered him to cut his smoking in half and to limit his work schedule to no more than four hours a day—an impossibility, of course, just weeks before D-Day and months before his potential nomination for a fourth term. Reporters pushed Admiral McIntire over rumors con-cerning the president's health, but he assured them that his patient suffered only from persistent bronchitis and otherwise enjoyed fine health "for a man of 62-plus."

Two weeks later, FDR disappeared for a month, telling official Washington and the compliant press that he had gone on vacation "somewhere in the South" to overcome the lingering effects of his al-leged bronchitis. He actually spent the entire time at Hobcaw, the 17,500-acre barony maintained by the financier and longtime presi-dential advisor Bernard Baruch—the same influential Washington and Wall Street figure Winston Churchill had tried to visit that night of his near-fatal Manhattan traffic accident thirteen years earlier.

"I had really a grand time down at Bernie's," Roosevelt told his aide Harry Hopkins, who had taken up part-time residence in the White House. "Slept twelve hours out of the twenty-four, sat in the sun, never lost my temper, and decided to let the world go hang. The interesting thing is the world didn't hang."

Eleanor, Anna, and the domestic staff at the executive mansion noted some improvement in his condition but occasional visitors still expressed alarm when they saw him. In June, Edward J. Flynn, former chairman of the Democratic Party and the suave, canny boss of the Bronx, came with his wife to spend a weekend in the White House. FDR wanted to talk out the challenges for a fourth-term campaign with the man who had engineered the successful campaign for a third, but both of the Flynns couldn't get past their worries over the state of the president's health. "We were both very unhappy about his condi-tion and sat up for two hours discussing it," Ed Flynn remembered. Pleading with the president not to attempt another race, he also urged the First Lady to use her influence to protect her husband's frail health. But both Eleanor and Franklin dismissed such worries and wanted to make plans for the convention and the contest in the fall.

"THE CONSPIRACY OF THE PURE OF HEART"

Unable to persuade FDR to pull back from his plans, Flynn quietly joined "the self-styled Conspiracy of the Pure of Heart," an informal alliance of some of the Democratic Party's most influential apparatchiks united for a single purpose: to protect the nation from the terrifying prospect of Henry Agard Wallace ascending to the presidency. As Secretary of the Treasury Henry Morgenthau bluntly told Roosevelt just two weeks before the convention: "If something happened to you, I certainly wouldn't want Wallace to be president."

Along with Flynn, the principal figures in the hastily assembled cabal included Postmaster General Frank Walker, another former chair of the Democratic National Committee, and party treasurer Edwin Pauley, a millionaire oilman from California (later a noted philanthropist and strong supporter of Governor Ronald Reagan). Bob Hannegan, the unofficial leader of the group, also counted as by far its youngest member: at forty-one, he looked to be a rising star in the Democratic Party, having already served FDR as commissioner of Internal Revenue and succeeded Walker as chairman of the DNC.

The son of a St. Louis police chief and a star athlete at St. Louis University, he played such a hyperactive role in Missouri politics that he became known as "Busyman Bob." Hannegan easily dominated any room he entered, charming even implacable opponents with his hearty manner, dazzling smile, broad shoulders, gleaming black hair, and a collection of shockingly loud neckties.

In 1940, Busyman Bob almost single-handedly rescued the state's junior senator, Harry Truman, from defeat in a bitter primary fight during his first campaign for reelection. Naturally, he considered Truman a potential replacement for Wallace on the ticket but initially he preferred another alternative—as did Truman himself. In fact, before the convention convened, Senator Truman had agreed to deliver the nominating speech for his friend Jimmy Byrnes and had nearly completed writing the high-profile address.

Despite his diminutive size, Byrnes loomed large in the preconvention maneuvering for a spot on the ticket because no other potential running mate could rival the breadth of his governmental experience or his personal connection with FDR. He had represented South Carolina with verve and distinction in both House and Senate, and even served as a justice on the Supreme Court, before Roosevelt picked him to take over the new Offices of Economic Stabilization and, later, War Mobilization. There, working in constant coordination with his chief, Byrnes earned the press nickname "Assistant President."

The problem with his candidacy stemmed from his record on labor issues (he sternly opposed sit-down strikes in wartime) and his typically southern, segregationist attitudes on race relations that even led to his ferocious opposition to federal antilynching laws. Moreover, Byrnes faced religious vulnerabilities: raised as a Catholic, he had converted to the Episcopal church in order to marry his wife. The Irish Catholic leaders of the Conspiracy of the Pure of Heart—Hannegan, Flynn, and Walker—worried that this much-discussed apostasy might scare away major delegate blocs they needed to replace Wallace.

In addition, Flynn worried that with the wrong running mate—either Wallace or Byrnes—FDR could actually lose the autumn election to the young, hard-charging Republican nominee, New York governor Thomas E. Dewey. After Roosevelt asked him to take a sounding of party leaders across the country, the worried Bronx boss came back with a report that key battleground states would be close. He clearly exaggerated the intensity of opposition to Henry Wallace, but he didn't have to exaggerate by much. In any event, FDR didn't protest, despite his prior commitments to both Wallace and Byrnes.

As Flynn recalled, he kept steering his discussion with Roosevelt back to the virtues of Harry Truman, especially citing his much-publicized performance in leading the special Senate investigating committee to expose waste and war profiteering in the defense industry. According to press accounts, the committee's work saved the government at least $10 billion and spared the lives of thousands of American troops after the war started. Flynn remembered that "we went over every man in the Senate, and Truman was the only one who fit." Aside from his success with the Truman Committee, "his labor votes on the Senate were good; on the other hand he seemed to represent to some degree the conservatives in the party, he came from a border state, and he never made any 'racial' remarks. He just dropped into the slot."

Roosevelt seemed to acknowledge that the Missouri senator might be the man "who would hurt him least" but simultaneously protested, "I hardly know Truman." He left it to the Conspiracy of the Pure of Heart to handle the mechanics of the nomination. In contrast to his role in selecting his ticket mate in 1940, when Roosevelt had firmly insisted on Wallace, the president now sought to avoid even a long-distance role in any fights that might emerge on the convention floor. He had already scheduled a trip to West Coast military facilities and then to Hawaii to confer with General Douglas MacArthur about the climactic stages of the war against Japan. He meant to deliver his brief convention acceptance speech by telephone hookup, thereby emphasizing the burdens of war leadership that kept him away from the grubby business of politics—like dumping a loyal vice president ardently admired by many of his fellow Democrats.

Despite all the uncertainties and distractions, as he rode in his high-security private train car toward California, FDR made a point of keeping his promise to his incumbent vice president and sent a letter on Wallace's behalf to the chairman of the convention, Senator Samuel Dillon Jackson of Indiana. Released to the public the same Monday the convention opened, its widely quoted concluding paragraph enigmatically declared:

> I have been associated with Henry Wallace during his past four years as Vice President, for eight years earlier as Secretary of Agriculture, and well before that. I like him and I respect him and he is my personal friend. For these reasons I personally would vote for his nomination if I were a delegate to the convention.

Roosevelt loyalists tried to read between the lines: was it an endorsement or not? The tepid tone offered a dispiriting contrast to the affirmation of four years before. Instead of insisting on Wallace's presence on the ticket, the president merely reflected on their comfortable long-term relationship. Rather than telling the delegates what they *should* do, FDR merely mused over what he *would* do—or might do—were he in their place.

Nevertheless, the pro-Wallace forces—representing a clear majority of the delegates, according to most on-the-scene sources—took comfort in the fact that the president hadn't named an alternate candidate and they resolved to fight as fiercely as possible to return both members of "the same old team" to the ticket.

"AND THEY STARTED ROARING, 'NO, NO, NO, NO'"

That cause took a major step forward with the vice president's seconding speech of FDR's nomination. Instead of the self-satisfied, orotund torpor that usually characterized his public utterances, Wallace summoned fire and passion, with an edge of righteous indignation, insisting on a progressive equality agenda sure to alarm the more conservative southern wing of the party.

"In a political, educational and economic sense there must be no inferior races," he roared. "The poll tax must go. Educational opportunities must come. The future must bring equal wages for equal work regardless of sex or race."

The vast crowd, approaching forty thousand, responded with delirious enthusiasm. They filled Chicago Stadium to capacity and well beyond, thanks to fifteen thousand counterfeit tickets printed by Chicago's mayor, Ed Kelly, who had arranged "the Voice from the Sewers" for Roosevelt four years before. Like other big-city bosses, he despised and distrusted Wallace, but to his chagrin many of the extra passes had gone to active union members from the left-leaning Congress of Industrial Organizations, who wedged into the galleries and then spilled onto the convention floor itself, chanting "We Want Wallace!" at every opportunity. After the president's formal nomination and his acceptance speech, which was transmitted to the hall from his railroad car in San Diego, they planned to stage an overwhelming demonstration to stampede the convention into an impulsive, preemptive renomination of Henry Wallace before other names could even be formally proposed.

With the plots and counterplots rippling through the jostling throngs, the noisy, overcrowded hall fell silent long enough to listen to the president. Many observers found something eerie and unsettling about hearing the familiar, resonant voice booming out from echoey speakers, while eyes watched the empty, ghostly podium spotlit at the front of the darkened auditorium.

He spoke about winning the war "overpoweringly" and implementing his dreams for a permanent peace. He sought an international organization that could "use the armed forces of the sovereign nations of the world to make another war impossible."

When he finished, and the lights came on in the sweltering space, a wild demonstration broke out immediately—not for Roosevelt, but for Wallace. The chants of "We Want Wallace!" reverberated everywhere and his troops began to sing. They bellowed the "Iowa Corn Song" until they grew hoarse, with its punch line ("That's where the tall corn grows!") meant to evoke their imposing candidate. At the nearby Blackstone Hotel, Busyman Bob Hannegan told his friend Harry Truman that instead of the vice presidential nominations going off as scheduled the next night, they had to be ready to put his name on the table immediately to counteract the emotional Wallace surge. Truman set off in search of his colleague Senator Bennett Clark, who had agreed to nominate him, but found the august legislator only after midnight, "cockeyed" drunk and barely conscious in "a hotel room he was not supposed to be in."

Meanwhile, Hannegan rushed to the hall, found Mayor Kelly, and conferred with Senator Jackson, the convention chairman, up at the crowded podium about what to do next.

Senator Claude Pepper, the feisty, cantankerous head of the Florida delegation, reacted to the chaos with something like euphoria, seeing, as the "Iowa Corn Song" proclaimed, "joy on ev'ry hand." Pepper, who went on to serve in Congress until 1989, always remembered that moment in 1944 when he had a chance to bend history.

"I sat there and watched the demonstration and I saw it growing in volume," Senator Pepper recalled. "I stood up on my seat, and I could see the whole convention hall then. And I said, 'You know, that's a *real* demonstration. . . .' So after it got into full speed and steam, I said, 'If we could bring this nomination up right now, we could nominate Henry Wallace.'" Together with other Wallace partisans, he resolved to force an immediate, unscheduled vote to take advantage of the exultation of the moment.

Claude Pepper began hopping up and down on his flimsy chair, waving the Florida standard to get the chairman's attention. He also picked up his floor microphone but it had gone dead. So he jumped down and started up the aisle toward the podium, shouldering his way through clots of delegates, spectators, and reporters who knew exactly what he intended to do, bulling ahead like a running back on a mission to score.

He recalled rushing the podium: "I got up to about the second step from the top going just as hard as I could to get up that stairway, and I saw the Chairman look over there. He had seen me coming up the aisle. And so, immediately—by this time I got about nearly to the first step—the Chairman said, 'Motion made for adjournment . . . All in favor of the motion, let me know by saying 'Aye, aye.' And, 'That's it.' And, 'The convention's adjourned.' And I by that time was just about to the top step. And they started roaring, 'No, no, no, no.'"

In fact, nearly all eyewitnesses (and earwitnesses) later agreed that the angry, frustrated shouts of "no!" sounded far more numerous and insistent than the tentative "ayes" for adjournment, but they couldn't stop the decisive *clop* of Chairman Jackson's gavel.

Afterward, Senator Jackson said that he had to shut down the convention just before Wallace's nomination because fire marshals insisted that the convention session had run too late. That explanation hardly worked because His Honor the mayor had been right there on the podium, with nearly all the other important city officials gathered in the hall, and if they wanted to allow the session to run past curfew, Chicago's famously pliant bureaucrats would have found a way.

Another excuse involved the radio and newspaper correspondents: Jackson apologetically told Pepper, his U.S. Senate colleague, that he had seen him the entire time he'd been pushing toward the podium, and knew what he had in mind, but he'd already promised the press that the vice presidential vote would be held the next day to give them the chance to prepare. The real reason for the early adjournment, according to David McCullough's marvelous Pulitzer

Prize–winning biography *Truman* (1992), was Bob Hannegan: he had already decided to terminate the proceedings to stop the seemingly irresistible surge to nominate Henry Wallace to a post just a few feeble heartbeats away from the omnipotent role of commander in chief.

Hannegan's crucial collaborator in this decision has been ignored by history. Samuel Dillon Jackson, a pastor's son and a prosecuting attorney in Allen County, Indiana, ran unsuccessfully for Congress in 1928, and then won an interim appointment to fill a Senate vacancy left by the sudden death of a two-term Democratic incumbent. Jackson served less than ten months in Washington before a successor could be elected, and he made no effort whatever to hold the seat for himself or to run for any public office after that. The appointment of the balding, earnest interloper as permanent convention chairman in 1944 had been intended to give the little-known Hoosier and temporary senator a bit of public recognition. Moreover, he'd been so briefly and slightly involved in national politics that he'd made neither significant enemies nor meaningful allies, so his fairness and impartiality seemed a good bet. He retired to the private practice of law after an unsuccessful governor's race later in 1944, and died just six years later. Without question, the pounding of his gavel to terminate the crucial session of the Chicago convention qualified as the most significant, far-reaching decision of his fifty-five years.

Certainly, Bob Hannegan understood the impact of his own role. Before his premature death from heart disease at age forty-six in 1949, he told several friends that his epitaph should read: "Here lies the man who kept Henry Wallace from being President of the United States."

"YOU ARE THE ONE IN TROUBLE NOW"

The day after the early adjournment and the puncture of the pro-Wallace delirium, the convention managed to return to normal. Hannegan and his associates plied the wayward Senator Bennett Clark with plenty of black coffee so he could deliver the speech nominating Truman in a close approximation of sobriety, though without

"WE DIDN'T EVEN KNOW HE WAS MORTAL": Last photograph of the
ailing FDR, April 11, 1945, Warm Springs, Georgia. He died the next day,
less than three months after his inauguration for a fourth term.

his normal oratorical flair. Though Wallace led on the first ballot, he
fell short of a majority, and it took the withdrawal of several favorite
sons in the next round to send enough delegates to Truman to put
him over the top. He hadn't wanted the nomination for vice president
and repeatedly told journalists and colleagues he didn't mean to accept it. Just hours before the convention opened, he attended a meet-

ing in Bob Hannegan's hotel room where the conspirators placed a prearranged phone call to the president in San Diego.

Roosevelt spoke with such volume and force on the telephone that listeners habitually moved the receiver away from their ears, so a whole room could hear the famous voice.

"Bob, have you got that fellow lined up yet?" the president thundered after they connected.

"No," said Hannegan. "He is the contrariest goddamn mule from Missouri I ever dealt with."

"Well you tell the Senator that if he wants to break up the Democratic party in the middle of the war, that's his responsibility." At that, FDR terminated the exchange—after Truman had listened to every word.

"I was floored, I was sunk," Truman later recalled. According to others who occupied the hotel room at the time, his very first words were "Oh shit."

After a few moments of uncomfortable silence, the senator from Missouri regained his composure. "Well, if that's the situation," Truman offered, "I'll have to say yes. But why the hell didn't he tell me in the first place?"

The answer to that question should have been apparent from the first sentence that the president delivered: by identifying his prospective running mate merely as "that fellow" he seemed to have forgotten Truman's name or, at best, indicated how little he knew or valued the prospective vice president. He wanted his associates to have a running mate "lined up," and with all the other pressures he faced at the moment, he didn't seem to care deeply who it turned out to be.

The most convincing explanation of Roosevelt's strangely indecisive conduct during the weeks when others arranged the Wallace-Truman switch came from Ed Flynn, one of the primary architects of the change. "I did not think President Roosevelt enjoyed the physical strength and mental vigor he had in the past. He had aged considerably," Flynn recalled. "I believe that in order to rid himself of distress or strife and rather than argue, he permitted all aspirants for the nomination to believe it would be an open convention."

Roosevelt and Truman went on to win the presidential race with less trouble than Flynn and other worried Democrats had predicted, prevailing over the Republican Dewey by a margin of 53 percent to 46 percent in the popular vote, with a landslide verdict of 432 to 99 in the Electoral College. Still, it represented the closest margin of victory since 1916, and a shift of some three hundred thousand votes in the right states (out of nearly fifty million cast) would have turned FDR out of office. In his unexpectedly gracious concession speech, Governor Dewey asked every American to join him in the expectation that "in the difficult years ahead Divine Providence will guide and protect the President of the United States."

The subdued wartime inauguration that followed featured no parades and the bare minimum of celebration. Truman took the oath of office as vice president from his predecessor, Henry Wallace. The new VP had already begun working on the first assignment from his boss: using his Senate friendships to secure confirmation for Wallace in a new job, secretary of commerce. To make up to Wallace for what the outgoing vice president considered a "stolen" nomination at the convention, Roosevelt had offered him any cabinet job he wanted in the new administration, other than secretary of state.

He chose the Commerce Department in part to confound the many detractors who believed that his populist, antibusiness, big-government attitudes equipped him more properly for service as a Russian commissar than an American commerce secretary. Truman worked earnestly to corral the Senate votes he needed, and even went along with a "reorganization" bill that trimmed the power of Wallace's new office. Nevertheless, thirty-two senators voted against Wallace, while fifty-six agreed to his confirmation.

Truman served only eighty-two days as vice president and met privately with Roosevelt only twice in that time period: once on March 8 and then on March 19, with both occasions brief and uneventful. Ten days after their last meeting, Roosevelt departed to his private retreat and polio healing resort at Warm Springs, Georgia, hoping to gather his strength to supervise the final stages of the war against Japan. Truman adjusted comfortably to his less consequential duties and enjoyed his ability to fraternize with old friends in both houses of Congress.

On the late afternoon of April 12, he presided over the Senate, feeling brutally bored by a seemingly endless, largely incoherent speech about water rights delivered by a bloviating senator from Wisconsin. The vice president discreetly took out paper and pen and pretended to be taking notes while actually scribbling a chatty note to his younger sister and his ninety-two-year-old mother back home in Missouri.

Afterward, he joined Speaker of the House Sam Rayburn for relaxation and liquid refreshment in the old "Board of Education" established by Cactus Jack Garner when he was Speaker during Prohibition. There, the VP received an urgent call from the White House, requesting his immediate presence. Riding the slow, rickety elevator up to the second floor and the First Family's residence, he found Eleanor Roosevelt waiting for him. She stood as he came in and placed a hand on Truman's shoulder.

"Harry," she said, "the President is dead."

Truman always remembered the moments of silence that followed.

"Is there anything I can do for you?" he finally responded.

"Is there anything *we* can do for *you*," the First Lady offered. "For you are the one in trouble now."

"'GETTING TOUGH' NEVER BROUGHT ANYTHING REAL AND LASTING"

Three months later, President Truman traveled to defeated Germany for a summit meeting in Potsdam on the future of Europe; four days after its conclusion he made the final decision to drop the atom bombs that finally ended the war with Japan. In the seven and a half years of his presidency that followed, Truman faced momentous decisions of such profound consequence that he shaped world history for more than a generation—organizing NATO, initiating the Marshall Plan, recognizing the state of Israel, and conducting a major war under the auspices of the United Nations to defend South Korea. He and his associates laid out the master plans to contain Soviet imperialism and to build the postwar prosperity that, followed by his eight bipartisan successors, won the Cold War.

He also scored the greatest political upset in American history to that time, winning a second term against the heavily favored Tom Dewey and unseating Republican majorities in both houses of Congress. In the more than sixty-five years since he left the White House, respect for the once derided "Give 'em Hell Harry" has risen to such an astonishing extent that twenty-first-century surveys of presidential "greatness" place him near the top of the list—among the first ten, almost always, deemed a "near great" by participating scholars and historians.

Watching this history unfold from his perch within the Truman cabinet, Henry Wallace mused over how the fractured and turbulent world might have been better—less polarized, more cooperative and peaceful—had Senator Claude Pepper run just a few seconds faster in rushing the podium at the Chicago convention and thereby succeeded in nominating Wallace for reelection as vice president.

We know Wallace would have taken a radically different approach to the postwar world because he expressed those thoughts freely and frequently, in print, interviews, and a private memo to the president dated July 1946 that was extraordinary for its open hostility toward the defense and foreign policies of the administration he served. The secretary of commerce ventured far afield from his official portfolio to demand radical cuts in defense spending and to warn that the world at large had come to believe "that we are trying to build up a predominance of force to intimidate the rest of mankind." He also deeply feared the "special relationship" between the United States and Great Britain, and resented the influence of Churchill (even after the prime minister had been voted out of power) because he considered Sir Winston a bombastic warmonger. "Aside from our common language and common literary tradition, we have no more in common with Imperialistic England than with Communist Russia," he declared in one notably Anglophobic address.

On September 12, he planned a major New York City speech that he hoped would rival the impact of the "Century of the Common Man" oration he had delivered to worldwide acclaim just four years earlier. Assembling a coalition of left-wing groups in a massive "Rally for Peace" at Madison Square Garden, the former vice president addressed a capacity crowd of twenty thousand. He sat on the stage beside Paul Robeson, the prodigiously gifted actor, singer, and African American activist—a longtime supporter of the Russian regime and later a winner of the Stalin Peace Prize and émigré to the Soviet Union. Wallace listened intently as his old friend Senator Claude Pepper of Florida warmed up the crowd by denouncing the anti-Communist excesses of the Truman administration in which Wallace retained a prominent post. "With conservative Democrats and reactionary Republicans making our foreign policy as they are today," Pepper shouted, "it is all we can do to keep foolish people from having us pull a Hitler blitzkrieg and drop our atomic bombs on the Russian people."

When the secretary of commerce took his turn, he praised "the tremendous emotional power which Marxism and Leninism gives to the Russian leaders" and asked his audience to "realize that we are reckoning with a force which cannot be handled successfully by a 'Get tough with Russia' policy. 'Getting tough' never brought anything real and lasting—whether for schoolyard bullies or businessmen or world powers."

Even while Joseph Stalin presided over one of the deadliest dictatorships in human history, Galahad comfortably compared Russia and the United States. "Russian ideas of social-economic justice are going to govern nearly a third of the world. Our ideas of free-enterprise democracy will govern much of the rest. . . . Under friendly peaceful competition the Russian world and the American world will gradually become more alike. . . . We who look on this war-with-Russia talk as criminal foolishness must carry our message direct to the people— even though we may be called communists because we dare to speak out."

The Madison Square Garden crowd roared its approval. They loved the speech; the president of the United States emphatically did not. Naturally, he demanded that Wallace resign, citing the fury of

ON APRIL 14, 1945, THREE POTENTIAL PRESIDENTS
MOURN FDR: James F. Byrnes (left), "Assistant President" and
future secretary of state; the new president Harry Truman
(center); and secretary of commerce and former vice president
Henry A. Wallace (right). At the Democratic Convention of
the previous year, each of them had drawn passionate
support for the vice presidency.

Secretary of State Jimmy Byrnes, who saw Wallace's speech as a direct attack on his diplomatic leadership. Wallace insisted that Truman himself had reviewed his speech in advance of its delivery and enthusiastically approved its contents, but it's impossible to imagine that the source of the Truman Doctrine would have sanctioned the more inflammatory passages of the explosive Madison Square Garden address.

"THE LORD IS WITH YOU, YOU MIGHTY MAN OF VALOR!"

Leaving the cabinet, Wallace took over the editor's post at the progressive flagship the *New Republic*, using its pages for regular blasts at his old friends in the administration. Other friends in the Kremlin no doubt regretted his departure from the cabinet, given his expressed eagerness to advance Soviet interests behind the scenes. In late 1945, the former vice president met with Russian diplomat Anatoly Gorsky, who also served as chief of the Washington station for the NKGB, precursor of the notorious KGB. Secret, decrypted Russian intelligence communiqués, released in the 1990s after the end of the Cold War, report that Wallace argued for the sharing of American atomic technology with Stalin's scientists and asked for Gorsky's assistance in besting the anti-Soviet elements in Truman's inner circle. In fact, less visible Communist operatives worked in close proximity to Wallace during much of his time in Washington. John Abt and Charles Kramer, subsequently identified as sources for Russian intelligence, both worked with Wallace during his years at the Department of Agriculture. At the end of 1947, when Wallace decided to run for president against Truman, Kramer signed up to become his speechwriter and Abt served as chief counsel to the campaign.

The political adventure in which they collaborated began with high hopes and lofty intentions, seeking to bring peace and cooperation between the United States and the Soviet Union, while establishing racial justice and economic equality on the domestic front. For Galahad, his candidacy amounted to a calling, not just a campaign. Wallace dubbed his loyal followers "Gideon's Army" in honor of the Old Testament hero who, with just three hundred godly and carefully selected men, prevailed over thousands of idol-worshipping Midianites. When an angel of the Lord appeared to Gideon, he greeted the hero with a ringing declaration: "The Lord is with you, you mighty man of valor!"

Henry Wallace seemed to hear similar voices, promising success for his efforts despite the gloomy history of third-party adventures. His followers took the name Progressive Party for the group that coalesced around the former vice president, even though the new organization bore scant resemblance to the old Progressive Party that conducted TR's gallant Bull Moose campaign in 1912. This time, luminaries from the world of arts and entertainment played a far more prominent role than elected officials or grassroots activists. Arthur Miller, Aaron Copland, Lillian Hellman, Dashiell Hammett, Pete Seeger, Artie Shaw, John Huston, Norman Mailer, Burl Ives, Clifford Odets, W.E.B. Du Bois, Judy Holliday, Frank Lloyd Wright, Lewis Milestone, and Thomas Mann all enlisted in Galahad's Crusade, and in the early stages of the complicated race, they seemed to believe he had a chance.

Polls at year's end in 1947 showed Wallace harvesting 20 percent of the vote, within striking distance of both the deeply unpopular Truman and Governor Dewey of New York, once again the standard-bearer for the Republicans. The energized Progressives staged a crowded, boisterous convention in Philadelphia, but many of the delegates seemed to feel more excited about Joseph Stalin than about Henry Wallace. Even for left-wing observers, the Communist influence became inescapable, and uncomfortable. Radical journalist I. F. Stone attended the convention and supported the nominee, but expressed deep skepticism about the people surrounding him. "The Communists have been the dominant influence in the Progressive Party," he wrote. "If it had not been for the Communists, there would have been no Progressive Party." Harvard-educated labor lawyer Lee Pressman, later publicly exposed as a Soviet spy since the 1930s, wrote the platform and then used underhanded tactics to get it approved.

At the convention, Rexford Tugwell, a prominent New Dealer and a key member of FDR's Brains Trust, became so disillusioned by the bullying tactics of the Stalinist left that he described himself as "heart sick" and told his wife he wanted to "disaffiliate" from the party. He never did campaign for Wallace and eventually denounced the Progressive campaign. Other New Dealers moved more quickly to reject the candidate's effort to present himself as Roosevelt's true heir. Harold Ickes, Francis Biddle, Archibald MacLeish, Herbert Lehman, and many others signed a statement calling on liberals to back Truman in November because "the Progressive party has lined up unabashedly with the forces of Soviet totalitarianism."

Most important, Eleanor Roosevelt, still an influential columnist and the official custodian of her late husband's legacy, spoke out repeatedly against the former vice president whose initial nomination she had helped to secure. "The American Communists will be the nucleus of Mr. Wallace's third party," she warned. "Any use of my husband's name in connection with that party is from my point of view entirely dishonest."

"A MESSIANIC FUMBLER"

In addition to the unsavory Stalinist associations and the unnecessary alienation of prominent New Dealers, the Progressive nominee left the Philadelphia convention with yet another burden that weighed down his efforts to wage a competitive contest. In Senator Glen Taylor of Idaho, Wallace had personally and purposefully recruited the most wildly eccentric running mate ever associated with a significant American campaign.

Senator Taylor attracted frequent attention in the press for his punishing, physical beatdowns of political enemies (and sometimes allies), his outrageous pompadour toupee, and his proud distinction as "the first ever professional actor ever elevated to the United States Senate." Known widely as "the Singing Cowboy," he campaigned with guitar, banjo, ballads of his own composition, and an array of western boots and headgear, mixed with radical populist visions of shattering the status quo. He finally won election to "the world's greatest deliberative body" on his third try in 1944—the same year the Democrats dumped Vice President Henry Wallace from their national ticket. Upon his arrival in Washington, he boldly rode his wonder horse, Nugget, up the steps of the Capitol, but humorless guards blocked the well-trained beast from joining its master in the Senate chamber. One of thirteen children born to an itinerant evangelist who traveled through Oregon, California, Montana, and Idaho, Taylor dropped out of school in eighth grade to join his brother in a traveling theater company that appealed to small-town crowds throughout the West. Just weeks after his arrival in Washington, he introduced an ambitious Senate resolution in the spirit of Wallace's utopian internationalism, calling for the dissolution of national boundaries and "favoring the creation of a world republic." He became the first Democrat to go on record in opposition to the Atlantic alliance that later became NATO. *Time* magazine lambasted him as "the banjo-twanging playboy of the Senate and an easy mark for far-Left propaganda."

Two years after running for vice president, Glen Taylor lost his Senate seat and made two unsuccessful attempts to win it back. At last, he abandoned Idaho and politics, retiring to Millbrae, California, where he went into business making male hairpieces based on the flamboyant rig he had designed for his own prematurely balding pate. "Taylor Toppers," also known as "Taylormade Hair Replacement," became an international sensation and an enduring American success story, based on a patented design that the former candidate's family assembled by hand.

Even with such a colorful and unconventional running mate, Henry Wallace couldn't distract attention from his own odd indulgences or dodge the sort of microscopic personal focus that comes, inevitably, with a presidential campaign. The "Guru Letters" finally surfaced, uncomfortably recalling the onetime agriculture secretary's blissful, bleary-eyed experience as a hypnotized follower of Nicholas Roerich. The acerbic right-wing columnist Westbrook Pegler gleefully featured long excerpts of this occultist correspondence, apparently provided by a member of Roerich's inner circle who felt betrayed by the candidate's estrangement from his long-ago rejected mentor. Pegler tagged Wallace as "a messianic fumbler" who was "off center, mentally."

Meanwhile, Wallace spoke relentlessly about the need for accommodation with the Soviets, hoping to mobilize Gideon's Army in what he called "the Fight for Peace." In the process, he defended every aggressive move by Stalin, including his brutal takeover of Czechoslovakia and his increasing pressure on Turkey and Greece. He blamed Truman for all international tensions and predicted that his "bipartisan reactionary war policy" would leave American soldiers "lying in their Arctic suits in the Russian snow." He warned that the United States faced an imminent Fascist takeover because "we recognize Hitlerite methods when we see them in our own land." Several reporters noted that long sections of Wallace's speeches appeared to be lifted directly from the editorials in the Communist Party newspaper, the *Daily Worker*. Arthur M. Schlesinger Jr. summarized the transformation of the once widely admired vice president: "He became in effect a Soviet apologist."

The Election Day results wrote a crushing conclusion to Wallace's political career: while Truman won his historic upset against Dewey, the man he had replaced as vice president drew a mere 2.37 percent of the national popular vote. His highest showing came in New York, where his 8.3 percent helped tilt the state to Dewey. In the South, where he dedicated weeks to braving hostile crowds and dodging hurled vegetables as a courageous and outspoken champion of civil rights, he found an appalling lack of support: drawing only one-tenth of 1 percent in South Carolina, or a mere 154 votes.

Looking back at Wallace's blasted hopes and disastrous campaign, revisionist historians cite the Democratic convention of 1944 as one of the tragic hinges of history, where America turned irrevocably toward immoral policies and unworthy leadership. In *The Untold History of the United States,* their twelve-part Showtime documentary series, and in the thick tome that accompanied it, film director Oliver Stone and American University historian Peter Kuznick identify a potential "President Wallace" as the nation's last, best hope. "Had [Claude] Pepper made it five more feet and nominated Wallace," Stone told *The Nation,* "Wallace would have become president in 1945 and . . . there might have been no atomic bombings, no nuclear arms race, and no Cold War." He might have added that Senator Pepper's push to the podium wouldn't have been necessary had the ailing and failing FDR simply provided his sitting vice president with the same sort of unequivocal endorsement that had forced him on the ticket four years earlier.

While Stone, Kuznick, and others believe that President Wallace might have guided the weary world to a golden age of cooperation and accommodation, most mainstream historians insist that America caught a major break when providence chose the right vice that sweltering night in Chicago.

Most important, they can call a star witness to help win their case before the bar of history.

That witness is Henry Wallace himself.

"SOMETHING UTTERLY EVIL"

After the thrills and horrors of his presidential campaign, Wallace retired to his sprawling estate in upstate New York, where he established his own experimental farm, developing highly successful hybrid chickens to go along with his world-changing hybrid corn. He also wrote regularly on agricultural science and history, including a definitive volume on the history of corn. Politically, he drifted back toward his family's Republican roots and publicly endorsed Dwight Eisenhower in his reelection run of 1956. He also initiated a warm correspondence with one of his successors as vice president: Richard Nixon. Though Wallace took no side in the spirited Kennedy-Nixon contest of 1960, JFK invited him to his 1961 inauguration—the first time the former vice president had attended such a ceremony since 1945. He wrote the young president to express his gratitude and told him: "At no time in our history have so many tens of millions of people been so completely enthusiastic about an Inaugural Address as about yours."

How could the most important advocate of Russian accommodation find common ground with a relentless Cold Warrior like Kennedy? The answer is that Henry Agard Wallace, against all reasonable expectations, turned out to be one of those rare souls with the ability and the courage to change his mind, publicly and completely.

In 1950, he broke with the remaining shell of his Progressive Party to support Truman when he led the United Nations effort to turn back North Korean aggression against the South. And then in 1952, he published an altogether remarkable piece in *This Week* magazine titled, simply, "Where I Was Wrong."

With stunning candor, he confessed to his long-standing naïveté and blindness regarding the crimes of the Soviet Union. "As I look back across my trip across Soviet Asia to China, I can see after reading accounts by former slave laborers who escaped from Siberia that I was altogether too much impressed by the show put on by high Russian officials, who as human beings seemed just like typical capitalistic 'go-getters.' . . . I had seen some evidence of the common man on the march in Asia in 1944, but what I did not see was the Soviet determination to enslave the common man morally, mentally, and physically for its own imperial purposes."

Rejecting his former savage assaults on the Truman administration and warnings about the advent of Fascism in the United States, he unequivocally declared: "So far as Asia is concerned, the US has never been an imperialistic nation. We freed the Philippines and will get out of Formosa and Japan when the danger of Red military aggression is certainly passed. The US has never engaged and will never engage in colonialism on the mainland of Asia."

In conclusion, he aligned himself with the Cold War consensus that empowered our presidents from Truman and Eisenhower through Reagan and Bush: "More and more I am convinced that Russian Communism in its total disregard of truth, in its fanaticism, its intolerance and its resolute denial of God and religion is something utterly evil."

In 1962, three years before he died at age seventy-seven of ALS—Lou Gehrig's disease—Wallace enjoyed a brief, earthy exchange with his old rival and nemesis Harry Truman. Fortunately for both men, they had reestablished a cordial relationship once they put politics behind them. Wallace sensed Truman's concern over lingering bitterness from their past battles and sought to reassure him. "I'm glad you fired me when you did," he declared.

Subsequent generations should share that gratitude for the way that fate, and ultimately Wallace himself, got things right.

"WE HAVE ALSO COME TO THIS HALLOWED SPOT TO REMIND
AMERICA OF THE FIERCE URGENCY OF NOW":
Martin Luther King Jr. delivers the "I Have a Dream" speech
at the Lincoln Memorial, August 28, 1963.

9

From the Mountaintop

Providence, Prophecy, and Dr. King

The night before a racist sniper cut him down with a single shot, Dr. Martin Luther King Jr. delivered a hauntingly eloquent speech—one that anticipated his own death.

After an evening of tornado alerts and slashing rain, Dr. King arrived late at the Mason Temple in Memphis to address a restless crowd of two thousand. They had waited two hours to hear him speak.

After thanking the audience for displaying their determination by braving the inclement weather, he delivered an emotional talk without notes, reassuring the city's striking sanitation workers that he would help them prevail in their struggle.

To put that battle in context, he cited great moments in history, from biblical times to the present day, expressing his gratitude "that God has allowed me to live in this period to see what is unfolding." Nearing his conclusion, he explicitly alluded to personal dangers and a flurry of threats from "some of our sick white brothers."

As the crowd hushed, his delivery assumed an air of exultation. At that point, the Nobel Peace Prize winner, just thirty-nine years old, began to reflect, as he often did, on his own mortality.

"Like anybody, I would like to live a long life. Longevity has its place. But I'm not concerned about that now. I just want to do God's will. And He's allowed me to go up to the mountain. And I've looked over. And I've seen the promised land. I may not get there with you. But I want you to know, tonight, that we, as a people, will get to the promised land!"

FOUR FATALISTS

This prophetic proclamation, combined with his cruel martyrdom the next day, helped secure King's place among the most admired of all Americans.

Only four individuals have been honored with federal holidays bearing their names: Christopher Columbus, George Washington, Abraham Lincoln, and Martin Luther King Jr. Though separated by nearly five hundred years of history and dramatically divergent backgrounds, those four shared a crucial common bond: an unshakable sense that their lives had been shaped by a higher power, to serve grand purposes.

Columbus took his first name seriously—it meant "Christ Bearer"—and he saw his voyages and discoveries as components of a divine mission.

Washington developed a similar sense of his own predestined role in a grand plan of cosmic significance. As a twenty-three-year-old lieutenant colonel in the Virginia militia, he emerged unscathed from the first major battle of the French and Indian War, in which nearly all of his fellow officers had been killed or wounded.

In Lincoln's case, a childhood of mournful, impoverished obscurity unfolded together with an instinctive expectation that he would play a significant part in the development of the young nation. As president, he repeatedly described himself as "an humble instrument in the hands of the Almighty."

A hundred years later, Martin Luther King came to perceive his role in similar terms, expressing a grim, persistent fatalism that Lincoln himself might have recognized. Like Honest Abe, Dr. King spoke to friends about numerous childhood scrapes that nearly killed him.

"SAVING HIM FOR US"

At age five, young Martin, known at the time as "M.L." or "Little Mike," fell—or jumped—from an upstairs banister and plunged headfirst to the floor more than ten feet below. The way his Pulitzer Prize–winning biographer Taylor Branch heard the story, the boy may have been upset over a household accident: his little brother A.D. (Alfred Daniel) slid down the banister of their comfortable home on Atlanta's Auburn Avenue and knocked over their beloved grand- mother, Jennie Celeste Parks Williams. According to family lore, M.L.'s small body bounced through an open door into the cellar. To the immense relief of his weeping relatives, the boy got back up to reassure them; miraculously, the damage to his limbs and skull was light.

A few years later, a car hit M.L.'s bicycle from behind, throwing him to the sidewalk. The accident destroyed the bike but spared the child. Six months later, on a new bike, he collided with another car and went hurtling over the handlebars, slamming his face against the street with a force that could have been fatal.

Years later, yet another blow to the side of his head came from a baseball bat that slipped from the hands of his younger but taller brother A.D. The guilty batter later recalled: "He was up right away and arguing that I was out because I'd missed on a third strike. M.L.'s got a hard head, all right."

A final episode represented perhaps the most serious and trou- bling test to his apparent indestructibility.

On a May Sunday in 1941, when M.L. was twelve, he slipped out of the house after church to watch a parade downtown. That same afternoon, his grandmother had agreed to deliver an inspirational talk for "Women's Day" at a neighboring Baptist church. Because of his furtive decision to see the parade, her "favorite grandson" missed the chance to hear her message.

When he returned at dusk, after hours of savoring the floats and marching bands near the center of the city, M.L. learned that his grandmother had been struck by a heart attack while waiting her turn to speak. She died on the spot at age sixty-eight. Overcome with guilt,

M.L. felt responsible for the terrible news. The stricken boy trudged up the stairs of his home and, echoing the incident of seven years before, impulsively threw himself out of a second-story window.

Years later, Martin Luther King Sr. recalled the incident, especially his son's distress as he "cried off and on for several days afterward and was unable to sleep at night." Daddy King tried to explain "that God had His own plan and His own way, and we cannot change or interfere with the time He chooses to call any of us back to Him."

The younger King remembered the events of that day as a personal turning point and, in an autobiographical sketch he composed at age twenty-two, recalled that they had a "tremendous effect on my religious development." He wrote that both his parents comforted him with assurances that "somehow my grandmother still lived," shaping his mature identity as "a strong believer in personal immortality."

Five years later that belief helped him face down regular death threats during the yearlong struggle that became known as the Montgomery bus boycott. To compel local authorities to abandon the long-standing rule that forced black people to the back of public buses, King, newly arrived in town, led local pastors in urging congregants to walk to work each day.

Among the weary crowds trudging through the wintry streets in 1956, one elderly woman expressed the growing sense among King's followers that the powerful young preacher had been dispatched and sustained by a higher power. She listened to some of her friends from church recounting the many close calls that spared him from death or serious injury during his eventful childhood. "The Lord had His hand on him even then," she concluded. "He was saving him for us. No harm could come to him."

When friends reported this comment to King himself, he felt too touched to dismiss it with a modest laugh or a shrug. After a pause, he basically concurred with the assumptions about heavenly protection. "Well, I guess God was looking out for me even then," he allowed. "He must have given me a hard head just for that purpose."

"THE MARK OF GREAT EXPECTATIONS"

King saw further indication of providential purpose in his dramatic renaming at age five.

His father had been born *Michael* Luther King, the son of a Georgia sharecropper and former slave. He named his eldest son after himself, recording his name as Michael Luther King Jr.—hence the nicknames "M.L." and "Little Mike."

In 1931, Daddy King succeeded his father-in-law as pastor of Atlanta's Ebenezer Baptist Church and quickly established himself as one of the most influential black preachers in the South. In that capacity, he got the chance for a grand, once-in-a-lifetime tour of Europe and the Holy Land before attending a weeklong meeting in Berlin with the Baptist World Alliance.

While in Germany, he felt inspired to visit some sites associated with Martin Luther, who, more than four hundred years before, changed the church and the world through the force of his faith and his rhetoric. The traveling minister felt a profound spiritual connection with the Great Reformer. When Daddy King returned home to his family and congregants, he brought with him a dramatic announcement.

Welcomed as a conquering hero by local clergy, Daddy King triumphantly announced that he would legally change his first name from Michael to Martin, in order to make his middle name (Luther) a more explicit, unmistakable reference to the founder of Protestant Christianity. At the same time, he naturally changed the name of his precocious and promising son, who now became Martin Luther King Jr.—a resonant designation that seemed to anoint him in advance as a fearless reformer ready to challenge the oppressive institutions of his time.

As Taylor Branch observed in *Parting the Waters: America in the King Years, 1954–63:* "The change of name was one of the most important events in the younger King's early life. For him it would be the mark of great expectations, a statement of identity that honored traditions in both religion and race. Name changes have always been part of religious history, used to announce the existence of a 'new person.'

Jacob became Israel, Saul of Tarsus became Paul, Simon became Peter, and the first act of every new pope is to choose a special name for his reign."

In King's case, the name selection made on his behalf by the father he greatly admired served not only to bring M.L. closer to the implacable, fearless Martin Luther, but to give his very existence a more godly and fateful dimension. After the name change, King had little doubt about his path in life. He had been raised, after all, to join the family business: his father, grandfather, and great-grandfather all served as preachers, as did his only brother and his father's brother.

Yet to him, the religious role he had been fated to fulfill shaped a prophet as much as a pastor. "Somehow the preacher must have a kind of fire shut up in his bones," he told that enraptured Memphis audience the night before his death. "Somehow the preacher must say with Jesus, 'The Spirit of the Lord is upon me, because he hath anointed me,' and he's anointed me to deal with the problems of the poor."

"THE RICHEST NEGRO STREET IN THE WORLD"

He sensed that anointing despite the unquestionably comfortable circumstances of his own upbringing.

Born in an upstairs bedroom of his grandparents' Atlanta home, King junior grew up in that same spacious two-story residence at 501 Auburn Avenue—a bustling boulevard celebrated by *Fortune* magazine in 1956 as "the richest Negro street in the world." Lined with respectable wooden houses with generous front porches, and boasting a rich array of thriving businesses, cafés, churches, and night-clubs, the avenue lent its name to a district of approximately eight square blocks known affectionately as "Sweet Auburn," home to the city's most prominent, prosperous black families. At a time when seg-regated housing patterns remained strictly in force, no level of success would have enabled the Kings to venture beyond the Sweet Auburn district for one of the leafy, privileged white neighborhoods springing up elsewhere in and around the city. In fact, black businesses and residents had first migrated to that refuge east of downtown when the bloody race riots of 1906 left twenty-seven dead, sending an unmistakable message that people of color couldn't feel welcome at the city's center.

Throughout boyhood and adolescence, young King remained ensconced in the cozy confines of his neighborhood. Ebenezer Baptist Church, the fortress of faith where his mother's father had preached the Gospel for a generation and his father continued to do so, stood less than three blocks from the family home. When King was thirteen, impressive test scores allowed him to enroll at Booker T. Washington High School, established just five years before his birth as Georgia's first public high school for black students. He rode the bus and dressed so formally in tweed jackets that he earned the nickname "Tweedy." He also quickly won a reputation for oratorical ability, earning a place on the school's debate squad and winning a local speech contest sponsored by the Negro Elks Club.

Despite his age (two years younger than most of his fellow students), and the compact stature that classmates derided as "shrimpy" (even as an adult, King never stood more than five foot seven), he loved sports and excelled at basketball. On the court, he became notorious as a "will-shoot"—a foolhardy but surprisingly effective outside gunner who hated to pass the ball. Yet even his most irrational shots, launched directly above the heads of defenders who usually towered over him, somehow managed to find their own implausible arc to the basket and to glory.

At age fifteen, M.L. followed another unlikely arc in his personal ascent: he completed his high school graduation requirements and won admission to Morehouse College. The onetime Baptist seminary had been generously sustained and developed by the devoutly religious oil tycoon John D. Rockefeller (an ardent abolitionist before and during the Civil War) and had already claimed its aspirational title as "the Black Harvard." Riding the bus between his family home and nearby classes at the Atlanta University Center, King wasted little time on distractions and single-mindedly pursued his goals: winning ordination as a Baptist minister and preaching part-time at his father's church, even before his graduation as a sociology major at age nineteen.

At that point, the young prince of Sweet Auburn ventured far from his hospitable home ground for the first time, enrolling at the Crozer Theological Seminary, a predominantly white Baptist institution near Chester, Pennsylvania, that gave him a taste of life outside the South. He graduated as class valedictorian in 1951 and then moved on to Boston University, where he acquired both a PhD (in Systematic Theology) and, more important, a wife.

SMALL STATURE, BIG DELUSIONS

Coretta Scott came from the small town of Marion, Alabama, where her father, Obadiah, had briefly served in the local police department before establishing himself as Perry County's most prominent black entrepreneur. Obie Scott owned a filling station and a trucking company, along with several hundred cotton-growing acres on which he built a gracious country house with his own hands. Coretta delighted her domineering daddy by displaying an early gift for music, mastering trumpet and piano and ultimately directing a local church choir. She developed a rich, velvety smooth, and powerful soprano voice and dreamed of an improbable career in the opera house or the recital hall, despite the lack of funds to secure the training she needed and the racial barriers that still confronted women of color. After following her sister to Antioch College, in Ohio, she earned a small scholarship to the prestigious New England Conservatory of Music in Boston.

There she met Martin Luther King Jr., the driven dynamo then pursuing his graduate studies at BU. Initially, Coretta found herself somewhat put off by the odd combination of small stature and big delusions of grandeur on the part of a twenty-two-year-old who was a full two years younger than she was.

In the memoir that she wrote shortly after his death, she recalled their conversation when he called her on the phone at the suggestion of a friend. He had seen her photograph and heard positive reports of her admirable qualities, so he aggressively demanded that they meet as soon as possible. "I'm like Napoleon," he announced. "I'm at my Waterloo, and I'm on my knees."

Won over by his pleading, she agreed to see him for lunch the next day, and as he drove her back to the conservatory he declared: "The four things that I look for in a wife are character, intelligence, personality and beauty. And you have them all." Apparently, it never occurred to him that any young woman with such attributes could possibly pass up the opportunity to drop her own ambitions and to come along on his predestined winged chariot ride to the spiritual leadership of his people.

Daddy King presided, regally, over his son's wedding on June 18, 1953, officiating on the spacious front lawn of Obadiah Scott's farmhouse. After a wearying reception with crowds of relatives and well-wishers, the young couple never got much of a chance for a romantic wedding night. With an exhausted M.L. sleeping in the seat beside her, Coretta did most of the driving in their five-hour, pre-interstate trek toward the King family home in Atlanta. They couldn't get a room anywhere in Alabama because long-standing tradition, backed by state law, prohibited motels and resorts from accommodating black people. They spent the first night of their marriage in a well-furnished funeral parlor that was owned by a friend of Coretta's family.

"I'VE BEEN CALLED TO PREACH"

During their first summer, the newlyweds busied themselves with the affairs of Daddy King's Ebenezer Church and participated in an eventful black Baptist convention in Florida, where younger leaders successfully challenged the stodgy establishment to force more aggressive efforts to demand civil rights. Back in Boston, M.L. tried to concentrate on finishing his PhD, but planned the next chapter of his life. He noted that by 1954, he had been "in school for twenty-one years without a break" and meant to begin his independent pastoral career at the same time he completed his doctoral dissertation.

He knew he could choose among any number of opportunities. A church in Massachusetts expressed interest in hiring him, as did another congregation in New York State, presenting the Kings with the chance to remain in the Northeast. A third church seemed to provide a more promising possibility, which would bring M.L. to Chattanooga, Tennessee—much closer to home. Three historically black colleges also corresponded with him over potential teaching or administrative positions, but after so many years of academia he leaned toward a pulpit position.

In the midst of these deliberations came an opportunity to preach a guest sermon at the historic Dexter Avenue Baptist Church in Montgomery, Alabama. The venerable congregation had been searching for a new pastor for more than a year. The previous incumbent, the turbulent civil rights pioneer Vernon Johns, had been forced from his post after riling the local white power elite and, more destructively, offending his own congregation's wealthiest and most influential members. Understanding the speaking invitation as a high-stakes audition, Daddy King strongly discouraged his son from making the appearance, naming the prominent families and overbearing individuals who would harass any newcomer to the prestigious pulpit.

The younger King nonetheless insisted that he could measure up to the challenge. He preached a sermon he'd already delivered as a guest in other black congregations. Under the title "The Dimensions of a Complete Life," he insisted that "if my life's work is not developed for the good of humanity, it is meaningless and Godless."

Impressed by his message, and by his precocious oratorical command, the pulpit committee at Dexter recommended that the church secure King's services as their new pastor. The members of the congregation unanimously endorsed the decision.

M.L. returned on May 2, 1954, to deliver his acceptance address to an expectant, excited crowd. "I come to the pastorate of Dexter at a most crucial hour of our world's history," he announced. Admitting that he addressed his task as neither a "great preacher" nor a "profound scholar," he nonetheless expressed unshakable confidence in the significance of his new mission. "I have felt with Jesus that the spirit of the Lord is upon me," he declaimed to his new congregants, "because he hath anointed me to preach the gospel to the poor, to heal the brokenhearted, to preach deliverance to the captives, and to set at liberty them that are bruised."

"THE MAN AND THE HOUR HAVE MET"

Within six months, the choice of this new pastor by a small but prestigious church in a provincial city had managed to change the world. Without King's leadership, the Montgomery bus boycott might have occurred, and even succeeded, but it never would have become a stirring, almost apocalyptic struggle that aroused the conscience of the country. And had he not moved to Montgomery at precisely the right moment, Martin Luther King might well have emerged, eventually, as a significant African American leader, but it's hard to imagine any way he could have achieved that dominating stature before the age of thirty.

At a very different confluence of historic forces in Montgomery, Alabama, former congressman William Lowndes Yancey proudly proclaimed: "The Man and the Hour have met." Ironically, Yancey—a notorious pro-secession "fire-eater" and unrepentant racist—used that phrase to hail the inauguration of Jefferson Davis as the new president of the Confederacy. That 1862 ceremony took place at the Alabama capitol, which literally cast its shadow on the very site where Dexter Avenue Baptist Church (originally Second Baptist Colored Church) began building its permanent sanctuary some fifteen years later.

As the proud "Cradle of the Confederacy" (the original capital city before Richmond took over the role), Montgomery remained one of the most strictly, fiercely segregated cities anywhere in the South. Civil rights activist Virginia Durr, who had just returned home after ten years in the nation's capital, described Montgomery as a venue of "death, decay, corruption, frustration, bitterness and sorrow. The Lost Cause is right."

But the city's black leaders found a new cause on the first of December in 1955.

Around six o'clock on that Thursday evening, a forty-two-year-old civil rights activist named Rosa Parks boarded the Cleveland Avenue bus after a long day of work as a seamstress in a downtown department store. Contrary to common depictions of the ensuing incident, Parks made no attempt to sit anywhere in the front ten rows of the bus, which were reserved, by law and custom, for white people. Instead, she made her way toward the back and, together with three other people of color, occupied seats in the row right behind the white section.

They rode quietly, and undisturbed, for two or three stops before a crowd of white people boarded the vehicle and filled up all the places reserved for whites at the front. This left one particular gentleman standing in place, glowering down at the black faces in the row right behind the "whites only" portion of the vehicle. The driver took note of the situation, stopped the bus, and walked toward the rear to confront the uncooperative black passengers. As Rosa Parks recalled some forty years later: "When that white driver stepped back toward us, when he waved his hand and ordered us up and out of our seats, I felt a determination cover my body like a quilt on a winter night."

In response to the bus driver's impatient orders, three of the black passengers in the contested seats stood up and quietly complied. Rosa Parks did not. It wasn't a question of her weariness, as much as a sense that she had reached a breaking point.

"I was not tired physically, or no more tired than I usually was at the end of a working day," she remembered. "I was not old, although some people have an image of me as being old then. I was forty-two. No, the only tired I was, was tired of giving in." The driver once more demanded that she vacate her seat but she politely declined. "And he told me he would have me arrested. And I told him he may do that. And of course, he did."

With the bus parked on the street and many of the other passengers angrily abandoning it, two policemen arrived and one of them asked Parks why she refused to stand. "I told him I didn't think I should have to stand up," she recalled. "And then I asked him, why did they push us around? And he said, and I quote him, 'I don't know, but the law is the law and you are under arrest.' And with that, I got off the bus, under arrest."

After friends from the NAACP bailed her out, she appeared in court the next day to face charges of disorderly conduct and violations of the city's segregation code. Her conviction took all of thirty minutes, with a fine of $10 plus $4 in court costs. By that time, news of her arrest had spread throughout the angry and exasperated black community, with activists drawing up plans for a one-day bus boycott at the beginning of the next week. Dr. King didn't know Parks personally, since he was new in town and she attended a different black Baptist church, but he recognized the importance of her reputation. "Mrs. Parks was ideal for the role assigned to her by history," he wrote years later, noting that "her character was impeccable and her dedication deep-rooted."

"SUBSTITUTE TIRED FEET FOR TIRED SOULS"

On the Sunday after her Thursday arrest, ministers in all the black churches preached sermons about Rosa Parks, and proposed a bus boycott for the next day.

That Monday protest proved unexpectedly successful: local newspapers reported that some 90 percent of the city's regular black passengers stayed off the buses and found alternate means to work. Later that afternoon, a mass meeting drew several thousand excited participants to the Holt Street Baptist Church and organized the Montgomery Improvement Association to extend the impromptu boycott to force concessions from the white establishment. They also chose Dr. King as its leader, despite his age (only twenty-six) and his status as a newcomer who had lived in the city less than two years. As Rosa Parks recalled, "The advantage of having Dr. King as president was that he was so new to Montgomery and to civil rights work that he hadn't been there long enough to make any strong friends or enemies."

He did make an immediate impression, however, on the jammed meeting that selected him. "Let us go out with a grim and bold determination that we are going to stick together," he roared to the big crowd at Holt Street Baptist Church. "Right here in Montgomery, when the history books are written in the future, somebody will have to say, 'There lived a race of people—a black people, fleecy locks and black complexion—a people who had the moral courage to stand up for their rights.'"

As he concluded and took his seat, the entire church rose and cheered, affirming their "grim and bold determination" in a sustained, emotional reaction. A prominent matron in the community named Idessa Williams Redden called out in piercing, soaring tones above the general tumult, "Lord, you have sent us a leader!"

That same night, the new Montgomery Improvement Association voted to extend the one-day protest. But no one expected the struggle to go on for more than a year. For most of the city's fifty thousand black residents, public transit offered the only way to get to work: though less than half of the overall population, they made up more than three-quarters of the ridership on local buses. Without these African American passengers, those empty vehicles rattled down the Alabama avenues like useless husks, inflicting daily financial losses on the capital city.

Meanwhile, King and his associates struggled to provide alternate means of transportation. Some of the boycotters drove horse-drawn wagons to make their way to work; others actually rode mules. The MIA worked frantically to organize car pools, eventually deploying more than three hundred automobiles with volunteer drivers, using donations from around the country to purchase a few new station wagons for that purpose.

But for the most part, the city's black population walked, making their way on foot to wherever they had to go. For many, this became a matter of choice as much as of necessity, creating indelible images for the international coverage that quickly focused on Alabama's capital. People of all ages and social strata, from teachers to cleaning ladies to mechanics, trekked defiantly to jobs or schools or markets, turning every day into a silent, communal, compelling march of protest. King seized upon profound symbolism of these quiet, determined, daily walks to work. "We came to see that, in the long run, it is more honorable to walk in dignity than ride in humiliation," he proclaimed. "We decided to substitute tired feet for tired souls, and walk the streets of Montgomery."

A week after the boycott began, a white librarian named Juliette Morgan wrote a letter to the editor of the *Montgomery Advertiser* expressing her conviction that "history is being made in Montgomery these days. . . . It is hard to imagine a soul so dead, a heart so hard, a vision so blinded and provincial as not to be moved with admiration at the quiet dignity, discipline, and dedication with which the Negroes have conducted their boycott."

The formal demands of this movement remained almost laughably modest: the MIA explicitly insisted on "courteous treatment by bus operators" and "first-come, first-served seating for all," but with no real expectation that black and white passengers would sit next to one another, in violation of Alabama's statewide segregation law. To avoid running afoul of that odious statute, King and his colleagues still accepted that whites would board from the front of each bus and blacks would board from the rear. But they insisted that if there were empty rows in the "whites only" section of the bus, black people would be allowed to sit in them rather than have to stand in the back with the other black passengers.

THE KITCHEN CONVERSION

Despite the reasonable and respectful tone of King and his colleagues, the politicians and bureaucrats of the local power structure pushed back with indignant ferocity. They disrupted the painstakingly assembled car pools in the black community with claims that their organizers had been operating an illegal taxi company; local insurance even canceled policies for the cars and drivers who transported the boycotters. During the 381 days of the ongoing struggle, law enforcement officials indicted King (and eighty other boycott leaders) for violating a 1921 law prohibiting conspiracies that interfered with lawful business. Worst of all, his family received up to thirty calls a day on their home phone threatening violence if he continued to battle the bus company. The angry, abusive callers invariably ordered him to leave town immediately or to suffer the bloody consequences.

King later identified the first moment he actually felt fear for his physical safety. On the afternoon of January 26, 1956, he was driving home from church with two of his congregants when the Montgomery police began following the young minister and eventually pulled him over. "Get out, King," they ordered. "You are under arrest for speeding thirty miles an hour in a twenty-five-mile zone."

To his astonishment and horror, they loaded him into a patrol car. "As we drove off, presumably to the city jail, a feeling of panic began to come over me," he remembered. "I had always had the impression that the jail was in the downtown section of Montgomery. Yet after riding for a while I noticed that we were going in a different direction. The more we rode the farther we were from the center of town. In a few minutes we turned into a dark and dingy street that I had never seen and headed under a desolate old bridge. By this time, I was convinced that these men were carrying me to some faraway spot to dump me off. . . . Then I began to wonder whether they were driving me out to some waiting mob, planning to use the excuse later on that they had been overpowered. I found myself trembling within and without. . . . By this time we were passing under the bridge. I was sure now that I was going to meet my fateful hour on the other side. But as I looked up I noticed a glaring light in the distance, and soon I saw the words 'Montgomery City Jail.' I was so relieved that it was some time before I realized the irony of my position: going to jail at that moment seemed like going to some safe haven!"

The sense of relief gave way to other thoughts as the jail doors slammed shut behind him. "For the moment strange gusts of emotion swept through me like cold winds on an open prairie. For the first time in my life I had been thrown behind bars."

Even after friends arrived to post his bail, King felt shaken, anxious, and, for the first time since the boycott began, uncertain. The next night, a Friday, he stayed late at church for another strategy session for MIA and came home to find Coretta and their baby daughter both soundly asleep. Before he could join them, the phone rang and he picked it up so the noise wouldn't wake his family. The unidentified voice on the line began with the same two words that launched most such calls: "Listen, nigger." The caller then growled out an unusually specific threat. "We've taken all we want from you. . . . If you're not out of this town in three days we're gonna blow your brains out and blow up your house."

By the time King hung up, his nerves felt too jangled for sleep. He walked into his kitchen, put on a pot of coffee, and then, with shaky hands, set it down on the kitchen table. What followed amounted to a decisive religious experience that he recounted many times, in writing and in sermons, over the crowded twelve years remaining in his life.

"I was ready to give up," he remembered. Staring at the untouched cup of coffee in front of him, he longed for a way to step aside from his position of leadership and vulnerability, without shaming his family or betraying his followers. He later recalled focusing especially on the fate of his newborn daughter, Yolanda, "the darling of my life," who could well lose her own life amid the threats of violence that increasingly surrounded him.

In his weakness and desperation, he realized he couldn't turn to his parents, 175 miles away in Atlanta. Instead, he could only "call on something in that person that your Daddy used to tell you about, that power that can make a way out of no way." At that point, he held his head in his hands and bowed over the edge of the kitchen table, praying aloud. "The words I spoke to God that midnight are still vivid in my memory. 'I am here taking a stand for what I believe is right. But now I am afraid.'" He spoke of the fear that his own failing courage would undermine the determination of the people who depended on him, causing all their hopes to collapse. "I am at the end of my powers," he confessed. "I have nothing left. I've come to the point where I can't face it alone."

And in response to that confession, King "experienced the presence of the Divine as I had never experienced Him before. . . . Almost at once my fears began to go. My uncertainty disappeared. I was ready to face anything. . . . I heard the voice of Jesus saying still to fight on. He promised never to leave me, never to leave me alone."

This transformational moment became known to King's friends, and later biographers, as his "Kitchen Vision" or "Kitchen Conversion." It occurred at precisely the moment King needed the help.

Three nights later, he delivered his keynote address to a mass meeting at Ralph David Abernathy's First Baptist Church. He spoke of his recent arrest at the hands of the Montgomery police. "If all I have to pay is going to jail a few times and getting about 20 threatening calls a day, I think that is a very small price to pay for what we are fighting for." Minutes later, as the meeting prepared to adjourn, King got word that a bomb had exploded at his home, with Coretta and their baby daughter inside.

"I WANT YOU TO LOVE OUR ENEMIES"

He rushed to the scene and pushed through a swelling, angry crowd to find his front porch nearly demolished and several windows shattered. His wife and baby daughter, who had been sleeping in the back room, remained blessedly unharmed. Stepping over broken glass to get to his living room, King found the city's mayor and police commissioner—staunch foes of the boycott—waiting for him with assurances that they condemned the bombing and hoped to find its perpetrators (they never did). Outside, leaping and shouting young men began waving fists in the air, as well as knives and firearms. They called for revenge, threatening the white policemen at the scene. King stepped up to his ruined porch and raised a hand to quiet the crowd. "Don't get panicky," he said. "Don't get your weapons. If you have weapons take them home. . . . We are not advocating violence. We want to love our enemies. I want you to love our enemies. . . . We must meet hate with love." As the crowd listened intently, he told them: "Go home and sleep calm. Be calm as I and my family are."

As the crowd dispersed, the mayor of Montgomery, W. A. "Tacky" Gayle, turned to M.L. and quietly, gratefully affirmed: "Preacher King, you saved our lives."

At that moment and others, even his enemies recognized King's power as extraordinary and unprecedented. His followers increasingly believed it stemmed from a divine, supernatural source.

King himself sensed the same thing. When he looked back on that tumultuous, potentially deadly night of January 30, he wrote: "Strangely enough, I accepted the word of the bombing calmly. My religious experience a few nights before had given me the strength to face it."

Increasingly, his rhetoric combined confidence and resignation, relying on divine protection and yet accepting fate's inscrutable master plan. As the exhausting boycott struggle approached its one-year anniversary, the Supreme Court of the United States affirmed a lower court decision that bus segregation laws violated the constitutional guarantee of equal protection. Though the Montgomery Improvement Association savored the moment of triumph, its leaders decided to continue the bus boycott until the court order for desegregation had been fully implemented.

The day after the high court announced its decision on November 13, 1956, King addressed a jubilant crowd at Holt Street Baptist Church and warned of the dangers that still lay ahead. "I'm aware of the fact that a week never passes that somebody's not telling me to get out of town, or that I'm going to be killed next place I move. . . . I don't have any guards on my side. But I have the God of the Universe on my side!" The audience roared in affirmation.

A few months later, the King family survived another serious attempt to kill them and destroy their home. On January 27—almost exactly a year since the last bombing attempt—the would-be killers planted a bundle with twelve sticks of dynamite on the front porch of the house but failed in their attempts to ignite the explosives. The *Montgomery Advertiser* ran the headline "'DUD' SPARES KING'S HOME ANOTHER HIT" and their readers understood exactly what had happened. The *Advertiser* also reported on the soaring sermon he delivered to his packed church the next day (under the headline "KING SAYS VISION TOLD HIM TO LEAD INTEGRATION FORCES").

For the first time, King spoke publicly about the "Kitchen Conversion" that had altered his life the year before, describing the voice he heard on a "sleepless morning" telling him to "stand up for the truth, stand up for righteousness."

"If I had to die tomorrow morning I would die happy, because I've been to the mountain top and I've seen the promised land!"

His language anticipated, almost word for word, the climax to the "I've Been to the Mountaintop" speech he delivered eleven years later, on the night before his death. More than a specific premonition of the next day's bloody events, King's phrases in both speeches expressed a general awareness of his own mortality. After the transformational kitchen encounter shortly after he turned twenty-seven, he gave voice frequently, almost constantly, to a sense of the limited time he had been granted to lead a transcendent cause. While he spoke of his faith in God's promised, personal protection, he also knew the protection wouldn't be permanent.

That knowledge of time running out for him—if not for his movement—drove his consistent focus on "the fierce urgency of now" so memorably invoked in the "I Have a Dream" speech. It also informed the theme and the title of his bestselling book the next year: *Why We Can't Wait.* As he resoundingly declared in his superb "Letter from Birmingham Jail": "We must use time creatively, in the knowledge that the time is always ripe to do right."

Rather than bask in the glory of his historic victory in Montgomery, the impatient leader immediately shifted his attention to a larger arena and a wider struggle. Barely a month after the formal end of the bus boycott and the official desegregation of the local transit system, King assembled sixty ministers and lay leaders at his father's church in Atlanta to organize the Southern Christian Leadership Conference to push for integration and voting rights. In May 1957, he made his first address to a national audience as featured speaker at the Prayer Pilgrimage for Freedom in Washington commemorating the third anniversary of the Supreme Court's unanimous school desegregation decision in *Brown v. Board of Education of Topeka.* He spoke to a large, peaceful crowd estimated at twenty-five thousand that gathered in front of the Lincoln Memorial—the same venue that drew a vastly larger crowd for the March on Washington for Jobs and Freedom six years later.

In the interim between those two mass events, King traveled incessantly and became an international symbol of black liberation. He journeyed to Africa to join in the mass celebrations when Ghana became the first black nation to gain its independence from colonial rule, then flew to India to meet with the prime minister and to connect with Mahatma Gandhi's inspired legacy of nonviolent resistance. *Jet* magazine estimated that in 1958 alone, King delivered 208 speeches—an average of four a week—and traveled some seventy-eight thousand miles.

"YOU WOULD HAVE DROWNED IN YOUR OWN BLOOD"

In one of those journeys, he faced the first attempt on his life that actually drew blood.

The incident came near the end of a high-profile trip to New York City to launch the promotional tour for his first book, *Stride Toward Freedom*, which told the triumphant story of the Montgomery bus boycott. On Friday night, September 19, 1958, King addressed a mass rally of some five thousand people in front of Harlem's twelve-story Hotel Theresa. The featured speakers for this grand occasion also included the governor of New York, Democrat Averell Harriman, and his ultimately victorious Republican challenger Nelson Rockefeller, both angling for the "Negro vote" in a hotly contested campaign. The legendary Duke Ellington and his orchestra provided music for the event and baseball immortal Jackie Robinson thrilled the crowd with his welcoming address.

For the most part, the event unfolded successfully, though a few noisy hecklers regularly interrupted the speakers. One particularly annoying troublemaker had managed to position herself behind the podium, where she attracted attention with her piercing voice and stylish, garishly colored, European wardrobe. A strikingly tall and powerfully built black woman, she also wore sparkling green sequined eyeglasses and dangling earrings as she yelled special hatred for the distinguished white visitors to Harlem, telling them they had no business invading a black neighborhood.

Perhaps because she was a fashionably dressed female who carried herself with a sense of purpose and authority, no one thought to silence or remove her, but King seemed to be addressing her hostility when he got up to speak. "Many of you had hoped I would come here to bring you a message of hate against the white man," he said. "I come here with no such message. Black supremacy is just as bad as white supremacy. . . . Don't let any man make you stoop so low that you have hate."

After the rally, Manhattan's black borough president, Hulan Jack, approached the dais with his principal aide and told King that in light of the agitation in the audience and backstage, he should have a bodyguard for the remainder of his trip to New York City. "Oh God, don't get a bodyguard!" the civil rights leader insisted. He then turned to the politician's assistant, William Rowe. "And don't you try to act like one either!"

After all, the next day, a balmy Saturday, was meant to be his last in the city. Dr. King's schedule called for a book signing at Blumstein's department store on West 125th Street in Harlem, and some fifty people already waited in line when he arrived at 3:00 p.m. He spent a few minutes chatting with each of his admirers and by 3:30 had worked his way through more than half of the patient crowd. At that point, a tall woman in high heels and a bright blue raincoat cut to the front of the line and made her own stride toward murder. She came directly up to the desk where King had been signing his books and boomed out a strange question. "Is this Martin Luther King?" she demanded.

Unfortunately, he failed to recognize her as the heckler from the night before and unhesitatingly responded, "Yes, it is."

Immediately she brought her hand out of her raincoat; in it was a gently curved Japanese blade about eight inches long, with an elegant handle of inlaid ivory—like a miniature samurai sword. Raising the weapon above her shoulder she brought it down full force and plunged it deep into King's chest. Fortunately, he raised his left arm just before contact, cutting his hand. She tried to pull out the knife to stab again but bystanders restrained her. "I've been after him for six years!" she shouted. "I'm glad I done it!" As horrified onlookers held the assailant and waited for the police, she kept repeating, "Dr. King has ruined my life. He is no good. The NAACP is no good, it's communistic. I've been after him for six years. I finally was able to get him now."

Her name was Izola Curry. A forty-two-year-old loner with a long history of mental illness, she was one of eight children born to sharecroppers in a tiny Georgia town and left school in seventh grade. After a brief marriage in her early twenties, she led an itinerant life that took her from Ohio to Missouri to West Virginia, back to Georgia, then to Florida, Kentucky, South Carolina, Florida again, and finally to New York City. There, she worked as a cleaning lady to pay for the gaudy clothes and earrings she habitually wore. She also developed paranoid delusions about Communist penetration of the "Negro Church" and repeatedly contacted the FBI about Communist agents who were constantly pursuing her.

On the day of the attack on King, she carried a fully loaded .32-caliber semiautomatic pistol in her purse but fatefully chose to remove her "samurai letter opener" from its ceremonial scabbard of carved, crimson-painted wood and stab him. With its blade sharpened to a deadly point, it was said to possess "the penetrating power of an ice pick."

Not yet fully aware of what had happened to him, or why, and with the handle still protruding from his chest, King staggered into a chair and struggled to reassure the near-hysterical crowd. "That's all right," he managed to say, with the gushing blood beginning to stain his crisp, white cotton shirt. "Everything's going to be all right." Some well-meaning people who hovered around him yelled for an effort to remove the blade, but fortunately, wiser heads prevailed. Doctors later affirmed that any such attempt would have almost certainly killed him.

At the hospital, the still-conscious but distinctly uncomfortable King received a parade of visitors, none of them particularly welcome. In the midst of his feverish reelection campaign, Governor Harriman came to offer comfort (and to strengthen his association with the popular black leader six weeks before the election). The chief executive of the Empire State stayed at the hospital for more than three hours, darting in and out of King's room with a mournful expression and occasionally squeezing the great man's hand.

Later, the police also brought in an even less appropriate guest: Izola Curry, the would-be assassin, now handcuffed but still ranting. The law enforcement officials wanted King to identify her as his assailant, before he lost consciousness or, as many expected, expired. Even though he was only twenty-nine, everyone counted his demise as a distinct possibility. King himself wrote later: "The razor tip of the instrument had been touching my aorta and that my whole chest had to be opened to extract it. 'If you had sneezed during all those hours of waiting,' [the chief of surgery] said, 'your aorta would have been punctured and you would have drowned in your own blood.'"

Reviewing the case against Izola Curry, prosecutors found her mental state so unequivocally deranged that she never stood trial. Instead, the authorities confined her to various psychiatric hospitals and rest homes where she lived to the age of ninety-nine. Her deranged condition didn't stop scores of white supremacists from sending donations to provide for her legal defense and to commend her "courageous blow" against a "nefarious advocate of race mixing." While still in the hospital, King himself issued a magnanimous press statement declaring that he bore "no ill will" toward his attacker and knew "that thoughtful people will do all in their power to see that she gets the help she apparently needs if she is to become a free and constructive member of society."

Meanwhile, King got the help he needed when his wife and mother arrived from Atlanta to supervise his care and lift his spirits. The press wrote glowingly of his forgiving spirit and gracious manners, featuring photographs of a smiling King wearing a shiny silk dressing gown he'd been given as a get-well gift. During his two weeks of recuperation, he developed a deepening sense that the bizarre sequence of events amounted to an important message: like his childhood scrapes with danger and injury, and the multiple attempts to harm his family in Montgomery, the knife near his heart reminded him of the proximity of death and of his purposeful, providential protection.

In fact, Dr. King later discerned physical evidence that reinforced the theme.

When the physicians finished their surgical work and stitched together the opening they had made in his body, they left behind a visible, raised scar that he bore for the rest of his life. At the center of his chest, this mark looked like a lowercase *t*. Others thought it resembled a plus sign. But looking at his own flesh, M.L. felt no doubt that he had been branded with the sign of the cross.

"I DON'T WANT TO DO THIS ANYMORE!"

The years that followed brought the honors and accomplishments that the nation recalls with reverence in observing the annual Martin

Luther King holiday. He guided his movement through the climactic, occasionally brutal struggle to desegregate Birmingham, followed by the March on Washington, with its unprecedented crowd of 250,000. He won designation as *Time* magazine's "Man of the Year" for 1963 and then received the Nobel Peace Prize presented in 1964. The passage of the most sweeping civil rights bill in American history brought bipartisan celebration, followed by dramatic confrontations in Selma that led to the Voting Rights Act, which enabled millions of African Americans to cast ballots for the first time.

Those years of lightning, thunder, and epic achievement gave King the status of international hero. More than a half century after his death, he looms in the national consciousness as such a monumental figure that it seemed natural to compare his martyrdom to Lincoln's. But while Lincoln perished at a moment of triumph, just days after victory in the Civil War and congressional passage of the Thirteenth Amendment, which abolished slavery, King's story concluded on an altogether different note: his last year brought the most stormy, painful, and frustrating months of his brief life.

PBS host Tavis Smiley underlined that point in his deeply sympathetic 2014 book *Death of a King: The Real Story of Dr. Martin Luther King Jr.'s Final Year.* Smiley characterizes that year as one of "unrelenting adversity" in which "everything and everybody turned against Dr. King." As British journalist Gary Younge noted in the *Guardian:* "Before his death in 1968, King was well on the way to becoming a pariah. In 1966, twice as many Americans had an unfavourable opinion of him as a favourable one."

By that time, the term "backlash" came to signify the mounting white resentment to the increasing militancy of a new crop of black activists—fiery voices that viewed Dr. King as increasingly irrelevant. Within the civil rights movement, younger leaders commonly referred to King as "De Lawd"—an ironic reference to his exalted reputation and grand biblical rhetoric. But the nickname also invoked the perceived distance between the revered international icon of brotherhood and the gritty realities that remained a daily challenge for the black community he sought to represent.

Without question, the inner-city explosions of looting, arson, and bloodshed that began with the Watts riots in Los Angeles in August 1965 did devastating damage to King's standing among blacks and whites alike. In the "long, hot summer" of 1967 alone, riots scarred 159 cities in every corner of the country, resulting in nearly 100 deaths, 2,100 serious injuries, more than 11,000 arrests, and untold billions in property damage. King, of course, never encouraged or condoned the nihilistic violence, but horrified observers of all races felt disappointed by the great civil rights leader's inability to stop the incidents. Many of his own supporters saw the riots as the ultimate rejection of Dr. King's uplifting emphasis on nonviolence and "the beloved community."

When the riots seemed to spread everywhere in the summer of 1967, King struggled to explain the violence without excusing it. "A riot is the language of the unheard," he proclaimed, but the *Chicago Tribune* rejected the line with an indignant editorial: "Every time there is a riot in the streets you can count on a flock of sociologists rushing forward to excuse the rioters." The newspaper concluded that King's "'nonviolence' is designed to goad others into violence." The *Dallas Morning News* similarly condemned him as "the headline-hunting high priest of nonviolent violence" whose "road show" resembled a "torchbearer sprinting into a powder-house." Even longtime allies and associates deemed the Nobel Prize winner suddenly, irrevocably, irrelevant. Adam Clayton Powell Jr., the pastor-politician who represented Harlem in Congress for more than a quarter century, contemptuously proclaimed: "I don't call for violence or riots, but the day of Martin Luther King has come to an end."

For King, the public attacks brought private despair—and a destructive pattern of self-punishment. His aides worried about "Doc" facing defeat in his ongoing "war on sleep": his exhausted body found it increasingly difficult to rise to the demands of his impossible schedule, especially with his growing consumption of cigarettes and alcohol—sometimes to excess. In the last two years of his life, he added at least twenty unhealthy pounds to his previously compact, muscular frame.

Financial challenges compounded the stress: he faced the constant demands of charitable fundraisers, paid speeches, and book deadlines to cover the bills for the chronically broke Southern Christian Leadership Conference in order to pay his staff and provide for his family. Perpetual travel and Dr. King's extramarital episodes also strained his increasingly remote marriage with Coretta. As early as November 1964, she'd been forced to confront evidence of his infidelity when she opened a package from an anonymous source that was addressed to his home in Atlanta. It contained tape recordings that featured snippets of off-color conversation and unintelligible, but clearly carnal, moans and exclamations. The packet also included a letter threatening imminent exposure:

> The American public, the church organizations that have been helping—Protestant, Catholic and Jews will know you for what you are—an evil, abnormal beast. . . . There is but one way out for you. You better take it before your filthy, abnormal fraudulent self is bared to the nation.

Historians and biographers now agree that high-ranking officials in the FBI penned and sent the "suicide letter," and that it was the FBI, with the authorization of Robert Kennedy's Justice Department, that bugged hotel rooms and gathered the tapes. For the final three and a half years of his life, M.L. lived not only with fear of death but with constant dread of blackmail and public humiliation.

No wonder he felt lost and wounded much of the time. His personal doctor believed he should see a psychiatrist, but his schedule and his pride made that impossible. A twenty-first-century psychiatrist, Dr. Nassir Ghaemi, author of the insightful study *A First-Rate Madness*, has examined the record and concluded: "He was increasingly damned, and increasingly depressed—not just sad, but clinically depressed." Seven months before he died, he was spending another sleepless night in a Virginia hotel room, drinking alone, when he woke up his colleagues in a desperate state. "I don't want to do this anymore!" he bellowed. "I want to go back to my little church!" He even discussed the possibility of leaving the United States altogether to take a peaceful pulpit somewhere in the English countryside.

"THE MOST RECENT UTTERANCE OF THE
ONCE-ESTEEMED LEADER"

Instead of indulging his fantasies of escape, King decided on a bold but risky bid to rescue his reputation and reenergize his ministry with a dramatic thrust in a contentious new direction: aligning himself with the most strident, passionate voices of opposition to the Vietnam War. In doing so, he not only abandoned his old allies in Lyndon Johnson's White House but indignantly attacked them.

On April 4, 1967, precisely one year before his death, he addressed a respectful crowd of left-leaning luminaries from New York's progressive elite who gathered at Riverside Church, the soaring, lavishly ornate, nondenominational neo-Gothic cathedral built by John D. Rockefeller Jr. in upper Manhattan. All of the building's 2,700 seats had been filled, together with more than 1,200 folding chairs to accommodate the eager overflow crowd. Instead of reciting patriotic phrases that emphasized America's legacy of liberty as he had in previous major speeches ("From every mountainside, let freedom ring!"), this time he denounced "the greatest purveyor of violence in the world today—my own government" and likened American troops to the Nazis, who employed "new medicine and new tortures in the concentration camps of Europe." He railed against this nation's corruption by "the giant triplets of racism, extreme materialism and militarism."

In retrospect, many of today's progressives deem the "Beyond Vietnam" speech as "visionary" and "prophetic," but Dr. King's much-discussed address drew scant public praise in 1967.

The *Washington Post* denounced the speech under the headline "A TRAGEDY," while the *New York Times* derided "the most recent utterance of the once-esteemed leader" as "wasteful and self-defeating." *Life* magazine voiced strenuous objection to Dr. King's apparent willingness to side with the enemy at the height of a bloody foreign conflict and described much of his speech as "a demagogic slander that sounded like a script for Radio Hanoi." Within days of King's "Beyond Vietnam" speech, the sixty-member board of the NAACP unanimously endorsed a resolution distancing themselves from its core message and condemning any effort to link the civil rights cause with opposition to the war.

In the face of collapsing support, and the constant struggle to pay the bills for his ongoing activism, he tried to refocus on the unresolved issue of economic inequality that afflicted impoverished Americans of all races. He planned a "Poor People's Campaign" for the summer of 1968 that would bring at least two thousand desperate and destitute protesters to Washington to construct shanties or pitch tents near the Capitol, refusing to depart until Congress had appropriated the money to lift stricken multitudes out of poverty. Meanwhile, his closest associates worried about King's painfully fragile moods and obsession with his own imminent demise. "He talked about death all the time," said Andrew Young, one of his most promising acolytes. He wept frequently, often inexplicably. Comedian and activist Dick Gregory recalled that King cried when he confided to him that he felt certain he'd be killed.

In this context of widespread public hostility and deepening private doubt, King's themes in the last major speeches of his life begin to make sense. He repeatedly anticipates his own death and tries to justify the value of his life.

On February 4, he preached on his home ground at Ebenezer Baptist Church in Atlanta in a truly remarkable sermon known as "The Drum Major Instinct" speech. The title refers to a famous homily delivered sixteen years earlier by a white Methodist pastor named J. Wallace Hamilton. The "drum major instinct," as King explained it, is "a desire to be out front, a desire to lead the parade, a desire to be first. And it is something that runs the whole gamut of life."

That instinct, he argued, could drive people to "lead the parade" in meaningless materialism, living beyond their means in the cars they drove or the clothes they wore in a bid to outdo their neighbors. Or, the same impulse could bring anyone closer to God and righteousness, by getting out in front in order to serve—as the New Testament demanded.

Inevitably, that brought him to reflections on his own life and the approaching end. "I don't want a long funeral. And if you get somebody to deliver the eulogy, tell them not to talk too long. . . . Yes, if you want to say that I was a drum major, say that I was a drum major for justice. Say that I was a drum major for peace. I was a drum major for righteousness. And all of the other shallow things will not matter. I won't have any money to leave behind. I won't have the fine and luxurious things of life to leave behind. But I just want to leave a committed life behind."

"I SEE GOD WORKING IN THIS PERIOD OF
THE TWENTIETH CENTURY"

His "committed life" lasted just two months more, with much of that time consumed by his involvement in the sanitation workers' strike in Memphis, Tennessee.

That bitter struggle began with the organization of a union representing the city's 1,300 trash collectors who suffered from unsafe working conditions, "starvation wages," and blatantly racist supervisors. From the beginning of their strike, the union leaders pleaded with King to come to town to rally support for their cause and to attract national attention; despite his undeniably diminished public standing, his celebrated name still commanded a unique ability to win publicity.

When he arrived on March 18, he addressed a wildly enthusiastic crowd of some twenty-five thousand at the Mason Temple and delivered the message that ending segregation was only the first step in his campaign for justice. "What does it profit a man to be able to eat at an integrated lunch counter," he asked, "if he doesn't have enough money to buy a hamburger?"

He returned ten days later to lead a march of some six thousand sanitation workers and their supporters to demand that the city negotiate in good faith. Dr. King marched resolutely at the head of the massive demonstration, but near the end of the line a group of black radicals who styled themselves "the Invaders" had their own plans. They began smashing downtown shopwindows and looting the merchandise while the police struck back with tear gas, beatings, and mass arrests. King fled the chaos, unable to stop the violence. The results proved devastating: 280 arrests, 62 serious injuries, and the death of a sixteen-year-old boy killed by a police shotgun blast.

To recover credibility and momentum for the strikers and their cause, King resolved to stage another march on April 8, determined to reaffirm the principles of nonviolence. Checking into the Lorraine Motel five days before the new demonstration, he planned to speak once again at the Mason Temple but felt reluctant to go due to his exhaustion, not to mention the rainstorm and tornado warnings that would obviously suppress the size of the crowd.

He tried to rest and dispatched his longtime colleague Ralph Abernathy, Jesse Jackson, and other lieutenants to take his place on the podium. But they called him from the venue and urged him to show up: two thousand supporters, mostly sanitation workers and their families, had turned out for the occasion expecting to hear King and they felt cheated by any substitute. He got out of bed, threw on his clothes, and rode through the torrential rain to the steamy, echoing rally site. He began his talk on an optimistic note that belied his late arrival and the sad current state of the strike.

"If I were standing at the beginning of time," he said, "with the possibility of taking a kind of general and panoramic view of the whole of human history up to now, and the Almighty said to me, 'Martin Luther King, which age would you like to live in?' . . . Strangely enough, I would turn to the Almighty, and say, 'If you allow me to live just a few years in the second half of the 20th century, I will be happy.' But I know, somehow, that only when it is dark enough can you see the stars.

"And I see God working in this period of the twentieth century in a way that men, in some strange way, are responding." The crowd murmured its enthusiastic assent, and King allowed: "I'm just happy that God has allowed me to live in this period to see what is unfolding. And I'm happy that He's allowed me to be in Memphis."

After calling for all his listeners to unite on behalf of the sanitation workers, after expressing full confidence that one more march, free of violence and doubt, would secure a victory for the downtrodden, he returned, as he so often did in his final years, to the theme of his own mortality.

He narrated in some detail the story of his Harlem stabbing by "a demented black woman" and described the way that "if I had merely sneezed, I would have died." After listing all the progress and triumphs he had witnessed in the intervening decade, he boomed in defiance: "I'm so happy that I didn't sneeze."

Swept up with the surging emotions of his audience, his face gleaming with perspiration from the steamy, damp evening, he soared to his famous conclusion.

"Well, I don't know what will happen now. We've got some difficult days ahead. But it really doesn't matter with me now, because I've been to the mountaintop. . . .

"And so I'm happy, tonight. . . .

"I'm not fearing any man!

"Mine eyes have seen the glory of the coming of the Lord!"

With that last jubilant exclamation, he seemed to fall, or at least to totter, toward his friend Ralph Abernathy, who caught him in a hug and helped him into a chair as the Mason Temple echoed with tumultuous applause, exclamations, and hallelujahs.

At that point he had less than twenty hours to live.

"PRECIOUS LORD, TAKE MY HAND"

He didn't use that time to rest or meditate or write, but instead opened a new front in his ongoing "war on sleep."

After catching up with the admiring clergymen who clustered around him at the Mason Temple, then patiently greeting a line of sanitation workers he had inspired, he drove off with his longtime personal assistant and traveling companion, Reverend Bernard Lee, and his closest friend, Abernathy, for what King's biographer Taylor Branch judiciously describes as "a long night on the town."

The revelry began with an intimate, after-midnight dinner at the home of an activist and hair salon owner who was eager to support the cause by entertaining her famous visitors. According to Abernathy's recollections, the after-feast festivities included private time for King behind closed doors in the bedroom of the hostess.

Finally, at 4:00 a.m., they took a cab back to the Lorraine Motel, where King spotted a car with Kentucky plates parked outside a room with all the lights still on. He immediately identified the vehicle with a recently elected member of the Kentucky legislature—the first woman and the first person of color ever to serve in the state senate. He knew that Georgia Davis had driven to Memphis in the company of his brother, Reverend A. D. King, but they had arrived too late for the earlier speech. So while Abernathy repaired, alone, to the room he shared with King, his friend spent the remainder of the night and most of the early morning in the company of Senator Davis. She later recalled that he preferred to spend time in her rooms because he felt certain that the FBI regularly bugged his accommodations wherever he traveled.

For twenty more years, Georgia Davis served in the state senate, stubbornly denying anything improper in her relationship with King. That changed in 1995, with the publication of her book *I Shared the Dream*, which detailed their passionate involvement in the months before his death. She also authorized release after her death (in 2016, at age ninety-two) of an interview describing her final hours with Dr. King.

After arising on April 4, M.L. spent most of his time with friends and staff (including his brother, Reverend Abernathy, and Georgia Davis), making arrangements for the forthcoming Poor People's Campaign and the thousands of protesters he expected to lead to Washington. King displayed mostly good spirits, eagerly wolfing down a plate of fried catfish that he shared with Abernathy, looking forward to a big dinner at the home of a local minister before a scheduled mass meeting to rally support for the upcoming march.

At one point, King and his brother placed a call to their mother back home in Atlanta, and she took real delight in the chance to speak with both of her boys at once. Afterward, M.L. expressed special concern over the menu for the evening's meal, asking for real "soul food" instead of some meager and purportedly healthful rations. He felt reassured when his hosts proudly summarized the menu of roast beef, sweetbreads, chitterlings, fried chicken, ham, pork chops, turnip greens, candied yams, corn bread, and corn pone, plus pies and cakes and cookies of every description.

In between the high spirits, the family fellowship, and big plans for the future, Senator Davis found King "unusually solemn."

"I think he was conscious that something was going to happen, I really do," she said in her long-concealed interview. "A lot of us were doing the talking. He was listening and had his eyes closed sometimes and it would just be like he was meditating." Of course, the closed eyes could also reflect the nearly sleepless night he had spent the day before.

In order to get "De Lawd" to arrive close to on time at the lavish dinner in his honor, his aides lied to him about the schedule, as they often did: they told him the organizers expected him at five, though the real start time was supposed to be six. But even as that later hour approached, the group was still assembling at the Lorraine Motel, trying to organize transportation and bantering back and forth about the glorious feed awaiting them. Georgia Davis sat at her mirror, applying makeup, while King stepped out of his room and onto the second-floor balcony. He stood at the railing, calling down to associates who were waiting on him in the parking lot below.

Jesse Jackson had been rehearsing a singing group to provide inspiration at the meeting later in the evening. He wanted Dr. King to greet the lead singer, Ben Branch, who was also a gifted saxophonist. "Oh yes, he's my man. How are you, Ben?" King called out from the balcony, recalling a number Branch had performed for another meeting in Chicago. "Ben, make sure you play 'Precious Lord, Take My Hand.' In the meeting tonight. Play it real pretty."

As Branch agreed, King's increasingly impatient driver, Solomon Jones, tried to hurry the great man to the car. "Dr. King, it's getting cool. You better get a coat."

At that precise moment, 6:01 p.m., witnesses heard the crack of a single rifle shot. A soft-point, metal-jacketed bullet ripped through King's right cheek and smashed through his jaw, shattering several vertebrae and severing his jugular vein in the process, before lodging into his shoulder. Losing consciousness instantly, King fell backward onto the balcony.

At St. Joseph Hospital, the doctors made a brief, vain attempt to resuscitate him before pronouncing him dead sixty-four minutes after the fatal blast.

"A TEN-CENT WHITE BOY"

After more than fifty years of conspiracy theories, and microscopic examination of every scrap of available evidence, there is still no reasonable doubt that James Earl Ray perpetrated the murder. An escaped convict with viciously racist attitudes, he'd been stalking King for nearly a month.

Less than a year older than his victim, Ray stands out among all the notable American assassins for the clearest pattern of criminality and the most prolific record of imprisonment. Arrested first at the age of fourteen for stealing newspapers, he dropped out of school the next year. When he was twenty-one, he began his first three-month jail term, for burglary. Longer sentences followed for armed robbery in Illinois and robbing a post office in Kansas. After he committed another armed robbery, his long string of offenses dictated a twenty-year sentence in the Missouri State Penitentiary.

In April 1967, after six years behind bars and two failed escape attempts, he hid himself in a large box that was supposed to be filled with fresh loaves from the prison bakery. When the bread truck rumbled past the prison walls on its regular route, Ray popped out and jumped off the back of the vehicle. Against the odds, he quickly found his way to Canada and from there to Mexico, where he made a brief attempt to film pornographic movies with local prostitutes.

Despite the obvious risks, the restless escapee couldn't keep himself from returning to the United States. He obtained a fake driver's license in Birmingham and bought himself a white '66 Mustang. He volunteered for George Wallace's "White Power" presidential campaign in Los Angeles, then headed for Atlanta, well known as the home of Dr. King. Two days later, he drove back to Birmingham, and using an alias, the escaped prisoner succeeded in purchasing a Remington Model 760 Gamemaster rifle, together with ammunition and a scope.

On April 2, Ray packed his weapon and drove the white Mustang to Memphis, after hearing about King's scheduled rally for the sanitation workers. On the morning of April 4, he read in the local newspaper that King and his party used the Lorraine Motel as their base of operations. At three in the afternoon, he got a room in a flophouse across a parking lot from the Lorraine. He paid $8.50 in advance for a week's rent and demanded a second-story room with a view of the motel.

Shortly after checking in, Ray left his room and bought a pair of binoculars. At about 5:55 p.m., he used them to spot King's small, neatly dressed figure on the balcony, in front of room 306.

It then took him several minutes to take out his rifle and to conceal it in a bedspread, then to walk down the hallway to the shared bathroom. Fortunately, for his purposes, it turned out to be unoccupied. He went in and locked the door behind him, stood in the bathtub, and removed the screen on the window facing the Lorraine. That way he could angle the gun for a plausible shot. To his relief, King was still there, lingering at the handrail overlooking the parking lot, chatting with his friends and associates.

According to Ray's confession, he shifted his feet until he got a sturdy, steady perch inside the bathtub. Unwrapping the deer rifle and lifting it to his shoulder, he lined King up in the scope he had attached to the gun. Then he squeezed the trigger, only once—the luckiest shot of his life, but for the nation one of the unluckiest in history.

Ray fled the scene immediately, leaving rifle and binoculars behind, and drove his Mustang to Atlanta. From there he took a Greyhound to Detroit and then a taxi to Canada. After lingering for a month in Toronto and securing a fake Canadian passport, he flew to England, then to Portugal, before returning to London. He successfully eluded capture for more than two months before authorities arrested him at Heathrow Airport when he tried to catch a flight to Belgium.

Extradited to the United States and charged with murder in Tennessee, he observed his forty-first birthday (March 10, 1969) by producing a full, detailed confession on how he went about murdering King. Less than a year had passed since the assassination, and Ray's agreement to accept a ninety-nine-year sentence saved him from likely execution by electric chair under the laws of Tennessee at the time. The plea deal also spared the state the cost and trauma of a long, sensational, and gruesome murder trial.

Three days later, Ray took it all back—retracting his admission of guilt and dispatching a letter to a local judge demanding a trial. He never got it, despite multiple motions and appeals, with the Supreme Court ultimately declining to review the case.

As his years behind bars in Brushy Mountain State Penitentiary began to accumulate, Ray made several escape attempts. In June 1977, nine years after his notorious crime, he led six other inmates over the wall and managed to avoid his pursuers, including some two hundred FBI agents dispatched by President Jimmy Carter, for nearly three full days.

After his return to custody, the legal system's continued refusal to give him the trial he wanted served to encourage his increasingly ardent insistence that he had been set up as an innocent "patsy." This argument intentionally echoed the claims of Lee Harvey Oswald shortly after his arrest in 1963, but for several reasons the conspiracy theories about the King assassination never gained the traction of similar suspicions surrounding JFK's murder. For one thing, Ray had provided a convincing confession to avoid electrocution, and had also compiled a long history of violent criminality and blatant racism that undermined his affirmations of innocence.

Nevertheless, some of King's closest associates always rejected the idea that a career convict like James Earl Ray had managed to kill the great man on his own. Reverend James Bevel, King's longtime colleague at SCLC, insisted that "there is no way a ten-cent white boy could develop a plan to kill a million-dollar black man."

"I BELIEVE IN PROVIDENCE"

More significantly, some of King's own children became entangled with swirling suspicions that their father had been slaughtered by a massive governmental conspiracy. In March 1997, M.L.'s second son, Dexter King, visited Ray in prison. He had been only seven years old when Ray shot his father and now confronted him directly. "I want to ask you for the record: Did you kill my father?" Dexter King demanded.

"No, no, I didn't, no," Ray haltingly responded. "But like I say, sometimes these questions are difficult to answer and you have to make a personal evaluation."

Satisfied by the denial, the younger King made an embarrassing (and well publicized) declaration: "Well, as awkward as this may seem, I want you to know that I believe you and my family believes you, and we are going to do everything in our power to try and make sure that justice will prevail. And while it's at the 11th hour, I've always been a spiritual person and I believe in Providence."

Dexter King has never explained what that belief meant to him, but anyone tracing the blighted path that took James Earl Ray from his prison escape in Missouri to his appointment with destiny in Memphis could see the role of coincidence and illogical twists that made King's murder possible.

If he hadn't succeeded in escaping the fourteen remaining years on his Missouri prison term, or avoided capture for a year, or returned, unimpeded, to the American South from refuge he had found in both Canada and Mexico, it's unlikely he would ever have felt the call or found the chance to kill a national celebrity. If a gun dealer in Birmingham had been less willing to sell him the fatal weapon, or if someone else had been locked in the shared bathroom at Ray's rooming house when King made his appearance on the balcony, or if M.L. had lingered for less time at that Lorraine railing, or heeded the prodding of his aides and arrived for dinner at the scheduled hour, then M.L. might have lived to enjoy that savory feast and gone on to other rallies and controversies. Above all, if Ray's single, difficult, standing-in-the-bathtub shot hadn't proven so fatally effective and had it missed its mark by a few feet or even a few inches, it's hard to imagine that he would have kept on firing before dropping his weapon and running away.

Any of these tiny alterations could have spared King's life on that

April evening. He might have survived the escaped con's unlikely shot just as he had all previous efforts to kill or injure him, but if he had, it's unlikely that his legacy would have taken on the monumental grandeur that it commands today.

As Gary Younge points out, in the last two polls before his death, King didn't even show up on Gallup's list of the most admired Americans of the year, but thirty years later, on the verge of the millennium, the same polling organization placed him second (behind Mother Teresa) on the list of the most admired people for the entire twentieth century.

PROVIDENTIAL LIFE, PROVIDENTIAL DEATH

It took time for the martyred King to make the transition from polarizing to unifying figure. In fact, the immediate reaction to his assassination brought ten days of devastating riots that erupted in 109 cities across the country. President Johnson worked with governors to deploy 58,000 National Guardsmen as well as dispatching regular troops from the army. At least 43 people died in the uncontrollable spasms of rage, with 3,500 injured and more than 27,000 arrested.

In response to the devastation, some public voices tried to connect King and his message to the arson and insurrection. William Tuck, a former governor of Virginia and an eight-term congressman from the Old Dominion, addressed the House of Representatives. While he allowed that "the killing of King" had been a misfortune for the nation, he went on to blame the civil rights hero for provoking his own murder because "he fomented discord and strife between the races." Representative Tuck went on to rip King's call for a Poor People's Campaign in the summer of '68 as a threat to national stability, in which Dr. King "was planning to invade Washington with a horde of the hosts of evil, to disrupt and stay the wheels of the government of the United States. Every sensible person knows, as he himself must have known, that such an act would result in wholesale property destruction, bloodshed, and death to this beleaguered city. This man trampled upon the laws of our country with impunity."

Consider, for a moment, that a United States congressman took the floor of the House of Representatives to depict Dr. King, just six days after his death, as a demonic figure who could call forth "a horde of the hosts of evil"—and not one of Tuck's congressional colleagues rose to object.

The power of "white backlash" in the late sixties helps to explain why the idea of a holiday in King's honor took so many years to gain meaningful momentum. In that first week after the assassination, Congressman John Conyers of Michigan, one of the founders of the Congressional Black Caucus, drafted legislation to observe King's birthday as a federal holiday but his initial effort attracted scant support. He persisted year after year, while Edward Brooke, a black Republican from Massachusetts, took up the fight on the Senate side of Capitol Hill.

In fact, once the Republicans took over both the White House and the Senate in the Reagan Revolution of 1980, the prospects for a King holiday seemed to brighten: young conservatives like the recently elected Georgia congressman Newt Gingrich picked up the cause with passion and eloquence. When Senator Jesse Helms of North Carolina tried to filibuster against the bill by citing secret FBI files about King's association with Communists and his "unnatural" sex life, several of his colleagues reacted with ferocious indignation. Bill Bradley, the Democratic senator from New Jersey, denounced the attacks on King's character: "They speak for a past that the vast majority of Americans have overcome."

As it turned out, that once confidential file made its public appearance in November 2017, disgorged as something of an afterthought along with previously classified material about the JFK assassination. Originally compiled in 1968, just three weeks before the assassination, the anonymous, top secret government report oozes with contempt and disgust, describing King as "a true, genuine Marxist-Leninist 'from the top of his head to the tips of his toes.'" It also alludes to "drunken sex orgies," abuse of prostitutes, extramarital affairs, and a "love child" with the wife of a dentist.

Considering that J. Edgar Hoover relentlessly expressed his hostility since the days of King's first emergence as a national figure, it's difficult to discern why the FBI director never planted such lurid stories with the pliant press. He may have collected the scurrilous details for precisely that purpose and waited for the right moment—like a discrediting defeat with the sanitation strike in Memphis. Of course, King's assassination just twenty days after the bureau completed its report preempted the potential smear. After his death, the idea of trashing his memory appealed neither to Hoover nor to the journalists who often feasted on leaks from the FBI.

That's another reason to argue that King not only lived a providential life but also died a providential death. His murder didn't put an end to his impact but served instead to amplify and extend it. Without question, King achieved his greatest influence after his demise, without the smears and quarrels and disappointments that would have almost certainly been inflicted on him had he lived through the years immediately following 1968. In this broader context, a pointless killing by a low-life murderer—a "ten-cent white boy" in James Bevel's phrase—could be seen to serve a larger purpose, just as could King's fateful decision to accept his first pulpit in racist and provincial Montgomery.

The House finally passed the King holiday bill in 1983 with a lopsided vote of 338 to 90, earning solid majorities of both parties. In the Senate, even South Carolina's crusty, onetime Dixiecrat Strom Thurmond (by then a Republican) supported the legislation, along with seventy-seven of his GOP and Democratic colleagues. In the signing ceremony, President Reagan aptly observed: "Dr. King had awakened something strong and true, a sense that true justice must be colorblind, and that among white and black Americans, as he put it, 'Their destiny is tied up with our destiny, and their freedom is inextricably bound to our freedom; we cannot walk alone.'"

Coretta Scott King followed the president with her moving remarks: "In his own life's example," she said of her husband, "he symbolized what was right about America, what was noblest and best, what human beings have pursued since the beginning of history. He loved unconditionally. He was in constant pursuit of truth, and when he discovered it, he embraced it."

BETWEEN MEMPHIS AND MONUMENT

And the nation he loved came to embrace that truth, gradually, incrementally in the years following his murder. Many states instantly welcomed the idea of a "King Day" and passed state legislation to authorize the holiday, but others resisted and quibbled for years. For complicated political reasons, the fight in Arizona proved especially contentious, with a dubious executive order of one governor rescinded by the next, two failed referenda, and punishing boycotts from national businesses—including the NFL, which stripped Phoenix of Super Bowl XXVII in 1993. Finally, in time to celebrate the new millennium in May 2000, South Carolina became the last state to authorize the King commemoration as a paid holiday for all state workers.

With all the progress he made in the electrifying twelve years between Montgomery and Memphis, attitudes toward King himself, and to black people in general, changed even more profoundly during the more than forty years between Memphis and monument.

In 2011, President Barack Obama presided over the dedication of the Martin Luther King Jr. Memorial on a four-acre site near the National Mall, within sight of previous monuments to Washington, Lincoln, and Jefferson. The cost amounted to $120 million to honor a man who left an estate for his widow and four children of less than $10,000.

More than 90 percent of the funds for the King monument came from private donations, including from some of the wealthiest and most prestigious corporations in the country. The parklike setting is dominated by an imposing granite centerpiece that shows a gigantic image of King, emerging from the raw rock like a force of nature and, with arms crossed across his chest, rising more than thirty feet from the ground. It's known as the "Stone of Hope" statue to honor a line from the "I Have a Dream" speech: "Out of the mountain of despair, a stone of hope."

The vision statement for the monument describes it as "a quiet and peaceful space" that "drawing from Dr. King's speeches and using his own rich language . . . will almost certainly change the heart of every person who visits."

"OUT OF THE MOUNTAIN OF DESPAIR, A STONE OF HOPE":
The Martin Luther King Jr. Memorial, dedicated by President Barack Obama
in 2011 on a four-acre site near the National Mall, has become one of
the five most-visited attractions in Washington, D.C.

Whether the memorial or the national holiday can actually change the heart of "every person" remains a dubious proposition, but no one can doubt the profound change of heart in the nation at large in the generations since his death. Skeptics might dismiss the holiday as a tacky, convenient excuse for winter sales or a three-day weekend just a few weeks after New Year's, but every January its messages—King's messages—seem more universally discussed, accepted, and honored in private and in public.

Critics may carp over the Stone of Hope sculpture at the memorial as "block-headed," "clumsy," and "propagandistic," but they can't deny its popularity with visitors to the nation's capital, or the reverence with which they stroll the grounds. It draws more than three million tourists every year, or nearly ten thousand per day, making it one of the top five most-visited attractions in Washington, D.C.

The other American heroes honored at or near the National Mall—Washington, Jefferson, Lincoln, FDR, and, soon to come, Eisenhower—are each associated with blatant, unmistakable American triumphs in war and peace. Assessing King's victories is more complicated, precisely because changed attitudes and altered patterns of daily life are far more difficult to measure or celebrate than victories on the battlefield. But the very existence of a national holiday and a popular monument to an individual who once inspired division and denunciation should serve as reassurance of the distance we've traveled. The troublemaker became a national treasure; the agitator is now an icon.

But the redemptive impact of his martyrdom remained obscure, if not inconceivable, in the weeks of horror that immediately followed the assassination. In fact, another murder a mere two months later convinced even chronically optimistic, reflexively patriotic Americans that the same God who had so reliably and prodigiously blessed their country may have irrevocably removed his special protection.

"GOD MIGHT HAVE WITHDRAWN HIS BLESSING FROM AMERICA": Senator Robert Kennedy, campaigning in the California primary days before his death. Novelist John Updike feared that RFK's assassination signaled the end of the Republic's providential protection.

10

"Forever Upward"

Grounds for Gratitude at the Edge of Apocalypse

"God might have withdrawn his blessing from America," novelist John Updike dramatically declaimed in response to the assassination of Robert Kennedy in June 1968.

The remark resonated with the public because Bobby's killing marked the third in a series of horrible murders after his brother's death five years earlier and just two months from the slaughter of Dr. King. When events fall into a discernible pattern, it's difficult to write them off as random and disconnected, and far easier to assume a cosmic shift, a vile curse, or some foul, toxic cloud descending on the American landscape.

"ROARING LIKE A BULL IN ITS WOUNDS"

To Norman Mailer, RFK's murder presaged a summer when "the Republic hovered on the edge of revolution, nihilism, and lines of police on file to the horizon. . . . And the country roaring like a bull in its wounds, coughing like a sick lung in the smog, turning over in sleep at the sound of motorcycles, shivering at its need for new phalanxes of order."

At the time, such descriptions of an afflicted America struck me with special force because I was there—present at the site of Bobby Kennedy's killing, perhaps twenty yards from the door to the kitchen where the senator fell.

As a nineteen-year-old "Kennedy for President" volunteer, I had pushed and slithered to the front of the joyous crowd of 1,500 jammed into the ballroom of the aging Ambassador Hotel in Los Angeles to celebrate the candidate's crucial win in the California primary. I had taken a leave of absence from my junior year at Yale, in order to jet to Los Angeles, where my parents and kid brothers lived, to work in the campaign.

That night, as the votes mounted in the close contest, the senator finally arrived to claim victory shortly after midnight. Standing near the podium with my two female friends from the campaign, I remember feeling struck by how small Robert Kennedy looked, surrounded by burly bodyguards and supporters like the huge pro-football legend Roosevelt Grier. RFK's complexion glowed notably pink, visibly sunburned from the afternoon he had spent at the beach with some of his ten children—his wife, Ethel, had an eleventh baby on the way. During one burst of cheering during his victory speech, I shouted out, "We love you, Bobby!" You can hear my voice on some tapes of the occasion.

He concluded his brief remarks with a pitch to heal the bitter splits in the Democratic Party and the nation at large. "I think we can end the divisions in the United States," Senator Kennedy insisted in a hushed, respectful tone. "What I think is quite clear is that we can work together in the last analysis. . . . We are a great country, an unselfish country, and a compassionate country. And I intend to make that my basis for running over the period of the next few months." The crowd erupted in sustained, confident cheers. "So my thanks to all of you, and now it's on to Chicago and let's win there."

He smiled, flashed a V-for-Victory hand gesture (which also counted as a peace sign in 1968), stepped down from the podium, and disappeared into a kitchen passageway to head upstairs for a televised press conference. I also wanted to exit the crowded ballroom as quickly as possible to go on to some of the private parties elsewhere in the Ambassador Hotel or already in session at nearby clubs. But then we all turned to the sound of popping balloons somewhere behind the podium—quick pops, in a staccato blast—followed by piercing screams and other voices crying, "Oh, no, no, no!"

My most vivid memory of the evening involves the sound of that crowd, as all its members instinctively grasped what had happened without being told. The moaning, shrieking, and gasping started at the front, where I stood, and spread to the back of the big ballroom, each individual cry blending into a terrifying animalistic roar. The panic hit the far wall, and then bounced back again, rolling like an all-engulfing tidal wave that gathered deadly force, with sobs and pleas now layered above the instinctive noises of fright and horror. An aura of risk and edge, danger and destiny, had attached itself to Bobby's crusade from the beginning, simultaneously firing and frightening his crowds.

After the shooting, when the shock had subsided, a woman in a light blue dress stepped to the podium and announced through the microphone what everyone already understood. "Senator Kennedy has been shot," she said, before adding the reassurance that everyone craved. "But he's all right. He's wounded and they've taken him to the hospital and they will be performing surgery." This produced light applause, but the attempt to cheer wilted even as it began, collapsing from a lack of confidence or conviction, stifled by the mood of desperation and doom that infested the gathering like a rank odor.

Like most of those present, I felt a powerful impulse to flee, suddenly sickened by the sheer creepiness of the Ambassador Hotel, with its chintzy, dated, old-Hollywood glamour—best known as the location of the once swanky Cocoanut Grove nightclub. Spectators to scenes of carnage may feel drawn to the site initially, but once you've gotten even a brief taste of the horror you want to get away.

Unfortunately, hotel and law enforcement officials made that impossible: they quickly sealed the building and no one was permitted to leave. As we wandered the hallways in a dreamlike daze, scrabbling for scraps of reassurance, word spread of multiple victims—five had been wounded, aside from Kennedy, by Sirhan Sirhan's eight shots. Rumors also circulated about multiple shooters, feeding groundless conspiracy theories that spread from the scene and survived, illogically, for decades. People watching their television screens at home had a far better grasp of what was actually going on than those of us trapped there on-site in our shell-shocked zombie state.

The cops began releasing people shortly before dawn. We waited in weary lines, forced to show IDs and to provide names and addresses before we could leave. The FBI duly contacted me some weeks later, but brief questioning made it clear I hardly counted as an important witness.

"TOMB OF OUR HOPES"

That morning, walking out into the bracing air through the doors of that sprawling old hotel, the phrase "Tomb of Our Hopes" came to mind. When I got into my parents' battered Mercury station wagon for the long drive home to West L.A., I heard the radio reports: doctors had been operating on Senator Kennedy's brain, removing bullet fragments. Some broadcasters suggested he stood a chance of recovery, but none of the survivors of the world's worst victory party could bring ourselves to believe it. I didn't believe it.

I drove down deserted Wilshire Boulevard in the dissolving darkness because it felt more fitting to creep along shadowy surface streets, with the city asleep on all sides, than to inject myself into the already quickening pulse of freeway traffic. I remember the sky fading from blue-black to pale gray, with hints of rose beginning to light the eastern horizon behind me, hauntingly reflected in the rearview mirror. Wearying of the repetitive and intensely depressing news reports on the car radio, I switched to Top 40 to listen to music of the moment.

One mournful ballad, Jimmy Webb's bizarre "MacArthur Park," oddly evoked the sense of ruined dreams. With its pungently plaintive punch line about irreversible loss ("I don't think that I can take it. . . . And I'll never have that recipe again, oh no!"), the song seemed to speak obliquely of the utter wreckage of that whole wretched year. By the time I finally arrived at my parents' suburban Westside neighborhood, I noted the children, gabbing and gathering just as usual, awaiting their school buses as they did on every normal morning. For them, at least, the world hadn't ended at the Ambassador Hotel.

My worried mom wanted to comfort me and feed me—equivalent processes in her mind, of course. The bulletins from the hospital told little new about Kennedy's condition. I tried to focus on what Bobby's situation would mean to the nation, to our history, but anxiety over my own exploded plans crowded out the larger speculation. I had meant to travel with the campaign all the way to the Democratic convention in Chicago and perhaps beyond—taking some part in the happy-ending Camelot restoration we all fully expected to celebrate after the November balloting. Now, that giddy, fairy-tale confidence felt ridiculous. What might have been a noble, world-shifting campaign, with fanfares and pennants flying, quickly dissolved into useless, desperate gestures of protest and vicious street fighting—which is just what happened in Chicago two months later.

Forty-two-year-old Robert Kennedy died at 1:44 a.m. the next day, Thursday, June 6, 1968, nearly twenty-six hours after his shooting. I had finally fallen asleep on a couch in the den when my father woke me with the news.

"He's gone," he sighed in an uncharacteristically high, wavering voice, and then wept. "Bobby's gone. Oh, my God. Our poor country."

OUR "SICK SOCIETY"

The months and years that followed brought so much bad news that it seemed entirely plausible that our once specially blessed Republic had become uniquely cursed. In place of spirited debate over Lyndon Johnson's utopian "Great Society"—the ambitious reform program introduced just four years before—conversation shifted to laments over our "sick society" and its suicidal trajectory. In campus conversation, it became almost impossible to invoke the neutral noun "society" without first deploying the inevitable identifying adjective "sick."

After assassinations, long, hot summers of urban riots, and the bloody, weekly "butcher's bill" in Vietnam came the grisly Manson murders and the general spread of crime and drugs. Domestic terrorism became a novel nightmare in American life, with wild-eyed, bearded revolutionaries planting deadly bombs in university mathematics buildings or staging bank robberies and kidnappings.

In politics, a vice president of the United States for the first time faced felony charges of kickbacks and corruption, then pleaded "no contest" and resigned his post. Spiro Agnew's boss, President Richard Nixon, simultaneously confronted accusations of his own in an alleged conspiracy to subvert the Constitution. On the verge of impeachment, he also left office in disgrace. Meanwhile, Soviet tanks rumbled into Prague to crush the first tentative stirrings of spring and independence, while Egypt and Syria used Russian weapons to stage a devastating Yom Kippur surprise attack on Israel, ultimately bringing the United States and the Soviet Union to a red-alert nuclear confrontation. The Arab oil embargo that followed produced shortages and gas lines for the first time since World War II, striking at the very soul of American independence—our cars.

None of this fit comfortably with cherished notions of a nation among nations, reliably and bizarrely blessed.

CONTRADICTORY SIGNS

Yet even amid all the epic disasters and sneering disillusionments, the news also brought some reassuring signs—for those who chose to seize on them.

Barely a year after Robert Kennedy's death, the United States succeeded in realizing his older brother's visionary goal by placing a trio of astronauts on the lunar surface, where they proudly planted the American flag. The machines worked perfectly, as did the adept and unflappable American heroes who operated them.

Then six years after that came a pair of stunningly strange incidents that provoked sighs of relief (and disbelief) rather than cheers and parades. Still they suggested that America hadn't yet exhausted her skein of illogical good luck as she approached her Bicentennial celebration.

Within the space of barely two weeks in September 1975, President Gerald R. Ford (who had assumed office after Nixon's resignation) made two trips to Northern California. During each of them, mentally disturbed women—one associated with the Manson Family, the other connected with a dubious FBI informants' program—drew a pistol on the stoic president of the United States in an attempt to gun him down. On September 5, in Sacramento, Ford walked from the Senator Hotel to the state capitol for a meeting with California's (perpetual) governor, Jerry Brown. As Ford made his way onto the capitol grounds, Charles Manson groupie Lynette "Squeaky" Fromme, wearing a Red Riding Hood getup and hoping to raise awareness of the threatened redwoods, tried to fire at him with her .45 Colt semi-automatic loaded with four rounds. Fortunately, an alert Secret Service agent wrestled her to the ground before she could rack a round into the firing chamber and take aim at the president of the United States.

Just seventeen days later, President Ford returned to California for a speech at San Francisco's St. Francis Hotel and this time came much closer to wounding or death. Sara Jane Moore, an unstable forty-five-year-old who had dabbled in the Bay Area's radical politics (and informed for the FBI) while racking up five divorces, used a .44-caliber revolver with 113 rounds of ammunition. She fired at the president from a distance of forty feet and barely missed him with her first shot, before an attentive bystander (and gay former Marine) spoiled her second try by batting away her arm. After this second threat to his life, President Ford followed the advice of the Secret Service and wore a thin bulletproof vest when he appeared in public.

As for his two would-be assassins, they both received life sentences and both escaped from the different prisons to which they had been committed—yet another coincidence that counted as beyond bizarre. After their respective recaptures, each received parole in the first decade of the new century, with Squeaky Fromme taking up residence with a fellow parolee (who happened to be a convicted killer) in a house cheerily decorated with human skulls.

Unlike the reaction to previous close calls—the attempted assassinations of President Andrew Jackson in 1835 and President-elect Franklin Roosevelt in 1933—the nation never celebrated the providential protection that shielded its recently installed leader (twice!) in the course of seventeen days. In part, the unsavory weirdness of the two deranged female assailants made it easier to minimize the seriousness of the threat.

"THE OUTCOME IS BY NO MEANS CERTAIN"

Nevertheless, for anyone who paid attention, President Ford's fortu-itous survival provided additional grounds for gratitude as the nation approached its two hundredth birthday bash in July 1976.

One hundred years earlier, at Philadelphia's gala Centennial In-ternational Exposition, huge crowds had gasped in awe and amaze-ment at Thomas Moran's vast canvas depicting the Mountain of the Holy Cross, seeing the natural wonder as supernatural confirmation of America's holy and predestined role in redeeming the world. By the time of the Bicentennial, the right arm of the snowy cross in the Rock-ies had already collapsed, as had the nation's unshakable confidence in its divinely directed destiny.

Nevertheless, one of America's most eminent historians used the occasion to deliver an important essay about the country's under-standing of unearthly, higher powers in shaping and sustaining the Republic. Arthur Schlesinger, a Harvard professor and onetime White House aide to President Kennedy, suggested that from the days of earliest British settlement two approaches had struggled for dominance. On the one hand, the first New Englanders believed they had been chosen by God for special favor and that his assistance would guarantee their success. "God hath covenanted with his peo-ple," said Increase Mather. "Without doubt, the Lord Jesus hath a pe-culiar respect unto this place, and for this people."

On the other side of the ongoing debate, Schlesinger arrayed the founders of the Revolutionary generation who viewed their handiwork as a human experiment—recognizing that every mortal undertaking can easily fail. Hence Washington's warning in his First Inaugural Address: "The preservation of the sacred fire of liberty and the destiny of the republican model of government are justly considered, perhaps, as deeply, as finally, staked on the experiment intrusted to the hands of the American people."

Yet it's worth noting that in the very passage Schlesinger uses to emphasize the pragmatic, earthly, secular emphasis of the founders, the first president pointedly describes the "fire of liberty" as "sacred."

Washington also spoke on innumerable occasions of the importance of acknowledging the "Invisible Hand" that guided the forces of liberty and reason to often unanticipated providentially provided success. In August 1778, for instance, as commander in chief of the Continental Army, Washington wrote to Brigadier General Thomas Nelson: "The Hand of providence has been so conspicuous in all this, that he must be worse than an infidel that lacks faith, and more than wicked, that has not gratitude enough to acknowledge his obligations." Note that the Father of Our Country saw obligation, not entitlement, as the primary product of God's intercession on America's behalf, even while acknowledging the possibility of failure for American endeavors.

Schlesinger concluded his memorable essay "America: Experiment or Destiny?" with an appropriate warning to the Bicentennial generation. "We can take pride in our nation," he wrote, "not as we pretend to a commission from God and a sacred destiny, but as we struggle to fulfill our deepest values in an inscrutable world. As we begin our third century, we may well be entering our golden age. But we would be ill advised to reject the apprehensions of the Founding Fathers. Indeed, a due heed to those ancient anxieties may alone save us in the future. For America remains an experiment. The outcome is by no means certain."

In the aftermath of the Bicentennial rejoicing, the American people felt no undue certainty about the success of the national enterprise, but they did begin to experience an increase in gratitude and confidence. In 1980, for example, they responded in massive numbers to a veteran Hollywood actor whose muscular, optimistic rhetoric provided the strongest possible contrast to a sour and besieged incumbent, Jimmy Carter, whose most celebrated public utterance had become known as "the Malaise Speech."

Ronald Reagan not only won the White House in a crushing landslide victory, but within a mere three months of his inauguration his gallantry in the face of danger and death brought the idea of providential protection back to the center of public—and presidential—consciousness.

On March 30, 1981, John Hinckley Jr., later diagnosed with "erotomania" for his fixation on impressing film star Jodie Foster, fired six shots from his revolver at Ronald Reagan as the president left a fund-raising speech at the Washington Hilton. The first five shots injured four men, delivering a grievous head wound to White House press secretary James Brady while striking a District of Columbia police officer and two Secret Service agents. A sixth bullet, fired before Hinckley could be subdued and disarmed, glanced off the side of the armored limousine where agents had tried to cram Reagan into the backseat for his protection. The ricochet struck the president under his arm and pierced his lung, before settling less than an inch from his heart. Instinctive, courageous, split-second decisions by his Secret Service detail combined with a series of inexplicably lucky breaks to save the president's life. For instance, had the party returned to the White House as Reagan initially demanded rather than sped directly to the nearest hospital, it's unlikely that "Rawhide" (the president's Secret Service code name) would have survived.

In retrospect, it's arguable that Reagan's near-death experience represented the most significant episode of his presidency, not only greatly deepening his bond with the public through his courageous display of gallantry and good humor, but also altering the chief executive's attitude toward his job and his life. All his biographers, based on interviews with intimates and, in some cases, with Reagan himself, affirm that from that point forward Reagan felt no doubt that God had spared his life to allow him to achieve higher purposes, strengthening the country and serving the cause of peace. "Perhaps having come so close to death made me feel I should do whatever I could in the years God had given me to reduce the threat of nuclear war," he wrote in retrospect.

That conviction also drew him closer to another world figure Reagan subsequently described as "my best friend": Pope John Paul II. Just six weeks after Reagan took a bullet in the chest, the Holy Father took two bullets in his abdomen, with two more striking his left hand and right arm. Shot by a well-trained Turkish gunman under circumstances that remain mysterious, John Paul went through five hours of surgery and lost three-quarters of his blood, but through strength and prayer survived for another twenty-four years of life and leadership.

In a remarkable collision of circumstances, the two individuals deserving the most credit for overcoming "the Evil Empire" and prevailing in the Cold War both absorbed potentially fatal shots from ruthless would-be assassins within six weeks of each other, and that coincidence impelled the development of a deep, productive friendship.

Their experiences unmistakably reflect the close calls of Winston Churchill and Franklin Roosevelt described in chapter 6 of this book, nearly a decade before their indispensable leadership in World War II. Over the course of fourteen months beginning during Christmas season in 1931, each of the two leaders came close to sudden death and, as with President Reagan and Pope John Paul II, subsequently became friends and allies, linked by an overwhelming sense of a common debt to destiny.

"A TEST OF THE OVERALL WORTH OF THE UNITED STATES"

In the final stages of the Cold War, that consciousness of playing a purposeful role in some grand, preordained plan echoed the same awareness of providential power that characterized the very beginning of the global struggle some forty years earlier.

In the profoundly influential "Long Telegram" of 1946, George F. Kennan, the brilliant chief of mission at America's Moscow embassy, urged President Truman to pursue a "containment" policy and prophetically delineated the contours of the conflict that unfolded, fatefully, over the half century that followed:

> The issue of Soviet-American relations is in essence a test of the overall worth of the United States as a nation among nations. Surely, there was never a fairer test of national quality than this. In the light of these circumstances, the thoughtful observer of Russian-American relations will find no cause for complaint in the Kremlin's challenge to American society. He will rather experience a certain gratitude to a Providence which, by providing the American people with this implacable challenge, has made their

entire security as a nation dependent on their pulling themselves together and accepting the responsibilities of moral and political leadership that history plainly intended them to bear.

Kennan lived to see the United States surmounting each of the challenges he anticipated, passing those tests with flying colors of red, white, and blue. He died at his Princeton home at age 101, widely honored and even revered, with his wife of seventy-one years at his side. Reagan and John Paul also lived to see and savor the ultimate victory in what John Kennedy called "the long, twilight struggle" that preoccupied nine presidents (from Truman to the first Bush) and five decades of our history.

In the wake of America's unalloyed triumph in that monumental, even existential confrontation, the idea of American decline in a slow-rolling apocalypse stands out as egregiously misguided. How could speculation of a "withdrawn blessing" possibly apply to an era of spectacular American success in our most consequential endeavors?

For seventy-five years, by far the longest stretch in modern history, the United States has remained the world's incontestably dominant power—militarily, economically, culturally. Past warnings of imminent displacement by Russia, Japan, or the European Union have turned out to be prime examples of wolf-crying; evidence strongly suggests that the current tendency to view China as the world's onrushing, unstoppable hegemon will prove similarly groundless.

In the years since World War II, America has helped our former enemies, Germany and Japan, rebuild as humane and prosperous democratic republics; succeeded in dismantling the brutal and dysfunctional Soviet Union and liberating its "captive nations" in Eastern Europe; fostered the rise of a "Europe whole and free" (in the words of President George H. W. Bush) for the first time in recorded history; modeled the economic approaches that lifted more than a half billion people from abject poverty in India and China into the middle class; conquered the ravages of AIDS on the continent of Africa and devised life-giving treatment for sufferers everywhere; developed a world-girdling industry of information technology that transformed daily life as radically as any innovation of the Industrial Revolution; dramatically improved the quality of air and water here in the homeland, while reserving millions of square miles as parkland and nature preserves; assisted in establishment of a vibrant, flourishing Jewish commonwealth with its capital in Jerusalem for the first time in two thousand years; and overcame some of its own lingering racist demons by building a flourishing African American middle class and electing its first black president *twice*—not bad, all in all, for a sick society purportedly perched at the edge of apocalypse.

In terms of measuring the living standards for America's own citizens, one statistic should suffice to indicate the overall direction of events. Since Harry Truman became president in 1945, life expectancy has risen by an astonishing seventeen years (from sixty-four to eighty-one). Anyone who denigrates that achievement is probably too young, or too dissatisfied with his own wretched existence, to understand what seventeen more years of living can mean to an ordinary American.

Of course, there are countertrends to decry and despise, with too many children raised outside of marriage or locked in failing public schools, and wretched homeless camps springing up in parks and parking lots almost everywhere. Americans die by their own hands almost twice as frequently as they're killed by others, while opioid overdoses claim more victims than suicides and homicides combined. Upward mobility remains the reality for most American families, but too many working people feel left out and left behind and their frustrations poison our politics. The demands of the twenty-four-hour news cycle encourage a sense of constant crisis, along with an insatiable appetite for polarization, scandal-mongering, and name-calling. Media naturally focus on picturesque and dramatic catastrophes; the peaceful, productive, and pleasant aspects of ordinary life can't possibly compete for attention. Our myopic vision serves to magnify signals of daily distress, while long-term progress and historical perspective look fuzzy and indistinct at best, or altogether unexamined at worst.

"THE LARGER IMPERATIVE THAT CALLS OUT
FROM THE MIRACLE"

Of course, the media do highlight occasional "feel good" stories, focusing at times on lottery winners—humble, struggling souls suddenly transformed into multimillionaires due to the random purchase of a lucky ticket at a neighborhood convenience store. One of the staples of such coverage involves tearful expressions of gratitude to God, since even nonreligious jackpot winners struggle to place their life-changing good fortune into some meaningful context.

And if Americans feel an urge to thank the Deity for some extra cash delivered through pure dumb luck, then why not express similar thanks—regularly—for winning life's lottery through your American birth or upbringing? You've already grabbed the golden ticket that half the world wants. You don't deserve the credit—though your grandparents or other ancestral arrivals almost certainly do. Nonetheless, it's you who gets the undeniable benefits that you never personally earned. Placing present-day predicaments in their proper global and historical context, comparing our own circumstances with those of the rest of humanity and all prior generations, should remind us of our freakish good fortune to live in the United States of America in the twenty-first century. It's not that the peoples of other lands or earlier eras can be scorned as losers; it's rather that we should rejoice in our status as winners, and embrace the obligations of gratitude and goodness that go along with it. When Lincoln spoke of Americans in 1861 as the Almighty's "almost chosen people," he argued that his countrymen had been chosen for special responsibilities, not special privileges; selected for duties rather than rewards.

George Kennan invoked the same idea when he summoned Americans in 1946 to accept "the responsibilities of moral and political leadership that history plainly intended them to bear." Playing the central role in the greatest struggles of the modern era may have been America's fate, but it wasn't necessarily a matter of choice, bringing with it as many burdens as benefits.

In 1956, Rabbi Joseph B. Soloveitchik of Yeshiva University, one of the most influential religious thinkers of the twentieth century, wrote of the profound obligation placed on those blessed by providential protection: "Miraculous grace places upon man an absolute responsibility to fulfill the larger imperative that calls out from the miracle." He was addressing the generation that had escaped the devastation of global war and mass slaughter. "Woe unto the beneficiary of a miracle who does not recognize it for what it is, and whose ear is deaf to the echo of the imperative that arises out of this metahistorical event. Pity the one who benefits from the miracles of the Master of the Universe but the spark of faith is not kindled in him, and his conscience is not stirred by the sight of this singular event."

To acknowledge such singular events isn't to expect them in every instance, or to deny the inevitable examples of national failure and fiasco. "Uncertainty about the future is not new to the U.S.," wrote Bard College's Walter Russell Mead in his 2018 Fourth of July column for the *Wall Street Journal*. "Our national anthem begins not with a triumphant assertion but an anxious question: Is the American flag still flying as night gives way to dawn?"

In the American context, the idea of heavenly favor for our national project has never meant guarantees of consistent victory or untrammeled success. After all, just three weeks before a worried Francis Scott Key rejoiced at dawn to see the Star-Spangled Banner still billowing in the breeze over Maryland's Fort McHenry, a major British invading force had marched into nearby Washington and burned the White House. In every era, calamities, setbacks, and stupidities interrupt, or even overwhelm, our positive progress, but they've never yet permanently altered the Republic's indomitably ascendant trajectory.

Despite disillusionment over present predicaments, Americans retain an instinctive affinity for the old faith in providential protection, and an honest examination of our history ought to make the case for its reclamation. The long-standing assumption that fate favored American endeavors always made more sense than its abandonment, however intense the contemporary choruses of discomfort and complaint.

"GOD IS ON VACATION"

With literally billions of dollars invested in negative advertising, every presidential election seems to bring new expressions of despair over the alternatives available to the electorate. Shortly before the 2016 confrontation between Hillary Clinton and Donald Trump, the conservative scholar Michael Barone tartly observed: "For two centuries, God or good luck provided Americans with brilliant leaders in times of crisis. It's beginning to look like our luck has run out or that God is on vacation."

Others blamed the public as much as any higher powers for the apparent decline in our political discourse. James Traub, the redoubtable biographer of John Quincy Adams, noted that "even a half century ago, the America of John F. Kennedy was expansive and forward-looking in its view of itself and the world. But the spirit of enthusiasm, the almost blind optimism about the future that made America so exceptional, has curdled recently into sour distrust. Many Americans are all too ready to believe the worst not only of their leaders but of one another. Standards of civility and mutual respect have given way to angry accusations of deception and bad faith."

Of course, the raging "civil war" over Donald Trump's embattled presidency only exacerbates that bad faith. His elevation to the nation's highest office seemed so shocking and unexpected that partisans on both sides rushed for supernatural explanations. White House press secretary Sarah Huckabee Sanders told the Christian Broadcasting Network: "I think God calls all of us to fill different roles at different times and I think that He wanted Donald Trump to become president, and that's why he's here." A Fox News Poll in 2018 showed that 25 percent of registered voters agreed with her in the proposition that Trump won the election by carrying "The One" constituency that counts most.

Even some of the president's most outspoken critics see a higher, potentially divine purpose to the degradation they see everywhere in his administration. David Brooks of the *New York Times* wrote in February 2019 that "Trump, personifying the worst elements in our culture, is like a providentially sent gong meant to wake us up and direct us toward a better path."

The most dispiriting aspect of the current polarization is the un-limited, godlike power that both sides impute to a single flawed and fascinating human being. In truth, Donald Trump can neither solely save nor single-handedly savage the most powerful nation on Earth. America may emerge from his time in office as notably stronger, or recognizably worse, than when he first came to power. To the disap-pointment of his admirers and the great relief of his critics, the nation won't be utterly transformed. He can't make America great again be-cause we never ceased being great and he won't be able to wreck all of our institutions because, as Adam Smith sagely observed in 1777, "there is a great deal of ruin in a nation."

Either way, the Republic will survive, and prosper, having endured far worse trials than a torrent of outrageous tweets and sometimes incoherent policies from the president, or accusatory excesses from his dreaded adversaries in fake news and the Deep State.

It does say something about the Republic's continued dominance on the world stage that the most apocalyptic fears of the moment focus on self-inflicted wounds rather than on foreign attacks or com-petition. Most often, that perversely appealing notion of impending, inevitable decline cites the likelihood that America will succumb, ul-timately, to a sickness of the soul (the "sick society" returns!), or to the curse of shabby and shortsighted leadership, or to waning worthiness for the protections of providence. At least those who speculate about such shattered prospects connect that fall to broken promises, ac-knowledging that the United States deserved and enjoyed fate's favor in the past.

"I know that it may sound naïve, even childish to think that any nation has a special destiny," wrote historical novelist Kevin Baker in an elegiac meditation in the *New York Times* the day after Donald Trump's inauguration. "I doubt if many of the other writers I know would admit that they believe in such a big, vague concept as 'Ameri-can exceptionalism.' But we do, most of us. It's inescapable, consider-ing what we are: the first republic of the modern age, a nation of immigrants, haven to so many peoples from around the world. We have, like no other country, for better and for ill, dominated the modern world through both our hard power and our soft, our weapons but also our ideas." Baker feared that America at the beginning of 2017 had become Belgium—a selfish, insignificant state no more precious than any other. To him, recent choices by the voters destroyed the "greater, almost spiritual faith that I had in my fellow citizens and their better instincts, something that served as my north star in all I wrote and all I did."

While Baker mourned American decay from the perspective of the center left, countless others have keened similar laments from the vantage of the religious right. The late Jerry Falwell, for instance, frequently quipped: "If God doesn't punish the United States of America soon, He's going to have to apologize to Sodom and Gomorrah!"

In other words, the same God who nourished his favorite nation in return for good behavior in the past would likely chastise it for bad conduct in the present and future. This reward-and-punishment concept of divine providence might comport comfortably with biblical notions of God's covenant with Israel, but it doesn't fit the idea of divine providence most regularly embraced by the founders and other great leaders of the Republic's past.

"TO LEAD THE LAND WE LOVE"

When Katharine Lee Bates wrote the inspired national hymn "America the Beautiful" in 1893, she deliberately emphasized an important word: "America! America! God shed His *grace* on thee." In the Christian tradition that shaped our national consciousness, "grace" is not reward: it is a gift from God that may or may not be merited, a freely bestowed favor that can't be earned. God grants grace to achieve his own goals, not because he necessarily approves of ours. In this perspective, it's reductionist and immature to see providence as the instrument of America's rise, and far more appropriate to view America as a key tool of providential processes.

If Dr. Martin Luther King is correct that "the arc of the moral universe is long, but it bends toward justice," then the United States, as he would be the first to recognize, has been an important mechanism in bending that arc.

At his fourth inauguration in 1945, Franklin Roosevelt spoke in similarly optimistic terms—despite the continued carnage of the war and his own gravely weakened condition. The scaled-down ceremonies overlooking the White House lawn called for only brief remarks, and FDR turned his thoughts to recollections of his prep school mentor Endicott Peabody, who had passed away just two months earlier.

The president told the nation and the world:

> I remember that my old schoolmaster, Dr. Peabody, said, in days that seemed to us then to be secure and untroubled: "Things in life will not always run smoothly. Sometimes we will be rising toward the heights—then all will seem to reverse itself and start downward. The great fact to remember is that the trend of civilization itself is forever upward; that a line drawn through the middle of the peaks and the valleys of the centuries always has an upward trend."...
>
> The Almighty God has blessed our land in many ways. He has given our people stout hearts and strong arms with which to strike mighty blows for freedom and truth. He has given to our country a faith which has become the hope of all peoples in an anguished world.

Just eighty-two days later, the president lay dead, leaving his unfinished work of victory and peace for other hands. That faith of which he spoke involved belief in America and its mission as much as it invoked confidence in God and his direction. American power has seldom been pursued as an end in itself, but has been seen instead as a means to higher ends and loftier goals.

During the Civil War, Abraham Lincoln purportedly responded to a question of whether God favored the Union cause. "Sir, my concern is not whether God is on our side," said the president. "My greatest concern is to be on God's side, for God is always right." That story—very possibly apocryphal—nonetheless makes an important point: we cannot reliably change the will and plans of God, but we can always alter our own.

In concluding his inaugural address, John Kennedy offered his fellow citizens an eloquent exhortation to do just that.

"With a good conscience our only sure reward, with history the final judge of our deeds," he told Americans in 1961, "let us go forth to lead the land we love, asking His blessing and His help, but knowing that here on earth God's work must truly be our own."

FROM ENDANGERED TO FLOURISHING: "Those who regularly predict impending doom for the United States of America should consider the signs and signals all around them—including the national symbol that now soars majestically above most states in the federal union."

PHOTO BY DIANE MEDVED

Messengers in the Sky

Appreciation and Acknowledgment

Three days after turning in the completed manuscript for this book, I jumped up in alarm when I heard my wife, Diane, screaming from the deck outside our kitchen. Running out to her in a panic, I felt intense relief to see her smiling broadly and pointing to the sky.

"Eagles!" she exclaimed. "Look at that—three bald eagles. Right here!"

Sure enough, there they were: three giant birds, boasting wingspans of six feet, hovering directly overhead and riding the air currents in slow, circular patterns. The silver-gray clouds drifting behind them on this Sunday morning in late March only rendered their aerial acrobatics more dramatic. Our national symbol, soaring emblem of American power and exceptionalism, appeared like a benediction, perhaps one hundred feet above our own backyard.

We live on a suburban island not far from Seattle, where our neighbors include some twenty-five thousand humans and, according to a regular survey, fourteen pairs of nesting bald eagles. The big birds, once on the verge of extinction, have made a spectacular comeback. Populations had dwindled to as few as 417 nesting pairs (in the contiguous forty-eight states) at the end of the 1950s, but thanks to sensible programs of conservation and protection, the American Eagle

Foundation now estimates at least twenty-eight thousand of the birds in the lower forty-eight, with perhaps double that number in Alaska and Canada.

In our home state of Washington, occupied eagle nests (which, amazingly, weigh more than one thousand pounds each) increased by 800 percent between 1980 and 2005, when authorities stopped counting. In 2007, the feds removed the species altogether from the official "List of Endangered and Threatened Wildlife."

It's an inspiring story, with a reassuring message for anyone willing to absorb it. Those who regularly predict impending doom for the United States of America should consider the signs and signals all around them—including the national symbol that now soars majestically above most states in the federal union.

The timing of our own eagle sighting proved especially encouraging on account of two important dates that also coincided with my completion of this book. Without planning it that way, I wrapped up my first draft on the tenth anniversary of my father's death. More than anyone else, he taught me to rejoice in the little gifts of everyday life, and encouraged limitless gratitude for our American homeland.

The day we lost my father also corresponded to the jubilant festival of Purim, which celebrates the unlikely deliverance of the Jewish people from the genocidal schemes of the wicked Haman, vizier of the Persian Empire in the fifth century B.C. The Book of Esther that we read each year to recount the story behind the festival is the Bible's only volume with no mention of God's name; we're left to look for signs and hints to discern his role in the unfolding story. As one favorite commentary describes the process, we're meant to assemble "God's Jigsaw Puzzle," which also pertains to my efforts here to identify pattern and purpose in past events.

As my father often insisted, that means learning from our own experience as well as drawing lessons from distant history. I quoted my dad about his boyhood hero, Franklin Roosevelt, to begin chapter 8, and then went on to describe the uncannily important substitution of Harry Truman for Henry Wallace as the vice presidential nominee at the Democratic convention of 1944.

My father couldn't vote in that election—he was still under

twenty-one—but he did cast his first presidential vote for Wallace when he ran as an independent Progressive in 1948. My dad even put in some hours as a volunteer for the dubious Progressive Party in its Philadelphia operation, but shortly thereafter he profoundly regretted the association—as did Henry Wallace himself.

By 1952, the onetime vice president acknowledged that his accommodate-Stalin platform had been a monumental mistake. My dad used to tell his sons the story of his own well-intentioned "youthful indiscretion" as a reminder of how wrong politicians and voters can be, even when they feel self-righteously certain of their own judgment. Only in retrospect can we place events, policies, and public personalities in proper perspective. I thank my late father, physicist-philosopher that he was, for that insight, and for so much more.

My kid brother, Harry Medved, helped to keep Dad's memory and influence alive, and makes heroic efforts to hold our far-flung family together. Harry also helped in choosing the title for this book and providing unstinting encouragement at every step in the project's progress. I'm also profoundly grateful to my brother Jonathan (a kindred spirit in distant Jerusalem) and brother Ben (in Silicon Valley) for their support and love. Aside from all the achievements by "my glorious brothers" (which was also the title of a novel about the Maccabees our late mom particularly cherished), I know our parents would be most proud that we've maintained not only connection but collaboration, despite the physical distance between us.

I'm also deeply grateful to Tina Constable, publisher and editor of Crown Forum, who has provided exemplary guidance and support on each of the five books we've produced together. For *God's Hand on America* in particular, she deserves special credit for the insight that the rich material presented here deserved a separate volume rather than hurried inclusion in the prior release, *The American Miracle*. My astute and preternaturally patient editor, Mary Reynics, has now managed to generate three books with me, at the same time she (even more significantly) produced two beautiful children with her husband, Richard.

My agent, Richard Pine, negotiated this project for me, as he has seventeen other books for my wife and me over the last forty-five years. That's an honorable, even admirable span for any business relationship—and I'm grateful for that endurance and consistency.

My radio family, meanwhile, continues to deserve gratitude every day for making my life and work possible. Producer Jeremy Steiner ("Pride of Hillsdale College") has been my indispensable partner in daily broadcasts for, amazingly, twenty-three years; "Rockstar Greg" Tomlin, my other producer and savvy social media counselor, has been part of the team for nearly fourteen years. It's a privilege to work with these brilliant and devoted brethren each weekday in framing responses to the breaking news, no matter how broken, as the "first draft of history." They've also helped initiate a new historical product— our three-times-a-week podcast *In Light of History*, which provides perspective from the past to apply to present, perplexing events.

Meanwhile, my assistant Karmen Frisvold (another pride of Hillsdale College) has played her usual crucial role in helping with research, organizing sources, securing visual imagery, proofreading, and much more in the demanding business at hand. She's managed all this while editing our weekly newsletter, tending to the needs of four-year-old Keller, and preparing to welcome a new baby to the family.

Finally, my immediate family contributed to this effort in ways they may not understand. Our daughters, Sarah and Shayna, are both gifted educators, one at the high school level and the other in early childhood education. Their dedication to their work encourages me to value the educational aspects of my history projects, as a potential source of inspiration and not just information. Meanwhile, Shayna's husband, attorney Mark Giuliano, provided considerable research help on my last book and has delivered solid advice on key issues with this one.

Even more important, Shayna and Mark, as well as our son, Danny, and his amazing wife, Richelle, have become our neighbors, establishing homes not far from the house where they grew up. Danny's demanding career in IT and responsibilities as a dad of two adorable little girls haven't kept him from serving as a crucial millennial sounding board on every aspect of this book. And Richelle, a nurse and mother, has helped to keep the author healthy (physically as well as emotionally) while this project moved ahead.

Finally, for my wife, Dr. Diane: no matter how gushing and over-the-top the words I deploy at this point, they couldn't equal the sense of gratitude and, yes, exaltation that I feel as your partner, collaborator, soul mate, and best friend these last thirty-five years. Despite all the post-midnight sessions proofreading and editing new chunks of this book, you somehow managed to complete your own acclaimed and important tome: *Don't Divorce: Powerful Arguments for Saving and Revitalizing Your Marriage*. You revitalize *our* marriage every day, with your kindness, brilliance, generosity, and sheer joy. In every aspect of our crowded life together, you look upward, taking note that even endangered eagles can not only survive but soar, while irresistibly indicating God's Hand on America.

FOR MORE ON THESE TOPICS:

Visit michaelmedved.com to sign up for our free weekly newsletter and our *In the Light of History* podcast, or to subscribe to our daily radio show. Also, go to MedvedHistoryStore.com for additional material on the themes of this book and deeper perspectives on the Republic's glorious past.

Sources

CHAPTER 1: THE MESSAGE IN THE MOUNTAINSIDE

BOOKS

Anderson, Nancy K. *Thomas Moran*. New Haven, CT: Yale University Press, 1998.

Bowles, Samuel. *The Switzerland of America: A Summer Vacation in the Park and Mountains of Colorado*. Boston: Lee & Shepard, 1869.

Goetzmann, William. *Exploration and Empire: The Explorer and the Scientist in the Winning of the American West*. New York: Alfred A. Knopf, 1966.

Hafen, LeRoy, and Ann W. Hafen, eds. *The Diaries of William Henry Jackson, Frontier Photographer*. The Far West and the Rockies Historical Series, 1820–1875, vol. 10. Glendale, CA: A. H. Clark, 1959.

Hayden, Ferdinand Vandeveer. *Sun Pictures of Rocky Mountain Scenery, with a Description of the Geographical and Geological Features, and Some Account of the Resources of the Great West [...]*. New York: Julius Bien, 1870.

Huber, Thomas P. *Hayden's Landscapes Revisited: The Drawings of the Great Colorado Survey*. Boulder: University Press of Colorado, 2016.

Jackson, William Henry. *Time Exposure: The Autobiography of William Henry Jackson*. New York: G. P. Putnam's Sons, 1940.

Jackson, William Henry, and Howard R. Driggs. *The Pioneer Photographer*. New York: World Book, 1929; Colorado Springs: Pikes Peak Library District, 2011.

Lawson, Michael L. *Little Bighorn: Winning the Battle, Losing the War*. New York: Infobase, 2009.

Wilkins, Thurman. *Thomas Moran: Artist of the Mountains*. Norman: University of Oklahoma Press, 1998.

ARTICLES

Alter, Jonathan. "Joe Biden Looks Back—and Forward." *New York Times Magazine*, January 22, 2017.

"American Transport Commission." *Daily Telegraph*, June 12, 1895.

Arave, Lynn. "Vail's Mountain Cross Inspiring." *Deseret News*, July 11, 2009.

Best, Allen. "A Divine Sanction." *Forest Magazine*, Spring 2005.

Blake, Kevin. "Imagining Heaven and Earth at Mount of the Holy Cross, Colorado." *Journal of Cultural Geography* 25, no. 1 (2008): 1–30.

Janiskee, Bob. "Pruning the Parks: Holy Cross National Monument (1933–1950)." NationalParksTraveler.org, December 17, 2010.

Lehman, Keith Allen. "William Henry Jackson." *Lighthouse Journal*, July 18, 2010.

"Manifested on the Mountain." TheHistoryBandits.com, April 26, 2015.

Van der Leun, Gerard. "The Mountain of the Holy Cross." AmericanDigest.org, March 19, 2017.

"William Henry Jackson (1843–1942), Career Chronology." Library of Congress, 2010.

SPEECHES

Coolidge, Calvin. "Inaugural Address." Washington, D.C., March 4, 1925.

Jefferson, Thomas. "First Inaugural Address." Washington, D.C., March 4, 1801.

POEMS

Longfellow, Henry Wadsworth. "The Cross of Snow." 1879.

CHAPTER 2: "NORTH TO THE FUTURE"

BOOKS

Alaska Blue Book, 1993–94, 11th ed. Juneau: Department of Education, Division of State Libraries, Archives & Museums.

Baker, George E., ed. *The Works of William H. Seward*, Vol. IV. Boston: Houghton, Mifflin and Company, 1884.

Dennett, Tyler, ed. *Lincoln and the Civil War in the Diaries and Letters of John Hay*. New York: Dodd, Mead, 1939.

Kluger, Richard. *Seizing Destiny: How America Grew from Sea to Shining Sea*. New York: Alfred A. Knopf, 2007.

Leonard, Elizabeth D. *Lincoln's Avengers: Justice, Revenge, and Reunion After the Civil War*. New York: W. W. Norton, 2004.

Seward, Frederick W. *Reminiscences of a War-Time Statesman and Diplomat, 1830–1915*. Creative Media Partners, LLC, 2018.

———. *Seward at Washington, as Senator and Secretary of State*. New York: Derby and Miller, 1891.

Seward, William H. *William H. Seward: An Autobiography*. New York: Derby & Miller, 1877.

Stahr, Walter. *Seward: Lincoln's Indispensable Man*. New York: Simon & Schuster, 2012.

Thayer, William Roscoe. *The Life and Letters of John Hay*. Boston and New York: Houghton Mifflin Company, 1908.

Weed, Thurlow, and Harriet A. Weed, eds. *Life of Thurlow Weed Including His Autobiography and Memoir*, Vol. 1. Boston: Houghton, Mifflin and Company, 1884.

ARTICLES

Gershkovich, Evan. "150 Years On, Russians Have Seller's Remorse." *New York Times*, March 31, 2017.

Haycox, Stephen. "Truth and Expectation: Myth in Alaska History." *Northern Review* 6 (Winter 1990).

"Homes: William H. Seward's House." Mr. Lincoln's White House, retrieved March 27, 2017. mrlincolnswhitehouse.org.

Kiffer, Dave. "Seward Was One of Alaska's First Tourists." SitNews.us, July 12, 2010.

Kizzia, Tom. "Now It Can Be Told: Seward's Role in Alaska's First Political Payoff Scandal." *Alaska Dispatch News*, November 24, 2012.

Kleber, Louis C. "Alaska: Russia's Folly." *History Today* 17, no. 4 (1967).

Maclean, Maggie. "Fanny Seward: Daughter of Abraham Lincoln's Secretary of State." CivilWarWomenBlog.com, January 10, 2014.

"The Russian Treaty." *Charleston Daily News*, April 12, 1867.

"William Henry Seward." Civil War Trust, retrieved February 8, 2017. civilwar.org.

Zemach, Heidi. "Biographer Calls Seward's Folly a Myth." *Seward Phoenix Log* 48, no. 33 (2014).

SPEECHES

Seward, William Henry. "Freedom in the New Territories." Washington, D.C., March 11, 1850.

LETTERS

Wilson, Joseph S. "Alaska Purchase." Washington, D.C., May 12, 1868.

CHAPTER 3: "THE LIGHTENING STANDS READY"

BOOKS

Ambrose, Stephen E. *Nothing Like It in the World.* New York: Simon & Schuster, 2000.

Bain, David Haward. *Empire Express: Building the First Transcontinental Railroad.* New York: Penguin, 2000.

Brown, Dee. *Hear That Lonesome Whistle Blow: The Epic Story of the Transcontinental Railroads.* New York: Holt, Rinehart & Winston, 1977.

Carver, Hartwell. *Memorial for a Private Charter, Asked for by Hartwell Carver and His Associates, to Build a Railroad from Lake Michigan to the Pacific Ocean.* Fairfield, WA: Ye Galleon Press, 1988. First published 1847 by J. & G.S. Gideon (Washington).

Dodge, Grenville Mellen. *Personal Recollections of President Abraham Lincoln, General Ulysses S. Grant and General William T. Sherman.* Glendale, CA: The Arthur H. Clark Company, 1914.

Gingrich, Robert. *The Role of Providence in the Founding of America: 99 Important Events That Shaped the United States.* Pennsauken, NJ: BookBaby, 2015.

Gordon, John Steele. *An Empire of Wealth: The Epic History of American Economic Power.* New York: HarperCollins, 2004.

Jacob, Kathryn Allamong. *King of the Lobby: The Life and Times of Sam Ward, Man-About-Washington in the Gilded Age.* Baltimore: Johns Hopkins University Press, 2009.

Jones, Helen Hinckley. *Rails from the West: A Biography of Theodore D. Judah.* San Marino, CA: Golden West Books, 1969.

Nichols, Joseph. *Condensed History of the Construction of the Union Pacific Railway*. Ann Arbor: University of Michigan Libraries, 1982.

Stevenson, Robert Louis. *Across the Plains with Other Memories and Essays*. London: Chatto & Windus, 1892.

Stewart, John J. *The Iron Trail to the Golden Spike*. Madison, CT: International University Press, 1984.

Utley, Robert M., and Francis A. Ketterson Jr. *Golden Spike*. Washington, D.C., US Department of the Interior National Park Service Division of Publications, 1969.

Whitman, Walt. *Leaves of Grass: The Original 1855 Edition*. New York: Dover, 2007.

Willumson, Glenn. *Iron Muse: Photographing the Transcontinental Railroad*. Berkeley: University of California Press, 2013.

Winchester, Simon. *The Men Who United the States: America's Explorers, Inventors, Eccentrics, and Mavericks, and the Creation of One Nation, Indivisible*. New York: Harper Perennial, 2014.

Wright, Ben, and Zachary W. Dresser. *Apocalypse and the Millennium in the American Civil War Era*. Baton Rouge: Louisiana State University Press, 2013.

ARTICLES

"Abraham Lincoln and Iowa." The Lehrman Institute Presents: Abraham Lincoln's Classroom, retrieved May 4, 2017. abrahamlincolnsclassroom.org.

Ambrose, Stephen E. "The Big Road." *American Heritage* 51, no. 6 (October 2000).

"A Brief History of Building the Transcontinental Railroad." Linda Hall Library, retrieved May 3, 2017. railroad.lindahall.org.

Burnett, Jim. "'The Last Spike': Separating Fact from Tradition at Golden Spike National Historic Site." NationalParksTraveler.org, April 30, 2013.

Crattie, C. Barton. "The Story of Theodore Judah." *American Surveyor* 9, no. 5 (2012).

"East and West: Completion of the Great Line Spanning the Continent." *New York Times*, May 11, 1869.

Gonchar, Michael. "A Nation on the Move: Exploring the Promise of the First Transcontinental Railroad." *New York Times*, March 18, 2015.

Harte, Francis Bret. "What the Engines Said: Opening of the Pacific Railroad." The Gilder Lehrman Institute of American History, retrieved May 4, 2017. gilderlehrman.org.

"Lincoln and Union Pacific." Union Pacific, Uniting the States of America, retrieved May 4, 2017. uprr.com.

"Pacific Railroad Acts." July 1, 1862. National Archives and Records Administration. cprr.org.

"Republican Party Platform of 1860–May 17, 1860." The American Presidency Project, retrieved May 4, 2017. presidency.ucsb.edu.

"Rev. Dr. John Todd's Dedicatory Prayer." Central Pacific Railroad Photographic History Museum, February 27, 2003. cprr.org.

Trumbore, Brian. "The Transcontinental Railroad—Link Up." StocksandNews.com, retrieved September 8, 2016.

SPEECHES

Lincoln, Abraham. "Lecture on Discoveries and Inventions." Jacksonville, Illinois, February 11, 1859.

CHAPTER 4: THE ABRAHAMIC ADVANTAGE

BOOKS

Adams, Charles Francis. *The Works of John Adams*. Boston: Little, Brown and Company, 1856.

Bermant, Chaim. *The Jews*. New York: Times Books, 1977.

Boudinot, Elias. *The Second Advent*. Trenton, NJ: D. Fenton & S. Hutchinson, 1815.

———. *Star in the West*. Trenton, NJ: D. Fenton, S. Hutchinson, and J. Dunham, 1816.

Bunker, Nick. *Making Haste from Babylon: The Mayflower Pilgrims and Their World; A New History*. New York: Random House, 2010.

Bush, George. *Life of Mohammed*. New York: J. J. & Harper, 1831.

———. *Valley of Vision*. New York: Saxton & Miles, 1844.

Bushman, Claudia Lauper. *Joseph Smith: Rough Stone Rolling*. New York: Alfred A. Knopf, 2005.

Davis, Moshe, ed. *America and the Holy Land*, Vol. IV, *With Eyes Toward Zion*. Westport, CT: Greenwood, 1995.

Dimont, Max. *The Jews in America: The Roots and Destiny of American Jews*. New York: Simon & Schuster, 1978.

Evans, Michael D. *The American Prophecies: Ancient Scriptures Reveal Our Nation's Future*. New York: Time Warner, 2004.

Frankel, Jonathan, ed. *Jews and Messianism in the Modern Era: Metaphor and Meaning*. Studies in Contemporary Jewry, Vol. VII. New York: Oxford University Press, 1991.

Gelernter, David. *1939: The Lost World of the Fair*. New York: Free Press, 1995.

Goldman, Samuel. *God's Country: Christian Zionism in America*. Philadelphia: University of Pennsylvania Press, 2018.

Hertzberg, Arthur. *The Jews in America: Four Centuries of an Uneasy Encounter: A History*. New York: Columbia University Press, 1997.

Himmelfarb, Gertrude. *The People of the Book: Philosemitism in England from Cromwell to Churchill*. New York: Encounter Books, 2011.

Johnson, Paul. *A History of the Jews*. New York: Harper & Row, 1987.

McTernan, John P. *As America Has Done to Israel*. Maitland, FL: Xulon Press, 2006.

Melville, Herman. *White-Jacket*. Evanston, IL: Northwestern University Press, 1970.

Oren, Michael B. *Power, Faith, and Fantasy: America in the Middle East, 1776 to the Present*. New York: W. W. Norton, 2007.

Radzinsky, Edvard. *Alexander II: The Last Great Tsar*. New York: Free Press, 2005.

Sanders, Ronald. *The Downtown Jews: Portraits of an Immigrant Generation*. New York: Harper & Row, 1969.

Smith, Ethan. *A View of the Hebrews*. Poultney, VT: Smith & Shute, 1823.

Telushkin, Rabbi Joseph. *The Golden Land: The Story of Jewish Immigration to America*. New York: Harmony Books, 2002.

Thackeray, William Makepeace. *The Works of William Makepeace Thackeray*, Vol. V. London: Smith, Elder, & Co., 1902.

Waldman, Steven. *Founding Faith: How Our Founding Fathers Forged a Radical New Approach to Religious Liberty.* New York: Random House, 2008.

ARTICLES

Aderet, Ofer. "The Quaker Farmer Who Was the First U.S. Consul in Jerusalem and a Jewish Convert." Haaretz.com, June 30, 2013.

Bass, Gary J. "Last Country Standing." *New York Times*, November 16, 2014.

Brooks, David. "The Week Trump Won." *New York Times*, October 27, 2017.

Evans, Albert. "The Golden Door." *The 5th Avenue Theater Program Booklet*, 2017.

Federer, Bill. "America's Unique Relationship with the Jews." AmericanMinute.com, January 26, 2017.

Fox, Frank. "Quaker, Shaker, Rabbi: Warder Cresson, the Story of a Philadelphia Mystic." *Pennsylvania Magazine of History and Biography* 95, no. 2 (April 1971): 147–94.

"From Haven to Home: A Century of Immigration, 1820–1924." JewishVirtualLibrary .org, retrieved July 3, 2017.

Green, David B. "This Day in History. A Quaker Convert to Judaism and Early Zionist Is Born." Haaretz.com, July 12, 2014.

———. "This Day in History, 1655. Colonial New Amsterdam Spurns 'Disgusting' Jews from Militia." Haaretz.com, August 28, 2015.

Greenspan, Jesse. "The Dutch Surrender New Netherland." History.com, September 8, 2014.

Isaacs, Eric D., and Robert Rosner. "How the Chicago Pile Helped the Manhattan Project Succeed." *Wall Street Journal*, December 2/3, 2017.

Klinger, Jerry. "Reverend William E. Blackstone." Jewish American Society for Historic Preservation, retrieved May 7, 2018. jashp.org.

Merkley, Paul Charles. "I Am Cyrus." *Christianity Today*, no. 99: *Faith & the American Presidency*, 2008. christianitytoday.com.

Windmueller, Steven. "Zion in America: This Nation's Unique and Historic Relationship to the Jewish Homeland." eJewishPhilanthropy.com, March 26, 2017.

SPEECHES

Benson, Ezra Taft. "A Message to Judah from Joseph." Calgary, Alberta, Canada, May 2, 1976.

CHAPTER 5: THE REAPER AND THE BULL MOOSE

BOOKS

Bennett, J. W. *Roosevelt and the Republic.* New York: Broadway Publishing Company, 1908.

Brands, H. W. *T.R.: The Last Romantic.* New York: Basic Books, 1998.

Garraty, John A. *Theodore Roosevelt: The Strenuous Life.* Rockville, MD: American Heritage, 1967.

Goodwin, Doris Kearns. *The Bully Pulpit: Theodore Roosevelt, William Howard Taft, and the Golden Age of Journalism.* New York: Simon & Schuster, 2013.

Grondahl, Paul. *I Rose Like a Rocket: The Political Education of Theodore Roosevelt*. Lincoln, NE: Bison Books, 2007.

Holsinger, M. Paul, ed. *War and American Popular Culture: A Historical Encyclopedia*. Westport, CT: Greenwood, 1999.

Long, John Davis. *America of Yesterday, as Reflected in the Journal of John Davis Long*. Edited by Lawrence Shaw Mayo. Boston: The Atlantic Monthly Press, 1923.

Marshall, Edward. *The Story of the Rough Riders*. New York: G. W. Dillingham, Co., 1899.

Merry, Robert W. *President McKinley: Architect of the American Century*. New York: Simon & Schuster, 2017.

Morris, Edmund. *Colonel Roosevelt*. New York: Random House, 2011.

———. *The Rise of Theodore Roosevelt*. New York: Random House, 2001.

———. *Theodore Rex*. New York: Random House, 2010.

Pietrusza, David. *TR's Last War: Theodore Roosevelt, the Great War, and Journey of Triumph and Tragedy*. Guilford, CT: Rowman & Littlefield, 2018.

Remey, Oliver, Henry Cochems, and Wheeler Bloodgood. *The Attempted Assassination of Ex-President Theodore Roosevelt*. Milwaukee: Progressive Publishing, 1912.

Roosevelt, Theodore. *Life of Thomas Hart Benton*. Boston: Houghton, Mifflin and Company, 1887.

———. *The Rough Riders*. New York: New American Library of World Literature, 1961.

Ruddy, Daniel. *Theodore Roosevelt's History of the United States: His Own Words, Selected and Arranged by Daniel Ruddy*. Washington, D.C.: Smithsonian, 2010.

———. *Theodore the Great: Conservative Crusader*. Washington, D.C.: Regnery, 2016.

———. *Theodore Roosevelt: An Autobiography*. New York: Charles Scribner's Sons, 1922.

Taubenfeld, Aviva. *Rough Writing: Ethnic Authorship in Theodore Roosevelt's America*. New York: NYU Press, 2008.

Thomas, Evan. *The War Lovers: Roosevelt, Lodge, Hearst, and the Rush to Empire, 1898*. Boston: Little, Brown, 2010.

Ward, Geoffrey C. *The Roosevelts: An Intimate History*. New York: Alfred A. Knopf, 2014.

ARTICLES

Brockell, Gillian. "Trump Says He Doesn't Take Vacations. They Couldn't Top Teddy Roosevelt's, Anyway." *Washington Post*, August 2, 2018.

Gores, Stan. "The Attempted Assassination of Teddy Roosevelt." *Wisconsin Magazine of History* 53, no. 4 (Summer 1970): 269–77.

Iglehart, Rev. Ferdinand C. "An After-Church Chat with President Roosevelt." *Christian Advocate*, January 30, 1919.

Johnson, Charles W. "Official Proceedings of the Twelfth Republican National Convention." Philadelphia: Dunlap Printing Company, 1900.

Russell, Robert Howard. "Mr. Dooley: He Reviews a Book." *Harper's Weekly*, November 25, 1899.

"Teddy Roosevelt." GraceReformedChurchDC.org, retrieved August 10, 2018.

"Theodore Roosevelt Dies Suddenly at Oyster Bay Home; Nation Shocked, Pays Tribute to Former President; Our Flag on All Seas and in All Lands at Half Mast." *New York Times*, January 6, 1919.

"T.R.'s Assailant Sorry He Failed to Kill." United Press International Archives, October 15, 1912. upi.com.

SPEECHES

Roosevelt, Theodore. "A Confession of Faith." Chicago, August 6, 1912.
———. "It Takes More Than That to Kill a Bull Moose." Milwaukee, October 14, 1912.
———. "The Right of the People to Rule." New York, March 20, 1912.

CHAPTER 6: TWO CLOSE CALLS

BOOKS

Alter, Jonathan. *The Defining Moment: FDR's Hundred Days and the Triumph of Hope.* New York: Simon & Schuster, 2006.
Black, Conrad. *The Flight of the Eagle.* New York: Encounter Books, 2013.
Burns, James MacGregor. *Roosevelt: The Soldier of Freedom: 1940–45.* San Diego: Harcourt Brace Jovanovich, 1970.
Dick, Philip K. *The Man in the High Castle.* New York: Mariner Books, 2011.
Freidel, Frank. *Franklin D. Roosevelt: A Rendezvous with Destiny.* Boston: Little, Brown, 1990.
Hamby, Alonzo L. *Man of Destiny: FDR and the Making of the American Century.* New York: Basic Books, 2015.
Hatfield, Mark O. *Vice Presidents of the United States, 1789–1993.* Washington, D.C.: U.S. Government Printing Office, 1997.
Picchi, Blaise. *The Five Weeks of Giuseppe Zangara: The Man Who Would Assassinate FDR.* Chicago: Academy Chicago Publishers, 1998.
Roberts, Andrew. *Churchill: Walking with Destiny.* New York: Viking, 2018.
Schlesinger, Arthur M., Jr. *The Crisis of the Old Order: 1919–1933; The Age of Roosevelt.* Boston: Mariner Books, 2003.
Smith, Jean Edward. *FDR.* New York: Random House, 2007.
Ward, Geoffrey C. *The Roosevelts: An Intimate History.* New York: Alfred A. Knopf, 2014.
Winik, Jay. *1944: FDR and the Year That Changed History.* New York: Simon & Schuster, 2015.

ARTICLES

Beinart, Peter. "Bernie Sanders Offers a Foreign Policy for the Common Man." *Atlantic,* October 15, 2018.
Burbridge, Richard. "Oliver Stone Rewrites History—Again." *New York Times,* November 21, 2012.
Chace, James. "The Winning Hand." *New York Review of Books,* March 11, 2004.
Churchill, Winston S. "My New York Misadventure." *Daily Mail,* January 4–5, 1932.
Cox, Patrick. "Not Worth a Bucket of Warm Spit." HistoryNewsNetwork.org, July 25, 2008.
DeLong, William. "Giuseppe Zangara Tried to Shoot FDR—but Missed and Killed Another Powerful Politician Instead." ATI, July 13, 2018. allthatsinteresting.com.
"F.D. Roosevelt Ill of Poliomyelitis." *New York Times,* September 16, 1921.

Glueckstien, Fred. "Contasino Meets Churchill, 1931: 'A World Aglare.'" Churchill Project, March 13, 2016. winstonchurchill.hillsdale.edu.

Greenfield, Jeff. "The Year the Veepstakes Really Mattered." Politico.com, July 10, 2016.

"He Shot at the President-Elect in Miami, and Almost Changed the Course of History." *Miami Herald*, February 11, 2019.

Lomazow, Steven. "Vice Admiral Ross T. McIntire: A Reassessment of an American Hero." *Navy Medicine*, July 2018.

MacKaye, Milton. "The New Crusade." *New Yorker*, October 22, 1932.

Medoff, Rafael. "What FDR Said About Jews in Private." *Los Angeles Times*, April 7, 2013.

Piket, Casey. "Attempted Assassination of FDR in Bayfront Park in 1933." Miami History, March 4, 2012. miami-history.com.

Rauchway, Eric. "Hard Times for Hoover, and FDR." *Wall Street Journal*, December 22, 2018.

Seal, Andrew. "What a Former Vice President Can Teach Democrats About Racial and Economic Inequality." *Washington Post*, June 8, 2018.

Simkin, John. "Giuseppe Zangara." Spartacus Educational, updated March 2018. spartacus-educational.com.

Walker, J. Samuel. "The New Deal and the Guru." *American Heritage* 40, no. 2 (March 1989): 92–99.

Wiener, Jon. "Oliver Stone's 'Untold History.'" *The Nation*, November 14, 2012. thenation .com.

Wolchover, Natalie. "Uncommon Man." *New Yorker*, October 14, 2013.

SPEECHES

Roosevelt, Eleanor. "Address to the 1940 Democratic Convention." Chicago, July 18, 1940.

Schlesinger, Arthur M., Jr. "History's Impresario." Boston, October 28, 1995.

CHAPTER 7: THE FIVE-MINUTE MIRACLE

BOOKS

Beevor, Antony. *The Second World War*. New York: Back Bay Books, 2012.

Carlson, Elliot. *Joe Rochefort's War: The Odyssey of the Codebreaker Who Outwitted Yamamoto at Midway*. Annapolis, MD: Naval Institute Press, 2011.

Churchill, Winston. *The Hinge of Fate*, Vol. IV, *The Second World War*. Boston: Houghton Mifflin Co., 1950.

Coale, Griffith Bailey. *Victory at Midway*. New York: Farrar & Rinehart, 1944.

Cressman, Robert J., Steve Ewing, Barrett Tillman, Mark Horan, Clark Reynolds, and Stan Cohen. *"A Glorious Page in Our History": The Battle of Midway, 4–6 June 1942*. Missoula, MT: Pictorial Histories, 1990.

Fuchida, Mitsuo. *Midway: The Battle That Doomed Japan; The Japanese Navy's Story*. Annapolis, MD: Naval Institute Press, 2001.

Hanson, Victor Davis. *Carnage and Culture: Landmark Battles in the Rise of Western Power*. New York: Random House, 2011.

———. *The Second World Wars: How the First Global Conflict Was Fought and Won*. New York: Basic Books, 2017.

Linzey, Stanford E. *USS* Yorktown *at Midway*. Maitland, FL: Xulon Press, 2004. Formerly published as *God Was at Midway* (Temecula, CA: Black Forest Press, 1996).

Lord, Walter. *Incredible Victory: The Battle of Midway*. Short Hills, NJ: Burford Books, 1967.

Lundstrom, John B. *The First Team: Pacific Naval Air Combat from Pearl Harbor to Midway*. Annapolis, MD: Naval Institute Press, 1984.

Miller, Donald L. *The Story of World War II*. New York: Simon & Schuster, 2001.

Morison, Samuel Eliot. *History of United States Naval Operations in World War II*, Vol. 4, *Coral Sea, Midway, and Submarine Actions, May 1942–August 1942*. Urbana: University of Illinois Press, 2001.

Mrazek, Robert J. *A Dawn Like Thunder: The True Story of Torpedo Squadron Eight*. Boston: Little, Brown, 2008.

Parshall, Jonathan, and Anthony Tully. *Shattered Sword: The Untold Story of the Battle of Midway*. Dulles, VA: Potomac Books, 2005.

Prange, Gordon W., Donald M. Goldstein, and Katherine V. Dillon. *Miracle at Midway*. New York: McGraw-Hill, 1982.

———. *God's Samurai: Lead Pilot at Pearl Harbor*. Washington, D.C.: Brassey's, 2003.

Roberts, Andrew. *The Storm of War: A New History of the Second World War*. New York: HarperCollins, 2011.

Symonds, Craig L. *The Battle of Midway*. New York: Oxford University Press, 2011.

Thompson, Roger. *Lessons Not Learned: The U.S. Navy's Status Quo Culture*. Annapolis, MD: Naval Institute Press, 2013.

Tillman, Barrett. *The Dauntless Dive Bomber of World War Two*. Annapolis, MD: Naval Institute Press, 1976.

Toll, Ian W. *Pacific Crucible: War at Sea in the Pacific, 1941–1942*. New York: W. W. Norton, 2012.

Wouk, Herman. *War and Remembrance*. New York: Simon & Schuster, 1978.

ARTICLES

Garnett, Robert R. "The American Guts and Grit That Sank Japan at Midway." *Wall Street Journal*, June 3/4, 2017.

Goldstein, Donald M. "Pearl Harbor Pilot Became Evangelist." *Stars and Stripes*, December 7, 2008. stripes.com.

———. "Putting the Midway Miracle in Perspective." *Naval History* 21, no. 3 (June 2007).

Noone, James A. "Warriors Return to Midway." *Naval History* 14, no. 1 (February 2000).

Symonds, Craig L. "Miracle Men of Midway Turn the Tide of WWII in the Pacific." *World War II Magazine*, June 2, 2017. historynet.com.

CHAPTER 8: THE RIGHT VICE

BOOKS

Culver, John C., and John Hyde. *American Dreamer: The Life and Times of Henry A. Wallace*. New York: W. W. Norton, 2001.

Donovan, Robert J. *Conflict and Crisis: The Presidency of Harry S. Truman, 1945–1948.* New York: W. W. Norton, 1977.

Hatfield, Mark O. *Vice Presidents of the United States, 1789–1993.* Washington, D.C.: U.S. Government Printing Office, 1997.

"If Elected . . ." Unsuccessful Candidates for the Presidency, 1796–1968. Washington, D.C.: Smithsonian Institution Press, 1972.

McCullough, David. *Truman.* New York: Simon & Schuster, 1992.

Schlesinger, Arthur M., Jr. *A Life in the 20th Century: Innocent Beginnings, 1917–1950.* Boston: Houghton Mifflin Co., 2000.

Smith, Jean Edward. *FDR.* New York: Random House, 2007.

Stone, Oliver, and Peter Kuznick. *The Untold History of the United States.* New York: Simon & Schuster, 2012.

Ward, Geoffrey C. *The Roosevelts: An Intimate History.* New York: Alfred A. Knopf, 2014.

Winik, Jay. *1944: FDR and the Year That Changed History.* New York: Simon & Schuster, 2015.

Woolner, David B. *The Last 100 Days: FDR at War and at Peace.* New York: Basic Books, 2017.

ARTICLES

Black, Conrad. "The Henry Wallace Rewrite." *National Review*, January 24, 2013.

Capshaw, Ron. "Henry Wallace: Unsung Hero of the Left." *National Review*, April 2, 2015.

Gross, Daniel. "Henry Wallace's Company and How It Grew." *Slate*, January 7, 2004. slate.com.

Kleinman, Mark L. "Searching for the 'Inner Light': The Development of Henry A. Wallace's Experimental Spiritualism." *Annals of Iowa* 53, no. 3 (Summer 1994): 195–218.

Luce, Henry R. "The American Century." *Life*, February 17, 1941.

Moreland, Will. "Portrait of Soviet Leader Josef Stalin." Vox.com, October 26, 2015.

Schlesinger, Arthur M., Jr. "Who Was Henry A. Wallace?" *Los Angeles Times*, March 12, 2000.

Wallace, Henry A. "Where I Was Wrong." *This Week*, September 7, 1952.

SPEECHES

Wallace, Henry A. "The Century of the Common Man." New York, May 8, 1942.

CHAPTER 9: FROM THE MOUNTAINTOP

BOOKS

Branch, Taylor. *Parting the Waters: America in the King Years, 1954–1963.* New York: Simon & Schuster, 1988.

Burrow, Rufus, Jr. *Martin Luther King, Jr., and the Theology of Resistance.* Jefferson, NC: McFarland, 2015.

Clayborne, Carson, ed. *The Papers of Martin Luther King, Jr.* Los Angeles: University of California Press, 1992.

Ghaemi, Nassir. *A First-Rate Madness: Uncovering the Links Between Leadership and Mental Illness*. New York: Penguin Press, 2011.

Jackson, Troy. *Becoming King: Martin Luther King Jr. and the Making of a National Leader*. Lexington: University Press of Kentucky, 2009.

Johnson, Charles, and John Lewis. *Martin Luther King, Jr.: 50 Years Later, a Leader Remembered*. New York: Life Books, 2018.

King, Coretta Scott. *My Life with Martin Luther King, Jr.* New York: Henry Holt, 1993.

King, Martin Luther, Jr. *Stride Toward Freedom: The Montgomery Story*. Boston: Beacon Press, 2010.

———. *Why We Can't Wait*. New York: Signet Classic, 1963.

Lincoln, C. Eric. *Martin Luther King, Jr.: A Profile*. New York: Hill & Wang, 1993.

Pearson, Hugh. *When Harlem Nearly Killed King: The 1958 Stabbing of Dr. Martin Luther King, Jr.* New York: Seven Stories Press, 2004.

Powers, Georgia Davis. *I Shared the Dream: The Pride, Passion and Politics of the First Black Woman Senator from Kentucky*. Far Hills, NJ: New Horizon Press, 1995.

ARTICLES

Amos, Owen. "Did Martin Luther King Predict His Own Death?" BBC News, March 27, 2018. bbc.com.

Bass, Jonathan. "Martin Luther King, Jr." EncyclopediaofAlabama.org, updated July 17, 2015.

Blakemore, Erin. "The Fight for Martin Luther King, Jr. Day." History.com, retrieved July 12, 2018.

Brooks, F. Erik. "Dexter Avenue King Memorial Baptist Church." Encyclopediaof Alabama.org, updated October 8, 2014.

Causey, Michael. "An Interview with Tavis Smiley." *Washington Independent Review of Books*, September 10, 2014.

Dear, John. "The God at Dr. King's Kitchen Table." *National Catholic Reporter*, January 16, 2007. ncronline.org.

"Dr. King's Disservice to His Cause." *Life*, April 21, 1967.

"Dr. King's Error." *New York Times*, April 7, 1967.

"Dud Spares King's Home; Another Hit." *Montgomery Advertiser*, January 28, 1957.

Dyson, Michael Eric. "Keeping the Faith—We Forgot What Dr. King Believed In." *New York Times*, April 1, 2018.

———. "The Shot That Echoes Still." *Esquire*, Winter 2018.

Eblen, Tom. "Interviews Reveal New Details of Martin Luther King's Affair with Kentucky Senator." *Lexington Herald Leader*, April 6, 2018.

Gates, Henry Louis, Jr. "Did MLK Improvise in the 'Dream' Speech?" PBS.org, retrieved July 2018.

Gizzi, John. "King Was Pressed to Run for President in 1968." Newsmax.com, August 28, 2013.

Grossman, Ron. "The Tense Months Before Martin Luther King Jr.'s Assassination." *Chicago Tribune*, April 1, 2018.

Habeeb, Lee. "King's Media Makeover." *National Review*, January 18, 2016.

Haygood, Wil. "This Powerful Stokely Carmichael Portrait Never Made It to the Cover of *Time* Magazine." *Smithsonian Magazine*, June 2016.

"Interview with Rosa Parks." DigitalHistory.uh.edu, June 2, 1995.

"King Says Vision Told Him to Lead Integration Forces." *Montgomery Advertiser*, January 28, 1957.

Kopkind, Andrew. "Soul Power." *New York Review of Books*, August 24, 1967.

Lehman, Dave. "Death of a King: The Real Story of Dr. Martin Luther King's Final Year." *NSRF Connections*, January 2015. nsrfharmony.org.

Lord, Debbie. "Who Was James Earl Ray, and Did He Really Kill Martin Luther King, Jr.?" *Atlanta Journal-Constitution*, April 3, 2018.

"Martin Luther King, Jr., on the Selma March." *Meet the Press*, NBCLearn.com, retrieved November 18, 2017.

"Montgomery Bus Boycott: 1955–1956." KingEncyclopedia.stanford.edu, retrieved March 20, 2018.

Nance, Kevin. "Tavis Smiley on 'Death of a King.'" *Chicago Tribune*, August 29, 2014.

Nave, Guy D. "Moving Beyond Rev. King's Dream." *Atlanta Journal-Constitution*, January 12, 2018.

Nugent, Tom, James S. Kunen, Jane Sanderson, and Elizabeth Velez. "A Bitter Battle Erupts Over the Last Hours of Martin Luther King." *People*, October 3, 1989.

Parr, Patrick. "The Man Who Would Be King." *Wall Street Journal*, April 21, 2018.

"People & Ideas: Martin Luther King Jr." PBS.org, retrieved July 2018.

Polk, James. "King Conspiracy Theories Still Thrive 40 Years Later." CNN.com, December 29, 2008.

Riley, Jason L. "Martin Luther King: 'We Can't Keep on Blaming the White Man.'" *Wall Street Journal*, April 4, 2018.

Risen, Clay. "'Death of a King,' by Tavis Smiley with David Ritz." *New York Times*, October 31, 2014.

Robinson, Nathan J. "Seeing Martin Luther King as a Human Being." *Current Affairs*, January 15, 2018.

Swanson, James L. "The Fateful NYC Visit That Left MLK 'Prepared to Die.'" *New York Post*, April 3, 2018.

Theoharis, Jeanne. "Don't Forget That Martin Luther King Jr. Was Once Denounced as an Extremist." *Time*, January 12, 2018.

Vanden Heuvel, Katrina. "Fifty Years Later, King's Warning Still Resonates." *Washington Post*, April 4, 2017.

West, Cornel, and Robert P. George. "Dr. King's Radical Biblical Vision." *Wall Street Journal*, April 6, 2018.

Whitehead, John W. "When Martin Luther King Reached the Point of No Return." *Huffington Post*, October 26, 2011.

"Williams, Adam Daniel (A.D.) (1861–1931)." KingEncyclopedia.stanford.edu, retrieved March 20, 2018.

Wolfensberger, Don. "The Martin Luther King, Jr. Holiday: The Long Struggle in Congress." Woodrow Wilson International Center for Scholars, January 14, 2008. wilsoncenter.org.

W.W. "A Blockheaded Memorial." *Economist*, August 30, 2011.

Younge, Gary. "Martin Luther King: How a Rebel Leader Was Lost to History." *Guardian*, April 4, 2018.

SPEECHES

King, Martin Luther, Jr. "Acceptance Speech." Montgomery, Alabama, May 2, 1954.

——. "Beyond Vietnam: A Time to Break Silence." New York, April 4, 1967.

——. "Drum Major Instinct." Montgomery, Alabama, February 4, 1968.

——. "God's Relation to the World." January 1, 1948, to December 31, 1954.

——. "Holt Street Address." Montgomery, Alabama, November 14, 1956.

——. "I Have a Dream." Washington, D.C., August 28, 1963.

——. "I've Been to the Mountaintop." Memphis, Tennessee, April 3, 1968.

Tuck, William Munford. "Opposition to Passage of Civil Rights Bill." Washington, D.C., April 10, 1968. *Congressional Record: Proceedings and Debates of the 90th Congress*, 2d sess., vol. 114, pt. 8.

LETTERS

King, Martin Luther, Jr. "Letter from Birmingham Jail." Birmingham, Alabama, April 16, 1963.

CHAPTER 10: "FOREVER UPWARD"

BOOKS

Clarke, Thurston. *The Last Campaign: Robert F. Kennedy and 82 Days That Inspired America*. New York: Henry Holt, 2008.

Mailer, Norman. *Miami and the Siege of Chicago: An Informal History of the Republican and Democratic Conventions of 1968*. New York: World Publishing, 1968.

Medved, Michael. *Right Turns: Unconventional Lessons from a Controversial Life*. New York: Crown Forum, 2004.

Scherman, Rabbi Nosson. *The Family Megillah*. Mesorah, 1982–90.

ARTICLES

Baker, Kevin. "The America We Lost When Trump Won." *New York Times*, January 21, 2017.

Barone, Michael. "The End of History Not Turning Out as Hoped." American Enterprise Institute, August 7, 2016. aei.org.

Blanton, Dana. "Fox News Poll: Did God Favor Donald Trump in 2016?" FoxNews.com, February 14, 2019.

Brooks, David. "Morality and Michael Cohen." *New York Times*, February 28, 2019.

Epstein, Edward. "Ford Escaped 2 Assassination Attempts/Both Happened in California—One in Capital, Other in S.F." *Chronicle Washington Bureau*, December 27, 2006.

Graham, Billy. "My Heart Aches for America." Billy Graham Evangelistic Association, https://billygraham.org/story/billy-graham-my-heart-aches-for-america/, July 19, 2012.

Kennan, George F. "The Sources of Soviet Conduct." *Foreign Affairs*, July 1947.

Klett, Leah Marieann. "Billy Graham's Daughter Anne Graham Lotz Warns God Is Removing 'Hand of Blessing' from United States." GospelHerald.com, April 18, 2017.

Mead, Walter Russell. "America's Decline Never Seems to Arrive." *Wall Street Journal*, July 3, 2018.

Milbank, Dana. "What Americans Have to Say to Putin." *Washington Post*, September 12, 2013.

Putin, Vladimir V. "A Plea for Caution from Russia." *New York Times*, September 11, 2013.

Schlesinger, Arthur M., Jr. "America: Experiment or Destiny?" *American Heritage* 28, no. 4 (June 1977).

Sherwood, Harriet. "The Chosen One? The New Film That Claims Trump's Election Was an Act of God." *Guardian*, October 3, 2018.

Starnes, Todd. "Can God Bless a Godless America." FoxNews.com, May 6, 2014.

Traub, James. "The First 'Rigged' Election." *Wall Street Journal*, October 29, 2016.

SPEECHES

Roosevelt, Franklin D. "Fourth Inaugural Address." Washington, D.C., January 20, 1945.

Soloveitchik, Joseph B. "Address on Yom Ha-Atsma-ut." New York, April 16, 1956.

LETTERS

Washington, George. "Letter to Brigadier General Thomas Nelson, Jr." August 20, 1778.

MESSENGERS IN THE SKY

BOOKS

The Megillah: The Book of Esther. ArtScroll Tanach Series. New York: Mesorah, 1976.

ARTICLES

Cecere, Al. "American Eagle Day." American Eagle Foundation, retrieved March 20, 2019. eagles.org.

Index

Midway Atoll, 48, 237–238, 242, 265

Midway Atoll National Wildlife Refuge, 238

Midway Occupation Force, 248

Military-Industrial Courier (magazine), 46

Milwaukee, Wisconsin, 129–134

Miracle at Midway (Prange), 253, 264

Missouri River, 58, 62

Mitsubishi Zeros, 248, 252, 256

Moley, Ray, 225, 230–231

Monongahela, Battle of, 158

Montgomery Advertiser, 322, 327

Montgomery bus boycott, 312, 319, 321–323, 327–329

Montgomery Improvement Association, 321, 322, 327

Moore, Sara Jane, 361

Moran, Thomas, 8–9, 13, 362

Mordaunt, Thomas Osbert, 158

Morehouse College, 315

Morgan, J. P., 117, 177

Morgan, Juliette, 322–323

Morgenthau, Henry, 287

Morison, Samuel Eliot, 251–252

Morley, Lord, 172

Mormon Tabernacle, 54, 74

Mormonism, 74–75

Morris, E. Joy, 99

Morris, Edmund, 147

Mosby's Rangers, 29

Mother Teresa, 347

Motion picture industry, 123–124

Mount Ararat, 96

Mount of the Holy Cross, 2, 4–13, 16, 362

Mrazek, Robert J., 262–263

Muir, John, 63

Murphy, John B., 135

Music, 122–123

NAACP (National Association for the Advancement of Colored People), 321, 336–337

Nachmanides, 91

Nagumo, Chuichi, 248–250, 252, 253, 257, 258

Nation, The, 305

National Forest Service, 172

National Park Service, 13

National Review, 231

Native Americans, 73, 96, 153

NATO (North Atlantic Treaty Organization), 297, 303

Naval History (journal), 262

Naval War of 1812, The (Roosevelt), 142

Nelson, Thomas, 363

New Amsterdam, 87–89

"New Colossus, The" (Lazarus), 112, 114–115

New Deal, 230, 270

New Netherlands, 89–90

New Republic, 224, 300

New York Board of Police Commissioners, 149, 153

New York Herald, 34, 41

New York Journal, 156, 161

New York State Assembly, 142

New York Times, 17, 72–73, 165, 198, 211–213, 218, 227, 282, 336, 370, 371

New York Tribune, 36, 40–41, 227

New York World, 219

New Yorker, 215

Newport, Rhode Island, 87, 92, 93

Niagara Gorge railroad, 62

Niagara River, 96

Nicholas, Sir Edward, 86

Nimitz, Chester, 244–245, 247, 253, 262, 263

Nixon, Richard M., 306, 360

Noah, Mordecai Manuel, 95–99, 106

Noah (biblical), 96

Nobel Prize, 172, 333

Notch Mountain, 5, 6, 10, 11, 13

Nourmahal (yacht), 224, 227, 230, 231

Nowaki (Japanese destroyer), 248

Obama, Barack, 350, 351, 367

Omaha, Nebraska, 58, 68, 70, 76

ABOUT THE AUTHOR

Since 1996, Michael Medved's daily three-hour radio show has reached a large, devoted national audience. He is the author of thirteen previous nonfiction books, including the bestsellers *The American Miracle*, *The 10 Big Lies About America*, *Hollywood vs. America*, *Hospital*, and *What Really Happened to the Class of '65?* He is a member of the *USA Today* board of contributors and a former chief film critic for the *New York Post*, and served for more than a decade as cohost of *Sneak Previews*, the weekly movie-review show on PBS. Medved is an honors graduate of Yale with departmental honors in American history. He lives in the Seattle area with his wife, clinical psychologist and bestselling author Dr. Diane Medved.

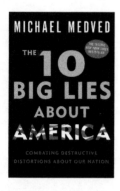